UNTANGLING BLACKNESS IN GREEK ANTIQUITY

How should articulations of blackness from the fifth century BCE to the twenty-first century be properly read and interpreted? This important and timely new book is the first concerted treatment of black skin color in the Greek literature and visual culture of antiquity. In charting representations in the Hellenic world of black Egyptians, Aithiopians, Indians, and Greeks, Sarah Derbew dexterously disentangles the complex and varied ways in which blackness has been coproduced by ancient authors and artists; their readers, audiences, and viewers; and contemporary scholars. Exploring the precarious hold that race has on skin coloration, the author uncovers the many silences, suppressions, and misappropriations of blackness within modern studies of Greek antiquity. Shaped by performance studies and critical race theory alike, her book maps out an authoritative archaeology of blackness that reappraises its significance. It offers a committedly anti-racist approach to depictions of black people while rejecting simplistic conflations or explanations.

SARAH F. DERBEW is an Assistant Professor of Classics in affiliation with the Center for African Studies and the Center for Comparative Studies in Race and Ethnicity at Stanford University. She was previously a Junior Fellow at the Harvard Society of Fellows.

UNTANGLING BLACKNESS IN GREEK ANTIQUITY

SARAH F. DERBEW

Stanford University

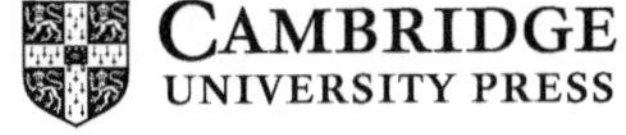

CAMBRIDGE
UNIVERSITY PRESS

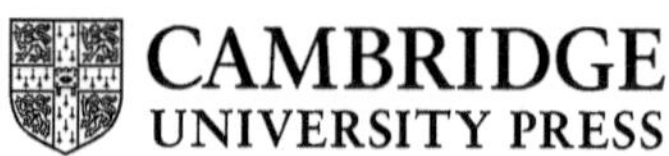

Shaftesbury Road, Cambridge CB2 8EA, United Kingdom

One Liberty Plaza, 20th Floor, New York, NY 10006, USA

477 Williamstown Road, Port Melbourne, VIC 3207, Australia

314–321, 3rd Floor, Plot 3, Splendor Forum, Jasola District Centre, New Delhi – 110025, India

103 Penang Road, #05–06/07, Visioncrest Commercial, Singapore 238467

Cambridge University Press is part of Cambridge University Press & Assessment,
a department of the University of Cambridge.

We share the University's mission to contribute to society through the pursuit of
education, learning and research at the highest international levels of excellence.

www.cambridge.org
Information on this title: www.cambridge.org/9781108817912

DOI: 10.1017/9781108861816

First published 2022
First paperback edition 2024

A catalogue record for this publication is available from the British Library

ISBN   978-1-108-49528-8   Hardback
ISBN   978-1-108-81791-2   Paperback

Contents

Figures

The descriptions of pottery listed below are taken directly from the
respective museum's online catalogue.

Tables

Acknowledgments

I relish the opportunity to acknowledge publicly those who helped bring this project to fruition. Many hands stirred this pot.

First, I thank those who read earlier chapter drafts and provided substantial feedback: Kim Benston, who embodies the trio of Haverford's tenets (trust, concern, and respect); Robert Cioffi, who kindly sent me drafts of his unpublished manuscript; David Elmer; Harriet Fertik; Milette Gaifman, whose excitement about my project rivaled my own; Shelley Haley; Andrew Johnston, whose visionary suggestions helped me see the book lurking behind the dissertation; Jason König, who graciously invited me to visit the University of St Andrews; Jessica Lamont, whose enthusiastic spirits buoyed me forward; Pauline LeVen; Denise Lim (Africanist extraordinaire); J. R. Morgan, who was generous with his time even in retirement; Kathryn Morgan; Camille Owens; Nancy Sorkin Rabinowitz; Phiroze Vasunia; and Tim Whitmarsh. Special thanks to Rebecca Futo Kennedy for reading through the manuscript in its entirety and providing detailed suggestions. I am also grateful to Aleydis Van de Moortel, Kathryn Morgan, Bret Mulligan, Liv Yarrow, Brian Breed, Grant Parker, Caroline Stark, Elena Giusti, Felipe Soza and Supratik Baralay, Harriet Fertik, Monica Park and Mathura Umachandran, Maura Heyn, Rebecca Futo Kennedy, Jeffrey Henderson, Susanne Ebbinghaus, Sara Forsdyke, Peter Struck, and April Pudsey for the opportunity to present my research to inquisitive audiences at the University of Tennessee, Knoxville, UCLA, Haverford College, Brooklyn College, the University of Massachusetts Amherst, Stanford University, the Center for Hellenic Studies, the University of Warwick, Harvard University, the University of New Hampshire, the Fifteenth Congress of the Classical Association/ Fédération internationale des associations d'études classiques, the University of North Carolina at Greensboro, Denison University, Boston University, the Harvard Art Museums, the University of Michigan, the University of Pennsylvania, and the Manchester Classical

Association, respectively. In addition, Denise McCoskey's *Race: Antiquity and Its Legacy* was one of the inspirations for this book. It was such a treat to meet her and present my research at Miami University in Ohio. Finally, a shout-out to the attentive audiences at Friends Seminary, the Brooklyn Latin School, and Brooklyn Emerging Leaders Academy.

Travel was an integral part of this project. I thank the staff at the following sites who ensured that I had access to relevant materials during my sojourns: the British Museum (especially Derek Welsby), the Louvre (special thanks to the guard who slowed down his rapid-fire French so I could understand his directions and locate the appropriate museum entrance), the Museo Nazionale Etrusco, the Ashmolean Museum, the Fitzwilliam Museum, the Sudan National Museum, and the Royal City of Meroe. In England, numerous scholars offered constructive feedback over cups of tea: Rosa Andújar, Pavlos Avlamis, Justine McConnell, and Jeremy Tanner. All of these international meetings would have been impossible without the financial support of the Whitney and Betty MacMillan Center for International and Area Studies, the Department of Classics at Yale, the Social Science Research Council, and the William F. Milton Fund at Harvard.

Beyond museum visits, I worked on this project in various cities. Kind hosts enabled me to focus on my work by providing me with a place to lay my head, tasty food, and top-notch company: Sym in Asan City, Julia in Sheung Wan, Nithya in Quito, my Sunshine family (Asteway, Lizayay, Rozit, Aman, and Nathania pre-Gelila and Moses) in Melbourne, SMLC in Brockley and Paris (along with Pascal and Esmé), Ifeanyi in London, Mahlu and Markos (plus Enana and Zinah) in Nashua, Unkie and Teddy in Chicago, Candace in Philadelphia, Denise and Ama in New Haven, and Tege and Suziyay in Addis Ababa. Thanks as well to Jeff Tecosky-Feldman, my undergraduate mentor (and calculus professor), who invited me back to my alma mater on numerous occasions. He was the first person to suggest that I consider a PhD in Classics. Had he not handed me a Mellon Mays Undergraduate Fellowship application in my freshman year of college, the financial sector would have had one more in its ranks.

During my graduate school years, numerous people had a positive impact on my academic experience. At the City University of New York Graduate Center, Gail Smith carved out time from her busy schedule to discuss African and African American literature with me. Once I moved to New Haven, Colin McCaffrey offered relevant book recommendations, Daphne Brooks and Tina Post gave helpful suggestions at an early stage, Steph Newell offered unstinting enthusiasm and an opportunity to present my research at the African Literature Association's annual meeting, Erica

James continually encouraged my academic interests, and Lisa Monroe always made me feel welcome in the Department of African American Studies. As a Black woman determined to thrive at a predominantly White institution, I benefitted from the wise counsel of Michelle Nearon, who provided me with a platform to discuss academic equity in constructive ways, and that of Patrice Rankine, who paved the way as the first Black person (from what I can tell) to receive a PhD from the Department of Classics at Yale. Mrs. Linda Dickey-Saucier's honest conversations and all-around joyous presence brightened my time in the Department of Classics. Despite her heavy workload and rich life outside of the department, she always supported me. The skirt she helped me sew during my final months as a graduate student is tangible proof that a PhD consists of more than books. In this vein, I give immense thanks to my graduate adviser Emily Greenwood. In addition to being a phenomenal academic advisor, she has had an enormous impact on my interdisciplinary academic pursuits and my diversity-related endeavors. After departing from meetings with her, I have murmured to myself more times than I can count, "How can one person consistently distill my scattered thoughts into such an elegant thread?" I am extremely lucky to benefit from the counsel of such a gracious and brilliant scholar. If I can inherit half of her expertise and rigorous work ethic, I will retire a happy woman. *Haba na haba, hujaza kibaba.*

My time in Cambridge provided me with the resources and precious time to revise the material in this book. I thank Wally Gilbert, Kelly Katz, and Ana Novak for their support during my time at the Harvard Society of Fellows. I am a grateful recipient of the William F. Milton Fund: what a joy it was to have the freedom to buy as many books (even hardcover!) as could fit on my shelves. It was a heartening experience to share my excitement about Nubia with Rita Freed at the Boston Museum of Fine Arts. Thanks as well to Sheldon Cheek for inviting me to explore the Image of the Black in Western Art archive to my heart's content. I have deep gratitude for the people who put together fabulous events at the Hutchins Center for African and African American Research, the Center for African Studies, and the Department of Classics at Harvard. These events provided stimulating and much-needed breaks from writing. As for the other Cambridge, I thank the astute referees as well as the editorial team whose wise counsel has strengthened this project. My time at Stanford University gave me the opportunity to sharpen my manuscript and benefit from the feedback of Ben Albritton, Hans Bork, Giovanna Ceserani, Jennifer DeVere Brody, Karen Fung, Grant Parker, Ato Quayson, Fatoumata

(Mata) Seck, Susan Stephens, and Jennifer Trimble. I am also grateful to Verity Walsh and Ellen Wert for their editing magic.

My love of reading began at P. S. 11K in Brooklyn. A heartfelt thanks to my elementary school teachers: Mrs. Jacobs, Mrs. Smiling, Mrs. Peterson-Ruffin, Ms. Frazier, Mrs. Stephens-Spellman, Ms. McGhie, and Ms. Holder. These women gave me a solid foundation and always encouraged me to be proud of my intelligence. I share a few snapshots from this well-rounded public education. It was in Mrs. Jacobs's kindergarten class that I read my first book, *If You Give a Mouse a Cookie*. In Mrs. Smiling's class, I was able to gobble up books and cookies from her seemingly endless stash. I vividly remember Mrs. Stephens-Spellman calling us to attention in the Akan language in fourth grade (*Ago? Amé*) and the gift of ankara fabric that she gave me when I did well on the New York citywide tests. I will never forget the fear I felt, and the lesson I learned, when my fifth-grade teacher Ms. McGhie threatened to call my parents after she caught me watching my friends throw wads of wet toilet paper onto the ceiling of the girls' bathroom; she told me that witnessing bad behavior and staying silent was the same as participating in the act. In sixth grade, Ms. Holder's passionate speech about the importance of capitalizing "Black" and scrutinizing the media's representation of Black people left an indelible mark on my impressionable eleven-year-old self. The Clinton Hill branch of the Brooklyn Public Library also deserves public acknowledgment. When they gave me a library card, they gave me a ticket to the world.

In my family, my brother jokes that he is the brains behind this project. To be fair, there have been times when I have followed his footsteps. At the age of three, I stubbornly (and successfully) insisted that I was ready for school so that we could be classmates. When I was twelve, I transferred to his school Friends Seminary, where I began learning Latin. By the time I reached college, he had already declared a major in Classics and normalized the study of ancient languages in our family. As a devoted member of Contingent XIX, he introduced me to Prep for Prep, where I wound up securing my first Latin teaching job. Turning to other members of my family, my aunt Mehret fortified me with her food deliveries and nurturing presence throughout my many years of schooling. Finally, four people deserve the biggest thanks: Baba (Derbew), Anguache, Aboy, and Aday. They gave me the greatest gifts I have ever received: my parents. እድሜና ጤና ይስጥልኝ፨ I dedicate this book to my grandmother Anguache (1944–2017), whose energetic voice and shrewd smile remain etched in my memory. To quote her wise words: ፍቅር ካለ፧ አንድ አንጀራ ለአንድ ሺ ይበቃል፨

Note on Nomenclature

With the necessary exceptions of the book's title, chapter titles, and
subheading titles, throughout the book I make a number of deliberate
distinctions among certain key terms, largely signaled by orthography
(uppercase or lowercase initial letters) and modifiers (such as "modern").
These distinctions are especially useful for detangling the categories of
ancient and modern people and identifying ancient and modern places –
and for studying them. In addition, I intend specific connotations for other
key terms, such as *race* and *identity*. I elaborate on these language choices
mainly in Section 3 of Chapter 1 but also in subsequent chapters. Below
I offer Table P.1 as a summary and visual reference.

Table P.1 *Key Terms: Orthography and definitions*

Term	Definition
Africa	A modern continent
Aithiopia	An ancient ethereal land that Greek sources sometimes conflate with a historical region; its geographical location roughly corresponds with modern Egypt and Sudan (spanning the First to the Sixth Cataract of the Nile)
ancient world	A broad term that refers to past communities whose geography need not correspond with the Mediterranean region
antiquity	A broad term that refers to past communities whose geography need not correspond with the Mediterranean region
blackness (lowercase)	A term that refers to the skin color of black (lowercase) people
Blackness (uppercase)	A term that refers to the skin color of Black (uppercase) people

Table P.1 (*cont.*)

Term	Definition
black face (lowercase)	A term that describes the faces of black people on Attic janiform cups
Blackface (uppercase)	A term that refers to the performances of nineteenth- and twentieth-century White minstrel actors
black people (lowercase)	People whose skin color is rendered black in ancient Greek literature and art; their phenotypic features usually include full lips, curly hair, and a broad nose
Black people (uppercase)	A modern, socially constructed categorization that denotes people with varying shades of melanin
brown face (lowercase)	A term that describes clay-colored faces on Attic janiform cups
Brown people (uppercase)	A modern, socially constructed categorization that denotes people of South Asian descent, among others
classical/classics (lowercase)	The study of ancient societies including and beyond the Mediterranean region
Classical/Classics (uppercase)	A problematic stand-in for the study of Greco-Roman antiquity
Classicist (uppercase)	A person who studies Greco-Roman antiquity
Egypt	An ancient country that spans from the Nile Delta to the First Cataract
Ethiopia	A modern nation located in the Horn of Africa, east of Sudan
Greco-Roman antiquity	A term used to denote the history of Greece and Rome from the eighth century BCE to the fourth century CE
Greece	A geographical marker of an ancient Mediterranean superpower that overlaps with the modern nation of Greece; also an umbrella term used to denote Greek-speaking cities such as Argos and Athens
Greek antiquity	A term used to denote the history of Greece from the eighth century BCE to the fourth century CE
Greek world	A geographical term that corresponds to ancient writers' amorphous mapping of Greek-speaking cities

Table P.1 *(cont.)*

Term	Definition
identity	An inward-facing category of self-evaluation (how you conceptualize yourself)
India	An ancient country located east of Aithiopia
modern Egypt	A modern nation located in northeast Africa, north of Sudan
modern India	A modern nation located on the Indian subcontinent
modern race	A doctrine that assigns fixed traits to groups of people loosely based on laws of hypodescent
Nubia	An ancient historical region whose geographical location roughly corresponds with modern Egypt and Sudan (spanning the First to the Sixth Cataract of the Nile)
Persian empire (Achaemenid)	An extensive empire that lasted from c. 550 BCE to 330 BCE; the lowercase "e" democratizes the privileged delineation of "empire"
race	An outward-facing category of evaluation (how you conceptualize others)
racism	The social practice of applying a double standard to people loosely based on their physical appearance; developed in the wake of the transatlantic slave trade
Roman empire (Augustan)	An extensive empire that lasted from 27 BCE to c. 476 CE; the lowercase "e" democratizes the privileged delineation of "empire"
Sudan	A modern nation located in northeast Africa, south of modern Egypt and west of Ethiopia
white (lowercase)	An objective color marker
White people (uppercase)	A modern, socially constructed group that exists in contradistinction to Black people

Abbreviations

I use the abbreviations of the *Oxford Classical Dictionary* (4th ed.) if they appear thereafter.

All Greek text is from the *Thesaurus Linguae Graecae*. Unless otherwise noted, all translations from the ancient Greek and Latin sources are my own.

For the student, nonspecialist, or the curious reader, immediately preceding the bibliography I also offer a list of recommended modern translations of the four primary sources on which I focus in this study: Aeschylus's *Suppliants*, Herodotus's *Histories*, Lucian's satires, and Heliodorus's *Aithiopika*. On this latter, I use a direct transliteration of the Greek spelling, rather than the common (Latinate) *Aethiopica*. I discuss my use of "Aithiopia" further in sections 1.3 and 6.3.

Aer.	Hippocratic treatise, *De aere, aquis, et locis* (*On Airs, Waters, and Places*)
Anach.	Lucian, *Anacharsis* (*Athletics*)
Argon.	Apollonius of Rhodes, *Argonautica*
Ars am.	Ovid, *Ars amatoria*
Astr.	Lucian, *On Astrology*
Ath.	Athenaeus, *Deipnosophistae*
Cyr.	Xenophon, *Cyropaedia*
Diod. Sic.	Diodorus Siculus, *Library*
Diog. Laert.	Diogenes Laertius, *Lives, Teachings, and Sayings of Ancient Philosophers*
Dionys. Per.	Dionysius of Alexandria, *Periegesis*
FGrH	Felix Jacoby and Stefan Schorn, eds. *Fragmente der griechischen Historiker.* 5 vols. Leiden:Brill, 1923–.
FHN	Tormod Eide, Tomas Hägg, R. H. Pierce, and László Török, eds. *Fontes Historiae Nubiorum: Textual Sources for the History of the Middle Nile Region between the Eighth*

Century BC and the Sixth Century AD. 4 vols. Bergen: University of Bergen Press, 1994–2000.

fr.	fragment
Hdt.	Herodotus, *Histories*
Heliod. *Aeth.*	Heliodorus, *Aithiopika*
Her.	Ovid, *Heroides*
HN	Pliny the Elder, *Naturalis historia* (*Natural History*)
Il.	Homer, *Iliad*
Ind.	Lucian, *Adversus indoctum* (*Ignorant Book Collector*)
Med.	Euripides, *Medea*
Met.	Ovid, *Metamorphoses*
Mor.	Plutarch, *Moralia*
Od.	Homer, *Odyssey*
Arist. [*Phgn.*]	Pseudo-Aristotle, *Physiognomies*
Pyth.	Pindar, *Pythian Ode*
Scyth.	Lucian, *The Scythian or the Consul*
Strabo	Strabo, *Geography*
Supp.	Aeschylus, *Suppliants*
Syr. D.	Lucian, *De Syria dea* (*On the Syrian Goddess*)
Tox.	Lucian, *Toxaris: A Friendship Dialogue*
Thuc.	Thucydides, *The History of the Peloponnesian War*
V A	Philostratus, *Vita Apollonii* (*Life of Apollonius of Tyana*)
Ver. hist.	Lucian, *Verae historiae* (*True Stories*)

CHAPTER I

Introduction
The Metatheater of Blackness

Untangling Blackness in Greek Antiquity charts the literary and artistic representations of black people in ancient Greece.[1] Delving into primary sources ranging from the fifth century BCE to the fourth century CE, I unearth numerous performances of blackness from ancient Greek literature and art. Ancient authors and artists create characters, contemporary scholars analyze these *personae*, and readers and viewers bring their own preoccupations to the fore. Running alongside this inquiry of portrayals of black people, a deep probing of race's precarious grip on skin color uncovers the silences, suppression, and misappropriation of blackness within modern studies of Greek antiquity. Shaped foundationally by performance studies and critical race theory, this project maps out an archaeology of blackness that rejects simplistic conflations. Altogether, this anti-racist study promotes a contextualized, critical approach to representations of black people in Greek antiquity.

1.1 Prologue: An Educational Revolution

In their 1968 memo, "On the Abolition of the English Department," lecturers Ngũgĩ wa Thiong'o (then known as James Ngũgĩ), Henry Owuor-Anyumba, and Taban lo Liyong spearheaded an educational revolution at the University of Nairobi. Eager to sweep out the vestiges of British colonialism from the university's English department, Ngũgĩ, Owuor-Anyumba, and Liyong proposed renaming their department "The Department of African Literature and Languages" and suggested

---

[1] Throughout the book, I make deliberate use of orthography and modifiers to differentiate between ancient and modern peoples and places, between colors and descriptors of socially constructed groups, and I assign specific connotations to certain key terms. I discuss my rationale for these choices in the second section of this introductory chapter, but I encourage the reader to consult the Note on Nomenclature and Table P.1, above, before reading this chapter and subsequent chapters.

a revised curriculum that emphasized the centrality of Africa via the study of its oral and written literature, art, and drama.[2] Building on this manifesto for literary emancipation, Ngũgĩ later drew attention to the immense significance of the written language in his collection of essays *Decolonising the Mind: The Politics of Language in African Literature* (1987). Here, the Kenyan scholar bid farewell to the English language as his literary medium and vowed to write all future works in Swahili and his native Gĩkũyũ. Instead of espousing colonial languages on the African continent, Ngũgĩ urged fellow African writers to develop literature in their mother tongues.[3]

This intentional erasure of Africa from the twentieth-century Kenyan curriculum serves as a reminder that unchallenged biases can lead to academic colonialism. Writing from a different context, I nonetheless heed Ngũgĩ's appeal for a plurality of voices in the literary archive.[4] His determined efforts to democratize the reading experience embolden me to prioritize representations of black people within the purview of ancient material. Moreover, Ngũgĩ's insistence that language connotes power compels me to interrogate both the written word and the dynamic power plays that undergird it.

Snapshots from Ngũgĩ's career underline the real-life stakes of literary liberation. After Kenya gained independence from Britain in 1963, Ngũgĩ worked with Kenyan farmers at the Kamĩrĩĩthũ Community Educational and Cultural Centre to create plays that examined unchecked political control in their country. Soon after the 1977 performance of *Ngaahika Ndeenda* (*I Will Marry When I Want*, 1997), a play that recounts a crumbling love affair between a poor woman and the son of her wealthy landlord, Kenyan government officials arrested Ngũgĩ. Following his release from prison and protracted exile, he returned to Nairobi and survived a violent assault. These glimpses into Ngũgĩ's life lay bare the challenging position in which writers find themselves. They cannot divorce

---

[2] Ngũgĩ (1973: 145–50). Ngũgĩ's linguistic emancipation extends to his name; by 1972, he had replaced his colonial name "James" with his Gĩkũyũ name "Ngũgĩ." Taking cues from Africanist scholars, I refer to this writer as "Ngũgĩ" throughout the book.

[3] Some of Ngũgĩ's contemporaries suggested that his linguistic choice privileged the Gĩkũyũ people over other ethnic groups in Kenya (discussed in Appiah [1992: 4, 199 n. 29]; and Sicherman [1990: 34]). Mũkoma wa Ngũgĩ (2018) highlights the importance of African languages in African literature (which I discuss further in Section 6.2); Warner (2019: 27–29) traces the ways that African, specifically Senegalese, writers "restage the literary" realm in response to linguistic schisms.

[4] Although Ngũgĩ's decolonizing efforts inspire my investigation of ancient Greek literature and art, I refrain from applying the language of decolonization to this inquiry because such an act would strip the methodology of its context for the sake of an inclusive, yet superficial, metaphor (Tuck and Yang [2012]). As for the language of the "archive," Hartman's (2008: 2) expansive definition of the archive as "an asterisk in the grand narrative of history" guides my use of this term.

themselves from their historical present. There can be rich synergy in self-aware, collaborative literary initiatives, as evidenced in Ngũgĩ's work at the University of Nairobi and the Kamĩrĩĩthũ Centre, but there are costly consequences associated with revolutionary undertakings.[5]

Classicists are not exempt from such visceral reactions to their work. For instance, Donna Zuckerberg and Sarah Bond have received praise for calling to task racist ideologies masquerading as relics of Greco-Roman antiquity.[6] They also have both spoken publicly about the death threats they have received following the publication of their articles about White supremacist receptions of Roman imperial history and polychromy on ancient Greek sculptures, respectively. Such vitriol reminds invested parties that much work remains to be done. The immense task of rehabilitating the academic terrain requires a vast community of thinkers who are willing to apply precision and historical depth to the subjects of their research.[7] I align my study with this trend in the hopes that my contextualized account of ancient formulations of blackness and their modern reception will encourage others to undertake similar research in the future.

1.2 Performances of Blackness

Throughout my contextualized account of blackness in Greek antiquity, I recognize that the twenty-first century is undeniably implicated in any iteration of "performances of blackness," a phrase that discloses my theoretical underpinnings. That is, I enlist the help of critical race theorists and performance studies scholars, both of whom continually interrogate categories of skin color and performance. From the 1950s onward, critical race theory has functioned as a complex methodology that breaks down polarizing categories. This relatively recent constellation of theories unsettles the prevailing argument that modern race is a form of objective science.[8] Committed to deconstructing rigid power dynamics, critical race theorists

---

5 Ngũgĩ's fight against colonialism spans many decades from the 1960s; see Ngũgĩ (1964); Ngũgĩ and Mugo (1976); Ngũgĩ and Ngũgĩ wa Mĩrĩĩ (1997); Ngũgĩ (2006); and Ngũgĩ (2018). Gikandi (2000) offers a comprehensive analysis of Ngũgĩ's career.

6 See Zuckerberg (2016) and Bond (2017).

7 This community includes Classicists (The Postclassicisms Collective [2020]), scholars of theater (Wetmore [2002]), English (Walters [2007]; Hairston [2013]; Barnard [2018]), modern Greek studies (Tziovas [2014]), and religion (Cahana-Blum and MacKendrick [2019]), to name a few.

8 Many scholars date the birth of critical race theory to 1952, the year that Frantz Fanon's *Peau noire, masques blancs* (*Black Skin, White Masks* [2008]) was published. I differentiate between "modern race" and "race" below, in Section 3 of this chapter. Haley (1993, 2005, 2009) and Bell (in press) offer models for integrating critical race theory into Latin literature and imperial Roman art, respectively.

embark on a two-pronged project: to analyze the broad scope of modern race and scrutinize the unstable valence of skin color. Theorists such as Frantz Fanon, Kimberlé Crenshaw, and Karen E. Fields and Barbara J. Fields have generated incisive theorizations of Blackness that refute simplistic analyses of Black people.[9] As I discuss in later chapters, their sophisticated conceptualizations of Blackness speak to a wide range of audiences beyond their own time period and field of expertise (medicine, law, sociology, and history, respectively). Performance studies, which emerged in the 1960s in the fields of anthropology, sociology, and theater studies, draws the writer, performer, and audience together into a tripartite relationship. Performance studies transforms literary and visual constructs into performers who manipulate their words and appearance to expose substantial challenges that they face. Despite performers' roles as fictional characters, their shrewd performativity grants them agency within circumscribed confines. Meanwhile, in terms of pragmatics, the term "performative," developed by the linguistic philosopher J. L. Austin in 1962,[10] helps to articulate the agential force of performers' semiotics (i.e. words, dress, and nonverbal gestures) as they wield different types of "language" to circumvent adverse situations.

Nestled within the realm of performance studies, the metatheater is another useful tool with which I parse performances of blackness. Coined by Lionel Abel, the metatheater is a self-referential form of drama that incorporates various instances of reflexive theatricality.[11] On a base level of theatrical engagement, playwrights create characters, characters enact performances, and performances attract viewers. Operating beyond these parameters, the metatheater recasts dramatists and the drama in which they participate as performers who warrant investigation. In other words, the metatheater houses characters who are aware of their own performances ("drama within drama") and offers a bird's-eye view of the dramatic performance itself ("drama about drama").[12] A horizontal mode of inquiry applies to all parties involved in these metatheatrical productions. In this vein, I treat each genre discussed in subsequent chapters as a stage on which

---

[9] See Fanon (1952), Crenshaw (1993), and Fields and Fields (2014).   [10] See Austin (2016).

[11] Abel (1963).

[12] Quotations are from Ringer (1998: 7). Abel (1963, 2003) interprets the latter form of reflexive theatricality ("drama about drama") as a manifestation of the playwright's disillusion with mimicry; he also distinguishes between the metatheater, which deals with the imaginary world, and tragedy, which deals with the real world. Dustagheer and Newman (2018) present a helpful survey of the metatheater; Taplin (1977) and Dobrov (2001) offer metatheatrical approaches to ancient Athenian tragedy.

performances of blackness take place. Art history, tragedy, historiography, satire, and the novel morph into sites of production.

Situated at the intersection of critical race theory and performance studies, Black performance studies informs my analysis of performances of blackness. The early genealogy of this interdiscipline dates to the mid-nineteenth century, and its formal introduction into the academy occurred in the 1990s.[13] Sometimes deemed performance historians, scholars of Black performance studies examine the movement and expressive culture of Black people, and they develop creative tools with which to animate Black performances that occur in a variety of settings.[14] Despite the wide range of their source material, Black performance scholars converge on what E. Patrick Johnson deems "the material, intellectual, and aesthetic matrix that is black performance."[15]

Along with their expansive take on performers, scholars of Black performance studies rework the timeline and location of performances. For example, Tavia Nyong'o conceptualizes performative hybridity as an untamed, time-bending trope that speaks to both the future and the past.[16] Nyong'o's temporal malleability is especially relevant to my twenty-first-century inquiry of representations of blackness in Greek antiquity. Furthermore, Nyong'o's inclusion of genres not traditionally associated with performance, such as historiography, in the domain of performance speaks to my theorization of genres as metatheatrical stages on which performances of blackness occur. Relatedly, I also build on Saidiya Hartman's analysis of quotidian performances enacted by enslaved Black people in the antebellum American south. Hartman traces an arc from

[13] This date corresponds to academic publications by the Black Public Sphere Collective (1995) and Dent (1998). Nonetheless, M. Gaines (2017) and Nyong'o (2019) expand on Black artistic production from the 1960s onward. Even still, earlier theorists of Black performances include Henry "Box" Brown (b. 1815; discussed in Brooks [2006: 66–130]), Pauline Hopkins (1859–1930), and Zora Neale Hurston (1891–1960; discussed in Hurston [1998]; and DeFrantz and Gonzalez [2014: 2–3]). When listing people's life span, I provide only a birthdate for cases where there is no death date available from a reliable source.

[14] Johnson (2006) and Colbert (2015) offer critical overviews of Black performance studies (which Colbert delineates as "African American Performance"). See also Brody (1998); the contributions in Phelan and Lane (1998); the contributions in Elam and Krasner (2001); Johnson (2003); Moten (2003); and Brown (2008). For a few examples of Black performance studies in practice: Brody (2008) treats seemingly minute gestures, such as the choice of punctuation, as performance pieces that trouble notions of stability; Young (2010: 7–12, 165–66) unearths meaningful dialogue buried underneath Black performers' silence; see also Benston (2000) and Fleetwood (2011: 33–70). These examples reflect only some of the current trajectories in the ever-growing realm of Black performance studies.

[15] Johnson (2006: 449). The lowercase "black" reflects Johnson's capitalization practices, not my own.

[16] Nyong'o (2009).

"scenes of subjection" into scenes of resistance, inspecting the ways in which Black subjects successfully transform small-scale acts such as work slowdowns and unlicensed travel into scenes that are part of the larger stagecraft of slavery. In the process, Hartman defamiliarizes expectations about what a typical theatrical performance looks like. For instance, she converts the inhumane site of the auction block into a scene from the "theater of the marketplace" where unwilling actors encounter a willing audience.[17] In this constrained context, enslaved people's refusal to bare their teeth or dance on command exposes the limitations of their self-authorizing performances. Hartman later elaborates that "what unites these varied tactics [of resistance] is the effort to *redress* the condition of the enslaved, *restore* the disrupted affiliations of the socially dead, *challenge* the authority and dominion of the slaveholder, and *alleviate* the pained state of the captive body."[18] Although a vast historical distance separates Hartman's source material from my own, her supple theorization of performances that redress, restore, challenge, and alleviate reimagines the scope of performance at the intersection of modern race and power.

Daphne Brooks offers another useful blueprint for excavating performances of blackness. Focusing on Black people's stage presence in the late nineteenth century, Brooks reworks the confines of performance to highlight linguistic and corporeal acts of dissent that occur among Black people who occupy seemingly marginal roles. She documents the phenomenon whereby, in spite of the strict social boundaries that govern their lives, they rupture the veil of Blackness under the guise of performance.[19] That is, their performative interventions destabilize presumed notions of inferiority based on skin color. Coupled with her investigative lens, Brooks's trope of dramatic interference informs my present inquiry of performers who upend audiences' expectations.

Equally convincing is Brooks's acknowledgment that there can be no singular, correct interpretation, as writers' intentions collide with those of performers, readers, and spectators. These multiple points of contact lead to numerous discoveries. Brooks's admission of her own position as spectator is especially liberating in its disavowal of authority.[20] Indeed, attempts to completely restore the "original" interplay between performers and their audience are futile, whether for performances of Blackness in the nineteenth century or for performances of blackness in Greco-Roman antiquity. Brooks's self-reflexive body of theory works well alongside

---

[17] Hartman (1997: 37, 43, 54, 78).   [18] Hartman (1997: 51; emphasis added).
[19] The language of unveiling evokes Du Bois (1903).   [20] Brooks (2006: 9–10, 66–206).

Classical reception theory to underline the many audiences who engage with ancient source material, including characters within the world of ancient Greek literature and art, their audiences, and twenty-first-century readers. As Lorna Hardwick and Emily Greenwood assert, even frail connections between the ancient and modern worlds can lead to substantial discoveries.[21] In other words, a confrontation between contemporary observations and ancient representations results in a vibrant metatheater.[22] Taking cues from Nyong'o, Hartman, and Brooks, I include a variety of performers and performances in this investigation. My subjects of inquiry include characters written for the theatrical stage, characters in literary texts, and characters who interact with viewers in the sphere of visual and material culture.

A well-known example illustrates ongoing permutations of performances in relation to skin color. In 2002, a recent graduate of Howard University sued her alma mater on charges of discrimination. After losing the case, she built her career around advocating for the Black community: her artwork focused on Black people, she taught in the Africana Studies Program at Eastern Washington University, and she became the president of the Spokane chapter of the National Association for the Advancement of Colored People. Her bronze-toned skin and curly hair suggested that she had Black ancestors. Further, in a 2015 interview with KXLY4 (a local news station in Spokane, Washington), she encouraged this link by stating that her son and father were Black.[23] Later that year, however, the truth began to tumble out once her birth parents revealed that their daughter, was White: Rachel Anne Doležal had accused Howard University of discriminating against her because she was White, among other reasons; she had started wearing artificial hair and cosmetically darkening her skin in 2009; her "son" was her adopted brother; and her "father" was a close friend.[24] Despite these revelations, Doležal continued to identify as Black. In 2017,

---

[21] See Hardwick (2003) and Greenwood (2010). I use the language of frail connections after Greenwood (2010: 1).

[22] Notable examples: Greenwood (2010) in the anglophone Caribbean; Rankine (2006) and McCoskey (2012) in the United States; Goff (2013) in anglophone West Africa; Parker (2017a) and contributions to his volume (2017b) in South Africa; McConnell (2013) in the African diaspora; contributions in Rizo and Henry (2016) in the hispanophone and lusophone worlds; Padilla Peralta (2020) in the Dominican Republic. Umachandran (2019) eloquently draws attention to the geographies of empire that have contributed to the global discipline of Classics.

[23] Humphrey (2015).

[24] A. Gaines (2017: 158–71). In the memorandum opinion and judgment of Doležal's appeal to the District of Columbia, the listed reasons for alleged discrimination are "race, pregnancy, family responsibilities and gender, as well as retaliation" (*Moore* v. *Howard U.*, 876 A.2d 640 [D.C. Cir. 2005]).

she legally changed her name to Nkechi Amare Diallo and published a memoir, *In Full Color: Finding My Place in a Black and White World*, on the cover of which she appears with bronze-toned skin, an Afro, and a colorful beaded necklace.

Even though Doležal's externally derived skin color, hairstyle, and accessories imply a performative aspect to her self-presentation, she has insisted that Blackness is not a costume to be worn or discarded. Instead, she has described her Blackness as a previously hidden part of herself that she intends to lay bare.[25] Conversely, her self-avowed unveiling runs counter to her adoption of artifices of Blackness, such as curly hair and brown skin. Regardless of her best efforts to fortify her status as a Black person, the uproar following the discovery of her lineage exposed the inescapable intersubjectivity of Blackness. In other words, socially constructed ways of seeing Blackness greatly affected her acceptance into the Black community. If skin color were the sole determinant of Blackness, Doležal's bronze-toned skin would have granted her swift entry. But the lack of a universally agreed-upon arbiter of Blackness made Doležal's assertion of Blackness difficult to accept in the public sphere. She muddled this already murky territory by combining visual markers with a variety of nonvisual elements, such as her public comments about negative interactions with police officers and her remarks about being a mother to Black men. Alisha Gaines separates Doležal's intentions from her actions by referring to Doležal's self-identification as an instance of "empathetic racial impersonation."[26] This phrase simultaneously underscores Doležal's yearning to understand perspectives outside of her own and the false consciousness that she has achieved. Indeed, Doležal has been adamant about her love for Black people, but the idea that there is a fixed criterion for becoming "Black," and that she has met this criterion, overlooks the complexities of reality. By reducing Blackness to particular tropes, Doležal has risked essentializing a historically fraught category for the sake of her project of self-discovery. At the same time, her malleable performance of Blackness highlights the unsteady platform on which Blackness stands. Those who decry her claims of Blackness solely because of her White parentage also

[25] "It [identifying as Black] felt less like I was adopting a new identity and more like I was unveiling one that had been there all along" (Doležal, 2017: 90–91; see also the documentary, *The Rachel Divide* [2018], dir. Laura Brownson).

[26] A. Gaines (2017: 158–71); see also Tuvel (2017). Sidestepping the impulse to offer a partisan response in support of or in indignation at Doležal, Hobbs (2015) focuses on contextualizing Doležal's performance.

subscribe to an essentialist fallacy – namely, their reliance on genealogy to determine Blackness privileges the laws of hypodescent, known as the "one drop rule" because it assigns the label "Black" to anyone with at least one Black ancestor.[27]

Doležal's story of chosen exile raises pressing questions of definition for any historical inquiry that examines the nexus of color and social categorization.[28] In addition, the aftermath of her transformation reveals potential consequences awaiting those whose identification with Blackness lacks a historically informed analysis of its contours. Although the Black–White constraint has no valuable application in ancient Greece, ancient writers and artists employ skin color and other visual markers in curious ways that speak poignantly to their own contexts as well as to the twenty-first century.[29] Therefore, as I begin this bidirectional inquiry into blackness in ancient Greek literature and art, careful handling of pertinent vocabulary is vital. In Section 1.3 of this chapter, my explication of geographical and chromatic terms reflects my own efforts to expose the relay between ancient and present contexts. My self-reflexive endeavor contributes to the democratizing force of this study; as scholars who inhabit a world in which we see through the prism of modern race, none of us are exempt from scrutiny. In Section 1.4, I interrogate the privileged status of two White scholars, Martin Bernal and Grace Hadsley Beardsley, alongside their scholarship about blackness in antiquity. Section 1.5 alerts readers to what lies ahead in the remaining chapters.

[27] Dating to the seventeenth century, the laws of hypodescent stated that no matter how diverse one's parentage, any Black parentage or ancestry determined one's categorization and that of his/her descendants. This drastically codified the assignation of Blackness and remains a powerful marker of social categorization in the twenty-first century.

[28] Wald (2000); Hobbs (2014). This overview of Doležal's story serves as merely one example of passing in America. Other examples of White people who passed as Black include Clarence King (b. 1842; discussed in Sandweiss [2009]), Ray Sprigle (1949), Grace Halsell (1969), Jessica Krug, and C. V. Vitolo-Haddad (both discussed in Flaherty [2020]). Despite this list, recorded instances of Black people passing as White outnumber those of White people passing as Black, presumably due to the social and financial benefits associated with membership in the White community. A notable example of this phenomenon includes Belle da Costa Greene (1883–1950), the daughter of Richard Theodore Greener, the first Black member of the American Philological Association (currently named the Society for Classical Studies), who identified as a White woman of Portuguese ancestry. Passing was also a popular phenomenon in apartheid-era South Africa; Michael Chapman's "Concrete Poem: The Chameleon Dance" highlights its ever-changing classifications (1986: 198).

[29] The Black–White binary refers to the categorization of people as either "Black" or "White." Even those who do not identify with either group are labeled as members of one or the other. In addition to creating social division, this binary model corrals all "non-White" people (a nebulous category in and of itself) into an amorphous group of "Black" people.

1.3   Building the Literary Landscape

In terms of geography, the borders of the Greek world were in flux from the fifth century BCE to the fourth century CE. Demarcations between regions were especially variable as hegemony in the Mediterranean region shifted from Athens to Rome. Although some Greek-speaking cities adopted an aggregative Greek identity during the Greco-Persian wars and later received the generic label of "Greece" after the battle of Corinth (146 BCE), "Greece" did not always reflect the geographic or political realities of individual cities.[30] Cognizant of the porous topography and extensive temporal scope of "Greece," I use "Greece" as an umbrella term that refers to a general location as well as specific Greek-speaking cities, such as Argos (Chapter 3) and Athens (Chapter 5).

Notwithstanding the complicated mapping of Greece, the temptation to fossilize historically specific labels persists in contemporary scholarship. For instance, many scholars assign the name of a modern country, Ethiopia, to an ancient region. The conflation between the only African country to successfully defend its sovereignty in the nineteenth century and a classical civilization whose popularity increased alongside nineteenth-century American Egyptomania is misleading, but not surprising.[31] To contextualize Ethiopia in the late nineteenth/early twentieth century: Liberia was the only other independent nation (under the auspices of the American Colonization Society) on the African continent, and many uprisings against European colonizers were underway, such as those led by Bambatha kaMancinza in South Africa, Henrik Witbooi in German South West Africa (present-day Namibia), Samory Touré of the Wassoulou empire (Guinea, Sierra Leone, Mali, and Côte d'Ivoire), Kinjikitile Ngwale in German East Africa (Tanzania), and John Chilembwe in Nyasaland (Malawi). Roughly concurrent with Ethiopia's victory against Italy in the Battle of Adwa (1896), Africans and African Americans adopted an iteration of the country's name ("Ethiopianism") during their quest for religious and political freedom.[32]

The term "Africa" has its own historical trajectory as well. In this book, I use "Africa" to refer to the modern continent (see Figure 1.1). This decision stems from the fact that extant Greek texts refer to the land

---

[30] Gleason (2006); see also contributions in Whitmarsh (2010). Jonathan M. Hall (1997, 2002) examines the transforming conceptions of ancient Greek identity from aggregative to oppositional.

[31] On Egyptomania, see Trafton (2004); Moyer (2011) helpfully frames interactions between Greece and Egypt as transactional, rather than protocolonial. I discuss my capitalization practices relating to "classics" and "Classics" below (p. 13).

[32] On Ethiopianism, see Nurhussein (2019: 1–20).

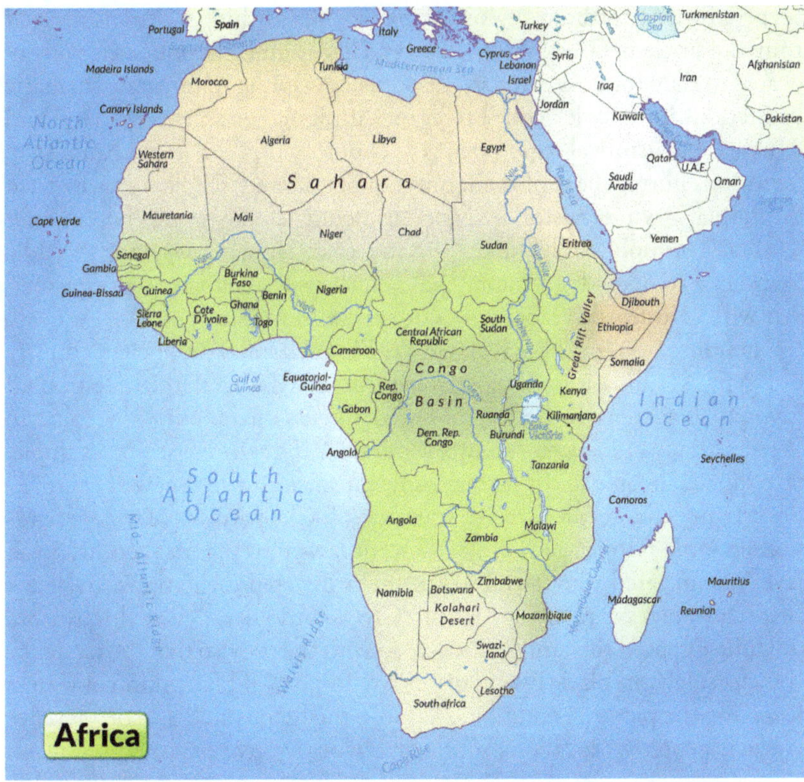

Figure 1.1 Map of Africa. © Panther Media GmbH/Alamy Stock Vector.

mass south of Greece as "Libya," not "Africa." The etymology of "Africa" suggests that Romans renamed the region they acquired from Carthage after the Aouriga, a group of people native to this region.[33] A fragment from Ennius's satires (239–169 BCE) provides the earliest recorded instance of "Africa" in Latin literature: *testes sunt . . . quos gerit Africa terra politos* ("there are elegant witnesses whom the African earth bears," *Saturae* 3.16). Subsequent iterations of "Africa" in Latin literature split Africa into *Africa Vetus* ("Old Africa") and *Africa Nova* ("New Africa").

As part of my ongoing opposition to anachronistic vocabulary, I denote the ancient region spanning two countries, the southern region of modern

---

[33] Mudimbe (1994: 72); Sellassie (1972: 45); Miller (1985: 6–14). Conybeare (2015) traces the first use of "Africanness" (*africitas*) to the sixteenth-century humanist Juan Luis Vives.

Egypt and the northern region of Sudan, as "Aithiopia" (transliterated from the ancient Greek *Aithiopia*), and I describe the modern country located in the Horn of Africa as "Ethiopia."[34] Opting to integrate thematic distinctions into my lexicon, I refer to "Aithiopia" as an ethereal land and "Nubia" as a historical region that is in contact with Greece and Rome. My definitions mirror those of modernity, in that literary scholars use the term "Aithiopia," while historians and museum curators generally prefer "Nubia," etymologically linked to the Old Nubian *napi* and Middle Egyptian *nbw* ("gold"). Due to the inconsistent labeling practices associated with "Kush," this label does not appear in my study.[35]

Extending from the Nile Delta to the First Cataract, the ancient country of Egypt is another part of this landscape.[36] In fact, the question of Egyptian blackness has often initiated discussions about skin color in Greek antiquity. Debates about Cleopatra VII's skin color, for example, have spurred people to sift through ancient sources with renewed energy.[37] Uncertainty about the precise identity of Cleopatra's paternal grandmother and a retrojection of hypodescent laws into the first century BCE have complicated the terrain. To be sure, representations of black Egyptians traverse many genres in Greek antiquity.[38] For this reason, I include Egypt in this study. But I do so with the proviso that the tendency to focus solely on black Egyptians in any inquiry of black skin color risks distorting the picture because it overlooks the literary and artistic presence of black people in locations south of Egypt. Moreover, an emphasis on

---

[34] Selden (2013: 329–31); Asso (2011).

[35] Selden (2013: 328); O'Connor (1993: 3, 37–41); Burstein (1995: 127); Raue (2019). The use of "Kush" as a temporal marker ranges from the eleventh century BCE to the mid-fourth century CE (as used by Eide, Hägg, Pierce, and Török [1994]), the eighth century BCE to the fifth century CE (as used by Török, 1997), and the third century BCE to the second century CE (as used by Morkot [1991]). Geographically, some scholars treat "Kush" as synonymous with Upper Nubia (as used by Buzon [2011: 21]; Faraji [2016: 223]). Even though I refer to "Nubia" as an ancient region, it is important to note that descendants of Nubians currently inhabit modern Egypt and Sudan, among other places (Emberling and Williams [2020: 2–3]). Sidestepping questions of nomenclature, Egyptologist Vanessa Davies created the Nile Valley Collective (https://nilevalleycollective.org/), an interdisciplinary group of scholars who promote the contextualized study of ancient civilizations along the Nile Valley.

[36] I distinguish between "Egypt," an ancient country, and "modern Egypt," a contemporary nation. As detailed in Table P.1, I also make this distinction for India.

[37] Debates about black Egyptians appear in scholarship on Greco-Roman antiquity (Lefkowitz [1997: 34–52]; Haley [1993]; McCoskey [2004]), Afrocentric research (Rogers [1946]; Clarke [1988]), African studies (Mudimbe [1994]), and archaeology (Bard [1996]).

[38] Examples include Herodotus, *Histories* 2.57, 104; *Tragicorum Graecorum Fragmenta*, Adespota F 161 (Snell, Kannicht, and Radt, 1971–2004; quoted in Vasunia [2001: 48]); the water jar (*hydria*) reproduced in Figure 1.2. With the student and nonspecialist reader in mind, I spell out the authors and titles of the ancient texts at first mention in text or notes and use the standard abbreviations of the *Oxford Classical Dictionary* thereafter. See the List of Abbreviations provided in the frontmatter.

Egypt alone risks reinforcing contemporary hierarchies that situate modern Egypt *in* Africa but not *of* Africa.[39] This prepositional shift highlights the tension between objective geography and subjective inclusion. By pulling Egypt out as the single exemplar of a powerful country south of the Mediterranean, scholars inevitably promote the current, problematic assessment of northern Africa as separate from and superior to the rest of the continent.[40]

As a visual corrective to isolationist renderings of Egypt, Fred Wilson's 1993 *Grey Area (Brown Version)* graces this book's cover. This installation features five plaster copies of the famous bust of the Egyptian queen Nefertiti. Sculpted around 1340 BCE, the original limestone bust depicts a woman with light brown skin wearing a tall, flat-topped blue hat and elaborate neckwear. Wilson's effigies differ from their ancient referent solely in terms of color palette. The color of each monochromatic head resembles the spectrum of human skin tones, ranging from off-white to dark brown.[41] Through his creative rendering of Nefertiti, Wilson questions the impulse to lighten the skin color of Egyptians, and he reframes the parameters of beauty as it relates to skin color. In one fell swoop, he rebuffs modern attempts to colonize Egypt without overlooking the historical context of his subject matter.

As reflected in my linguistic and geographic choices, I remain convinced that language can contribute to an overhaul of Greece and Rome's monopoly of antiquity. Its revolutionary potential governs my approach to the following terminology: "Greek antiquity" and "Greco-Roman antiquity." I use these terms throughout the book to denote a time period that spans from the eighth century BCE to the fourth century CE. These terms diminish the monopoly that Classicists inadvertently reinforce when they consider the unmarked phrases "ancient world" and "antiquity" as synonyms for Greco-Roman antiquity. For my purposes, "ancient world" and "antiquity" are broad terms that refer to past communities whose geography need not correspond to only one region of the world. In addition, I treat the uppercase "Classics" as shorthand for "the worlds of Greece and

---

[39] I use this language after W. E. B. Du Bois who, upon reflection on his graduate school years, states that he was "in Harvard, but not of it" (quoted in Provenzo [2002: 36]). See also Kamugisha (2003).

[40] I note a few examples of these geographic manipulations: ethnologist C. G. Seligman (1930: 96–156) attributed all of Egypt's cultural developments to the Hamites, whom he describes as "Caucasians," and Egyptologist Flinders Petrie proposed a theory of an influential "New Race" that entered Egypt during the Old or Middle Kingdom (see Challis [2013: 167–85]). The location of Egyptian objects in the British Museum also contributes to this lopsided history, which I discuss in Section 2.4.

[41] Excavated from Amarna (Egypt), Nefertiti's bust is currently a part of the Egyptian Museum in Berlin's collection: Reid (2015: 87–93).

Rome in antiquity," and "Classicist" as a synonym for "the person who studies Greco-Roman antiquity." Rather than fossilize "Classics" or prop it up as an exemplar of the past, this capitalization of "Classics" aims to decenter the Greco-Roman monopoly of antiquity.[42] By marking "Classics" as a (problematic) stand-in for ancient Greece and Rome, this orthographic practice enables the lowercase "classics" to encompass societies including and beyond the Mediterranean region.

I have thought carefully about the orthography of blackness I use in this book. I have adopted a referential practice in which I shift between "black" and "Black." Lowercase "black" denotes people with black skin and phenotypic features including full lips, curly hair, and a broad nose in ancient Greek literature and art, while uppercase "Black" refers to a modern, socially constructed group of people whose melanin is merely one of its distinguishing traits.[43] Due to the numerous Greek terms employed to categorize black people, a transliterated label is not a suitable alternative. Color-based vocabulary varies, such as *melangchimos* ("black," *Supp.* 719), *melangchrōs* ("black-skinned," Hdt. 2.104), *kuaneō*, and *aithaleō* ("blazing" and "dark," Dionys. Per. 22, 1111). Some of these terms share etymological roots via the Greek adjective *melas*, while others have their own derivational history. Geography-based markers are also slippery, in that writers describe black Egyptians (Hdt. 2.57), Aithiopians (Hdt. 3.101), Indians who live near Aithiopians (*Supp.* 285), and Colchians (Hdt. 2.104; *Pyth.* 4.212). Adding to this convoluted matrix, chromatic markers did not always correspond to phenotypic features. Some colors became personal nicknames that were passed down to descendants even when physical characteristics no longer applied.[44] Therefore, I define "black people" as an inclusive term for geographically diffuse peoples with black skin, as they are rendered in ancient Greek literature and art.

Despite my best efforts to sharpen my vocabulary, this visual application of "black" inevitably lends comparison to current politics surrounding skin color. Undeniable similarities linking "black" people and "Black" people aside, "Black" is not a direct referent for "black." Marked differences warn against the elision of the two, such as the near-universal phenomenon of assuming commonalities among Black people that does not directly map onto Greek antiquity. Even more, the structural inequalities that Black people face are specific to their historical context. Philosophers of modern

---

[42] Greenwood (2010: 12–13).

[43] Haslanger (2012: 7) and Crenshaw (1993: 1244 n. 6) influence my capitalization practices.

[44] Cameron (1998). Funke (2018) examines the ways that nineteenth- and twentieth-century cultural linguists analyzed ancient Greek color terminology.

race have attempted to identify the particular register of Blackness in the twenty-first century. As Charles Mills wryly observes, "the conceptual and theoretical cataracts on the white eye" prevent the Black experience from being philosophically visible. That is, one cannot enjoy an unencumbered view of Blackness without an invasive operation of the "white eye."[45] If left untreated, the eye's "theoretical cataracts" will build up and eventually obscure Blackness altogether. The process of erasure operates differently for representations of black people in Greek antiquity. Contemporary audiences examine representations of black people through a modern lens that threatens to cloud their vision.[46] In an effort to provide a clear-eyed outlook, my manipulation of "black" and "Black" keeps the particular historical context of each term in view at all times.

Productive, albeit unanswerable, questions arise from a confrontation between the terms "black" and "Black": when does the objective color "black" become conflated with the polarizing marker "Black"? What is the process by which attributing visual significance to a group transforms into labeling a group based on this marker? Attempts to pinpoint this shift fall short, as there was no sudden transition. The process required time, ruthlessly creative minds, and malleable power dynamics. In their quest to justify the violence they meted out to fellow humans, European enslavers generated socially constructed categories which gave "Black" an abstract, yet stringent, chromatic valence. The emergence of anti-Black racism, developed in European countries, propelled this shift.[47] Centuries later, their designated categories still resonate. In his analysis of various labels used to describe people of African descent, such as "colored," "Negro," "Afro American," and "African American," Robert B. Stepto envisions each designation as part of a metaphorical family tree whose branches connote specific time periods. He warns readers of the pitfalls that

---

[45] Mills (1998: xvi). See Morrison (1993); Jacobson (1998); Boxill (2001); the contributions in the inaugural issue explored by the Racial Imaginary Institute (2017); the contributions in Taylor, Alcoff, and Anderson (2018); and Glasgow et al. (2019).

[46] Examples of this clouded vision include the treatment of the "Apollo of the Belvedere" statue as an epitome of White beauty (refuted by Bond [2017]) and the intense denunciation of chromatic diversity in Roman antiquity following the BBC's cartoon of a black soldier from Roman Britain (dispelled by Beard, as discussed in Zhang [2017]).

[47] Heng (2018). Whitaker (2019) argues that the mirage-like notion of "black" as morally deficient and "white" as morally sufficient can be traced to the European and English Middle Ages; the contributions in Albin et al. (2019) encourage audiences to resist the weaponized nostalgia that has fallen under the banner of the "Middle Ages." See also scholars who examine the presence of Black people in the early modern European period, such as Hall (1995) and Habib (2007) for England; Cohen (1980) for France; the contributions in Hering Torres, Martínez, and Nirenberg (2012) for the Spanish Atlantic world; and the contributions in Bethencourt and Pearce (2012) for Portugal and lusophone countries.

can come with alterations in nomenclature.[48] Stepto's observation prompts me to probe the modern label "Black." The racist coupling of "Black" and inferiority is a problematic reality in the twenty-first century, but readers retain the freedom to question the relevance of such vocabulary within a wider historical scope. In our era, scholars have reclaimed and adapted the term "Black."[49] Christina Sharpe's practice of anagrammatical blackness is especially helpful in outlining my nomenclature. Her ability to "anarrange" (arrange anew) terminology inspires my imposition of new meaning onto historically trenchant vocabulary. As part of my anagrammatical project, I wade through the recent past – that is, the debris of "Blackness" in the wake of the twenty-first century – in order to access the deep past, that is, the plurality of "blackness" in the world of Greek antiquity. Simply put, I assert that "black" people are in dialogue with, but not a replica of, "Black" people.[50]

1.3.1   Uncoupling Blackness from Race and Racism

"Race," a term that modernity has conflated with skin color, requires similarly rigorous evaluation. As early as the 1940s, scholars opted to use "ethnicity" rather than "race" as the primary determinant of group membership.[51] In *Man's Most Dangerous Myth: The Fallacy of Race*, Ashley Montagu bristles against the "tyranny of race" because of the emotional responses it engenders. He prefers the socially dynamic label of "ethnic group" due to its noncommittal and flexible status.[52] Bridget M. Thomas echoes Montagu's assertion that "ethnicity" is more suitable

---

[48] "Each change that defines a generation may well cut off that group from what has come before" (Stepto [1991: xiii]). Keita (2000: 27) also challenges the conflation of "'Africa' = 'colored' = 'Negro' = 'black.'"

[49] The négritude movement marked a pivotal rehabilitation of Blackness in the twentieth century. Articulated by Léopold Sédar Senghor, Léon-Gontran Damas, and Aimé Césaire, négritude explored the unity and rich complexity of Black identity. Premised on the inherent value in Blackness, négritude spoke back to the hostile rendering of Blackness on the part of racist societies. On the debts of the négritude movement to earlier attempts to reclaim the term *nègre*, see Miller (1998: 33–41). On women's pivotal role in the négritude movement, see Sharpley-Whiting (2002) and Joseph-Gabriel (2020).

[50] Sharpe (2016: 75–77, 80, 87, 118, 122–23), which looks back to Spillers (2003: 209) and Moten (2003: 1). I use the language of the wake after Sharpe (2016).

[51] Examples include Hall (1997); Smith (2003); the contributions in McInerney (2014) (in particular, those by McInerney, Munson, Siapkas, Luraghi, and Papadodima); and Figueira and Soares (2020).

[52] Montagu (1997: 521–30). In the 1951 revision of the 1950 UNESCO Statement on Race, Montagu and his fellow authors removed any mention of "ethnicity" and repeatedly used "race," even as they discussed their failed attempts to find another word to adequately replace the contentious term (UNESCO [1969a, 1969b]). In the most recent UNESCO Declaration on Race and Racial Prejudice (1978), "race" and "ethnic group" each appear numerous times.

than "race."[53] Thomas links "ethnicity" to its implied etymological precedent, the ancient Greek noun *ethnos*, thereby belying the deeper complexities of *ethnos* for the sake of general legibility.[54] Furthermore, Thomas's and Montagu's shared desire to sidestep the power differential embedded into "race" renders words unruly time bombs that require detonation rather than time capsules in need of constant upgrading. Calling to task both those who liken race to skin color and those who dismiss the term outright, Denise McCoskey demands that scholars consider other criteria for the charged term "race." In her salient assessment, she explains:

> Although scholars in other fields have insisted on the status of race as an organizing principle whose precise contours change over time, Classicists have continued to reduce the broader concept of race to its narrow modern "biological" form, one that holds skin color as its primary sign. Recognizing rightly that ancient Greeks and Romans did not base identities on skin color, Classicists have not asked instead whether racial identities were based on other criteria, but have instead dismissed the term "race" altogether.[55]

Indeed, it is only through breaking down and rebuilding categories that scholars can write responsible, historically specific studies. For this investigation of Greek antiquity, I propose a definition of the mechanism we deem "race" as an outward-facing category of evaluation. During the act of racial formation, to use Omi and Winant's language, people label others as a way to bolster their own self-importance.[56] In turn, these subjective classifications lead to the establishment of unequal power paradigms. This open-ended definition of race subsumes seemingly disparate content signifiers of race, including visual and non-visual elements in the sphere of culture (dress, religion, language, etc.), under a single entity. This grouping of seemingly fixed and variable features reinforces my general claim that race is a slippery phenomenon in ancient Greek literature and art.

---

[53] Thomas (1998: 74).

[54] Jones (1996) traces the various meanings of *ethnos* in Herodotus's *Histories*.

[55] McCoskey (2003: 104–05); see also McCoskey (2012: 27–34). Beyond Classics, historians explore factors that shape the construction of modern race (Kidd [2006]), and sociologists emphasize the changing parameters of modern race (Dixon and Telles [2017]).

[56] I use the concept of "racial formation" after Omi and Winant (1994). My inclination to broaden "race" beyond chromatic markers builds on a forthcoming analysis by Rebecca Kennedy of race as a system of institutionalized inequality "based on imaginary and moving signifiers for human difference" and Heng's (2018: 3, 27) treatment of race as "a structural relationship for the articulation and management of human differences." See also Murray (2021). My thanks to Rebecca Kennedy for sharing a draft of her chapter "Race and the Athenian Metic Re-visioned" to appear in *Identities in Antiquity*, edited by Vicky Manolopoulou, Joseph Skinner, and Christina Tsouparopoulou (Routledge).

Broadly conceived, my reframing of "race" is not solely reducible to skin color, and at times it has little connection to skin color.[57] Instead, my iteration of "race" replaces restrictive ideologies with polyvalent possibilities. Multiple axes of difference are far more determinative of someone's race than skin color alone, which itself is rarely the most important or consistent marker of race in Greek literature and art. Although it may initially seem disorienting to rework the definition of race within a book whose thematic issue is black skin color, my semantic shift pushes back against the limiting treatment of race as nothing more than chromatic appearance. In other words, "race" encompasses a number of factors that mark groups of people as distinct from each other, and skin color is but one part of a larger mechanism of hierarchical difference in an expansive system of race.

A final caveat on "race": due to my insistence that the study of race in Greek antiquity is inescapably dialogic and diachronic, it follows that the conception of race with which I work here is inevitably contingent on the view of the present and thus a work in progress. My current recasting of "race" is the product of my own wrestling with this term for the purposes of Greek antiquity. This is not an admission of negligence or defeat. Rather, this frank disclosure serves to point out the importance of continual reflection and wide-ranging viewpoints. It is my hope that readers will assume the role of conversation partners in the ongoing projects of revising race within and beyond Greek antiquity.

In tandem with the intersubjective status of race, "identity" is a product of social relations. Unlike "race," which is prone to interpretation without the input of the racialized person, "identity" refers to people's self-ascribed conceptualization of themselves. People articulate their own identities with varying levels of consultation from others.[58] Together, "race" and "identity" reveal the mixture of social projections and self-declared moments of assertion at play during performances of blackness. More capacious than our current vocabulary, these intentionally overlapping terms usher readers

---

[57] Some nineteenth-century scientists manipulated a non-chromatic approach to modern race to the detriment of their field; among them was Samuel Morton, who defended his biased view of Black people's inferiority based on the size of their crania: see Selden (1998: 191–95).

[58] Swain (1996: 10); Appiah (2018). The voluminous literature on Greek identity includes Hall (1997), who pairs it with ethnicity; the contributions in Whitmarsh (2010) which probe its local permutations; and Hartog (1988) and Hall (1989), who assert that a binary model governs its construction in Greek history and tragedy, respectively. In relation to Roman identity, Dench (2005) offers a chronological examination; others examine geographic permutations in the west (Revell [2016]; Johnston [2017]), east (Woolf [1994]; Andrade [2013]), north (Mullen [2013]), and south (Mattingly [2011]) of the Roman empire.

into a world in which assigned and chosen categories collide as characters struggle to equate their conception of themselves with others' views of them.

Etymologically linked to race, "racism" calls for careful attention. Fields and Fields helpfully define racism as a social practice of applying a double standard, "the missing step between someone's physical appearance and an invidious outcome."[59] They treat modern race, part of a brutally convenient doctrine that assigns fixed traits to groups of people, as the principal unit of racism, but they wisely caution against conflating "race" and "racism." Instead, Fields and Fields coin the term "racecraft" to refer to the way in which racism produces modern race as its object of knowledge. Racecraft highlights the presence of racism while simultaneously obscuring the agents of racist acts.[60] Fields and Fields's methodology is instructive in teasing apart Benjamin Isaac's repackaging of racism into "proto-racism," a term that Isaac developed to describe a fixed model of discrimination in Greco-Roman antiquity. In *The Invention of Racism in Classical Antiquity* (2004), Isaac's use of proto-racism alongside his assertion that ancient Greeks and Romans viewed all black people as fixedly marginal reproduces anachronistic assumptions about the perceived marginality of people based on skin color. Moreover, his insistence that black people had minimal impact on Greco-Roman antiquity overlooks significant interactions between Greece/Rome and Nubia, evidenced in Ptolemy II's campaign to capture Nubian elephants and the discovery of Roman remains in Meroe, the capital of Nubia spanning the period c. 300 BCE–300 CE.[61] On a visual note, the art used for the cover of Isaac's book eerily evokes racecraft's contortions of the Black male body (see Figure 1.2). The image features a large, naked, muscular dark brown man strangling and trampling on light brown men. The coding of dark brown skin as innately threatening has no historical roots in the sixth century BCE.[62]

---

[59] Fields and Fields (2014: 27, 15–17). I treat the concept of racism as a phenomenon of reception and not as a datum about ancient Greece and Rome.

[60] Beyond the academy, racecraft is seared into the public's consciousness, as is evidenced in national coverage on the criminalization of Blackness: "Driving while Black" (LaFraniere and Lehren [2015]), "Napping while Black" (Caron [2018]), and "Jogging while Black" (Futterman and Minsberg [2020]), all of which can be subsumed into the ontological category "Living while Black" (Henderson and Jefferson-Jones [2020]).

[61] Isaac (2004: 33, 49–50); conversely, see Samuels (2015: 730). I prefer to use terms such as "discrimination" or "prejudice" to describe violent opinions based on ancient Greek notions of fundamental difference because they do not invoke contemporary color-based rhetoric. Burstein (2008a) and Casson (1993: 249 n. 6) discuss Ptolemy II's elephant campaign; Török (1989–90) and Doxey, Freed, and Berman (2018: 152) examine Roman remains in Meroe.

[62] Irwin (1974); Sassi (2001: 1–33); Eaverly (2013); Olya (2021). I discuss "brown" as a color marker below (p. 33). To complicate matters further, the color palette has been altered on Isaac's cover; the

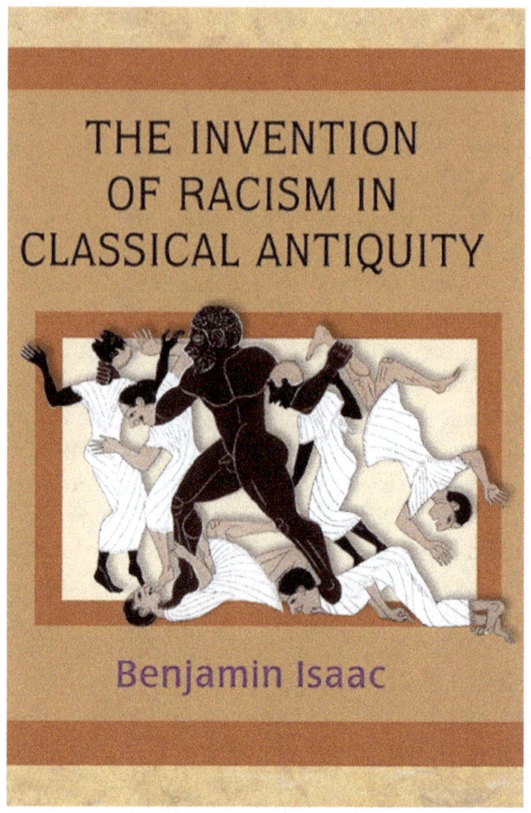

Figure 1.2 Cover of *The Invention of Racism in Classical Antiquity* by Benjamin Isaac (2004). © Princeton University Press.

Only a viewer with specialized knowledge of Attic vase paintings understands this image as a reference to Hercules fighting against Egyptian priests whose king, Busiris, has ordered them to sacrifice the demigod. Those unfamiliar with the water jar (*hydria*) on which this image is based may miss this allusion and instead assume a link between the central figure's dark color and a propensity for violence.[63]

central figure on the original *hydria* is red (Hemelrijk [1984: 54]; Miller [2000: 417–22]; Derbew [2018]).

[63] Productive reviews of Isaac (2004) include those by Lambert (2005), Haley (2005), and McCoskey (2006). Isaac admits that "Greek vases do not always make an effort to render skin color realistically, as may be seen" (2004, figure 1). Haley responds: "it is clear that the vase painter had enough contact with people of African descent to render them realistically and not as caricatures" (2005: 453). In

While the concept of racism, developed in the wake of the transatlantic slave trade, has no direct ancient equivalent, Isaac's erasure of black people coupled with a jarring visual complement is a questionable interpretative move. The superficial nod to chromatic diversity on his book cover may lead to better sales, but such a depiction belies the scant engagement with skin color within the book's pages.[64] This cover mirrors an underlying tension in Classics between what the field is doing versus what the field markets itself as doing. In essence, Isaac's avoidance of a loaded topic demonstrates the simultaneous hypervisibility of black skin color in the twenty-first century and oversight of the complex representations of black people in ancient Greece.

1.4 Privileged Perspectives

Dissenting from dismissive views of black people, I propose a two-way approach to blackness that situates black people in their particular context without ignoring the conceptual filter of Blackness. This bidirectional methodology is attentive to the interference of modern projections, not to mention the potential risk of circularity in examining a phenomenon under an oft-used term. In this vein, an inspection of a few twentieth-century thinkers illustrates the ways that anachronistic biases about contemporary Blackness can seep into scholarship about representations of blackness in Greek antiquity.[65]

Reiterating ideas previously espoused by Black scholars, Martin Bernal caused a great stir in the academy with the publication of his three-volume *Black Athena* (1987, 1991, 2006).[66] Bernal elucidated two main models of

a later publication, Isaac (2009: 49) laments the difficulty of discussing skin color due to its slipperiness and elasticity. On an encouraging note, Isaac (2017) points out anachronisms that exist in modern studies of ancient empires.

[64] McCoskey (2006: 251–52). See also the image of a bust of Socrates wearing a Malcolm X cap on the cover of Lefkowitz's (1992) earliest review of Bernal's *Black Athena*. Lefkowitz (2008: 38) has stated that she was not consulted about this cover design and learned about it only when she received a hard copy of her article.

[65] There was nineteenth-century interest in this topic as well, such as Löwenherz's (1861) study of black people in ancient Greek art.

[66] Some of Bernal's Black predecessors include Phyllis Wheatley (1773), Edward Wilmot Blyden (1869), Martin Delany (1879), Anténor Firmin (1885), Marcus Garvey (1925), Drusilla Dunjee Houston (1926), Cheikh Anta Diop (1955), Engelbert Mveng (1972), and St. Clair Drake (1987–90). Keita (2000) and Malamud (2016) offer a fuller list of Bernal's African and African American predecessors. In 1968/9, the rise of Afrocentrism, an academic movement that grew out of the African Heritage Studies Association, also led to a growing number of Black interlocutors. Moses (1998) and Burstein (2002) offer useful overviews of Afrocentrism that sidestep Howe's (1998) and Asante's (2007) polemic portrayals.

Greek history: the "Ancient Model," which suggested that Egypt and Phoenicia were the progenitors of ancient Greek civilization; and the nineteenth-century "Aryan Model," which denied Egyptian and disputed Phoenician influence in ancient Greece.[67] Toggling between material from the ancient and modern worlds, Bernal also called the field of Classics to task for ignoring the racist ideologies that informed nineteenth-century conceptions of the discipline. Although Bernal's general argument about Egypt's considerable impact on ancient Greece and his criticism of nineteenth-century prejudices are persuasive in their own right, Bernal's publications are not relevant to this book, for a few reasons.[68] First, Bernal was not the first scholar to recognize that people from Greek cities interacted with those living along the Nile Delta. Decades before Bernal penned his thesis, Black writers had taken a keen interest in the representation of black people in Greco-Roman antiquity.[69] Bernal's status as a White, Cambridge-educated professor based at Cornell University perhaps influenced the amount of serious engagement that Classicists afforded to his work over that of his Black predecessors. Bernal himself mused on his privileges:

> Certainly, if a Black [*sic*] were to say what I am now putting in my books, their reception would be very different. They would be assumed to be one-sided and partisan, pushing a Black nationalist line, and therefore dismissed. My ideas are still so outrageous that I am convinced that if I, as their proposer, did not have all the cards stacked in my favor, I would not have enjoyed even a first hearing. However, being not only white, male, middle-aged, and middle-class but also British in America has given me a tone of universality and authority that is completely spurious. But it's there! So I must thank my lucky stars, rather than any talent that I may possess for having got this far, even if this is as far as I go.[70]

Notwithstanding Bernal's positionality, his quest to lessen "European cultural arrogance," as he deems it, stands in stark contrast to his brief mentions of non-Egyptian civilizations situated along the Nile Valley.[71] His decision to spotlight Egypt implies that nineteenth-century European arrogance was limited to Egypt when in fact, European bigotry spread far

---

[67] Bernal (1987: 437) preferred to align himself with Black intellectuals such as W. E. B. Du Bois, Ali Mazrui, and George James rather than those he deemed "the academic orthodoxy"; Bernal's religious identity as a Jewish man also informed his critique of the Aryan model. For a sample of scholarship in direct response to Bernal's publications, see Levine (1989); Lefkowitz and Rogers (1996); Berlinerblau (1999); Adler (2016: 113–72).

[68] Bernal received a fair amount of criticism that refuted his archaeological and linguistic evidence, such as that of Morris (1996) and Jasanoff and Nussbaum (1996).

[69] See note 66 above.   [70] Bernal (1989: 20).   [71] Bernal (1987: 73).

beyond this region. His brief mentions of "Ethiopia," a label he uses to describe the region south of Egypt, reifies this geographic bias.[72] That is, Bernal's fulsome survey of Greece alongside his sparse discussion of "Ethiopia" promotes a world map that positions Egypt closer to its northern neighbors and further away from civilizations along the Nile Valley.

Bernal's deployment of ancient Greek literature as a source of historical facts poses additional challenges. For instance, Bernal concludes that Aeschylus's portrayal of Danaus in the *Suppliants* reflects Aeschylus's belief that Danaus was a Hyksos ruler who colonized Argos in the second millennium BCE.[73] This conflation of a fictional character and a historical event encourages readers to disregard context for the sake of cohesion. As a final critique, Bernal's proposed models assign a discriminatory undertone to the Aryan Model and an idyllic one to the Ancient Model. His binary distinctions oversimplify the uneven tropes of power that govern both of these models.[74] Subsequently, recent publications have moved beyond the debates surrounding "Black Athena" to trace the overlapping relationships between Egypt, Nubia, Greece, and Rome.[75]

Predating Bernal's publications, renewed interest in representations of black people in Greco-Roman antiquity led to publications by Classicists Grace Maynard Hadley Beardsley (b. 1896), Frank Snowden, Jr. (1911–2007), and Lloyd Thompson (1932–97). Based at Goucher College, Howard University, and the University of Ibadan (Nigeria), respectively, these scholars contributed to academic discourse about representations of black people in Greco-Roman antiquity. As Black Classicists, Snowden and Thompson were both keenly aware of the high stakes associated with their research, and they constantly fought against contemporary attempts to colonize Greco-Roman antiquity.[76] Part of this fight included shared criticism against the work of their White predecessor, Beardsley. Under the

---

[72] Bernal refers to "Ethiopia" five times, focusing on its linguistic, specifically Semitic, features (1987: 11, 56–57, 344, 353, 431).

[73] Bernal (1987: 88–98).

[74] See Mudimbe (1994: 95), as a comment attributed to McCoskey, and E. Hall (2002), who cautions against substituting one faulty model (Aryan Model) for another (Ancient Model). Edith Hall (2002: 149) helpfully reframes the binary framework with the following questions: "who on earth did Greeks *think* they were? Why did they think it? And what is it about the late twentieth century which renders the issue so important to *us*?"

[75] Such as: Byron (2002); Török (2009); contributions in Orrells, Bhambra, and Roynon (2011); McCoskey (2012); Hatke (2013); Vasunia (2016); Ashby (2020); contributions in Moyer, Lecznar, and Morse (2020).

[76] Snowden (1947, 1948, 1970, 1981, 1983, 1988, 1997, 2001, 2010); Thompson (1989, 1993). Parmenter (2021) situates Snowden's scholarship in its historical context. Thanks to archival work pioneered by Michele Valerie Ronnick, it is possible to place Snowden and Thompson in a wider timeline of Black male Classicists, beginning with Richard Theodore Greener (1844–1922), Edward Wilmot

supervision of David Moore Robinson, an archaeologist who edited the series in which her book was published, Beardsley wrote a dissertation that eventually became *The Negro in Greek and Roman Civilization: A Study of the Ethiopian Type* (1929).[77] Relying on 1920s terminology, she argued that Negroes occupied a servile position beneath Caucasians, her nomenclature for their Greek counterparts.[78] Throughout her discussion of "tribal dances" and "grotesque depictions" of black people in Greco-Roman antiquity, Beardsley reinforced anachronistic, negative stereotypes. Conversely, Snowden vehemently defended Greco-Roman antiquity from any claims of prejudice against black people with an extensive analysis of ancient Greek and Latin sources. As a Black scholar in twentieth-century America, he recognized the cultural importance denied to members of his community, and he exonerated ancient representations of black people from the negative prejudices that Black people were forced to endure. Resisting Snowden's outright rejection of a chromatic hierarchy, Lloyd Thompson concluded that Romans had diverse views of black people.[79] Despite their ideological divergence, Thompson echoed Snowden's disapproval of Beardsley's prejudicial attitude. In his censure of Beardsley's language, Thompson explains, "many of her observations offer crude revelations of a mental and intellectual enslavement to the norms and assumptions of her own society."[80]

Among her Classicist peers, Beardsley's work received many positive reviews.[81] But her tendentious descriptions did not go completely unnoticed

---

Blyden (1832–1912), and William Sanders Scarborough (1852–1926). See Scarborough's autobiography (2005), scholarly writing (2006), and Greek textbook (2018) for unparalleled insight into the career of the first professional Black Classicist in the United States. Ronnick (2016) lists some of the earliest known Black female Classicists, such as Anna Julia Cooper (c. 1858–1964) and Helen Maria Chesnutt (1880–1969).

[77] Fraser (1929: 426) suggests that Robinson chose Beardsley's research topic for her. Despite Robinson's unscrupulous advising practices, brought to light decades later, Robinson supported Beardsley's career (Kaiser [2015]); Robinson's support was perhaps due to his own academic interest in representations of black people in Greco-Roman antiquity.

[78] In 1929, Black people also used the term "Negro" self-referentially.   [79] Thompson (1989).

[80] Thompson (1993: 25–26). Other critiques of Beardsley: "Beardsley told us far more about her own America of the 1920s than she did about Rome when she put forward the silly view that the Roman practice of decorating ordinary household objects and personal trinkets with depictions of blacks is clear evidence of a contemptuous attitude towards blacks as a 'race'" (Thompson [1993: 21–22]), and "Beardsley's pseudo-sociological forays . . . [are] hardly more than effusions (however unconscious) of the American racism of her own milieu" (Thompson [1993: 25]); see also Snowden (1947: 288–90) with n. 120). Surprisingly, Mudimbe (1994: 25) offers a favorable view of Beardsley.

[81] Generally positive reviews include those by Fraser (1929); Mylonas (1929); Chapouthier (1930); Dugas (1930); and Verhoogen (1932). Among the slightly critical reviews, Myres (1930: 513) bemoans the limitations of Beardsley's study ("unfortunately Dr Beardsley does not carry the study of negroid types far enough to throw any light on the sources"); and Smith (1930: 511) remarks on Beardsley's

by a wider circle of Black academics. In October 1929, the *Journal of Negro History* published a book review that criticized her assumptions. The reviewer, William M. Brewer, encouraged Beardsley to concentrate on literary and material evidence in her scholarship, rather than personal beliefs. He accused her of tainting her research with discrimination and ended with the following insight:

> When one observes that this work is the production of one of our accredited universities [Johns Hopkins] noted for scientific investigation he must wonder how a book so meretricious should receive the approval of that institution. This may be due to the fact that in America, we have paid such a little attention to ancient Africa and know such a little about it that almost any unscientific production may impress us as valuable.[82]

Brewer's review involves a critique of modern race-thinking interposing itself in a book about Greco-Roman antiquity. This public reckoning of Beardsley's uncritical scholarship continually prompts me to sort through the ways that contemporary ideology can masquerade as history.

1.5 Overview of Chapters

Illustrative rather than exhaustive, this book unearths sophisticated tropes of blackness spanning from the fifth century BCE to the fourth century CE. I explore how writers and artists create a world in which performers rework blackness alongside claims of foreignness and Greekness. In the following chapters, black skin color appears among other determinants of race (outward-facing categories of evaluation) as Argive Greeks, royal Aithiopians, curious Scythians, and athletic Athenians participate in heterogeneous performances of blackness. Together, the sustained accounts that I offer in the following five chapters highlight the wide range of performances in Greek antiquity. I conclude each chapter with a contemporary comparandum that generates new avenues of connection between the Black archive and the ancient Greek tradition. My thematic scope may be jarring for any readers expecting a chronological guide to blackness. This interdisciplinary premise, however, is well equipped to

---

"almost irresponsible hunt after replicas" and the "occasional jarring phrase and some awkward passages."

[82] Brewer (1929: 533–34). Black scholars J. A. Rogers and W. E. B. Du Bois also commented on Beardsley's study: Rogers (1967: 79–82) used Beardsley's research to buttress his argument that black people existed in Greco-Roman antiquity, and Du Bois referred to Beardsley's book as a "stupid combination of scholarship and race prejudice" (uncited quotation in Keita [2000: 50 n. 22]).

illuminate performances of blackness that speak back to the discipline's myopia regarding skin color.[83]

Due to my desire to untangle blackness from the virulent narrative of anti-Black racism, I devote considerable attention to black Aithiopians.[84] I limit my discussion of black Indians, highlighting their literary presence only in relation to their western neighbors in Aithiopia. This brevity does not discount the significance of India in Greco-Roman antiquity. Instead, this choice to focus on Aithiopia emphasizes the different stakes for ancient subjects when they are mapped onto twenty-first century topography. In other words, the pervasiveness of anti-Black racism in the twenty-first century compels me to foreground representations of black people whose geographic location maps onto the (modern) African continent. That being said, the performative framework laid out in the following chapters provides a useful starting point for those interested in representations of other black people in Greco-Roman antiquity.[85]

Chapter 2, "Masks of Blackness: Reading the Iconography of Black People in Ancient Greece," analyzes visual paradigms of blackness in Greek antiquity as they appear on fifth-century BCE janiform cups that depict black and brown faces on opposite sides. Lopsided projections are all the more pronounced when dealing with visual constructs of black skin color in Greek antiquity. Disputing the uncomfortable ease with which some art historians presume a fixed connection between black people and bumbling inferiority, I argue that black faces are part of a repertoire of sympotic performance. Similar to theatrical masks, faces on janiform cups enable drinkers in the symposium to adopt new identities. Ensuing discourse about the chromatics on janiform cups leads to a broader inspection of museums' display of the iconography of black people in ancient Greek art. An extended examination of museum displays reveals the temporal clash that can occur when modern audiences view the iconography of black people in Greek antiquity. In particular, a visit to the British Museum lays bare the institution's troubling tendency to privilege ancient Egypt as a powerful nation at the expense of Nubia.

---

[83] Good sourcebooks already exist, such as those by Mveng (1972); Schneider (2004); Kennedy, Roy, and Goldman (2013); and Grundmann (2019).

[84] Apposite to my language of "untangling," Grundmann (2019) offers a sociocultural examination of hair alongside skin color in ancient Greece, and Hodder (2011, 2012, 2016) elaborates on modern entanglement theory.

[85] For readers interested in black Indians, see the sophist Philostratus's *Life of Apollonius of Tyana* and the poet Nonnus's *Dionysiaca*. Parker (2008), Seaford (2016), Cobb (2018), and Stoneman (2019) discuss encounters between India, Greece, and Rome; Vasunia (2013) analyzes the role of Classics in modern India.

Maintaining the lens of performance, Chapter 3, "Masks of Difference in Aeschylus's *Suppliants*," examines the role of black skin color in this tragedy (c. 463 BCE) which details the story of Danaus's fifty black daughters, referred to as the Danaids, who flee from Egypt to Argos to escape a forced marriage to their Egyptian cousins. Their knowledge of Greek religious rites convinces Pelasgus, the ruler of Argos, that they are distant kin even though their black skin seemingly denies their identity as Argive Greeks. This chapter asserts that the Danaids are sophisticated performers who successfully diminish the relevance of their physical alterity and declare their hybrid identity as Egyptians and Argive Greeks. They emerge as supple and subtle ethnographers of the Argives to whom they are making a supplication. Conversely, their Argive audience – the intradramatic spectators of the Danaids' alterity – proves to be less able to comprehend their hybridized Argive Greek identity. An exploration of political resonances, particularly in relation to Athenian metics, draws Aeschylus's fifth-century audience away from the distant mythical realm and toward their own political reality. Altogether, the drama speaks to the complicated exteriority of race and identity in one Athenian tragedy.

In line with the previous chapter's refashioning of foreignness, Chapter 4, "Beyond Blackness: Reorienting Greek Geography," delves into the historical portrayal of Greece's distant neighbor, Aithiopia. Herodotus's iteration of Aithiopia simultaneously looks back to Homer's utopian Aithiopia and positions it as a historical allegory that critiques Athenian imperial aggression (Hdt. 3.17–26). Through the Aithiopian king's comments to Egyptian spies, Herodotus undermines any fixed, negative assumptions about Aithiopians that may lurk in the minds of his fifth-century readership. Moreover, Herodotus labels people as Aithiopians based on their height, longevity, and skin color, thereby complicating a facile rendering of black people's external categorization (i.e. their race). A reciprocal ethnography of Scythians further exposes the instability of race as two Scythian men, Anacharsis and Scyles, wear Greek clothes and maintain their Scythian identity (Hdt. 4.76–80). Their untimely demise reveals the dangers that Hellenocentric Scythians face once they return to their xenophobic homeland.

The fluctuation between Scythians and Greeks reverberates in Chapter 5, "From Greek Scythians to Black Greeks: A Spectrum of Foreignness in Lucian's Satires." In this chapter, I explore Lucian's (c. second century CE) complex model of difference that relies unevenly on skin color, attire, and language. Lucian's trio of Scythian satires features characters who rework the relationship between race (external categorization) and identity within their specific contexts. The categories of "Greek" and "foreigner" become muddled as Greeks and Scythians share their impressions about black people in their midst: Greeks conflate blackness with Aithiopians or liken it to their own appearance with ease, while one Scythian man marvels at the sight of black Athenian athletes. These varied observations lead to a collective questioning of blackness in relation to Greek identity under the guise of humor.

Chapter 6, "Black Disguises in an Aithiopian Novel," continues to upend the limiting Greek–foreigner binary model. Heliodorus's novel *Aithiopika* (c. fourth century CE) traces the peripatetic journey of Charicleia, an Aithiopian princess rejected at birth because of the dissonance between her white skin and her parents' black skin. In this novel, which is the earliest extant example in the Greek language of a plot in which black skin constitutes cultural privilege, skin color is a volatile element: Charicleia exploits color as a disguise (Heliod. *Aith.* 6.11.3), her companion Theagenes uses skin color as a marker of trustworthiness (7.7.6–7), and a prophecy destabilizes both perspectives (2.35.5). Throughout the novel, Heliodorus wields skin color as a negotiable ethnographic tool that does not necessarily correspond to identity. This flexibility underscores Charicleia's own fluidity between several performative categories. She can be a beggar and a princess, a docile woman and the leader of her entourage, the daughter of a Greek man and an Aithiopian man. Readers are forced to be patient as Heliodorus masterfully exploits time to create a gap between what his characters know and what his readers have already grasped. In addition, this chapter situates Meroe, Charicleia's homeland and place of ultimate arrival, as a vibrant historical site in the classical world.

The Conclusion, "(Re)placing Blackness in Greek Antiquity," reiterates the invisible ontologies that haunt current assessments of black skin.[86] A final look at the poetry of Langston Hughes and Gwendolyn Brooks offers suggestive models for revamping polarizing approaches to Greek antiquity in the twenty-first century. Prefiguring Ngũgĩ's pioneering liberation work discussed at the start of this chapter, Hughes transforms insults into subversive jabs in "The Black Clown," and Brooks untangles preconceived misconceptions from the root in "To Those of My Sisters Who Kept Their Naturals."

---

[86] I also discuss invisible ontologies in Section 2.1. Haunting can lead to "that dense site where history and subjectivity make social life" (Gordon [2008: 8]).

CHAPTER 2

Masks of Blackness
Reading the Iconography of Black People in Ancient Greece

In fifth-century BCE Athens, the symposium provided a convivial space for various *polis* inhabitants, including poor Athenian men, metics, and perhaps women, to indulge in boisterous activities.[1] More than a homogeneous drinking party, the symposium was a pseudo-microcosm of the *polis* that reflected its heterogeneity.[2] Public performance, an integral part of the city, found its counterpart in the private world of the symposium. Within this world, guests played games and professed their erotic desires, sometimes at the same time. For instance, *kottabos*, ostensibly a game of skill that measured how accurately a drunk person could fling wine from a vessel onto a specific target, offered symposiasts a way to profess their love for someone in whose name they dedicated their throw. Participants engaged in these lively pursuits, all the while consuming copious amounts of wine from a variety of cups. Among these cups, revelers came face to face with various characters depicted on their drinkware, including janiform[3] (two-faced) drinking cups which fused brown and

---

[1] Jones (2014) asserts that non-elite people composed and performed musical pieces at Athenian symposia; conversely, Steiner (2002: 375–76) remarks that although there was a democratization of the symposium after Cleisthenes's reforms, there was no mixing between elite and non-elite people. Burton (1998) and Kennedy (2015) argue for the presence of women in the symposium; Corner (2012) argues against women's presence; and Goldman (2015) challenges the hypersexualization of the *aulētris* ("flute girl") in symposiastic spaces. Ancient Greek sources suggest a diverse group of symposiasts: the lyric poet Archilochus bemoans the presence of an uninvited Myconian who gorges on unmixed wine (fr. 124b [Ath. 1.7f–8b], as numbered in Gerber [1999b]), the narrator of the *Theognidea* welcomes a Scythian to the symposium (fr. 825–30, as numbered in Gerber [1999a]), and the lyric poet Anacreon asks his companions to desist from Scythian-like drinking practices (fr. 356b [Ath. 10.427b], as numbered in Campbell [1988]). In Plutarch's *Dinner of the Seven Wise Men*, Anacharsis's sympotic *persona* suggests that Scythian customs are more consistent and sensible than their Greek counterparts (*Mor.* 146e–164d; Hobden [2013]: 73–116, esp. 107–16; Hartog [1988]).

[2] I build on Corner's (2010: 356) reading of the symposium as a microcosm of the *polis* and Hobden's (2009) treatment of the symposium as a subversive reflection of the *polis*.

[3] The term "janiform" invokes Janus, the two-faced Roman god: one face looks to the past, and one looks to the future. See Appendix 1 for a list of extant janiform cups.

black faces together. In addition to functioning as vessels from which drinkers could imbibe alcohol, these cups allowed symposiasts to try on different faces within the privacy of their party. Through their use of cups, carousers came into close contact with brown faces, black faces, gods, and satyrs. The physiological effects of the wine within the janiform cups further blurred the sharp distinctions between the drinker and the life-like faces in his or her midst.

Millennia after their production, many of these janiform cups are now housed in American and European museums. Curators have struggled to extricate a suitable label for these objects, sometimes opting to delineate one face of the cup as "White" and "beautiful," and the other as "Negroid" and "humorous." The tendency among Classicists and art historians to slip between the categories of (ancient) black people and (modern) Black people further exacerbates these imprecisions.[4] More broadly, the whitening of ancient Greek bodies has created a pervasive hierarchy that relegates black bodies to its lowest rungs. Moving towards a balanced treatment of blackness, in this chapter I offer a reparative account of the iconography of black people on Attic pottery, in particular fifth-century BCE janiform drinking cups used in symposia. Visual representations of black people on Attic janiform cups invite viewers to the stage of the symposium, a site where performances of blackness occurred.

At the beginning of this chapter, I probe the scholarly inclination to apply modern categories to Attic janiform cups. Namely, my proposed nomenclature for janiform cups, brown and black faces, resists contemporary attempts to divorce these cups from their historical context. Next, I investigate janiform cups in their current location: museums. Various museums become performance spaces where ancient iconography meets contemporary reception. Both the objects themselves and paratextual details, such as their captions, contribute to the entanglement of (ancient) blackness and (modern) Blackness in the twenty-first century. As part of this inquiry, I examine the British Museum's display of objects from Nubia, a historical region associated with black people. I close the chapter with a look at recent museum exhibits and exhibitions that reinforce the importance of critical curation,

---

[4] I remind the reader to consult Section 1.3, the Note on Nomenclature, and Table P.1 on my deliberate use of orthography to differentiate between colors and descriptors of socially constructed groups, as well as my specific connotations for key terms.

particularly when displaying the iconography of historically overlooked groups.[5]

2.1 Seeing Brown and Black Faces

Twenty-five centuries after its production, a two-handled janiform drinking cup that might have been used in a convivial symposium sits in the Boston Museum of Fine Arts (MFA, Figure 2.1a–c). It affords numerous observations, not the least of which is its name: *kantharos*.[6] I refer to this object as a "cup," rather than *kantharos*, because "cup" prioritizes its function in the symposium. Furthermore, "cup" transports the object out of the museum, out of the sole purview of art historians, and away from the limitations imposed by disciplinary boundaries. The museum's label of this cup reads: "high-handled *kantharos* in the form of two heads." From bottom to top, the cup features a short base and a stylized body shaped to resemble two conjoined faces gazing in opposite directions. Loose curls peeking out of a black headband (*sakkos*) frame the face on one side, and tight curls sit atop the other. The delicate eyebrows and lack of facial hair on both faces suggest that they represent women. Greek text runs along the rim of the cup (ΚΑΛΟΣ Ο ΠΑΙΣ, Ο ΠΑΙΣ ΚΑΛΟΣ, "attractive is this boy, this boy is attractive"), and a neat arrangement of palm fronds appears on the neck's central section. A pair of handles is fused onto the sides of the cup: the handle bases are located directly above the ears on both of the faces, and the upper ends of the handles are fused with the palmettes. Finally, geometric square designs decorate the lip of the cup.

Over time, presumptions about skin color have bled into scholarly commentary about this janiform cup. Popular labels for the left-hand side of Figure 2.1c include: "white," "White," and "Greek." A proponent of the term "white," Frank Snowden, Jr. defends his preference: "It is likely that many Greeks referred to the blacks of these [janiform] vases as *melanes* and the white as *leukoi*, a terminology that would have been a natural development of the dramatic contrast between the black glaze and white paint, as well as a logical extension of the *melas–leukos* antithesis of the environment theory."[7]

---

[5] In line with museum terminology, I use "exhibit" to denote permanent museum displays and "exhibition" to refer to temporary installations.

[6] Nineteenth-century art historians Theodor Panofka and Eduard Gerhard were instrumental in the modern codification of these two-handled cups as *kantharoi*. More tenuous linguistic connections include: the harbor of Piraeus (Κανθάρου λιμήν: Aristophanes, *Peace* 145; Plutarch, *Phocion* 28.6.2) or Kantharos being the name of a potter who made these cups (Ath. 11.474d–e; discussed in Richter and Milne [1935: 25]).

[7] Snowden (1988: 61).

(a)

(b)

(c)

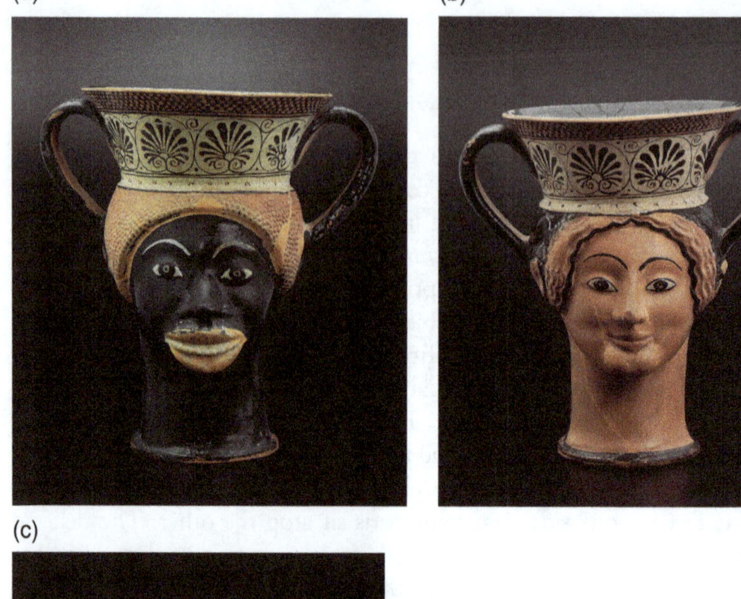
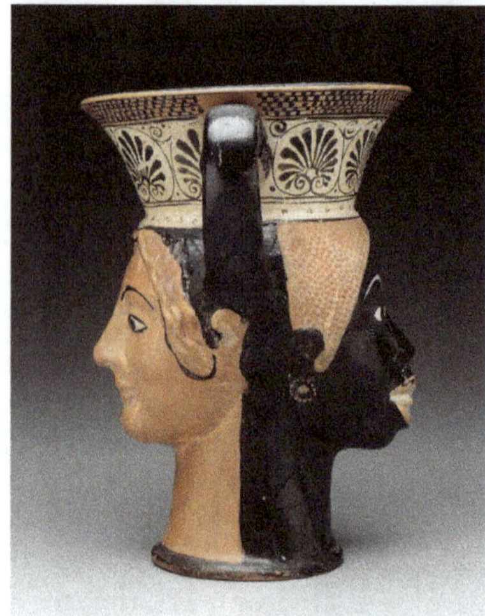

Figure 2.1a–c High-handled *kantharos* in the form of two heads, Attic black-figure ceramic, attributed to the London Class, c. 510–480 BCE. H. 19.2 cm, 98.926. © Museum of Fine Arts, Boston.

Upon closer inspection, Snowden's *melas–leukos* ("black–white") model falls apart. Barring the sclerae of both sets of eyes and the teeth of the right-hand face, the color "white" does not account for the visual composition of the cup at all. Even more, the term *leukos* ("white") is not an adequate signifier of skin color for all depictions of Greek people.[8] Greek iconographic tradition attributes white skin to Greek women and girls, not Greek men, and environmental treatises pair Scythians and white skin (*Aer.* 20). Snowden's conflation of the visual experience of seeing the color "white" and the constructed categorization of people as "White" (uppercase) ignores the historically specific context of the latter term.[9] The Black–White binary does not have an ancient visual referent. "White," an imprecise label that folds the amorphous category of "Greeks" into a contemporary group made up of a range of skin colors, reflects modernity's fixation on artificial categories. From the fifteenth century onward, careful policing of the parameters of "Whiteness" has enabled a subjective category to gain currency. Expanding this language of economics, Harryette Mullen compares Whiteness to legal tender.[10] Within Mullen's model, Whiteness operates as a transactional category in which power is doled out to select individuals. Its historical roots date back to the advent of the transatlantic slave trade, during which people formulated imbalanced equations of power that resulted in the supremacy of Whiteness. Due to this relatively recent timeline of calculated "Whiteness," it remains an ill-suited term to apply to ancient Greek iconography. Another popular label, "Greek," may initially seem promising because it coincides with an ancient group of people. Even with the temporal relevance of "Greek," this designation suggests a singular, fixed phenotype associated with "Greek" people that does not address the contested nature of this term.[11]

My proposed label for the face on the left-hand side of Figure 2.1c, "brown face," resists anachronistic presuppositions. Closely related to its material referent "clay-colored," "brown" subsumes different shades of color (i.e. light brown and dark brown) into one category. Although the lowercase "brown" loosely overlaps with "Brown," a modern social categorization used to describe people of South Asian descent among others, the lowercase term focuses on color while also alluding to metamorphoses of chromatically inflected language.[12] In other words, the emphasis on the

---

[8] Snowden's inclusion of "white" coincides with Knox's (1993: 26) labeling of ancient Greeks as "undoubtedly white or, to be exact, a sort of Mediterranean olive color."

[9] See Skinner's (2012: 98) description of "the face of a Caucasian woman" on a janiform cup and Winckelmann's preference for ancient Greek statues that appeared unpainted and marble-white; Harloe (2013); Hägele (2013: 253).

[10] Mullen (1994: 80–81). Mullen expands the financial metaphor in her description of White people of humble financial means benefitting from what she deems "color capital," a system of accounting that subtracts more from non-White people than from their White counterparts.

[11] Princeton University Art Museum's online catalogue refers to a face on a janiform cup as "Greek" (https://artmuseum.princeton.edu/collections/objects/20038; see Figure 2.4a–c).

[12] Prashad (2001) and Harpalani (2015) explore the use of "Brown" to refer to people of South Asian descent. Davé (2013) examines the phenomenon of "Brownface," a term she developed to describe

visual composition of "brown" sidesteps the warped mutations of "white."
I use the second word of this description, "face," to acknowledge the
anthropomorphic imagery on the cup. "Face" refers to the two-
dimensional subject of my investigation, the frontal area that spans from
the forehead to the chin, whereas a term like "head" encompasses the three-
dimensional body part above the neck. Taken together, "brown face"
resists the impulse to consider the left-hand side of the cup as historical
evidence of a particular group's phenotype. Instead, this designation
highlights the limited color palette in the artist's workshop. More broadly,
this nomenclature pushes back against a project of erasure that has overlooked what is immediately visible for the sake of mapping contemporary
binaries onto ancient Greek iconography.[13]

Descriptions of the color associated with the cup's right-hand face
(Figure 2.1c) oscillate between "African," "black-glazed," and "Black."[14]
Again, these terms include a neutral color marker and a highly polemic
label. The first proposed label, "African," is unsuitable because it has no
clear assignation in the fifth century BCE. Even still, the geographical
prominence of one region ignores black people's literary presence in
Greece (Chapter 5), India (chapters 4 and 6), and Colchis (Hdt. 2.104;
Pyth. 4.212). The technical term "black-glazed" reflects the manipulation of
oxygen during the cup's firing process. Potentially appealing because of its
focus on color and material composition, "black-glazed" nonetheless lacks
the ideological heft needed to confront the onslaught of modern bigotry
associated with this color. The next label, "Black," promotes an anachronistic understanding of skin color in Greek antiquity. Karen E. Fields and
Barbara J. Fields help to (re)visit this vocabulary with their coinage of
"racecraft," the mode of thought that consists of the unseen and vivid, the
imagined and real, what Fields and Fields deem "invisible ontologies."[15]
This framework applies to the application of "Black" to this cup's right-
hand face, in that racecraft immediately summons the modern hierarchy of
skin color when examining the deep past.

The term I offer for the right side of the cup, "black face," aims to bring
together the world of color and that of people (who have faces), thereby

White actors who exaggerate the accent, mannerisms, and color of South Asian people in American
film and television.

[13] Haley's translation of *albus* as "pale brown" inspires my language choices; Haley (2009): 31–34.

[14] An earlier investigation of these terms appears in Derbew (2018); see also Ako-Adounvo (1999) and
Gaither et al. (2020).

[15] Fields and Fields use "invisible ontology" after Appiah, who describes the act of pouring liquor onto
the ground for ancestors as a literal belief in a symbolic act, that is, the ontology of invisible beings;
Appiah (1992: 113–34); Fields and Fields (2014: 5–6, 203).

humanizing representations of black people in Greek antiquity. My orthographic practice, using lowercase "b" and a single space between "black" and "face," aims to distinguish "black face" from nineteenth-century minstrelsy. Although it is naïve to imagine that "black face," paired with this face's full lips and broad nose, does not evoke comparison with "Blackface," a term used to describe nineteenth- and twentieth-century White minstrel actors, there can be meaningful dialogue between the two terms. Despite their wildly different historical settings, both exist within the world of performance: Blackface actors in front of theatrical audiences, and black faces on janiform cups before an eager group of symposiasts. In addition, both introduce their audiences to a diverse array of characters in a jovial atmosphere.[16]

Scholarship about janiform cups of the fifth century BCE benefits from a continual push against an oversimplistic Black–White model of skin color. The notion that Black people are a "prototypical minority group" against which all non-Black minority groups are weighed is irrelevant to any interpretation of these cups. Emily Greenwood cautions against the dangers of adopting a modern hierarchy: "The conjoined head vases speak to the desire on the part of many modern scholars, from the civil-rights era and the era of decolonization onwards, to realign and to level the social and political hierarchies that existed between raced bodies."[17] Contemporary ideas are all the more pronounced when dealing with visual constructs of skin color in Greek antiquity and therefore require constant interrogation. The scholarly tendency to slip between time periods creates an inaccurate and potentially damaging picture of Greek antiquity. For example, in J. D. Beazley's discussion of "negro heads" of extant janiform Attic cups, he explains that a black face on a single-handled cup wears an expression "of one born to serve, and to suffer confusedly: a drudge."[18] This linkage of skin color and abject subservience reflects perspectives that dominate Beazley's historical context, not that of the cup. More than eighty years later, Beth Cohen echoes Beazley's sentiments. In her appraisal of iconography of black people carrying large birds on fifth-century Attic cups, she concludes that these representations would have been amusing. There is an uncomfortable ease with which Cohen assumes a fixed association between

---

[16] It is worth noting that Blackface actors and black faces on janiform cups exist within performances; they do not offer direct historical anecdotes. Richlin (2019) offers a thought experiment pairing Blackface minstrelsy and third-century BCE Latium. Despite her cogent analysis of the role of Carthaginians in the *palliata*, Richlin's discussion of "Blackface" without contextualization of loaded terms ("African," "black") left this reader wanting.

[17] Greenwood (2013).

[18] Beazley (1929: 42). Compare with the Archaeological Museum of Polygyros's label for Figure 2.5a–c: "*kantharos* with the heads of a negro and a girl (from Akanthos)."

black people and bumbling inferiority. To be sure, there are depictions of enslaved black people in ancient Greek art, and there is a correlation between small stature and humble status.[19] Cohen's assured reading, however, exceeds the speculative basis of her observation.[20] Her cited evidence does not adequately substantiate her argument, in that she bases her argument on uncritical scholarly remarks.[21] Her commentary ignores ancient Greek iconography depicting black people in numerous roles as soldiers, followers of Isaic and Bacchic rituals, and musicians.[22] Lopsided readings like Beazley's and Cohen's stand to gain from contextualized evaluations of visual representations in Greek antiquity. In this vein, I offer this reading to replace infiltrations of contemporary color dynamics with historically informed analyses of iconography of black people in Greek antiquity.[23] Although gender coding by skin color was pervasive on Attic pottery, Greek women depicted with white skin and their male counterparts with black skin, janiform cups depicting faces of different colors were more than supplemental illustrations of subjugation.[24] A careful inspection of these cups within their specific contexts offers alternative ways to read these brown and black faces.

2.2   Facing Blackness in the Symposium

When people gathered for social activities and entertainment in the symposium, they utilized a variety of decorated pottery to aid with their

[19] Cohen (2012: 468). Cohen is perhaps alluding to Theophrastus's *Characters* 21.4.2, in which a man of petty ambition (μικροφιλότιμος) acquires an Aithiopian attendant in order to fulfill his desire for prestige; Wrenhaven (2011: 105–07) and Oakley (2000) discuss the link between height and status in Greek art.

[20] Counteracting Cohen's myopia, Ramgopal points out the need for humane approaches to enslaved people. In the context of their mobility in ancient Rome, Ramgopal (2019: 133) cautions: "where studies of mobility are concerned, to set aside the little evidence we have for the movements of slaves is to treat their sufferings as trivial and to tacitly regard slavery as an acceptable feature of empire."

[21] Cohen cites Metzler and Hoffman (1977: 7–10, 18 n. 12); Bäbler (1998: 73–74); and Lissarrague (2001: 105–07). Metzler and Hoffman (1977: 9) hesitatingly describe a horn-shaped cup (*rhyton*) depicting a black person being eaten by a crocodile as amusing without clear reasoning for doing so; Bäbler (1988: 73–74) does not provide evidence for her claim that enslaved Aithiopians' "peculiar appearance" was amusing to their owners; and Lissarrague (2001: 106) remarks that the black glaze of a Sotadean horn-shaped cup accentuates the "negroid characteristics" and "caricatural aspect of the statuette."

[22] Snowden (1981: 415–18; 2010: 141–250) offers a fuller list of black peoples in Greco-Roman iconography.

[23] Although I focus on janiform cups (*kantharoi*), images of black people in Greek antiquity show up in numerous media. Contributions in Bindman and Gates (2010) discuss hundreds of representations of black people in Greco-Roman antiquity; Volz (2012: 114–55) examines janiform objects from various parts of the world, including Africa, China, Papua New Guinea, and the Solomon Islands.

[24] Tanner (2010: 30–31). See also Irwin (1974), Sassi (2001: 1–33), and Eaverly (2013).

consumption of wine: a mixing bowl (*kratēr*) to mix the wine with water in order to ensure its potency was not overwhelming, a wine cooler (*psyktēr*) to keep the beverage at the appropriate temperature, and a variety of drinking cups. Of the approximately ninety-five extant head-shaped cups, seventy-five are janiform (see Table 2.1).[25]

The process of making these janiform cups began with the preparation of the clay. Attic clay, rich in iron (which contributed to its reddish-brown color), came from nearby clay pits. In order to purify the clay, workers used the pits as settling basins in which they mixed the excavated clay with water. This allowed the impurities, such as sand and small stones, to fall to the bottom. After skimming the top layer and pouring it into a new basin of water, and repeating the process numerous times, workers left the mixture untouched in order to allow some of the water to evaporate. Damp blocks of clay were later mixed with older clay, then partially dried before use. Once the clay was malleable, the shaping process consisted of three steps: forming the object, decorating it, and firing it.[26] First, the potter shaped a piece of clay on a wooden wheel to form the cup's body and molded another piece of clay to form the foot. To make the faces and handles, the potter pressed clay into a hand-shaped terracotta mold and shaped the handles by hand. The potter then used slip (a mixture of clay

Table 2.1 *Distribution of janiform cups*

	brown face (female)	black face[27]	satyr
satyr	23	1	-
brown face (female)	21	11	-
Hercules	13	2	2
Dionysus	1	-	1

---

[25] Lissarrague (1995: 6; 2001: 108–09). I have slightly amended Lissarrague's count of ninety-four cups to ninety-five, to include a janiform cup bearing a satyr and a black face that he omits. For a list of extant single-headed cups featuring a black face, see Appendix 2.

[26] Noble (1988: 16–18, 75–78, 166–67). This was at least a two-person job: the potter threw and shaped the clay, and the vase painter decorated the objects (Noble [1988: 10–11]). Balachandran (2019) helpfully points out that the pottery process was a communal one and that each stage had its own "sensory signature." For instance, see Lissarrague's (1994) discussion of a cup that is signed by a painter (Epiktetos) and a potter (Python). Noble (1988: 25–34) provides detailed pictures of the pottery process; see also the Getty Museum's instructional video (www.youtube.com/watch?v=WhPW5or07L8).

[27] Due to the inconsistent labeling of the gender of black faces in museum collections, I have not been able to categorize the black faces by gender.

and water) to attach the cup's various components. During the decoration process, the shaped clay was painted with additional slip. If the painter chose to give the faces curly hair, this procedure included pressing clay dots into the surface of the cup and coating the dots with slip as well.[28] Following this step, the kiln master carefully fired the cup, oscillating between preventing air from entering the kiln and allowing it to enter. Upon removal from the kiln, the oxygen-rich parts of the cup had a matte finish and the oxygen-poor parts a black-glazed finish. It is worth stating that this glossy black exterior differs from "black face," a term I use to denote the iconography of people with black skin, a broad nose, and full lips on janiform cups. The former focuses solely on material composition, and the latter relies on a combination of chromatic and phenotypic features.

In addition to symposiastic ware, ongoing intersections between the iconography of black people and performance exist throughout antiquity.[29] Four examples elucidate the numerous stagings of blackness among artists who predate and postdate fifth-century potters.[30] First, a wall painting in the palace of Knossos includes one of the earliest visualizations of black people in the Mediterranean. A twentieth-century reconstruction of this palace, which flourished between 1700 BCE and 1400 BCE, features the "Captain of the Blacks" fresco of three figures in flight. From left to right, three men run in close succession towards the right side of the frame. They are almost identical, except for skin color and height: the two men in the rear have black skin, as is visible in the legs of both figures and the head of one, and are taller than the leader of the trio, who has brown skin. Barring a piece of fabric around their waists and two bands around each of their ankles, they are all naked. The shorter man leading the group holds two long, narrow objects in his right hand, and he wears a feather in his hair. Arthur Evans, the lead excavator at this site, concluded that the fresco portrayed a Minoan commander leading Nubian soldiers to fight against Greece.[31] Viewers gazing at the fresco would presumably marvel at the men's shared performance of military might.

---

[28] Pedley (2012: 193); Cohen (2006: 107).

[29] As noted in Table P.1, I use the generic term "antiquity," rather than "Greek antiquity" to acknowledge the inclusion of ancient Minoan civilization.

[30] Athenian craftspeople began to create cups with divine, satyr-like, and mortal faces at the end of the sixth century BCE.

[31] Snowden (2010: 143). The extant wall painting reveals the left leg of the man in the rear, both legs of the central figure, and the full profile of the leading figure; Newman (2017: 219–22); Gere (2009: 112–17).

Approximately seven centuries later, on a relief carved onto the eastern staircase in the Apadana (palace hall) of Persepolis, three short men march behind a man who dwarfs them. From right to left, the tall man bears a staff in his left hand and holds his right hand behind him, the first diminutive figure holds the hand of the lofty man in front of him, the second one holds a cylindrical jar, and the third wields a curved object that resembles an elephant tusk in his left hand and the leash of an okapi that trails the group in his right. Alongside other political imagery in the Apadana, this relief is a visual microcosm of Persian imperial might. In other words, it enacts a performance of Persian domination.[32] Eric Schmidt understands the gifts in this scene – an okapi, an elephant tusk, and a vessel presumably filled with gold – as proof that the three figures are Aithiopians bringing tribute to the Persian ruler. In its current state, this relief does not retain traces of color. Therefore, Schmidt relies on the figures' gifts, curly hair, and what he deems to be "Negroid features" to support his claim.[33] While the animal imagery and hairstyle of the iconography suggest affiliation with Aithiopians, people whose skin color is frequently associated with blackness, it is unclear what undergirds Schmidt's assertion of the figures' "Negroid features." Schmidt perhaps bases this label on their rounded noses and their prominent chins, but their physical appearance does not differ greatly from the figure identified as Persian on this relief. Even so, if both Evans's and Schmidt's identifications are correct, the fresco and relief endorse the Minoans' and Persians' empire-building initiatives. As these superpowers co-opt their warrior neighbors into the world of political performance, the skin color and portable items in the "Captain of the Blacks" fresco and the Apadana relief, respectively, translate into costumes that help viewers identify the figures.

Three-dimensional depictions are another part of the iconographic tradition of performances of blackness. Horn-shaped cups (*rhyta*) depicting a black person engulfed in the jaws of a crocodile enhance the performative atmosphere of the symposium.[34] As revelers drink wine from these cups, they bring animals onto the lively stage of the symposium. The horn-shaped cups grant them a sense of security, allowing them to witness black people trying to escape the clutches of reptiles without putting

---

[32] Kuhrt (2007: 469) interprets the images alongside the text of the Apadana.

[33] Schmidt (1953: 90); Valdez and Tuck (1980); Hdt. 3.96. Based on their short stature and beardless state, Reimer (2013) describes the three figures as boys.

[34] True (2006); Lissarrague (1995). *Rhyta* were the subject of a 2018–19 Harvard Art Museums exhibition, "Animal-Shaped Vessels from the Ancient World: Feasting with Gods, Heroes, and Kings"; see Ebbinghaus (2018).

themselves in danger. In fact, the sight of the violent fate of the black figures on the horn-shaped cups perhaps encourages drinkers to curb their drinking habits to avoid drowning in wine. Alternatively, a travel warning may lurk behind this iconography: any reveler who intends to travel across the Mediterranean may find him or herself caught in the mouth of a hungry crocodile whose appetite has been whetted by human flesh.

An implicit call for restraint among wine-guzzling symposiasts also appears on scenes painted onto wide-mouthed cups (*skyphoi*) from the sanctuary of the Kabeiroi in Thebes (Boeotia). At this site, five of these cups recall a memorable scene from the *Odyssey*, in which the nymph Circe coaxes Odysseus to drink a potion that will transform him into a pig (10.302–47).[35] On one of these late fifth-/early fourth-century cups, both Circe and Odysseus are depicted as squat, black figures (Figure 2.2). Barring some fabric draped over his left arm and his brimmed hat, Odysseus is completely naked. His erect penis, pronounced nipples, and potbelly are on full display. Holding a sword in his right hand and its sheath in his left, he seems poised

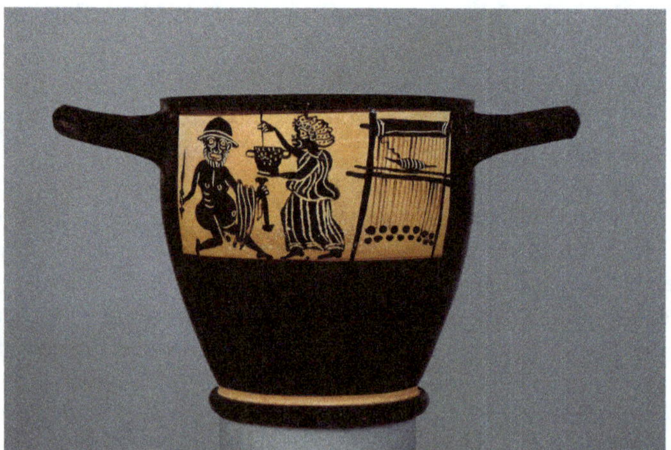

Figure 2.2 *Skyphos* depicting Odysseus at sea and with Circe, Boeotian black-figure ceramic, attributed to the Cabirion Group, c. fourth century BCE. H. 15.4 cm, AN1896–1908 G249. © Ashmolean Museum, University of Oxford.

---

[35] Dosoo (2020: 262–67); Snowden (2010: 168); Bedigan (2008: 285–89); Blakely (2006: 38–54); cf. references to Circe in Walcott's epic *Omeros*: Walcott (1990: 64 [v. 1.11.1]; 96 [*Od.* 2.18.1]; 155 [*Od.* 3.29.3]; 204 [*Od.* 5.40.2]; 250 [*Od.* 6.49.3]). Worshipped mainly in Asia Minor and northern Greece, the Kabeiroi promoted fertility and protected seafarers: Bedigan (2008: 282–89).

to attack Circe. Unlike her nude houseguest, the curly haired Circe wears a *chitōn*-like dress. Abandoning the loom behind her, she holds a wide-mouthed cup in her left hand and a stick with which she mixes a potion in her right. Even though Odysseus shares Circe's skin tone and phenotypic features, Kirsten Bedigan construes Circe as a "Negro[,] an object of derision" and Odysseus as a symbol of Greek superiority.[36] Bedigan's conclusion ignores the unusual portrayal of Odysseus as a chubby and lustful houseguest, and it also disregards the heady combination of wine and magic at Circe's disposal. Circe's modest appearance disguises the power with which she transforms Odysseus's men into utterly helpless creatures, thereby taking on the role of omniscient director who supervises an unfolding drama. The contrast between her unassuming looks and her cunning talents mirrors the deceptively powerful role of wine in the symposium.[37] In the event that revelers underestimate this seemingly innocuous drink, the depiction of Circe on these wide-mouthed cups gently cautions drunken symposiasts to pace themselves, lest they risk transgressing acceptable limits of intoxication and ending up in dire straits like Odysseus's men-turned-pigs.[38]

As was the case for the four visual renditions of black people discussed above, janiform cups do not require the physical edifice of a theater to be part of a performance. In their own right, they wield transformative power. A drinker reaching for a two-handled janiform cup encounters a pair of eyes looking back at him or her. This direct gaze casts the drinker in the role of an audience member who watches the face on the cup. As the drinker brings the cup to his or her mouth, the face-as-actor becomes less and less visible. By the time the drinker's lips touch the rim of the cup, the drinker is rendered mute and blind, his or her throat filled with wine and his or her gaze obscured by the interior of the cup. At this moment of physical contact between the drinker and the mask-like face, the interactive performance is underway. Although most cups do not indicate whether there was a preferred way in which the drinker should hold them, one janiform cup currently held in the collection at the Fitzwilliam Museum at the University of Cambridge provides some clues. Labeled "janiform

---

[36] Bedigan (2008: 285) insists on Odysseus's superiority, despite describing his appearance as "pot-bellied … disproportionate … slightly gormless … child-like … rat-like … stocky"; see also Bedigan (2013).

[37] I describe Circe's looks as modest and unassuming not to apply modern, Eurocentric notions of beauty to an ancient character, but to acknowledge that her appearance differs from depictions of goddesses on extant Attic pottery. That is, painters of Attic pottery typically depict Greek goddesses with narrow noses, thin lips, and well-proportioned limbs.

[38] Osborne (2014: 60) interprets wine as a disguise: "intoxication also both revealed the true individual, and bonded the group. The intoxicated both put on and took off their mask."

kantharos belonging to the Class G of the head vases," this cup features two female faces: the black face is wearing a fitted headdress and her slightly open mouth reveals her teeth, and the brown face wears a headband from underneath which her loose curls escape (Figure 2.3a–c).[39] This cup has a slight indent on the lip directly above the black face (Figure 2.3a), which suggests that the drinker turned the black face of the cup towards himself or herself and the other guests observed the brown face. In this way, the black face of this cup morphs into a mask for the drinker. The metamorphosis extends to the symposium, which is recast as a stage on which the drinker's companions turn into the drinker's audience.[40] Emboldened by liquid courage, the symposiasts enter a world of alcohol-induced mirth and performance.

Close scrutiny of another janiform cup foregrounds the realm of performance in which these cups existed. One cup currently in the Princeton University Art Museum's collection (Figure 2.4a–c), labeled as "janiform *kantharos* with addorsed heads of a male African and a female Greek," presents two female faces. A curly haired black face with full lips and a broad nose appears on the left-hand side, and a headband-wearing brown face with thin lips and a narrow nose on the right (Figure 2.4c). The fused clay, most apparent at the neck of the cup, draws attention to the inexorable connection between the two faces. On the whole, the cup invites multiple versions of difference, in that viewers may understand the two faces as opposing or complementary. In my effort to redress the scholarly tendency to elide difference and inferiority, I regard these two faces as complementary masks. They reinforce the jocular atmosphere, in that they invite many performers to the party. Moreover, the interconnected faces circumvent cultural chauvinism. As a unit, the two faces embody an intertwined performance in which the symposiasts partake.[41] Separately, each face resembles an actor performing for an audience of symposiasts.

---

[39] Similar to my analysis of the janiform cup currently held at the Boston Museum of Fine Arts (Figure 2.1a–c above), I interpret the delicate eyebrows and hairless faces on both sides of Figure 2.3a–c as indicators of gender.

[40] Frontisi-Ducroux (1989: 151) discusses the inversion of the one-way relationship between subject and object in depictions of a frontal-facing Dionysus on the tondo of a shallow cup (*kylix*). Although art historians frequently point to eye cups (*kylikes* with pairs of eyes painted on the exterior) when conceptualizing masks in the symposium, a drinker must lift an eye cup in order to transform his or her drinkware into a mask, whereas janiform cups require no intervention on the drinker's part in order to resemble a mask.

[41] An emphasis on antagonistic juxtaposition risks playing into the modern polarization of skin color. Lewis (2002: 170) rightly questions the anachronistic conflation present when scholars describe depictions of women on janiform cups as marginal figures who stand "in opposition to the white citizen symposiast."

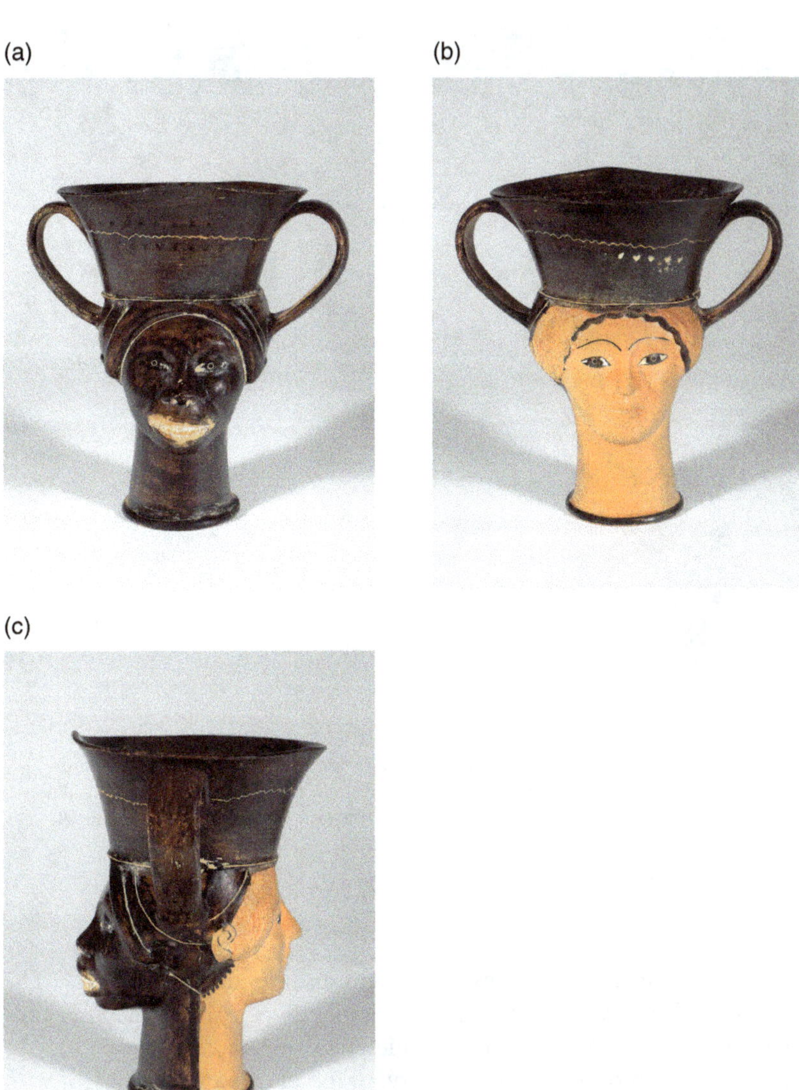

Figure 2.3a–c Janiform *kantharos* belonging to Class G of head vases, Attic red-figure ceramic, attributed to the London Class, c. 470 BCE. H. 20 cm, GR.2.1999. © Fitzwilliam Museum, University of Cambridge.

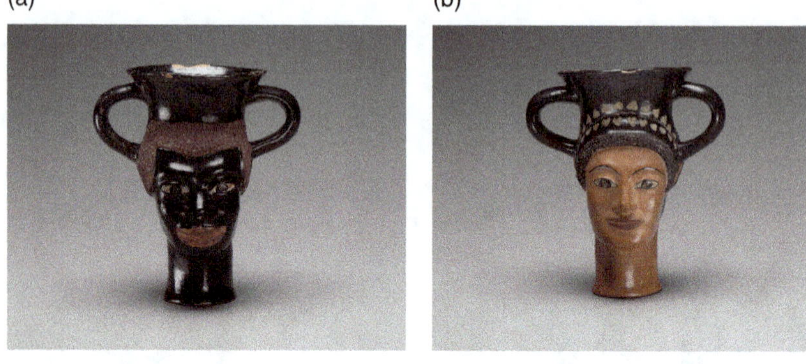

Figure 2.4a–c Janiform *kantharos* with addorsed heads of a male African and
a female Greek, Attic red-figure ceramic, attributed to the Princeton Class, c. 480–
470 BCE. H. 14.9 cm, 33.45 (y1933–45). © Princeton University Art Museum/Art
Resource, NY.

When the drinker lifts the cup, he or she subsumes this role of actor. The
depiction of two faces fused onto one janiform cup simultaneously pro-
vokes and cuts across any permanent hierarchy of color that viewers may be
tempted to map onto Greek antiquity. Skin color works in tandem with
other visual markers to serve as a mask for symposiasts. In the minds of
modern viewers who are not aware of the ways that cultural conditioning
can infiltrate their perspective, there may appear to be an imbalanced
presentation of the different faces on these cups. The sharp lines that
distinguish each face from the other may mislead them to perceive the

cup as a vivid antecedent of nineteenth-century Jim Crow laws. In spite of this problematic shorthand, there is no simple Black–White binary at work here. To be sure, color was part of a larger apparatus of distinction on Attic pottery, but its valence was not perpetually fixed. Instead, the faces on these cups represent semiotic markers of the diversity and flexibility at play in symposiastic performances.

2.3 Interrogating Claims of Beauty and Humor

It is curious that none of the documented janiform cups, with the exception of Figure 2.5a–c, discussed below, features a brown male face on either side of the cup. Jeremy Tanner argues that the brown male face, a visual representation of a "Greek man," stands in contrast to different modes of alterity present on these cups.[42] This merging of many groups into a "not Greek male" category requires probing. There is little evidence to support Tanner's claim that Greek people, a contested grouping in and of itself, have a specific phenotype or that all non-Greeks shared enough similarities to warrant their grouping in the symposium. Furthermore, Tanner's desire to extrapolate historical fact from Attic pottery undermines the flexible nature of performance in the symposium. In line with Tanner's treatment of the cups' faces as historical relics, François Lissarrague states that the brown faces reflect Greek women's position as wine pourers at the symposium, and the black faces represent servants at the symposium. Here, Lissarrague does not reflect on the conjectural nature of his assessment. The twin assumptions that the iconography of black people always depicts subjugation and that this visual iconography consistently corresponds to historical evidence misrepresent the evidence at hand.[43] If such misconstrued conclusions remain unchallenged, it is all too easy to translate a subjective stance into an unalterable fact. Even still, the inaccurate notion that the conflation of inferiority and skin color has a historical antecedent could easily morph into a justification of bigotry. Conversely, Claude Bérard proposes to render both faces on janiform cups with a brown and a black face as a shared site of unmarked and exotic beauty.[44] Based on his exploration of a wine jar (*amphora*) depicting Memnon receiving battle equipment from his black

---

[42] Tanner (2010: 31).

[43] Lissarrague (1995: 6; 2001: 108–09). Skinner (2012: 98) comments that "representations such as the African face that features on one side of an Attic red-figure head-kantharos . . . are frequently cited as evidence of a derogatory juxtaposition of idealized Greek and ugly barbarian." Rotroff (2014: 167) briefly summarizes various interpretations of these cups.

[44] Bérard (2000: 396–405, 411). See also Gruen (2011: 211–20, esp. 219).

squires and a rotund wine jar (*pelikē*) portraying Andromeda flanked by black servants, Bérard deduces that skin color is a malleable tool that localizes people to Aithiopia.[45] While Bérard's use of these cups as evidence regarding people's beauty standards or geographic specificity is speculative, his scrutiny of each face of the cup in its own context offers a refreshing alternative to the conclusions posed by Tanner and Lissarrague.

The need for even-handed coverage extends to inscriptions on janiform cups. Various types of inscriptions appear on Attic cups: signatures of artists, captions that identify figures, dedications, and acclamations.[46] *Kalos* inscriptions are found on roughly 1,000 extant pieces of Attic pottery.[47] They appear in a number of locations, including the base of a cup's neck (Figure 2.1a–c) and its lip (Figure 2.5a–c). These inscriptions indicating beauty, *kalē* for women and *kalos* for men, were usually painted onto cups in the workshop.[48] The generic formula *ho pais kalos* ("this boy is attractive," Figure 2.1a–c) was a popular inscription that enabled an older lover (*erastēs*) to offer a romantic compliment to a younger lover (*erōmenos*), a fitting gesture at the convivial symposium.[49] With this combination of stunning imagery and textual labels, inscribed cups catered to all levels of literacy.

A janiform cup currently held at the Archaeological Museum of Polygyros (Figure 2.5a–c) described as a "*kantharos* with the heads of a young woman and a negro from Akanthos," reveals the lopsided treatment of inscriptions in modern scholarship. From left to right, a light brown female face wears a headband over loose curls, and a dark brown

---

[45] Full descriptions of the pottery featuring Memnon and Andromeda (respectively): terracotta neck-*amphora*, attributed to an artist near Exekias, c. 530 BCE, New York, Metropolitan Museum of Art 98.8.13; Attic red-figure *pelikē*, related to the workshop of the Niobid painter, c. 460 BCE, Boston, Museum of Fine Arts 63.2663. Snowden (1970: 154) suggests that Andromeda may have been black in Greek mythology; later descriptions of her imply that her skin is the same color as black Indians (*Andromedan Perseus nigris portarit ab Indis*, "Perseus carried Andromeda away from the black Indians," *Ars am.* 1.53). Unencumbered by polarity, Greek myth emerges as a genre in which various mythological characters (Memnon, Andromeda, Hercules, and Busiris) are rendered in complex ways. For example, the scene on a red-figure rotund wine jar of the Egyptian Busiris attempting to sacrifice Hercules is both Greek and anti-Greek, in that Busiris uses Greek sacrificial tools but causes an orderly, revered process to descend into chaos; Lissarrague (2001: 123–24).

[46] The earliest inscriptions on Attic pottery date to the mid-sixth century BCE; the latest inscriptions date to 420 BCE; see Lissarrague (1999: 362). *Kalos* inscriptions rarely appear on Attic pottery made after 440 BCE; Shapiro (1987: 117–18).

[47] Lissarrague (1999: 362).

[48] Steiner (2002: 358–61) insists that these inscriptions were not scratched on afterwards; conversely, Ebbinghaus (2008) identifies them as graffiti.

[49] Lissarrague (1999: 364–66). In his analysis of thirty-seven pieces of Attic pottery, mainly oil flasks (*lekythoi*) with *kalos* inscriptions and a patronymic name, Shapiro (1987) suggests that these inscriptions had political resonances.

(a)   (b)

(c)

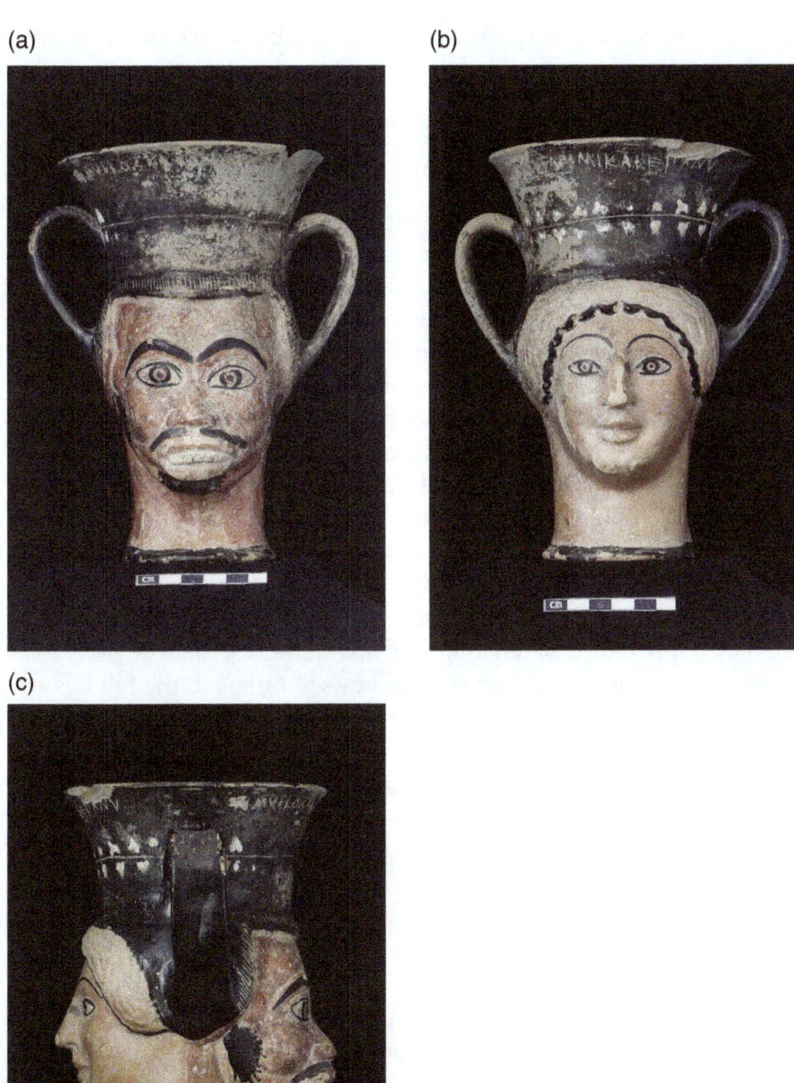

Figures 2.5a–c *Kantharos* with the heads of a young woman and a negro from
Akanthos, Attic red-figure ceramic, c. 480–470 BCE. H. 18.6 cm. Archaeological
Museum of Polygyros, I.D.Y. 8. © Hellenic Ministry of Culture and Sports,
Ephorate of Antiquities of Chalcidice and Mount Athos.

male face with sideburns sports a mustache and beard that frame an open mouth. An inscription running horizontally along the lip of the cup reads:

Ἐρόνασσε εἰμί καλὲ πάνυ[.] Τίμυλλος ὡς τό[δε τ]ὸ πρόσωπον καλὸς[.]

I am Eronassa, the most beautiful . . . Timyllos is as handsome as this face.

The text describing Eronassa runs above the light brown face, and that describing Timyllos runs above the dark brown face. It is instructive to examine first the scholarly labeling practices applied to the dark brown face (hereafter referred to as "Timyllos's face"). Despite the presence of two brown faces of different shades on this cup, scholars tend to distance Timyllos from Eronassa, whose skin color they conflate with "Greek." The Archaeological Museum of Polygyros likens Timyllos to an "African man"; the Archaeological Museum of Thessaloniki, where the cup was held before it moved to Polygyros, identifies him as a "a negro"; the Beazley Archive, a comprehensive online database for Attic pottery, lists him as a "black youth"; and Lissarrague categorizes him as "black." Aware that Timyllos is "a deep reddish brown color, rather than the usual shiny black," Ada Cohen nonetheless insists that he is a "black man." She provides a rationale for Timyllos's appearance by arguing that his non-black skin offers a color contrast to his black facial hair and eyebrows.[50] Although the full lips and broad nose of Timyllos's face correspond to those on the black faces of other cups (figures 2.1a–c, 2.3a–c, and 2.4a–c), classification as "negro" or "black" is an oversimplification. Scholars import hypodescent laws into Greek antiquity when they describe Timyllos's face with these terms.[51] By prioritizing their historical present, they have elided (ancient) blackness into (modern) Blackness. Nomenclature benefits from self-reflexive labels that historicize the unavoidable preoccupation with color dynamics in the twenty-first century without reproducing it. Therefore, my decision to refer to Timyllos's face as brown encourages viewers to pair him with Eronassa rather than superimpose the appearance of a Black man onto him.

In his analysis of the inscriptions on the janiform cup at the Archaeological Museum of Polygyros (Figure 2.5a–c), Lissarrague understands the inscription associated with Eronassa as a compliment and that of Timyllos as an ironic twist.[52] Lissarrague insists that the potter has

---

[50] Vokotopoulou (1996: 236); Lissarrague (2001: 109–10); Cohen (2011: 480).

[51] Scholars may also be relying on gender codes in ancient Greek art that associate Greek women with white skin and Greek men with black skin.

[52] Comparable to Lissarrague (2001), Ebbinghaus (2008: 153) interprets the male face as a parody of the standard *kalos* inscription.

caricatured the features on Timyllos's face because of Timyllos's prominent teeth.[53] Exposed teeth are a popular feature of archaic Greek pottery, but there is no consensus about them indicating a simple and/or ugly person.[54] Even so, Lissarrague identifies Eronassa as Greek and therefore not subject to ridicule. His inclination to construe only Timyllos's face as a parody resonates with twenty-first-century labeling of Black people as "other."[55] His insistence that Timyllos's face can only exist in inadequate response to Eronassa's traps the viewer in a modern historical conundrum without consideration of the world in which the cup existed. The lack of convincing evidence to support Lissarrague's claim that Timyllos is inherently comedic leaves viewers to draw their own conclusions about this conflation, which may lead them to make uninformed connections between Timyllos's exposed teeth in the fifth century BCE and the iconic teeth-baring grin of Blackface actors in the nineteenth and twentieth centuries. Admittedly, the presence of the first person ("I am Eronassa") and third person ("Timyllos is handsome") adds a playful quality to this cup. The variability may emphasize an interpersonal play between the reader of the inscription and the face on the cup.[56] Taking this switch between persons further, Eronassa may be the speaker of both inscriptions. If this is the case, she remarks on Timyllos's appearance after she admires her own beauty. This reciprocal exchange fits in well with the general theme of malleability that dominates the metatheatrical stage of the symposium.

Despite Ada Cohen's argument that Eronassa's face represents a *hetaira* who is teasing her companion because of his dark brown complexion, the relationship between *hetairai* and prostitution is more complicated than Cohen acknowledges.[57] Mapping an egalitarian stance onto both sides of

[53] Lissarrague (2001: 109–10). With his caricaturing of Timyllos, Lissarrague (1999: 364) contradicts an earlier statement: "there is practically no painted inscription, as far as I know, that is derisory or insulting – all belong to the field of praise."

[54] Rotroff (2014: 168–70). See Isaac's (2017: 20) warning about the emotional weight that can be hidden behind a presumed sense of humor.

[55] Gruen (2011) offers an excellent reworking of the category of "other" in Greco-Roman antiquity. See also Mitchell (2009: 198), who interprets a depiction of an "African youth" grooming a horse on an Attic cup from the fifth century BCE as a reflection of the social marginalization of animal groomers rather than an indication of humor. Nonetheless, Mitchell's (2009: 3–4) ready labeling of foreigners on Attic pottery as comedic lacks the careful consideration that he applies to other groups depicted on Attic pottery.

[56] Martin (2014) inclusively suggests that there is irony in both inscriptions.

[57] Cohen (2011: 478–82). True (2006: 268) describes a brown woman on a janiform cup as a prostitute "depicted with both grace and beauty." Neils (2000: 226) reduces women to their sexual prowess in her suggestion that Greek men had a begrudging admiration for the "liberated and liberating acts of such women [who worked as prostitutes] … because they do, and do well, something that men admire." Burton (1998: 150–54) provides a wide range of evidence that many women in Athens were

the cup, I interpret the inscriptions as attempts to highlight the plurality of performances without privileging either side. Whether humor is part of this cup's pictorial value is unclear. Nonetheless, if there is a comedic element, it applies to both faces. The potential etymology of their names hints at this balance: Eronassa as "lovely duck" (ἔρος + νᾶσσα) and Timyllos as "honorable Egyptian mongoose" (τιμή + ὕλλος).

The art historical perspectives discussed above deny modern viewers a contextualized understanding of black skin color on janiform cups. Counteracting the historical lapses in their arguments, I treat the cups' black faces as masks that people adopted during symposia. Whenever symposiasts wielded these janiform cups, they were able to enact performances in which new characters entered their private party. Altogether, my analysis prompts viewers to look beyond the facile renderings of skin color. Furthermore, my recasting of the iconography of black people in Greek antiquity as performances of blackness offers contemporary audiences a new model for confronting their own historicized positionality without immediately grafting it onto antiquity.

2.4 Ancient Blackness in Modern Museums

As is apparent in art historians' lopsided treatment of black and brown faces on janiform cups, contemporary influences contribute to the uneven treatment of iconography of black people in public-facing settings. For instance, in the Beazley Archive, the world's largest online database of photographs of ancient Greek pottery, descriptions generally concentrate on the color of the black face and female gender of the brown face, thereby nullifying the gender of the former and the color of the latter.[58] This reductive shorthand invariably privileges the male gender and brown faces, the latter of which many art historians liken to a Greek phenotype.

conspicuous in a nonsexualized manner at drinking and dining occasions where men were present. Although Corner (2012) appreciates Burton's examination of men and women eating together outside of the symposium, he nonetheless argues for the exclusion of women who were not *hetairai* as part of the symposium's function. More generally, Goldhill (2015) situates the *hetairai* within the marketplace of sex while Kennedy (2014b: 68–96) redefines a *hetaira* as a foreign woman of wealth who interacts with elite Greek men.

[58] The Beazley Archive is physically housed in the Ioannou Centre at the University of Oxford. For examples of the uneven labeling practices applied to the iconography of black people in Greek antiquity, see appendices 1 and 2. Cf. Jim Crow laws that rendered the gender of Black women irrelevant. Hartman (2019: 37–42, esp. 38) vividly describes Ida B. Wells's experience on a train trip in Tennessee during which she was dragged out of the ladies' train car and forced onto the smoky, filthy segregated car where White men could enter freely and engage in lewd behavior without consequence.

In this way, the Beazley Archive reinforces the popular notion that the Greek male is the artistic norm. Other faces are remarkable only in comparison to this standard. No label provides a singular "correct" or "accurate" insight into the world of the fifth century BCE. On the contrary, they flag the multiple layers of comprehension that collide when modernity and antiquity interact. Indeed, it is impossible to isolate the past while living in the present, but it is the responsibility of curators and academics to confront twenty-first-century notions of Blackness before making conclusive remarks about the representations of blackness in Greek antiquity.

The inconsistent analysis of janiform cups reaches its apex in the labeling practices of contemporary museums. In the authoritative guide for museum professionals *Exhibit Labels: An Interpretative Approach*, Beverly Serrell exhorts label writers to avoid generalizations based on singular examples.[59] In this vein, in the remainder of this chapter, I rely on new museum ethics, a subfield of museum studies that calls for museums to create democratized social spaces and amend ideological barriers that perpetuate subjugation based on skin color.[60] Nascent attempts to achieve this goal are apparent in the Princeton University Art Museum's online description of a janiform cup with a black face and a brown face as presenting "a male African and a female Greek" (Figure 2.4a–c). Combining a metaphorical and literal approach to color, the online catalogue of the Boston Museum of Fine Arts (MFA) notes an unusual "joining of black and white female heads" on another janiform cup (Figure 2.1a–c). In the MFA's entry, the cataloguer situates the cup within the wider context of "white (i.e. Greek) women." The cataloguer's parenthetical inclusion "(i.e. Greek)" anachronistically collapses the distinction between white and Greek while also creating a false color dichotomy that ignores the cup's color palette. In fact, there is more white on the black face than on its brown counterpart.[61] The Fitzwilliam

---

[59] Serrell (2015: 37, 63–65). In a study of labels from seventy-three British museums, Sorsby and Horne (1980) conclude that many contained vocabulary and sentences that were too difficult for the average reader. For a cautionary tale about the dangers of ironic museum labels, see Butler (2011). Museum ethnologist Marjorie Halpin (1983: 268–73) describes her and her colleagues' phenomenological approach to the University of British Columbia's Museum of Anthropology.

[60] Marstine (2011); Kreps (2015).

[61] The black face has white eyebrows, teeth, and sclerae of the eyes; the brown face has white sclerae. The MFA's full description of this cup reads: "The joining of black and white female heads is unusual. On black-figure vases, white (i.e. Greek) women are often painted with the same white slip (liquid clay) as that used on the mouth of this cup, but on head vases they are always left in the reddish and more lifelike color of the clay, heightened somewhat by a wash of yellow ochre, so the

Museum's online catalogue eliminates any mention of color or gender with a generic label: "Class G of the head vases; the London Class" (Figure 2.3a–c). The cataloguing practices of the MFA and the Fitzwilliam Museum deny the viewer contextualized information about the cups. Even the color- and gender-inclusive categorization of the Princeton University Art Museum's online catalogue poses challenges due to the historical variations generally attributed to the term "Africa." Altogether, these labels reveal the complex interactions between modernity and antiquity that occur within museums.

Returning to the language of performance, I construe the museum as another stage on which performances of blackness occur. Quotidian productions ranging from the smallest captions to the most expansive layouts can have a lasting impact on the general public.[62] These performances of blackness appear in the greatest numbers in museums' Nubian collections.[63] In concert with the unequal treatment of skin color on janiform cups discussed above, museums situate Nubian iconography in ways that subvert a clear understanding of their relevance. Generally, Nubian objects are part of a Greco-Roman exhibit, an Egyptian exhibit, or have their own display.[64] The display of Nubia and Egypt together is understandable since Lower Nubia, the northern region of Nubia, and Upper Egypt, the southern region of Egypt, shared a border. This emphasis becomes problematic, however, when Egypt functions as a legitimizing force in the presentation of Nubian objects. Tracing a visitor's experience in the British Museum highlights the visual cues that can subordinate Nubia to Egypt.[65]

flesh is red, eyes white, and the iris black. The African woman smiles with her teeth showing; her eyes and eyebrows are white. Her hair is a mass of dots, with traces of red paint."

[62] Dubin (2006); Hooper-Greenhill (2006); Karp and Kratz (2006); Marstine, Bauer, and Haines (2011, 2013). In his 1992 "Panta Rhei" exhibition at Metro Pictures, New York, artist Fred Wilson manipulated titles as a way to shift his audience's focus. Namely, he sculpted renditions of Greek gods and relabeled them with the names of their Egyptian predecessors; Karp and Wilson (1996: 253–58). See also Wintle (2013), who traces colonial legacies in the museum-like British Empire and Commonwealth Institute (this entity is now a registered charity under the name Commonwealth Education Trust).

[63] On the nomenclature of Nubia, see sections 1.3 and 6.3.

[64] The Fitzwilliam Museum pays scant attention to Nubia in its "Rome and Ancient Sudan" exhibit (Room 24) on the lower ground floor next to the toilets, whose pungent odors wafted into the space during my visit in October 2016. The Egyptian wing in the Metropolitan Museum of Art features the Temple of Dendur from Lower Nubia (Gallery 131), animal horns from the tombs of Nubian mercenaries (Gallery 117), and a facsimile wall painting of Nubians carrying tributes (Gallery 135). The Ashmolean Museum of Art and Archaeology at the University of Oxford, the British Museum, the Oriental Institute Museum at the University of Chicago, and the MFA in Boston each have at least one room dedicated to Nubian objects.

[65] Many museums house collections of Nubian objects: the Ashmolean, the MFA, the Fitzwilliam, the Michael C. Carlos Museum at Emory University, the Oriental Institute Museum, the University of Pennsylvania Museum of Art and Archaeology, the Walters Art Museum in Baltimore, and Yale

Upon entering the British Museum, the visitor almost immediately becomes aware of Egypt's looming presence (Figure 2.6). Centrally located beyond the main entrance, a gift shop, and a room featuring Assyrian sculptures (Room 6), the "Egyptian Sculpture" (Room 4) consist of three interconnected rooms that display the Egyptians' artistic prowess from 2686 BCE–395 CE.[66] Here, massive lion sculptures, temple pillars, and busts of pharaohs appear alongside sarcophagi, tomb reliefs, and the Rosetta Stone.[67] It is easy to overlook the small area in the third segment of Room 4 (furthest from Room 6) that addresses Egypt's relationship with Nubia. Off the main walking path and up a short ramp, the more determined visitor encounters a small area entitled "Political Fragmentation: Third Intermediate Period (21st–25th Dynasties)." The term "Third Intermediate Period" suggests that the Twenty-Fifth Dynasty (c. 720–664 BCE), in which Nubian rulers Shabaqo, Shebitqo, and Taharqo successively ruled Egypt, was a brief anomaly between the New Kingdom and the Late Period.

A closer look at interpretive remarks on the panel titled "Political Fragmentation" reveals the implicit assumptions that the curator passes on to viewers:

> King Piankhy of Kush *took advantage* of Egypt's division [into multiple regional kingdoms] and invaded. He and his successors, the 25th Dynasty, *imposed themselves as overlords* on the local rulers. Napata was the capital in Kush, and Memphis became its Egyptian twin. The Kushites *embraced*

Peabody Museum of Natural History. In an upcoming project, I expand the scope of this discussion to put several of these museums in dialogue with museums located on the Nile corridor, such as the Nubia Museum in Aswan (Egypt) and the Sudan National Museum in Khartoum.

[66] In the British Museum, five rooms are dedicated solely to Egypt: "Egyptian Sculpture" (Room 4, partitioned into three interconnected rooms), "Egyptian Life and Death: The Tomb-Chapel of Nebamun" (Room 61), "Egyptian Death and Afterlife: Mummies" (Rooms 62–63), and "Early Egypt" (Room 64). Separate galleries on the upper floors are dedicated to "Sudan, Egypt and Nubia" (Room 65), "Ethiopia and Coptic Egypt" (Room 66); and "Africa" (Room 25, partitioned into three interconnected rooms) is in the basement. When I inquired about this disparate layout of neighboring regions during a personal interview in 2017 with Derek Welsby, a keeper (curator) in the British Museum's Department of Ancient Egypt and Sudan, he explained that the ground-floor location of "Egyptian Sculpture" (Room 4) was a practical choice: the museum building could not support large objects on upper floors. He also stated that that the ad hoc room assignments of other objects led to the odd position of Egyptian objects on the upper levels. Caygill (1992) and Wilson (2002) offer a comprehensive history of the British Museum.

[67] The Rosetta Stone has an enviable location: its placement in the middle segment of Room 4 grants visitors access to its display from Room 8 and the Collections Shop. Visitors who approach the Rosetta Stone from the Collections Shop will also see the entrance to the Parthenon galleries (Room 18) directly behind the glassed case that houses the trilingual *stela*.

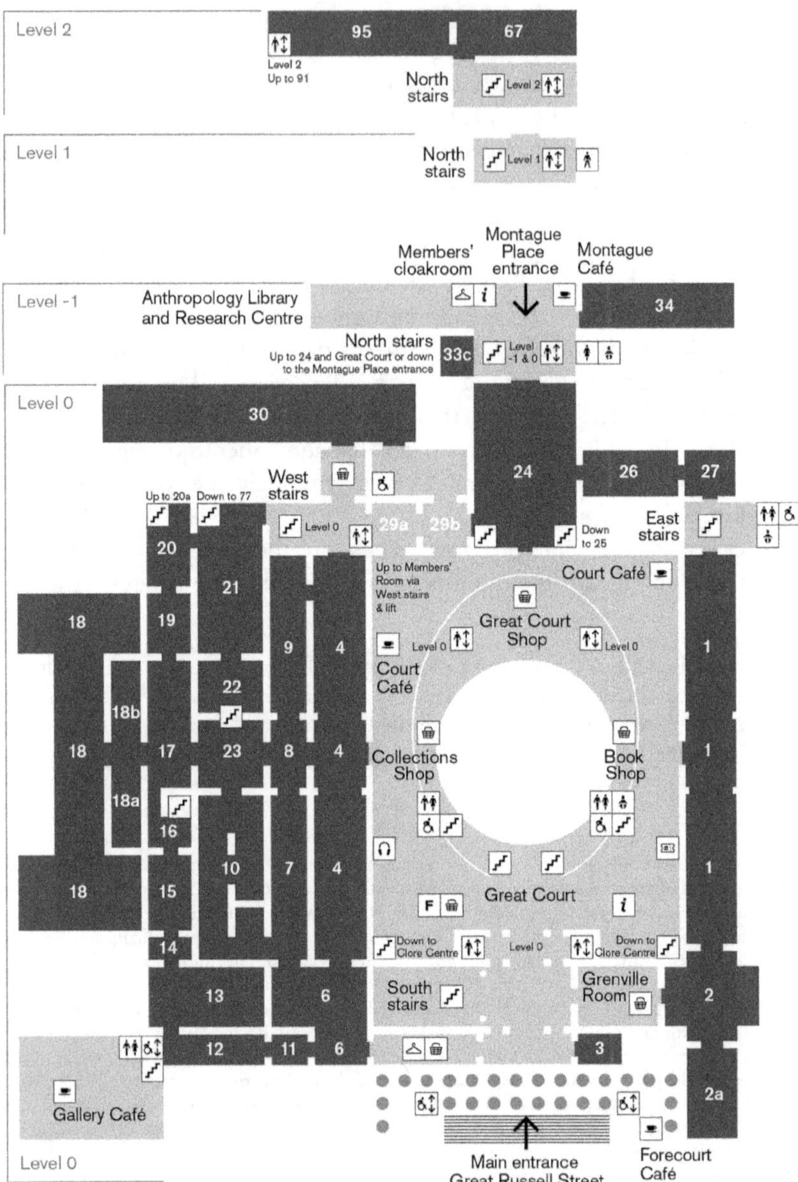

Figure 2.6   Ground floor layout of the British Museum, 2016. © The Trustees of the British Museum.

Egypt's culture and artistic expression, as their own had been *transformed* by past pharaonic domination.[68]

This wall text foregrounds Egypt and pushes Nubia to the periphery, which in turn renders Nubia's rule of Egypt an irregularity. According to the author of this text, Nubia gained power because it "took advantage" of preexisting conditions. Therefore, unfortunate political circumstances, rather than Nubia's military prowess or Egypt's inadequate efforts to unify itself, led to the end of Egyptian rule. The characterization of Nubians who "imposed themselves as overlords" likens them to ruthless invaders whose sinister plots threatened to destroy the political landscape. These Nubians disregarded the position of "local rulers" and forged ahead with their deceitful rule. The writer of this text implies that Nubian rulers could not even create their own northern capital; they merely appropriated an Egyptian one. A superficial glance at the extent of the Twenty-Fifth Dynasty (approximately sixty years) may buttress the argument that brute force and sheer luck fueled Nubian rule since the Egyptians regained control of their kingdom to found the Twenty-Sixth Dynasty (c. 664–525 BCE). But even with Egyptians' periodically successful local uprisings, it is impossible to ignore the centuries of Persian and Greek domination of Egypt that followed.

The reverence for Egyptian rule extends to the closing words of the wall text, in that the violent Nubians somehow "embraced" Egyptian culture. Here, the writer intimates that Egypt's "culture and artistic expression" compelled the Nubians to take a "transformed" perspective. These comments are especially puzzling in light of the panel's earlier account of pugnacious Nubians. It is difficult to make sense of brutal and luck-driven Nubians, as the wall text characterizes them, who somehow set aside their belligerent ways and welcome their former oppressors. The repeated glorification of Egypt in Room 4 prevents a contextualized understanding of the relationship between Egypt and Nubia. Even though archaeological evidence points to sustained cultural exchange among Nubians and Egyptians, especially those living in proximity to each other near the First and Second Cataracts of the Nile, the false impression of a one-way stream of culture from Egypt to Nubia overshadows the realities of acculturation.[69] Outside of this

---

[68] I recorded the interpretive material from Room 4 during a 2019 visit to the British Museum. The emphasis is my own. Unless otherwise noted, quotations from museum signage and interpretive material derive from my notes during in-person visits.

[69] Nubian acculturation to Egyptian practices occurred as early as the late Bronze Age: O'Connor (1993: 56–57). Smith (2003) and Török (2009) examine the two-way cultural transfer between Egypt and Nubia, especially in frontier regions.

"Political Fragmentation" display, the presence of Nubia in Room 4 mostly serves to aggrandize Egypt.[70] The omission of the two-way exchanges among these neighboring groups robs visitors of the opportunity to view Nubia as a region rich with its own history. The intense focus on Egypt is understandable since these objects are part of the "Egyptian Sculpture Galleries." Nonetheless, the direct and indirect emphasis on Nubia's perceived inferiority detracts from the educational value of Room 4 as a whole. Regardless of whatever the curatorial team's goals may have been for this room, this layout reduces Nubia to a primitive outpost of Egypt and promotes an Egyptocentric understanding of Nubia.

Coinciding with its limiting portrayal of Nubia in the "Egyptian Sculpture" gallery, the British Museum presents a skewed display of visual representations of black people in Greek antiquity. For a visitor interested in this iconography, a short walk from "Egyptian Sculpture" through "Assyria: Nimrud" (rooms 7–8), "Greek and Roman Sculpture" (Room 23), and "Nereid Monument" (Room 17) leads to a series of rooms (14–16) displaying ancient Greek pottery. In "Athens and Lycia" (Room 15), the British Museum's only janiform object with a brown face and a black face on display is a stout perfume bottle (*aryballos*).[71] Part of a glassed collection entitled "Africans," the label for the perfume bottle reads: "5th-century Athens was dominated by citizen males. Foreigners and women were both

---

[70] The region of Nubia is mentioned eight times in Room 4's object labels, including the caption for a pair of statues depicting Amenhotep III as a lion found in "foreign soil … [in] the conquered former kingdom of Kush"; statues of Senwosret II, who "campaigned in Nubia"; a statue of Teti, whose "grandfather and great-grandfather had been viceroys of Nubia"; a sarcophagus of Merymose, who was "a king's son of Kush, a viceroy ruling the whole of conquered Nubia"; a sarcophagus lid of Setau, "the viceroy of Nubia for Ramesses II"; a statue of Montuemhat, who was a "vassal of the Kushite kings [until] he switched loyalty as Psamtek I of Sais phased out all foreign domination by Assyria and Kush"; a libation bowl of Montuemhat that "probably stood in the temple … [where there was] a chapel that feature[d] him and King Taharqo, his original Kushite overlord"; and a sarcophagus lid of Sisobek, a "vizier of Lower Egypt after King Psamtek I had freed the land of Assyrian and Kushite rule." The region of Nubia is mentioned four times on wall text in Room 4: "Theban kings also faced incursions from the southern kingdom of Kush, after it seized Egypt's former Nubian possessions" (panel "Decline and Hyksos Rule: Second Intermediate Period"); "Campaigns in the south put an end to the kingdom of Kush and the whole of Nubia was annexed" ("The Age of Empire: Early New Kingdom"); "[Ramses II's temples include] two rock temples at Abu Simbel, in Lower Nubia … [in the Twentieth Dynasty,] Egypt also lost control of Nubia" ("The Ramessides: Late New Kingdom"); and "Psamtek I gained recognition across Egypt, forging the country's independence from both Assyrian and Kushite domination" ("Independence and Occupation: The Late Period").

[71] In addition to the stout perfume bottle in Room 15, I found another janiform object that depicts a black face and a brown face in the British Museum holdings (see Appendix 1). I also identified one janiform object from Naukratis: a sixth-century *aryballos*. The British Museum's online collection describes the turquoise bottle as a depiction of "an African and a western Asiatic male's head" (www .britishmuseum.org/collection/object/G_1847-0806-20).

therefore political outsiders." Comparable to Tanner's observations,[72] the description presumes selective political resonances. This collection features other objects from the fifth century BCE: a bronze statue of a kneeling boy holding a sponge in his right hand and a boot in his left, a terracotta figurine of a boy sitting cross-legged with his right leg propped up and his hands folded over his right knee, and a mixing bowl (*kratēr*) depicting a brown Andromeda with her servants. Barring the mixing bowl, these objects all feature renditions of people with a broad nose and full lips. The general caption portrays a semi-divine group of people who swiftly descend into the substratum of society:

> The Mediterranean sea washes the shores of north Africa where Greek colonists came into contact with the native peoples of the African continent. Ethiopia (the land of burnt faces) held a special fascination for the Greeks as a fabled land, favoured by the gods and the presumed source of the Nile. Africans enter Greek art as figures in myth or as studies in human physical type. African residents in fifth-century Athens will have been mostly slaves.[73]

In her survey of the British Museum, Page DuBois astutely points out curators' myopia regarding ancient Greek and Roman slavery.[74] These blind spots lead to swift elisions, as is evidenced in Room 15's pairing of African residents and an enslaved status.[75] The decision to categorize the four objects in the "Africans" display as depictions of enslaved people unhelpfully applies a restrictive modern lens to the diverse enterprise of Greco-Roman slavery. Although the attribution of some black people as enslaved in the fifth century BCE is plausible, there is no sure signification among these objects of their enslaved status. The bronze statue may reflect a person of humble means, and the pose of the terracotta sculpture bears similarities with a pondering philosopher. The physical distance between the Nubian objects in "Sudan, Egypt and Nubia" (Room 65, two levels above Room 15) and those in Room 15 reinforces the inaccurate conflation of black people and servitude. The humble presence of Nubia against the backdrop of monumental Egyptian objects in Room 4 further heightens

---

[72] See above on p. 45.

[73] I recorded captions from Room 15 during my 2017 visit to the British Museum.

[74] DuBois (2008: 65–88, 113).

[75] In her study of ancient Greek iconography, Wrenhaven (2011: 97, 112–14) asserts that enslaved people were identifiable based on their hair color, tattoos, and skin color; she also distinguishes between the actual presence and the artistic presence of enslaved people. Despite her contextualized approach, Wrenhaven (2012: 81, 83, 109) equates black faces on janiform cups with "the supposedly wild and exotic 'Others'" (p. 82).

this divide. A trip upstairs to Room 65, a room dedicated to Nubia, provides a more thorough assessment of the iconography of black people on display in the British Museum.

The panel at the entrance of the Raymond and Beverly Sackler Gallery "Sudan, Egypt and Nubia" (Room 65; see Figure 2.7) recognizes the importance of Nubia beyond its association with Egypt.[76] It reads: "[Nubia] was a vital link between central Africa, Egypt, and the Mediterranean world." This bidirectional connection with its northern and southern neighbors frees Nubia from the shadows of Egypt into which it was previously thrust on the ground floor. Walking through the room, a visitor comes across stunning pieces that highlight Nubia's long-lasting presence: rock art of a long-horned cow that dates to the second millennium BCE, a remarkable reproduction of a frieze from the thirteenth century BCE in which black Nubians carry tribute to the Egyptian pharaoh Ramses II, and a first-century BCE sculpture of a defeated enemy with an ironic inscription in the Meroitic language: "This is the king of the Nubians."[77] The gallery's title conveys the geographic scope of Nubia (spanning Sudan and modern Egypt) without presuming that Nubia depends on Egypt for political relevance.[78] The displays in this room reveal a somewhat expansive coverage of Nubian history including burial practices in Kerma, Pan-grave culture, Meroitic writing, the Twenty-Fifth Dynasty, and rescue archaeology in Abu Simbel. Some panels, however, promote a one-sided relationship, such as "Towns and Temples in Occupied Nubia" and "Egyptian Fortresses in Occupied Nubia."[79] These curatorial choices do not acknowledge that Nubia was a powerful entity in relation to all of its neighbors. In particular, the omission of Aksum (also spelled "Axum"), Nubia's southern neighbors who annexed Nubia in the fourth century CE,

---

[76] I give the full names of galleries to acknowledge the increasingly influential role of modern philanthropy in museums. Giridharadas (2018: 154–200, esp. 176–83) cautions against allowing plutocrats to become quasi-oligarchical stakeholders who weaponize philanthropy for their own ends.

[77] My visits to Room 65 yielded different observations. During my first visit, in August 2016, the podium on which millennia-old Nubian rock gongs sat was marked with stains from the coffee cups of unscrupulous visitors. During my second visit, in October 2016, the podium was scrubbed clean. During my third visit, in November 2016, the captions were difficult to read because of broken light fixtures. The skylights that had helped to illuminate the room on previous visits were insufficient because the sun had already set. I inquired about the lighting situation and a helpful guard, Mr. Ernest Johnson, explained that imminent repairs would remedy the lighting problems in the entire wing. I was unable to confirm whether the lights had been fixed during my fourth and fifth visits, in May 2017 and May 2019, because there was still daylight when the museum closed (around 9 p.m.).

[78] In 1988, Vivian Davies (a keeper at the British Museum) changed the name of the Department of Ancient Egypt to the Department of Ancient Egypt and Sudan to reflect sustained interest in Nubia.

[79] To be fair, many of these labels were part of the "Egyptian Imperialism in Nubia" display.

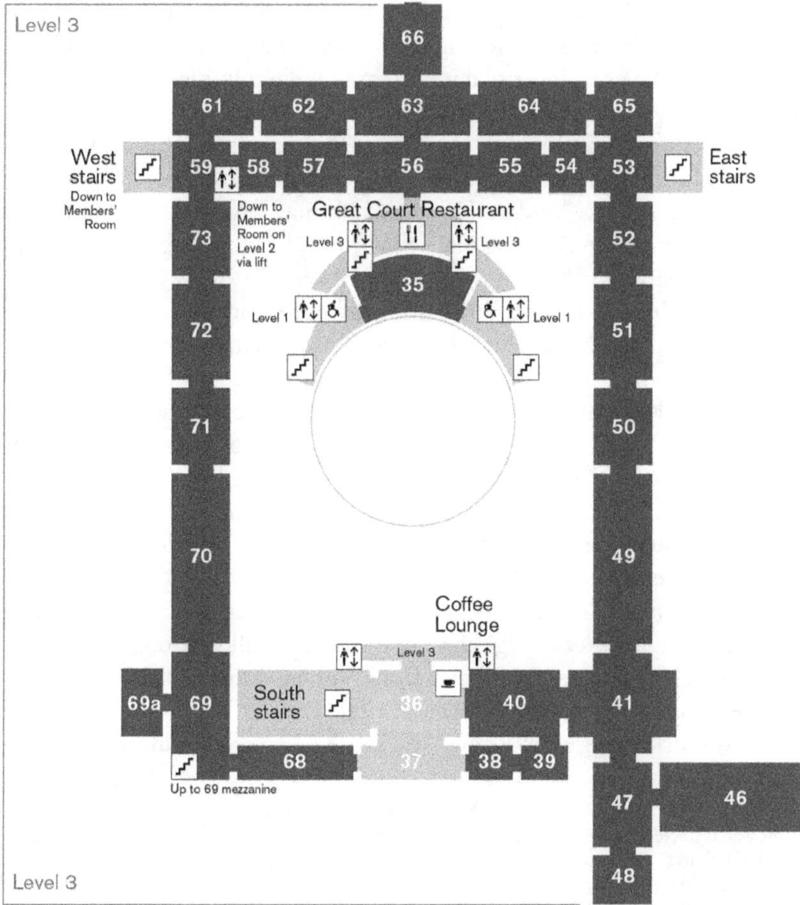

Figure 2.7 Level 3 layout of the British Museum, 2016. © The Trustees of the British Museum.

risks providing viewers with an incomplete picture of Nubia's history. None of the text in Room 65 mentions Aksum's contentious encounters with Nubia or its prominent role in Nubia's demise. Instead, the wall text explains that the collapse of Meroe, Nubia's capital city from c. 300BCE–300CE, was "apparently brought about by a decline in trade and persistent raiding by desert nomads."[80]

---

[80] When, in 2017, I asked keeper Derek Welsby about the omission of Aksum in Room 65, he stated that Aksum did not single-handedly lead to Meroe's demise; see Welsby (1996: 196–205) and Hatke

The British Museum's placement of Augustus's bronze head from Meroe further downplays the might of Nubia. Rather than use this piece to elevate Nubia as a powerful nation that literally trampled on the Roman emperor (due to the bust's original location, buried underneath the steps leading to a temple in Meroe), the British Museum treats this bronze head as a relic of Rome and places it in Room 70, "Roman Empire," eight rooms away from Room 65, "Sudan, Egypt and Nubia."[81] With this layout, only informed visitors are able to situate the bronze head among other Nubian objects and envision Nubia as a formidable region in its own right. For those determined to contextualize this head in its findspot, a brief side trip to Sudan reveals the relativity of the categories "center" and "periphery." Currently, a replica of Augustus's head is on display at the Sudan National Museum in Khartoum. The object's label omits any discussion of the head's replica status or the current location of the original bust.[82] It was only during a tour of the Royal City of Meroe, the site from which the head was excavated, in January 2020, that I was able to ascertain any information about the object's current location. Upon my inquiry, the local guide, Ms. Neema, located it "somewhere in England."[83]

The location of "Sudan, Egypt and Nubia" in Room 65 frames Nubia in relation to its northern neighbors: one literally walks through Egypt (in rooms 64 and 63) in order to travel from Nubia (Room 65) to its southern neighbor, Ethiopia. In "Ethiopia and Coptic Egypt" (Room 66), located in a narrow corridor between Room 63 and the north stairs, curators leapfrog

(2013: 143–47). Welsby also explained that this hotly debated topic was too complex for inclusion in the wall text. Nevertheless, the Ashmolean Museum explicitly lists Aksum as part of Nubia's history in the wall text "Dynastic Egypt and Nubia" (Room 23): "Around AD 350, an invading army from Aksum in Ethiopia brought an end to the Meroitic kingdom." See Burstein (1981), who suggests that Ezana completed his Aksumite predecessor's attempts to subdue Nubia.

[81] The object label for Augustus's head at the British Museum reads: "Bronze head from an over life-sized statue of Augustus (The Meroe Head): Statues of the emperor, together with images of him on coins and painted panels, were essential to imperial propaganda. They showed his far-flung subjects who he was and reminded them of his power … The Kushites intended the burial [of Augustus's head underneath the entrance of a temple] to be a sign of triumph over the Roman Empire and its emperor. But by a twist of fate it ultimately preserved this fascinating symbol of power."

[82] The object label for Augustus's head at the Sudan National Museum reads (in Arabic, then English), "Bronze head of Emperor Augustus discovered buried beneath the threshold of a temple in the royal city of Meroe, probably formed part of the plunder taken by … queen Amani Rinas during their raids [sic] upon Egyptian frontier in the late first century B.C." The British Museum also has its own replica of the bust, which curators put on display in Room 70 when the original bronze head was included in various traveling exhibitions (the National Museum of Western Australia in Perth in 2016, the National Museum of Australia in Canberra in 2016/17, and the Victoria Gallery and Museum at the University of Liverpool in 2018).

[83] I visited the Sudan National Museum and the Royal City of Meroe in January 2020. I interpreted Ms. Neema's lack of specificity as a shrewd way to circumvent England's geographic hegemony beyond the country's borders.

over Nubia to pair two countries (Ethiopia and Egypt) whose people cannot access each other without traversing Nubia. "Ethiopia and Coptic Egypt" highlights the prominence of fifteenth-century CE Ethiopian crosses and Christian art alongside objects from fourth- to sixth-century CE Wadi Sarga in Coptic Egypt. Despite the religious overlaps in this room, the chronological leap unfortunately perpetuates the perception that Egypt alone has a meaningful ancient history. The British Museum's rendering of Egypt as a singularly remarkable country remains undisturbed, as the sole exhibit featuring objects from modern Egypt, Sudan, and Ethiopia is located in the Sainsbury African Galleries.[84] Only a brief note in "Ethiopia and Coptic Egypt" invites viewers interested in Ethiopian textiles to visit the African galleries.[85]

A visit to the basement brings this museum adventure to an end. Located in Room 25 on Level -2, "Africa" displays objects from over forty African countries (including four pieces from modern Egypt and nineteen from Sudan). Ivan Karp and his colleagues Fred Wilson and Corinne Kratz assert that the display of African objects in a museum's basement encourages visitors to perceive non-European civilizations as nebulous tributaries that feed into "the great stream culminating in Western civilization."[86] The British Museum unfortunately reinforces this troubling current with its presentation of the Benin Bronzes (c. sixteenth century CE) in Room 25. Stolen from the royal palace in Benin City (southern Nigeria) as part of British troops' punitive expedition in 1897, the British Museum treats these brass plaques as exotic war booty. The title wall sanitizes the British troops' destruction of Benin City and reflects imperial arrogance with the introductory title: "The Discovery of Benin Art by the West." The panel continues to identify positive aspects of the British invasion: "Benin treasures caused an enormous sensation [in the West], fuelling an appreciation for African art which profoundly influenced 20th century Western art." The exploitation extends to the final lines of the caption: "Between the 1950s and 1970s the British Museum sold around 30 objects to Nigeria." This closing comment underlines the

---

[84] I refer to "modern Egypt" and "Sudan," rather than "Egypt" and "Nubia," to emphasize the temporal shift in the labeling practices of the Sainsbury Galleries.

[85] The British Museum catalogue reinforces this hegemonic portrayal of Egypt, in that the "Ancient Egypt" category has six entries, including "Sudan, Egypt and Nubia" (Room 65) and "Ethiopia and Coptic Egypt" (Room 66). The museum catalogue lists only one entry under the "Africa" category: Room 25.

[86] Karp and Wilson (1996: 263–64); Karp and Kratz (2000: 194). For the perspective of the curators of the Sainsbury Galleries, see Spring, Barley, and Hudson (2001).

continued profiting of former colonial powers that occludes an egalitarian relationship between African and European nations.[87]

2.5   Conclusion: Critical Curation

Invisible ontologies pervade contemporary scholarship about ancient Greek iconography. Any exploration of blackness calls to mind broader histories of skin color, but representations of blackness in Greek antiquity need not mirror modern connotations of skin color. In referring to janiform cups with black and brown faces as portable performance pieces within the symposium, I refrain from making general claims about the occupation of black people in the general iconographic world or in Greece as a whole. Adopting a new identity in a symposiastic setting is not the same as learning about or interacting with foreigners. Rather, my focus on a subset of artistic renditions of black people has aimed to encourage a wider exploration of the theatricality and flexibility of blackness. When symposiasts interact with a variety of faces on their cups, they tap into the performative nature of the symposium. In turn, the faces become part of a drinker-turned-actor's repertoire. This act of transformation reflects the power of performance, in that it enables drinkers to adopt, and guests to accept, a new identity.

Writ large, modernity's inconsistent fixation with skin color translates to museums' unequal presentation of black people in Greek and Nubian antiquity. At the British Museum, the general portrayal of Nubia promotes a rigid hierarchy that relegates it to a secondary position under Egypt. This limiting approach is tempered with a slightly more impartial handling of Nubia in "Sudan, Egypt and Nubia" (Room 65). On the whole, I question not the intentions of the curators, but the implementation of their goals.[88]

---

[87] Cuno (2008) and Jenkins (2016) examine the larger debate surrounding the repatriation of museums' dubiously acquired objects; Coombes (1994: 7–42), Ogbechie (2011: 173–207), and Hicks (2020) contextualize the Benin Bronzes. Although most of the Benin Bronzes remain in European and American museums' collections, museum officials from various European countries have worked with Nigerian officials to create the Benin Dialogue Group. As a result of this group's advocacy efforts, some European museums have agreed to arrange for a long-term loan of the Benin Bronzes to be displayed at the Edo Museum of West African Art in Benin City, Nigeria (currently under construction). Calls for full restitution of stolen African objects continue to dominate public discourse. There has been some progress, as France returned twenty-six artifacts looted from Benin in November 2021.

[88] The British Museum's keepers Anna Garnett and Derek Welsby discuss their admirable goals for the recently revised layout of "Sudan, Egypt and Nubia" (Room 65) in the British Museum's newsletter of July 2016: "[this room aims] to showcase the diversity of the Nubian and Sudanese civilisations and further highlight the great cultural and political flowerings in this region over more than six millennia ... it is hoped that these displays will enable visitors to better understand the

In their brilliant evaluation of museum exhibits, Ivan Karp and Corinne Kratz outline the net positive results of critical curation:

> Ideally, exhibitions created with such recognition [that all people, even museum curators, are members of other cultures] would not only tell visitors about cultural diversity and include several perspectives, but also show the process through which curatorial judgments were made, that those judgments are contingent and contestable rather than final, and that there are other stories that were not included but might have been.[89]

Karp and Kratz exhort curators to think rigorously about categorizations of material culture and the issues they implicitly flag with their classifications. Otherwise, curators can too easily overlook the privileging of their own perspectives in their exhibits and exhibitions. Identifying blindspots in curatorial practices can address some of the dangerous consequences of slippage between different time periods. A reciprocal gaze that erodes the power dynamics in museums is especially important for any visual display of the iconography of black people in Greek antiquity.

Recent projects that promote equitable museum practices have begun to bear fruit. In 2019, Marenka Thompson-Odlum spearheaded "Labelling Matters: Activating Objects", a collaborative project that identifies colonial language in the Pitt Rivers Museum's labels. This endeavor culminated in a series of podcasts featuring fifteen- and sixteen-year old students from Oxford Spires Academy, a state-funded secondary school in England, who scrutinized the museum's curatorial practices.[90] Another instance of critical curating appears at the Ashmolean Museum at Oxford. This museum houses the Christian Levett Family Gallery "Dynastic Egypt and Nubia," which presents Nubia's vast relationships with its neighbors in a balanced manner. The wall text in this exhibit underscores Nubia's interactions without any Egyptocentric fanfare. The placement of the Nubian ruler Taharqo's massive shrine in the middle of the exhibit pushes back against

---

developments in Nubian and Sudanese history while gaining a new appreciation of the beauty and diversity of the material cultures of those who lived and died along the Nile Valley south of the First Nile Cataract"; Garnett and Welsby (2016: 17).

[89] Karp and Kratz (2000: 221).

[90] Thanks to Mai Musié for bringing "Labelling Matters" to my attention; see www.torch.ox.ac.uk /labelling-matters#/. Other creative museum projects include: the Museum of Westminster Street (a 3D pop-up museum in Providence, RI, www.themuseumonline.com/westminsterstor/index.php /museum/), the US-based movement "Decolonize This Place" (https://decolonizethisplace.org/), the Dutch initiative "Decolonize the Museum" (https://twitter.com/Decolonizemusea), and "Museum Detox" in the United Kingdom (www.museumdetox.org/). See also Bielenberg's (2018) shrewd analysis of an object label ("a bust of a boy, negroid type") at the Rhode Island School of Design Museum.

the portrayal of Nubia as an appendage of Egypt. In a tripartite display that examines Egypt's encounters with Nubia, the Levant, and the Mediterranean, a subheading entitled "Conflict" emphasizes the trilateral balance of power in this region of the world.[91] At the Oriental Institute Museum at the University of Chicago, the Robert F. Picken Family Nubian Gallery provides visitors with a balanced assessment of Nubian history through its chronological series of displays, including "Meroitic Pottery," "Nubian Archers," and "Dress and Adornment in Meroitic Nubia." The panel "New Kingdom," which encompasses the period of Egyptian occupation of Nubia from 1550 to 1069 BCE, emphasizes the two-way traffic of goods and people.[92] This evenhanded methodology applies to the variety of objects on view, such as a Qustul incense burner with Egyptian iconography and wheel-made (Egyptian-style) pottery with Nubian designs.[93]

The exhibition "Ancient Nubia Now," which ran from October 2019 to January 2020 at the MFA, offers a final example of critical curation.[94] In possession of the largest Nubian collection outside of Sudan, the MFA highlighted Nubia's extensive networks via displays of imported Egyptian, Greek, and Roman objects found in Nubian tombs. Wall text throughout "Ancient Nubia Now" outlined Nubia and Egypt's intertwined history without subjugating the former. Near the entrance of the exhibition, the museum incorporated its own history into the narrative. Part of the "Nubia, History, and the MFA" panel, the wall text read:

> Until recently, Nubia's story has been told in large part by others – beginning with the ancient Egyptians, whose propaganda cast their enemies in a negative light. In the early 20th century, scholars and archaeologists often brought racial

---

[91] The Ashmolean's subheading reads, "The ancient Egyptians represented foreigners as tribute bearers or defeated enemies. However, archaeological evidence suggests that trade and immigration played a much greater role in inter-cultural affairs during most of the Middle Kingdom and the Second Intermediate Period." I recorded this caption during my visit to the Ashmolean in May 2017.

[92] The Oriental Institute Museum's panel reads: "An Egyptian governor administered the country [Nubia] and ensured the flow of Nubian gold to Egypt. Nubia also contributed exotic products such as animal skins, ivory, and ebony as well as dates, cattle, and horses prized for their quality. Despite being required to send rich resources to Egypt, Nubia prospered during this period. Many Egyptians settled in Nubia, and Nubians moved north to Egypt." I recorded this caption during my visit to the museum in January 2017.

[93] Located between the First and Second Cataracts of the Nile, Qustul was the site of a royal cemetery with finds that date to c. 3200 BCE.

[94] A brief note about these museums' acquisition history: the Oriental Institute Museum acquired its Nubian collection mainly through rescue archaeology in advance of the completion of the Aswan High Dam in the 1960s; the Ashmolean acquired most of its Nubian collection from the excavations led by Sir Francis Llewellyn Griffith in the early twentieth century; the Boston MFA built its Nubian collection from the excavation work led by George A. Reisner from 1913 to 1932.

prejudice to their work, influencing interpretations of Nubia for decades. This exhibition, drawn entirely from the MFA's collection, examines some of the ways in which Nubia's history has been obscured and misinterpreted – and the Museum's own role in that particular history.[95]

The MFA's explicit grappling with its colonialist history serves as a model for precisely the sort of reflexive work that Karp and Kratz invoke. In other words, the museum's accountable stewardship helps museum-goers construct their own restorative performance of blackness.[96] Channeling this bidirectional methodology, in the next chapter I explore a performance of blackness on a tragic stage: black protagonists in Aeschylus's *Suppliants* (c. 463 BCE) repurpose the mask of difference that their audience foists upon them. In line with these savvy ancient performers, Black characters in nineteenth-, twentieth-, and twenty-first-century literature wriggle out of the straitjacket of alterity into which others have forced them.

---

[95] I recorded this text during my January 2020 visit to the "Ancient Nubia Now" exhibition at the MFA.

[96] I use the language of accountable stewardship after Besterman (2011).

CHAPTER 3

Masks of Difference in Aeschylus's Suppliants

> We wear the mask that grins and lies,
> It hides our cheeks and shades our eyes, –
> This debt we pay to human guile;
> With torn and bleeding hearts we smile,
> And mouth with myriad subtleties.
>
> (Dunbar [1895: 21, vv. 1–5])

In his poem "We Wear the Mask," published in 1895, Paul Laurence Dunbar named and claimed the mask that obfuscated his people's collective face. With this imagery, he brought to the forefront the transformation that occurred when he and his fellow Black people packaged themselves as performers who entertained their audience. This artificial disguise allowed them flexibility: in private, they could step out of these assumed roles to fulfill self-determined ones; in front of their audience, they became actors extraordinaire. The mask reified unequal power dynamics in that the stakes were high for those without power, and their survival hinged on a convincing performance. At the same time, the undercurrent of guile ("myriad subtleties") hinted at the subversive power lying beneath the nebulous mask. Dunbar's famous poem poses probing questions about the versatility and veracity of those who stand before the public gaze at the mercy of their audience. Similarly, characters in fifth-century BCE Athenian tragedy invite audiences to rethink and broaden their perspectives of other people.

Unlike Dunbar's performers, who can presumably remove their masks when they are among themselves, the protagonists of Aeschylus's *Suppliants* (c. 463 BCE) do not exist beyond the world of theater because they are representations of blackness, not real people.[1] Nevertheless,

---

[1] In the second stanza of "We Wear the Mask," Dunbar hints that the mask is removed in certain company: "Let them only see us, while / We wear the mask." Before 1952, many scholars thought that the *Suppliants* was Aeschylus's first tragedy (dating it to the 470s BCE), citing elements such as the prominent role of the chorus and the clumsy handling of the second actor (Garvie [2006: 88]). In

Aeschylus's literary constructs push the boundaries of performance when they transform into astute performers who force their intratextual audience to contend with their perceived differences. In turn, these performers entice people outside of the world of the tragedy to destabilize their own definition of alterity. In what could be read as a case study of reorienting otherness, Aeschylus's Danaids perform an Argive Greek identity that seemingly contradicts their black skin and place of immediate origin in Egypt.[2] In the first play of Aeschylus's tetralogy, the Danaids – the fifty black daughters of Danaus – travel from Egypt to Argos in order to escape a pending marriage to their cousins, the sons of their paternal uncle Aegyptus.[3] The Danaids' performance of a hybrid identity is initially irreconcilable with the Argive ruler Pelasgus's externally driven assessment of their identity – that is, their race. Although their skin color and clothes expose their visual alterity, the Danaids transcend these physical differences and confuse normative categories with their words and actions.

1952, the discovery of *P. Oxy.* 2256.3, a fragment from the late second/early third century CE, suggested a later production date because it lists Aeschylus's tetralogy alongside "Archedemus," the archon of Athens from 464–63 BCE: ἐπὶ ἀρ[χεδημίδου . . . ἐνίκα [Αἰ]σχύλο[ς | Δαν[αί]σι Ἀμυ[μώνη | δεύτ[ε]ρ[ο]ς Σοφοκλῆ[ς ("in the time of Archedemus . . . when Aeschylus [won first prize] with the *Danaids* and *Amomyne*, Sophocles was in second place," fr. 1–4). Unless otherwise noted, all translations from ancient sources are my own.

  Some scholars have disagreed with the amended date: Diamantopoulos (1957) asserts that the play was composed (c. 492 BCE) much earlier than the production date (460s BCE), while Taplin (1977: 192) maintains that the *Suppliants* was Aeschylus's earliest play. Following Sicherl (1986), Sommerstein (1997) argues for a later date of 461 BCE. Along with Rösler, Sommerstein also challenges the order of the plays: Sommerstein (2008: 283–89) lists the *Aegyptians* as the first play of the tetralogy and the *Suppliants* as the third, while Rösler (2007: 182–83) places the *Suppliants* second.

2 More than a blank slate onto which Greeks can paint their anxieties about others, Egypt is a conduit for both a real and an imagined place (Vasunia [2001: 73–78, 288]); Mudimbe (1994: 167–81) and Said (1978) elaborate on the idea of a foreign country as a blank slate. In Euripides's *Helen* (412 BCE), the only extant Athenian tragedy set in Egypt, the tragedian inverts the familiar myth of Helen's departure to Troy and instead situates her in Egypt, a country inhabited by frenzied sexual predators. The play alludes to stereotypes about the lustful nature of Egyptian men via Theoclymenus's eager desire for Helen (see also Hdt. 2.89); Vasunia (2001: 73) remarks that Egyptian men in Athenian tragedy do exactly what Greek men wish they could do.

3 I take the *Suppliants* to be the first play in a tetralogy that included the *Aegyptians*, the *Danaids*, and the satyr play *Amomyne*; the *Suppliants* is the only extant one. The plots of these lost plays are currently thought to be as follows: the *Aegyptians* focuses on the events leading up to the murder of the forty-nine bridegrooms (Garvie [2006: 196]); the *Danaids* covers the Danaids' fatal wedding day (Zeitlin [1996: 169]; Bachvarova [2009: 289]); and *Amomyne* recounts the experiences of Amomyne, Danaus's daughter, who resists a satyr's attempt to rape her and later conceives a child with Poseidon (Garvie [2006: 233]; Sommerstein [2008: 281–84]). The *Suppliants* is the earliest of a group of extant tragedies that center on the reception of fugitive suppliants in Greek cities, followed by Aeschylus's *Eumenides* (458 BCE), Euripides's *Medea* (431 BCE), Euripides's *Daughters of Heracles* (430 BCE), Euripides's *Suppliants* (422 BCE), and Sophocles's *Oedipus at Colonus* (401 BCE).

In this chapter, I extend my inquiry of representations of blackness to the literary realm. Through my extended examination of the Danaids' metaphorical mask of difference alongside transhistorical iterations of this guise, I draw connections between ancient Athenian tragedy and twentieth-century literature without sacrificing the specific context of each. Scrutiny of the Danaids' black skin in Greek iconography reinforces the performers' unique reworking of color and identity. Following this foray into the visual realm, a close examination of the written text of the play reveals the Danaids to be obedient daughters and versatile ethnographers who successfully waylay Pelasgus's attempts to label them as foreigners (*Supp.* 222–46, 274–90). I also consider the Danaids' metic status alongside the resonances of metics in fifth-century Athens. Finally, I put the Danaids' intersectional approach to identity into dialogue with Suzan-Lori Parks's "New Black Math," a poetic essay in which the narrator redefines the parameters of a "Black play."[4]

Aeschylus's *Suppliants* is the only extant tragedy from Greek antiquity that features characters who explicitly reflect on their skin color.[5] However, those who are eager to treat blackness as the driving force in this Athenian tragedy may be disappointed: my focus on the Danaids' black skin does not indicate a centrality afforded to this trope in the *Suppliants*. In other words, my sustained analysis of blackness in this tragedy reflects my own centering of skin color rather than any ancient Greek preoccupation. The Danaids redirect Pelasgus's prejudice, which includes a detour through the visual difference of skin color, but they swiftly move to other domains, including geography, attire, and gender expectations. Nonetheless, their ability to weave black skin in and out of their Argive Greek identity enables modern readers to encounter a performance of blackness in an unexpected setting.

---

[4] See Parks (2005).

[5] While Aeschylus's *Suppliants* stands alone in this respect, there are fragments of other Athenian tragedies featuring black characters. In Sophocles's *Inachos*, Zeus appears in the guise of a black stranger (fr. 269a53–54, as numbered in Lloyd-Jones [1996]); Euripides's *Archelaus* (fr. 1. 3–4, as numbered in Collard and Cropp [2008]) refers to black Aithiopians, and his *Phaethon* features Merops, king of the black people who live in the East (line 4, as numbered in Collard and Cropp [2009]; discussed in Hall [1989: 140]). Although the geographer Strabo (15.3.2) claims that Memnon was Aithiopian and both Sophocles's and Euripides's *Andromedas* feature an Aithiopian princess, the actors performing as Memnon and Andromeda probably wore white masks (Hall [1989: 140–43]). Furthermore, black characters appear in other genres: Odysseus and his herald Eurybates in the *Odyssey* (16.175, 19.246; discussed in Dee [2003–04: 161–62]) and the Aithiopian gods in Xenophanes of Colophon's lyric poetry (fr. 16, as numbered in Edmonds [1931]). Metaphorical blackness, as a way to depict strangeness, also applies to the Erinyes in Athenian tragedies (Aeschylus, *Agamemnon* 461–67; Aeschylus, *Eumenides* 183, 370).

3.1 Masks of Difference

In the fifth century BCE, masks were an integral part of Athenian tragic performances. Of religious origins, masks had become purely theatrical phenomena by that time.[6] They were made with linen soaked in a stiffening agent of plaster or animal glue and pressed into negative molds, and the only extant visual examples consist of fifth-century pottery and terracotta replicas.[7] Despite the popular interpretation of masks' wide-open mouths serving as vehicles for unhindered passage of the actor's voice, elaborate theatrical design such as careful construction of the theater site, the circular arrangement of the seating area, and the presence of the fourth wall also contributed to actors' auditory range.[8] As an invisible wall that created a barrier preventing any interaction between the actors and the audience, the fourth wall recast the *orchēstra* and *skēnē* as actual sites of action.[9]

In Aeschylus's *Suppliants,* the actors playing the Danaids wore dark masks and long, dark robes to symbolize their chromatic alterity.[10] The incongruity of the Danaids' skin color and their Argive Greek identity foregrounds the ambiguous relationship between inner being and outer guise. The Danaids use the former to overpower whatever the latter may suggest. Donning these masks as (re)presentations of skin color, the Danaids' appearance initially clashes with their proposed affiliations. In their lengthy opening speech (*Supp.* 1–175), they unsettle prejudicial judgments by invoking the Greek god Zeus, patron of suppliants, while also pointing out their foreign status: Ζεὺς μὲν ἀφίκτωρ ἐπίδοι προφρόνως | στόλον ἡμέτερον νάιον ... ἀπὸ προστομίων λεπτοψαμάθων | Νείλου ("may Zeus the suppliant gladly look upon our naval voyage ... from the soft, sandy mouth of the Nile," 1–4).[11] They perform their diverse

---

[6] Halliwell (1993: 197–99, 207). See also Wiles (2007: 255–56): "we need to distinguish the understandings of a modern book-based society, whereby the visual illustrates or fleshes out the written text, from the practices of an oral society, where language served to animate the visual image."

[7] Wiles (2007: 15–43, 62). Aeschylus introduced color to these initially plain white masks (Wiles [2007: 15]). Frontisi-Ducroux (1989) examines depictions of masks on Attic pottery.

[8] Duncan (2006); Easterling and Hall (2002).

[9] McCart (2007: 249–50, 253); Spatz (1982: 11); Wiles (2007: 131); Sommerstein (2010: 17–31). The Danaids may have stood in the *orchēstra* rather than the *skēnē*, since they were members of the chorus. Regardless of where they stood, both locations would have been distinct from the world of the audience, and the fourth wall would have remained intact.

[10] I describe the masks as "dark" to reflect the opacity regarding where on the color spectrum these masks fell (whether they were completely black or merely a dark shade).

[11] Zeus is mentioned thirteen times in the Danaids' opening speech (*Supp.* 1–175) and fifty-six times in the entire play. It is curious to note that in the Athenian context, Zeus is associated with foreigners and metics.

knowledge of Greek religion and Egyptian geography through these verbal markers. Even though their black skin is one of many elements that prevent Pelasgus from believing their declaration of Argive Greek ancestry, their wide-ranging fluency in the language and customs of Greece helps them gain access into his world.

In this linguistic vein, Frantz Fanon acknowledges that mastery of the French language enables his fellow Black Antilleans to benefit from certain privileges. Fanon highlights the price that Black people in the French Caribbean pay when they adopt the language of the colonizer. In their futile effort to become part of the elite, they become "slaves of their archetypes."[12] He explains the dangers associated with this linguistic choice: "[this] means imprisoning the black man and perpetuating a conflictual situation where the white man infects the black [*sic*] man with extremely toxic foreign bodies."[13] No amount of verbal skills can alter the Antilleans' appearance. An integration of the colonized and colonizer's language might occur, but this violent cohesion prohibits any redistribution of power. The semiotics of the transatlantic slave ship that haunt the Lesser Antilles do not have a direct parallel in Argos. Nevertheless, as I discuss in greater detail in Section 2 below, the Danaids prefigure the Antilleans' contested status when they struggle to convince Pelasgus of their shared ancestry solely with their words.[14] In their efforts to reconcile Pelasgus's uncoupling of their words and appearance, the Danaids speak knowledgeably about Greek religious rites. Their verbal acuity bristles against their phenotypic alterity, undoing Pelasgus's attempts to assign a mask of difference to them.

In his essay "Change the Joke and Slip the Yoke," which originally appeared in 1958 in the *Partisan Review*, Ralph Ellison argues that White Americans force their Black counterparts to wear a metaphorical mask (of joviality and servility, among other traits) that usurps their lives. The mask strips Black people of their versatile identities and projects onto them one that maintains an unequal power paradigm. Ellison deconstructs the subversion lurking beneath the mask: "Here the 'darky' act makes brothers of us all. America is a land of masking jokers. We wear the mask for purposes of aggression as well as for defense, when we are projecting the future and preserving the past. In short, the motives

---

[12] "L'esclave de leurs archétypes": Fanon (1952: 47); trans. Philcox, Fanon (2008: 18).

[13] "C'est enfermer le Noir, c'est perpétuer une situation conflictuelle où le Blanc infeste le Noir de corps étrangers extrêmement toxiques": Fanon (1952: 48); trans. Philcox, Fanon (2008: 18–19).

[14] I use "semiotics of the slave ship" after Sharpe (2016: 21).

hidden behind the mask are as numerous as the ambiguities the mask conceals."[15]

According to Ellison, Black people's calculated response of "accommodation + resistance" troubles the inequitable society that treats them like indistinguishable relatives ("brothers of us all").[16] Daphne Brooks's work on the 1903 minstrel musical *In Dahomey* presents a refreshing analysis of the ways in which Black people harnessed previously ascribed roles to turn claims of primitivism inside out.[17] In this musical, with lyrics written by Dunbar, vaudeville stars Bert Williams and George Walker assume the roles of two Black men traveling from Boston to Florida to return a family heirloom to its rightful owner. They decide to relocate to their final destination, the Dahomey kingdom (modern-day Benin).[18] The revised ending of the play concluded with a cakewalk, a plantation dance originating in the antebellum American south that became a popular staple in minstrel shows. The cakewalk consisted of a song-and-dance competition in which formally attired enslaved Black people imitated their White masters' dance moves in order to win a prize (cake) from their master.[19] The performance itself was a parody: White masters viewed the dance as an admiring emulation of themselves while Black people used it to mock their oppressors. With their reenactment of a cakewalk, Williams and Walker

[15] Ellison (1995: 109). Dunbar's literary corpus, including poems in standard English and in African American Vernacular English, also complicates any clear division between one's words and appearance; Braxton (1993).

[16] I use the calculation of "accommodation + resistance" after Gilroy (1995: 16). Sharpe points out that a "terrible calculus" continues to exist in the current afterlife of slavery (2016: 97, 100; after Hartman [2008: 6]). On minstrelsy, see Toll (1974), Lott (1993), Lhamon (1998), Meer (2005), and Thompson (2021).

[17] Brooks (2006: 207–80).

[18] Widespread interest in the Dahomey kingdom grew out of "The Dahomey Village" exhibition at the 1893 World's Columbian Exposition in Chicago, during which people from Dahomey were displayed as part of a living museum (Rydell [1987]; Reed [2000]). Also present at the World's Columbian Exposition was Nancy Green, a formerly enslaved woman who performed as Aunt Jemima to promote a ready-made pancake mix.

[19] Shipp (1903); Baldwin (1981); Carter (2008: 56–68); Brooks (2006: 207–80, esp. 271–73). It is reported that British audiences of *In Dahomey* became so raucous after the cakewalk that the cast had to sing "God Save the King" to restore order (Brooks [2006: 207, 212, 278]). The intersection of satire, masks, and skin color has another modern parallel: in Jean Genet's 1958 play *The Blacks: A Clown Show*, which examines the murder of a White woman through a community's reenactment of the death scene, the notes for the play demanded at least one White actor, or someone wearing a white mask (Genet [1994: 4]). Despite this prerequisite, the American premiere of this play in 1961 featured an all-Black cast, with chorus members wearing masks of white faces with black bands (Genet [1994: 4, 8]). Genet's play bears an uncanny resemblance to Langston Hughes's 1931 poem "The Black Clown" (see Hughes [1995]), which was expanded into a musical featuring an all-Black cast in 2018 (*The Black Clown*, music and lyrics by Davóne Tines and Michael Schachter, dir. Zack Winokur, American Repertory Theater, Cambridge, MA, August–September 2018).

blurred the distinctions between Black and White in an entertaining, subversive way. The play was ostensibly made for a White audience, yet the all-Black cast transformed the objectification of their people into that of their masters.[20]

Despite the vast differences between twentieth-century America and ancient Argos, the Danaids utilize comparable tactics as Williams and Walker in their quest for refuge. The Danaids' survival hinges on their ability to erase any distinction between their assigned identity (i.e. their race) and their asserted identity. They cannot hope for protection from Pelasgus if he retains a binary understanding of the two. By putting their mastery of Greek religion on display, they eventually erode the label of "foreign" that Pelasgus has ascribed to them. Fanon recognized that a similar transformation offered Black Antilleans a chance to leave behind their unjust society. In line with Fanon's francophone Antilleans, the Danaids reject their former environment and adopt a linguistic register that implies association with a powerful group. At the same time, they recognize the disconnect between their appearance and lineage. They bridge this gap with a syncretic model of their identity: Argive Greek, black, and Egyptian. For all of the groups discussed (African Americans, Antilleans, and the Danaids), their survival depends on their successful manipulation of their assigned masks of difference.

As the sole extant play featuring the merging of the categories of Argive Greek, Egyptian, and black, the *Suppliants* tempts twenty-first-century readers to read the Danaids' skin color as an allegory for presumed Egyptian presence in fifth-century BCE Athens. The mythical setting, however, discourages twenty-first-century audiences from grafting the Danaids' physical countenance onto the perceptions of all Egyptians in fifth-century Greece. Such a hasty conclusion assumes that skin color was a sharply polarizing phenomenon and that the *Suppliants* is a documentary text, neither of which is true. Within the mythical realm, then, the question of whether the Danaids' skin color is indicative of all written representations of Egyptians arises. The Danaids employ color self-referentially when they describe themselves as members of "a black, sun-struck people" (μελανθὲς | ἡλιόκτυπον γένος, *Supp.* 154–55) with "tender, Nile-warmed cheeks" (τὰν ἁπαλὰν Νειλοθερῆ παρειάν, 70).[21] They push back against the label of foreigner to Argos by crafting an image of

---

[20] Tapping into the restorative power of creative writing, Jess (2016: 130–42) revisits Williams's and Walker's relationship with minstrelsy.

[21] This sun-related vocabulary implies a link between the Danaids, a people from the south who have traveled north, and Helios, who traverses long distances as the sun rises and sets. Their invocation of

themselves that can exist in both Egypt and Argos: they have arrived from
the Nile but are descendants of the Argives: "from the mouth of the Nile
with fine sand . . . we arrived on Argive land, what is more, the land from
where our people [came]" (ἀπὸ προστομίων λεπτοψαμάθων | Νείλου . . .
κέλσαι δ᾽ Ἄργους γαῖαν, ὅθεν δὴ | γένος ἡμέτερον, 3–4, 15–16). In this vein,
the following exploration of the Danaids' artistic context unveils more
fruitful information about their unique visual presence.

Attic pottery depicting the Danaids mainly portrays them as water
carriers, a nod to the famous myth in which they killed all but one of
their bridegrooms on their wedding night and suffered punishment in the
underworld, condemned to carry leaky water jars for eternity.[22] Despite the
lack of confirmed iconography depicting black Danaids, one fourth-
century BCE mixing bowl (*kratēr*) provides potential insight into the
physical appearance of their Egyptian cousins (Figure 3.1). Many scholars
identify the central figures on this Apulian mixing bowl as Orestes killing
Aegisthus or Hercules murdering Busiris. Writing against the grain, both
Frank Snowden, Jr. and Phiroze Vasunia identify the curly haired, full-
lipped naked figure wielding a dagger near the center of the scene as
Lynceus, the son of Aegyptus, and the crouching figure on his left as
Danaus.[23] The generous amount of red-figure painting on this object
makes it difficult to glean any information from the skin color of the
female figure brandishing a long, narrow tool in the upper-right register.
Her violent stance suggests her solidarity with the other curly haired figures
in the scene. If Snowden's and Vasunia's hypothesis is correct, this female
figure is Hypermnestra, Danaus's daughter who disobeyed her father's
command to kill her husband Lynceus on her wedding night. Her assumption of violence likens her to her husband, while her Greek *chitōn* and loose
curls mark her as drastically different from him. In this way, the composite
representation of this figure (color, pose, clothes, hair) embodies the
multifaceted performance that the Danaids enact.[24]

the sun as their savior (καλοῦμεν αὐγὰς Ἡλίου σωτηρίους, "we call the rays of the sun our savior,"
Supp. 213) also fortifies this connection.

[22] Keuls (1974).

[23] Snowden (2010: 176); Vasunia (2001, fig. 2). For surviving accounts of this story, see Horace's lyric
poetry (*Odes* 3.11) and Ovid's epistolary poems (*Her.* 14).

[24] Keuls tentatively identifies a depiction of Danaus and one of his daughters on a fourth-century
volute mixing bowl (*kratēr*). A kneeling man, presumably Danaus, clasps the knees of a seated man,
potentially Pelasgus. Keuls (1986: 342) describes the figures in the lower register as "a youth, woman
with hydria and negro carrying stools." There are many challenges associated with interpreting this
scene: the kneeling man has also been identified as Agamemnon, Atreus, or Chryses, and it is
difficult to determine whether the black person is a Danaid (Beazley [1927: 224 n. 8]). If this is
indeed a depiction of a daughter of Danaus, the pairing indicates an iconographic relationship

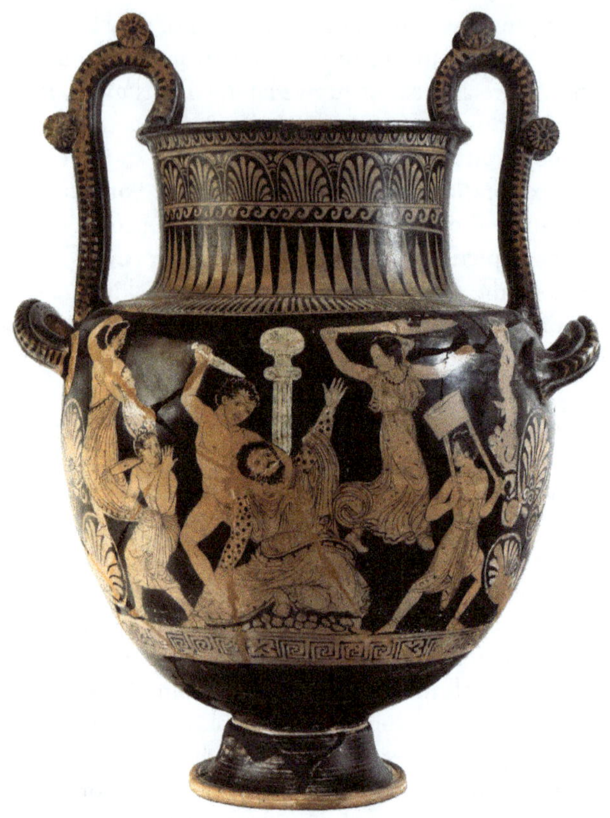

Figure 3.1 Apulian *kratēr* depicting Lynceus killing Danaus, Attic red-figure ceramic, attributed to the Brooklyn-Budapest Painter, c. 350 BCE. H. 49 cm, 2667. © Akademisches Kunstmuseum Bonn.

As it appears in the *Suppliants*, the Danaids' black skin breaks the iconographic tradition on Attic black-figure pottery in which gender determines characters' color: black skin for Greek men and white skin for Greek women, as seen in the "two-handled *amphora* depicting a woman in a swing and four men" (Figure 3.2).[25] This inversion of normative artistic expectations

between the Danaids and blackness. Vasunia (2001, fig. 1) examines iconography of the Danaids preparing to deliver gifts to Pelasgus.

[25] The Greek women's white skin also pulls them closer to their epic and tragic counterparts (Cohen [1989: 6–8]). The presence of black people on Attic pottery, however, was not always a clear signifier of foreignness.

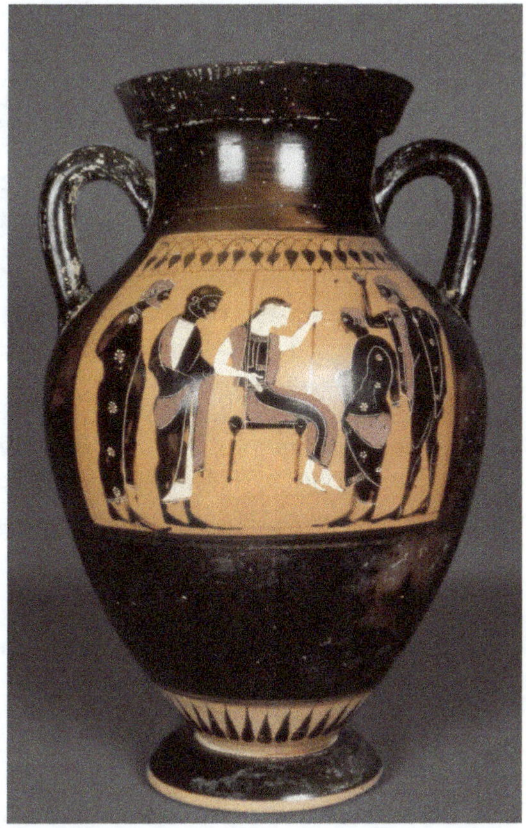

Figure 3.2 Two-handled *amphora* depicting a woman in a swing and four men, Attic black-figure ceramic, attributed to the Swing Painter, c. 540–520 BCE. H. 40.1 cm, 98.918. © Museum of Fine Arts, Boston.

potentially indicates that the Danaids' skin color is solely a condition of their environment. In her discussion of their inability to change their skin color, Nancy Sorkin Rabinowitz attributes the Danaids' phenotype to their location and concedes that their Greek mannerisms could presumably lighten their skin.[26] Her provocative remark alludes to the play's confounding relationship with color. When the tragedy begins, the Danaids' color is noteworthy, but by the closing scenes, the color distinction is of minimal relevance. The Danaids

---

[26] Rabinowitz (2014: 7). The sun also alters the skin color of the Argives (*Supp.* 746–47). See also Hall (1989: 172–74), who interprets the Danaids' skin color as a result of their environment.

themselves propose the idea that their skin color is black due to the sun's rays (μελανθὲς | ἡλιόκτυπον γένος, "black, sun-struck people," *Supp.* 154–55). Their black skin likens them to Greek women whose socioeconomic status made it necessary for them to earn an income. That is, poor Greek women held occupations that demanded their presence outdoors, such as wage laborers and food vendors. The prolonged periods of time that they spent outside would have affected their skin color. Greek women of higher socioeconomic status also departed from their homestead, however, for outdoor religious festivals (like the Thesmophoria) and funeral processions. Together, these two groups reveal the flimsiness of a strict relationship between identity and skin color in Greek antiquity, in the case of Greek women, and in Athenian tragedy, in the case of the Danaids.[27] Their shared sun-kissed appearance refutes strict assignations of color. Below, I point out the ways in which the Danaids, with their father's help, privilege nonvisual components of Argive Greek identity over its visible element, thereby reworking their mask of difference to their benefit.

3.2   Sophisticated Suppliants

Once he and his daughters arrive in Argos, Danaus prepares to seek assistance from the Argive people. Before leaving his daughters, he delivers a passionate speech to them in which two goals stand out: to enumerate the threats that his nephews pose to his family and to build an affinity between the Danaids and the Argive people. Danaus draws attention to contrasting traits that distinguish his daughters from his nephews: pious, peaceful, and willing versus impious, brutal, and obstinate. His decision to focus on their differences from their cousins helps to align the Danaids closer with other dutiful (Argive Greek) women and further away from their despicable (Egyptian) relatives. For Danaus, family ties and identity are two categories that he can manipulate and reconcile. Employing hortatory directives among other rhetorical tactics, he aims to impress this point to his daughters so that they can circumvent the intractability of lineage even in his absence:

πάντων δ' ἀνάκτων τῶνδε κοινοβωμίαν
σέβεσθ'· ἐν ἁγνῷ δ' ἑσμὸς ὣς πελειάδων

---

[27] In addition, outward appearance does not always correlate to moral qualities. As the epic hero Odysseus explains, a man can be physically unimpressive but endowed with the invisible gift of speech (*Od.* 8.169). In fact, when Odysseus arrives at Troy at the head of the embassy to bring back Helen, his powerful words affect the Trojans more than his appearance (ἀϊδρεΐ φωτὶ ἐοικώς, "resembling an ignorant man"; ὄπα τε μεγάλην ἐκ στήθεος, "great words from his heart," *Il.* 3.219, 221).

ἵζεσθε κίρκων τῶν ὁμοπτέρων φόβῳ,
ἐχθρῶν ὁμαίμοις καὶ μιαινόντων γένος.
ὄρνιθος ὄρνις πῶς ἂν ἁγνεύοι φαγών;
πῶς δ' ἂν γαμῶν ἄκουσαν ἄκοντος πάρα
ἁγνὸς γένοιτ' ἄν; οὐδὲ μὴ 'ν Ἅιδου θανὼν
φύγῃ ματαίων αἰτίας, πράξας τάδε.
κἀκεῖ δικάζει τἀμπλακήμαθ', ὡς λόγος,
Ζεὺς ἄλλος ἐν καμοῦσιν ὑστάτας δίκας.
σκοπεῖτε κἀμείβεσθε τόνδε τὸν τρόπον
ὅπως ἂν ὑμῖν πρᾶγος εὖ νικᾷ τόδε.

You all, honor the altar that is common to all of the gods!
Sit on the holy seat like a flock of gray doves
who are frightened of their fellow birds, the hawks,
enemies to their relatives and defilers of their kin!
How could a bird who gnaws on a part of another bird be pure?
How could a man who marries an unwilling bride against her father's wishes
be pure? Not even a dead person in the underworld
flees the blame of the impieties if he does these things.
Even there, as the story goes, a different Zeus judges the offenses,
the last judgments among the dead.
Consider the situation and reply in this particular way
so that this action may turn out victorious for you all.

(*Supp.* 222–33)

In the beginning of his speech, Danaus firmly instructs his daughters to obey his words. Rather than merely ask them to honor the gods, he demands that they maintain their religious duties in his absence (σέβεσθ' … ἵζεσθε, "honor! … sit!", *Supp.* 223, 224). It is vital that the Danaids show due respect during their father's absence in order to invoke divine protection from the gods and pity from the Argives. Intent on thoroughly preparing his daughters, Danaus ends his speech by advising the Danaids to act respectfully so that their actions (πρᾶγος, 233) can speak favorably for them if their words do not suffice.

Throughout his exhortation, Danaus heightens the tension between his innocent daughters and his evil nephews. Despite the Danaids' shared lineage with Aegyptus's sons, Danaus distances his obedient, serene, and eager daughters from their disrespectful, forceful, and brutish cousins. The difference between his daughters and his nephews speaks volumes about each group's character: the Danaids obediently sit at the holy altar (ἐν ἁγνῷ, *Supp.* 223), while their sinister cousins are unable to comport themselves dutifully (πῶς … ἁγνὸς γένοιτ' ἄν, "how could [such] a man be pure?", 227–28). Their desired defilement of the Danaids further pits them against their dutiful relatives. By alluding to an awful deed, Danaus characterizes his nephews' desire to do something lawful – namely, marry their relatives, as a heinous crime. He cannot command his daughters to respect men who brashly try to inflict violence on their own family. He may be a visitor to Argos, but he holds certain Greek traits, like familial piety, in high regard.

According to Danaus, birds of a feather need not flock together. In his comparison of his family to winged creatures, his daughters are a frightened congregation of gray doves whose cousins are dangerous hawks.[28] Even though the Danaids' cousins share the same bloodline (ὁμοπτέρων, "similarly feathered," *Supp.* 224), some family members cannot be trusted. The bond between parents and children is apparently exempt from this observation, in that Danaus insinuates that the only person whose actions his daughters need to emulate is himself. This running theme contorts the Greek-centered mindset that welcomes natives and questions foreigners. Danaus's vilification of outsiders and questioning of peaceful familial ties promotes a new world-view in which foreigner and family can overlap.[29] His description of his nephews as despicable underscores the slipperiness of these categories (ἐχθρῶν ὁμαίμοις, "enemies to their relatives," 225).[30] According to Danaus, his nephews are uncouth men who disregard the laws of humanity. They are unafraid to pursue vicious courses of action, metaphorically devouring the Danaids like carnivorous birds (ὄρνιθος ὄρνις . . . φαγών, "a bird gnawing on a part of another bird," 226).[31]

Aegyptus's sons endeavor to commit crimes so heinous that not even death could free them from punishment for their misdeeds (οὐδὲ μὴ 'ν Ἅιδου, "not even in the underworld," *Supp.* 228). Such clever imagery speaks louder than any direct remark concerning their cruelty. These relatives are so despicably wicked that not even Hades can grant them reprieve. The more Danaus portrays the cousins in a negative light, the easier it becomes to view the Danaids in a positive one.[32] Danaus does not

---

[28] Doves are also associated with sanctuary (Sandin [2005: 139]; Johansen and Whittle [1980: 179]). Maintaining this animal imagery, the Danaids refer to their cousins as spiders (*Supp.* 887).

[29] Danaus's speech highlights the relativity and flexibility of the term "foreign." Compare the Persians' outlook that the farther away a group is from Persia, the more unsophisticated their customs (Hdt. 1.134.2), as well as Greeks' and Indians' disgust with each other's burial practices (3.38).

[30] Manuscript M (Laurentianus xxxii 9) reads ἐχθρῶν ὁμαίμων ("hated relatives"), which further suggests a discomfiting relationship between family and enemies.

[31] This ornithological polyptoton (ὄρνιθος ὄρνις) underscores the animalistic nature of the Danaids' cousins, in that animals can commit such cannibalistic acts, but decent humans do not stoop to such levels of depravity (Hesiod, *Works and Days* 276–80).

[32] Danaus's focus on the agonistic relationship between the Danaids and their cousins extends to his hope for a victorious outcome (ὅπως ἂν ὑμῖν πρᾶγος εὖ νικᾷ τόδε, "so that this deed may lead to

directly name his nephews as his accursed relatives in this speech; instead, he obliquely attacks their violent proposal when he questions the purity of a man who forces a woman into marriage. Neither the woman's nor her father's wishes are important to men who whisk away whomever they choose (ἄκουσαν ἄκοντος πάρα, "[who marry] an unwilling bride against her father's wishes," 227). This polyptoton complicates the agency that people of different genders possess. Danaus implies that the preference of a young woman and a father are equally important in the choice of suitor, which does not mirror historical or mythical Greece. Attic legislation did not require a prospective bride's consent before marriage unless all of her male relatives were dead, and numerous literary examples reveal the dastardly outcomes that occur when women chose their own partners.[33] Even though the Danaids are not historical figures, Aeschylus's reworking of these characters corresponds to historical, Egyptian-born women who do not submit to the will of men. This is a fine line to tread, especially because Danaus and his daughters continually align themselves with Argive Greeks via their shared ancestry and religious practices. A possible hidden agenda lies behind the Danaids' refusal of marriage: Danaus may be on a quest to find Argive husbands for his daughters and a tyranny for himself.[34] This creative theory requires more evidence than is readily apparent from the play's text because Danaus does not openly disclose his reasons for referencing a woman's agency. Regardless, he undeniably highlights the kindred thoughts between

your victory," *Supp.* 233). In addition, the verb νικᾷ ("lead to victory") suggests an intertextual reference to the footrace that Danaus organizes for potential suitors in Pindar's victory paean (*Pyth.* 9.112–16).

[33] Johansen and Whittle (1980: 183); MacKinnon (1978). Two examples of unfortunate female-dictated choices: Clytemnestra's relationship with Aegisthus, Medea's marriage to Jason. Grammarian Nonius Marcellus Melanippus and the narrator of the early epic *Danais* describe the Danaids' rearing as abnormal and unfeminine (*Grammatici Latini* 757; fr. 1, as numbered in West [2003]). It is unclear whether the Danaids are vehemently opposed to any marriage, or solely marriage to their cousins. Rather than view their refusal of marriage as a sign of their complete devotion to Artemis, Elisei (1928) understands their dislike as a form of loyalty to their father, who is nursing a grudge against Aegyptus (discussed in Garvie [2006: 215]). Following von Fritz (1936), Winnington-Ingram (1961: 144) explains, "the violent approach of the sons of Aegyptus has warped the feminine instincts of the Danaids and turned them against marriage as such." Zeitlin (1996: 153–60) treats the Danaids' refusal to marry their cousins either as a dislike of the savage form of sexuality that Egyptian men represent or as an erotic yearning for the divine. Despite the lack of evidence about precisely what they are refusing, the Danaids have undeniably refused a conventional and legitimate, albeit forceful, marriage proposal. They follow in the tradition of other tragic women who rebel against the institution of marriage, such as Electra (Euripides, *Electra* 695–98) and Cassandra (Aeschylus, *Agamemnon* 1202–12). Focusing on Danaus's agency, Sicherl (1986) understands his unwillingness to marry off his daughters as a result of an oracle, delivered later in the tetralogy, that reveals that his son-in-law will kill him.

[34] Kennedy (2014b: 31–32). Shipton (2018) examines intergenerational relationships in Athenian tragedy.

a father and daughter.[35] Whether or not his own daughters agree with him is irrelevant. In his eyes, his perception eclipses their own.

Pelasgus regards his own perspective in equally high esteem. Despite his confidence, the following passage shows the breakdown of his reliance on visual cues to determine who the Danaids are. Upon first meeting them, he is unsure where they have come from. A closer look at his address uncovers the particular visual markers that confound him:

Πελασγος: ποδαπὸν ὅμιλον τόνδ' ἀνελληνόστολον
    πέπλοισι βαρβάροισι κἀμπυκώμασι
    χλίοντα προσφωνοῦμεν; οὐ γὰρ Ἀργολὶς
    ἐσθὴς γυναικῶν οὐδ' ἀφ' Ἑλλάδος τόπων.
    ὅπως δὲ χώραν οὔτε κηρύκων ὕπο
    ἀπρόξενοί τε νόσφιν ἡγητῶν μολεῖν
    ἔτλητ' ἀτρέστως, τοῦτο θαυμαστὸν πέλει.
    κλάδοι γε μὲν δὴ κατὰ νόμους ἀφικτόρων
    κεῖνται παρ' ὑμῶν πρὸς θεοῖς ἀγωνίοις·
    μόνον τόδ' Ἑλλὰς χθὼν συνοίσεται στόχῳ
    καὶ τἄλλα πόλλ' ἐπεικάσαι δίκαιον ἦν,
    εἰ μὴ παρόντι φθόγγος ἦν ὁ σημανῶν.

Χορος: εἴρηκας ἀμφὶ κόσμον ἀψευδῆ λόγον·

PELASGUS: From what country is this company whom I address,
    wearing unGreek clothes and flaunting foreign robes and headbands?
    The clothes of these women are not Argive, and they are not from any place in Greece.
    This is a marvel, how you all have fearlessly dared to come to this land,
    although you were neither presented by the heralds nor a sponsor,
    and you came without any guides.
    Yet the boughs, according to the law of the suppliants,
    are certainly arranged beside you before the gods in assembly.
    It is a reasonable guess that your land is Greece in respect to this alone.
    And for the other matters, it would be customary to guess many things still
    if there were not a voice informing me as I stand beside you.

CHORUS: You have spoken not falsely about our clothes.

(Supp. 234–46)

Pelasgus does not directly refer to the difference between the color of his own skin and the Danaids'. Instead, he focuses on other visual markers of difference. He is puzzled because the Danaids' attire indicates their foreign status, yet their suppliant branches imply familiarity with

---

[35] The Danaids follow their father's lead when they describe their cousins as dangerous men from whom they must be saved (*Supp.* 529–30, 751, 887).

Greek supplication rites. When he describes the Danaids as women who luxuriate in foreign clothes (*Supp.* 235–36), he discerns certain hubristic emotions that align with fifth-century Greeks' view of foreigners.[36] Oblivious to Danaus's recent departure, Pelasgus also marvels at the complete novelty of the solitary female travelers, without any local or foreign guides (238–39).[37] From Pelasgus's perspective, the Danaids are in dire straits in that they are bereft of any allies inside or outside of the city.

Pelasgus's remark about the Danaids' divergence from Greek sartorial standards (ἀνελληνόστολον, "unGreek clothes") is striking.[38] He simultaneously mobilizes a broader Hellenic identity by rendering the *polis* of Argos a microcosm of the entire Hellenic world, and he positions the Danaids in opposition to his people with the alpha privative *an-* ("not-"). The etymology of the *hapax legomenon anellēnostolon* demonstrates a common way to determine someone's race: by examining their clothes. Additionally, this word evokes the confining boundaries in which Pelasgus's language exists. The Danaids are either Greek or not Greek; flexibility is not an option. The repetition of alpha privatives and negative enclitics that Pelasgus sprinkles throughout his speech has a twofold result: they distance the Danaids from him and foreground the limitations of his own knowledge (ἀνελληνόστολον … οὐ γὰρ Ἀργολὶς | οὐδ᾽ ἀφ᾽ Ἑλλάδος τόπων … οὔτε κηρύκων ὕπο | ἀπρόξενοί, "unGreek clothes … not Argive and not from any place in Greece … neither presented by the heralds nor a sponsor," *Supp.* 234, 236–37, 238–39).[39] Although the presence of negations (ἀν-, οὐ, οὐδ᾽, οὔτε, ἀ-) alongside geography can suggest that Argos and Greece are distinct locations, Pelasgus emphasizes the cohesion of Greek customs in sharp contrast to the Danaids' unidentified foreignness. His fixed Hellenocentric lens prevents him from exploring the possibility of the Danaids' dual identity as Argive Greek and Egyptian.[40] The Danaids complicate any simple attribution further when they speak knowledgeably about the Argive shrines and Greek rituals. In this way, they enact an

---

[36] In particular, this comment likens the Danaids to the Persians, a group that Greeks characterize as excessively ostentatious. See Derbew (in press) for a joint assessment of the Danaids and the Persians in Aeschylean tragedy.

[37] Κήρυκες are foreigners, πρόξενοί and ἡγητῆρες are local inhabitants; Sandin (2005: 142).

[38] A brief intertextual glance to Hdt. 4.76–80 provides useful insight into the signifying power of attire. This passage ostensibly serves as a warning to Scythians to reject foreign practices but more discreetly highlights the precarity of identity in ancient Greek literature. I discuss this Herodotean passage further in Section 4.2.

[39] The Danaids confront Pelasgus's binary assessment of them with their use of the alpha privative in ἀψευδῆ ("not falsely," *Supp.* 246).

[40] Unlike other tragic characters, such as Andromache, who laments that the Greeks have invented barbarian wrongs (Euripides, *Trojan Women* 764), Pelasgus cannot easily merge the two groups.

anagrammatical performance in which they rearrange the category of "unGreek" (ἀνελληνόστολον) to suit their needs.

Inspired by Sharpe's creative index of anagrammatical Blackness, my rendering of *anellēnostolon* as "unGreek" is an attempt to translate Aeschylus's esoteric language into English.[41] A challenge that all anagrammatical projects face is the sticking power of new definitions. The Danaids must tread carefully until Pelasgus accepts their novel performance. They need to tap into Pelasgus's perception of "Greek" in order to destabilize his notion of "unGreek." They begin to strategically dismantle his foisting of an identity onto them (i.e. race) when they confirm his suspicion that their clothes are not Greek and avoid immediately answering any of his questions (*Supp.* 246). They grant Pelasgus a small victory when they admit that their clothes indicate foreign heritage, but they do not equivocate or apologize for how they look. Simply put, the Danaids "play the other" on their own terms.[42] Given the uneven power dynamics at this early stage of playing the other, they must proceed cautiously. They opt to momentarily distract Pelasgus from his queries and encourage him to recount his lineage (249–73). Only after he has finished a lengthy account of his family line do they provide reticent answers about their own fatherland (274–76) and eventually recalibrate the role of "the other" to convince Pelasgus of their Argive Greek identity.[43]

As an observer and pseudo-arbitrator, Pelasgus has difficulty seeing that "Greek" and "foreigner" are sometimes overlapping groups. It is up to the Danaids to utilize their sophisticated fluency in order to translate their story into a form that is legible to him. Their fluency encompasses diachronic and synchronic views of history. Their ability to trace their lineage back to Io, an Argive princess, speaks to their diachronic capabilities while their practice of current Greek religious rites reflects their synchronic mastery. Their skills mirror those of Herodotus, an ethnographer who analyzes the world through, and sometimes in, time.[44] By the time Herodotus pens his *Histories*, Greek identity has transformed from one based primarily on descent to one based on customs. In the *Suppliants*,

---

[41] See Sharpe (2016).   [42] I use the language of "playing the other" after Zeitlin (1996).

[43] Cf. the late second-/early third-century CE funerary relief of Lucius Julius Mutacus, a man whose hair, attire, and adornments suggest the self-conscious performance of a Gallic identity while the Latin inscription (including his *tria nomina*) indicates a hybrid performance; Johnston (2017: 231–35).

[44] Herodotus explains the lineage of Lydia, spanning thousands of years, and proposes ethnographies of his contemporaries from distant places.

however, the Danaids recognize both modes of identity construction, genealogy and shared practices.

Pelasgus strives to lessen his confusion about the Danaids' background by asking them to narrate their life stories. But he has already presumed their race (his perception of their identity), and his findings disrupt potential expectations: the Danaids are sartorially distinct rather than unmarked or local (πέπλοισι βαρβάροισι, "with foreign robes," *Supp.* 235), brave instead of meek (ἔτλητ᾽ ἀτρέστως, "you fearlessly dare," 240), pious as opposed to sacrilegious (κατὰ νόμους ἀφικτόρων, "according to the laws of the suppliants," 241), and female where he might expect men (γυναικῶν, "women," 237). Adopting a concept from critical race theory, intersectionality calls for a negotiation of the Danaids' compounding aspects altogether.[45] Each sphere of difference further entrenches the Danaids as separate from Pelasgus. If they were merely dressed in foreign attire or had courageously entered Argos without escorts, perhaps he would be able to figure out who they are. As it stands, Pelasgus is stuck in an intersectional dilemma. In critical race theory, an intersectional dilemma is a situation in which one is unable to prove discrimination due to the intersecting nature of the bias. Pelasgus cannot fit the Danaids into his schema of "Greek people" because they have foreign attire *and* they boldly entered the city without guards *and* they are familiar with Greek religious practices. Their layered deviations from his norm overwhelm him, and he chooses to begin his investigation with an intense focus on the visual aspect: their foreign attire. It proves difficult for his essentialist point of view to recognize their multiple identities. Below, I outline Pelasgus's transformation from a stubborn ruler to an eager pupil, hopeful to learn about the Danaids under their guidance.

3.3 The Convergence of Autopsy and *akoē*

Χορος: βραχὺς τορός θ᾽ ὁ μῦθος· Ἀργεῖαι γένος
  ἐξευχόμεσθα, σπέρματ᾽ εὐτέκνου βοός·
  καὶ τῷδ᾽ ἀληθῆ παντὰ προσφύσω λόγῳ.

Πελασγος: ἄπιστα μυθεῖσθ᾽, ὦ ξέναι, κλύειν ἐμοί,
  ὅπως τόδ᾽ ὑμῖν ἐστιν Ἀργεῖον γένος.

---

[45] Crenshaw (1989) focuses on the ways in which the intersection between modern race and gender affect employment opportunities for Black women while Crenshaw (1993) delves into an exploration of the same intersection's potency to inflict violence on Black women. Nash (2019) offers an intellectual history of intersectionality, tracing its migration from Black feminist studies to the wider US academy.

Λιβυστικαῖς γὰρ μᾶλλον ἐμφερέστεραι
γυναιξίν ἐστε κοὐδαμῶς ἐγχωρίαις·
καὶ Νεῖλος ἂν θρέψειε τοιοῦτον φυτόν·
[Κύπριος χαρακτήρ τ' ἐν γυναικείοις τύποις
εἰκὼς πέπληκται τεκτόνων πρὸς ἀρσένων·]
Ἰνδάς τ' ἀκούων νομάδας ἱπποβάμοσιν
εἶναι καμήλοις ἀστραβιζούσας χθόνα
παρ' Αἰθίοψιν ἀστυγειτονουμένας,
καὶ τὰς ἀνάνδρους κρεοβότους τ' Ἀμαζόνας,
εἰ τοξοτευχεῖς ἦτε, κάρτ' ἂν ἤκασα
ὑμᾶς. διδαχθεὶς δ' ἂν τόδ' εἰδείην πλέον,
ὅπως γένεθλον σπέρμα τ' Ἀργεῖον τὸ σόν.

CHORUS: This speech will be plain and short.
    In respect to our lineage and to the seed of the cow who bore a fine son (Epaphus),
    we proclaim that we are Argives.
    And I will speak entirely trustworthy words in this speech.

PELASGUS: You all are uttering unbelievable words for me to hear, strangers,
    how this [*pointing to them*] is the Argive people.
    Rather, you resemble Libyans very much
    and not our native women in any way,
    and the Nile might have borne such a crop (as you).
    [The impressed mark of Cyprus has been similarly stamped
    into womanly shapes by male craftsmen;]
    I hear that there are Indian nomads who ride over lands
    while saddled on camels that resemble horses
    and live in the town neighboring the Aithiopians.
    and if you all were arrow-shooters,
    I would liken you to the meat-eating, man-hating Amazons.
    If I were taught further, I would know this,
    namely how your people and seed are Argive.

(Supp. 274–90)

In the passage above, many themes deserve close attention, the first of which is that of truth and fiction in relation to identity and race. The Danaids state that they are telling the truth about their identity (ἀληθῆ, *Supp.* 276), but Pelasgus finds it hard to swallow their story (ἄπιστα, 277). With the first word he utters, Pelasgus again describes the Danaids by explaining what they are not.[46] Rather than unGreek-attired women

---

[46] The initial and final words of Pelasgus's speech succinctly summarize his main point: "your claim is unbelievable" (ἄπιστα . . . σόν).

(ἀνελληνόστολον, 234), they are strangers who have delivered an unbelievable speech (ἄπιστα … ξέναι, 277). His delayed uttering of the word *genos* (278) implies an extreme reluctance to entertain the Danaids' assertions. He also points out that their bodies and physical appearances do not correspond to the Argive people with the deictic neuter adjective *tod'* (278). Beyond agreement with *genos*, the neuter adjective arguably denies the Danaids their female gender. They say that they are women and (distant) relations of Pelasgus, but the Argive ruler wields the power to determine the veracity of their statements. Although he rejects their declaration of an Argive Greek identity, his view is not completely uncompromising. Once they outline their genealogical relationship to Io, Pelasgus's Hellenocentric view no longer clouds his perspective, and he is willing to entertain the Danaids' claims (325–36).

This passage poses another exciting consideration for Pelasgus's understanding of the Danaids. In his eyes, they are passive women who require the opposite gender to create their *character* (*Supp.* 282–83). As it stands, Danaus has guided his daughters in the same manner that male artisans shape coins.[47] The reference to *Kuprios* may imply a connection between Aphrodite and the Danaids. Pelasgus makes it clear, however, that he does not view the Danaids as lovers of men. In fact, he emphasizes their dislike of men by comparing them to the remote, man-shunning Amazons. Even though the Danaids refuse to marry, they see value in male leadership, as they dutifully follow their father to a potential safe haven. Nonetheless, Danaus's limitations suggest that men are not infallible leaders.[48] He remains conspicuously quiet when his daughters confront Pelasgus, and he is nowhere to be found when Aegyptus's sons arrive in Argos and try to kidnap the Danaids. Oliver Taplin considers Danaus's silence in these scenes to be purposefully dramatic.[49] Danaus's voice during these exchanges would dilute the power that the Danaids start to claim for

---

[47] Due to their confusing content (Cyprus was considered both a quasi-Greek place and a conduit to Egypt, numismatic depictions of female figures usually depict goddesses or nymphs, "womanly" [γυναικεῖοι] typically refers to wives instead of daughters), some editors see lines 282–83 as an interpolation and excise them from the text (Johansen and Whittle [1980: 223–26]) while others retain them (Sommerstein [1997]; Bakewell [2013]). I treat these lines as part of the play's text but recognize that they may be a later addition in this tragedy's life cycle.

[48] Invoking Spivak's 1988 essay, "Can the Subaltern Speak?" (see Spivak [1994]), Wohl (2010: 410) interprets the extended interaction between the Danaids and Pelasgus as a "narrative of white men saving brown women from brown men." See also Zeitlin (1996: 140), who describes the paradox of men causing violence due to women's rejection of violent suitors as a "contest of phallic pride."

[49] Taplin (1977: 204–06).

themselves. In the absence of their father, they morph into their own heroes.

Initially, Pelasgus cannot envision these foreigners as relatives so he supplies the Danaids with a menu of options in relation to their homeland. In other words, he assigns various masks of difference to them. While rewriting the Danaids' history, he lumps together numerous peoples who are geographically distant from each other: Λιβυστικαῖς ... Νεῖλος ... Ἰνδάς ... παρ' Αἰθίοψιν ... καὶ ... Ἀμαζόνας ("Libyans, Nilotic people, Indians near Aithiopians, and Amazons," *Supp.* 279–87).[50] Such a quick succession of potential homelands for the Danaids spans the limits of Greek knowledge and blurs any line of separation between these places.[51] In addition to revealing the extent of his ethnographic gaze, Pelasgus again confronts the restrictions of his own language as he utters the *hapax legomenon astrabizousas* to describe the ways that Indians mount their camels ("riding on a saddle," 285). By explaining that he has heard about some of these groups, Pelasgus cleverly attributes any linguistic shortcomings or glaring omissions to his sources and not to himself (ἀκούων, "I hear," 284).[52] Pelasgus's uneven toggling between autopsy (visual perception) and *akoē* (aural-derived information) likens him to Aeschylus, who incorporates large-scale importation of Achaemenid official art and the oral tradition into his staging of the Persian ruler Darius in the *Persians*.[53] Similar to Aeschylus, Pelasgus cannot travel

---

[50] Egyptians and Indians are described elsewhere as having black skin: Hdt. 2.57 (Egypt) and 3.101 (India). Pelasgus's reference to the Nile encourages a brief glance at a discussion of Egypt in a broader context: Herodotus marvels at the ways in which Egyptian women resemble Greek men (a few examples: they urinate while standing up, they work outside; Hdt. 2.35–50). In a similar vein, the Danaids resemble Greek men in their bold actions, such as refusing a marriage proposal and advocating for themselves in their father's absence. Furthermore, Pelasgus's mention of Aithiopia suggests that the Danaids are affiliated with an intertextual locus for divine travel (*Il.* 1.423; *Od.* 1.23–24). In addition, the Danaids' environmentally derived skin color (*Supp.* 154–55) corresponds with the etymology of Aithiopia (αἰθώ, "I blaze").

[51] Hall (1989: 2) treats descriptions of foreigners in Athenian tragedy as cultural authorizations that provide insight about the person making the assertion rather than the group they are describing. In fact, Pelasgus's speculations follow a counterclockwise journey around Argos: Libya to the southwest, the Nile to the south, India to the east, and Themiscyra (the home of the Amazons in Pontic Asia Minor) to the northeast (Johansen and Whittle [1980: 220–21, 229–31]). See Kennedy (2014a), who categorizes Aeschylus's geographic markers into three groups: formulas, itineraries, and maps.

[52] All of the countries on Pelasgus's list are part of Greece's wider trade networks in the fifth century BCE. His subsuming of many countries into one category corresponds with Malkin's (2011) argument that physical divergence can lead to cultural convergence. See also the growing trend among Aeschylus's contemporary Athenians to funnel many non-Greek groups into "the straitjacket of the great 'Other'" (Miller [2000: 441]).

[53] Kennedy (2013: 69–78). Autopsy as a conduit for ethnographic knowledge of distant communities calls to mind the story of Candaules and Gyges (Hdt. 1.7–12). Embarking on a morally dubious quest, Candaules concocts a scheme that enables his bodyguard Gyges to see his wife naked and

everywhere and meet everyone. Therefore, autopsy and *akoē* are the tools
with which he grasps information about other people and places.

Pelasgus highlights the vast divide between the foreign Danaids and his
own Argive Greek identity with such wide-ranging speculations. Unlike
the Danaids, who possess a flexible mindset evidenced in their ability to
activate different parts of their identity at different times, Pelasgus fails to
engage with multiple perspectives. He seems to have a malleable mindset at
the outset of his speech when he listens to the Danaids' unbelievable claims
(ἄπιστα … κλύειν, *Supp.* 277), but his inflexible outlook later compels
him to focus solely on their appearance. After he has exhausted various
options, he echoes his request to know what group they call their own
(277–78, 289–90). Once the Danaids explain their background, Pelasgus
shifts from a rigid stance to a versatile one. In other words, he cedes his
opinion of the Danaids' race (i.e. his perceived categorization of them) to
the Danaids themselves.

The Danaids are subtle and supple ethnographers of Argos. They
disassociate themselves from the world of stories (ὁ μῦθος, *Supp.* 274)
that Pelasgus inhabits and assert that their speech will be a different sort
of tale (λόγῳ, 276). This is not to say that *mythos* and *logos* are mutually
exclusive terms or that one holds an objectively preeminent position.
Rather, the Danaids' choice to call their story a *logos* connects them to
the world of public speechmaking in the Athenian *polis* and indirectly
evokes the epistemological weight that visual proofs held in ancient
Athenian law courts. The Danaids exploit forensic language to their
advantage because visual proofs will not support their general declaration
of Argive Greek heritage: ἀληθῆ προσφύσω λόγῳ ("I will speak trustworthy words in this speech," 276).[54] They speak about Argive Greek
customs with ease while Pelasgus reveals his linguistic and geographic
limitations. He cannot discern their native land, and his sole criterion for
it is foreignness to or distance from Argos. Once Danaus informs them that
the Argives have approved their request for refuge, they silence their
foreign lips (ξενίου στόματος, "mouth of a foreigner," 627–28) and
honor Greek gods (625–709).[55] After unsuccessfully positing a wide range

thereby validate her beauty. Never considering that his wife might seek revenge for this nonconsen-
sual display, the Lydian ruler privileges vision over hearsay.

[54] An intertextual glance at Aristotle's rendering of rhetoric as a tool employed when there is a lack of
clear-cut rules in a discussion (*Rhetoric* 1357a) complements the Danaids' employment of it as
a weapon within their verbal arsenal. McClure (1999) elaborates on women's speech in Athenian
drama; Zeitlin (1996: 160–64) discusses the Danaids' relationship with *mythos* and *logos*.

[55] Although the Danaids have foreign lips, Pelasgus never questions their ability to speak Greek
fluently.

of predictions, Pelasgus assumes the role of a student eager for instruction (διδαχθείς, "if I were taught," 289) from his polyphonic teachers, the Danaids.

One lesson that the Danaids impart upon their pupil is the legitimacy of their claim of an Argive Greek identity. Intent on discarding the mask of difference that Pelasgus has attempted to impose on them, they present the myth of Io, an Argive princess and their genealogical predecessor, as proof of their lineage. In this myth, Hera connives to keep her lustful husband away from Io by sending a gadfly to hound the princess all the way to Egypt, at which point Zeus finds and impregnates her. Channeling their father's advice (*Supp.* 222–33), the Danaids transform the unstable categories of identity and genealogy into persuasive tools that aid their quest for refuge. That is, they employ language to alleviate any tension that may surround their asserted identity and perceived descent. But the story of Io as an allegory for the Danaids reveals a few hiccups in their logic. First, the Danaids surprisingly choose to align themselves with Io, a victim of Zeus's lust, instead of a mythical figure who actively shapes her own destiny.[56] Their selective appropriation of Io enables them to rewrite the myth, however, and neatly align themselves with an Io of their own creation. Second, it is curious that the Danaids pray to Zeus for safety because the god of suppliants and travelers is also the god who abducted and raped Io, the exact fate from which the Danaids hope to escape. Notwithstanding this correlation, the Danaids' frequent association with Zeus calls to mind his positive relationship with Aithiopians (*Il.* 1.423). Although the Danaids never discuss their affiliation with Aithiopia, Pelasgus encourages this connection in his list speculating on the Danaids' homeland (*Supp.* 281, 286). Third, once the Danaids successfully prove their familial ties with the people of Argos, this kinship also applies to their violent cousins from whom they have fled.

Perhaps as part of their endeavor to separate themselves from their cousins, the Danaids beg the gods to throw their black suitors into the sea: λίμνᾳ δ' ἔμβαλε πορφυροειδεῖ | τὰν μελανόζυγ' ἄταν ("ram the black-seated ruin [of our cousins' ship] into the purple sea!", *Supp.* 529–30). In this description, the Danaids overlook the fact that color-wise, they resemble Aegyptus's sons. Drawing attention to the association between his nephews and blackness, Danaus emphasizes their black bodies

---

[56] Murray (1958) expounds on the story of Io as an allegory; Brill (2009: 172–76) investigates the tension between the genealogical and mythological story of Io; Stephens (2003: 20–73, esp. 25–26) examines the special relationship between Egypt and Greece articulated through the myth.

(μελαγχίμοις, "black-limbed," 719). This chromatic resonance culminates in the occupation of Danaus's nephews: they are sailors whose black skin resembles their ship and whose white clothes parallel their ship's sails (743–44).[57] Unlike the rays of sunshine that cause the Danaids' black skin, these men derive their skin color from the nautical world. The separation between the lofty sun and the deep sea mirrors the distance that the Danaids seek to create between themselves and their cousins. Such divergent origin stories of blackness complement the Danaids' insistence that black skin is a dynamic feature. This multiperspective outlook regarding skin color becomes increasingly important in the Danaids' quest to convince Pelasgus that they are long-lost relatives worthy of protection from their violent cousins.

As the plot of the *Suppliants* progresses, the Danaids develop into their own agents of change. Namely, they threaten suicide in and pollution of the city if Pelasgus does not heed their request (*Supp.* 455–67).[58] Resolute in their ultimatum, the Danaids unseat Pelasgus from any position of power he occupies. Even though he tries to deny their Argive heritage, they adamantly insist it to be true. It is difficult, then, to determine who ultimately determines whether the Danaids are Argive Greek, Pelasgus or the Danaids themselves. The Danaids recognize the importance of successfully convincing Pelasgus that their race (an outward-facing category) and identity (an inward-facing category) coincide. Otherwise, Pelasgus has little incentive to protect them from any aggressors. Once they make the treacherous promise to commit suicide in front of the altar of Zeus, however, they effectively turn the tables. That is, if Pelasgus refuses to protect the Danaids, he risks polluting his entire city. Their threat of inciting Zeus's wrath spurs Pelasgus to acquiesce to their requests.[59] In this way, Pelasgus relies on interest convergence to choose his course of action. Derived from critical race theory, "interest convergence" reflects

---

[57] See the Danaids' parallel color palette: their black skin (μελανθὲς ἡλιόκτυπον γένος, "a black, sun-struck people," *Supp.* 154–55) and white boughs (λευκοστεφεῖς ... νεοδρέπτους κλάδους, "white-wreathed branches with freshly plucked leaves," 334).

[58] This signals one difference between the characters of the well-known myth and the flexible characterization of the Danaids in Aeschylus's retelling (Bednarowski [2010: 203]; Taplin [1977: 27]).

[59] Vidal-Naquet (1988: 265–66). Within her exploration of interruption tropes in Athenian tragedy, Honig (2013) helpfully emphasizes Antigone's political staying power in contemporary receptions of Sophocles's *Antigone*. Her omission of any African/Black diasporic receptions of this tragedy, however, misses an opportunity to engage fully with this trope (such as her overlooking of the 1973 play *The Island* by South African playwrights Athol Fugard, John Kani, and Winston Ntshona, discussed in Goff and Simpson [2007: 271–320]. Honig [2013: 276 n. 67] limits discussion of Goff and Simpson to a brief note about postcolonial modernity in ancient Greek texts).

the self-interest of a powerful party, not a concern for the powerless. Derrick A. Bell, Jr. coined this term in his analysis of the 1954 ruling *Brown* v. *Board of Education* that prohibited racial segregation in American public schools.[60] He argued that desegregation occurred because it was advantageous to White communities: it provided credibility for America's image among developing nations, it offered economic and political advantages to the country, and it lessened the fear among White people that Black Second World War veterans would rise up in rebellion upon returning home. This mutually advantageous framework helps to clarify Pelasgus's actions. He has not somehow grown affectionate for his long-lost relatives. Instead, their interests have converged because of the threat of violence that looms over both of them.

In Athenian tragedy, the trope of female characters committing suicide is a familiar one. Some stab themselves, others jump into a flaming pyre, and many opt for strangulation. Hanging enables tragic women to co-opt the garments that mark their gender (headbands, veils, and belts) in their quest to master their death.[61] Nicole Loraux understands these decisions as the ultimate recourse to those under great duress. Indeed, tragic women possess the free will to choose to end their lives, yet their power is confined to the room associated with their gender – the bedchamber.[62] During this "fatal entanglement of words and deeds,"[63] tragic women recast themselves as key players in their future life (and death) choices. At the final stage of their lives, they can dictate their own fate. They have forced other characters, and their audiences, to see what happens when they have no other option and violently create new ones. Even though self-inflicted death is a sacrilegious act, these tragic women assume complete agency over their lives with their bold stance. In their pursuit of safety, the Danaids rework the "language of lamentation" to their own ends.[64] Unlike others, who follow through with their suicides, the Danaids impressively receive what they demand while preserving their lives. Their threat reframes the limited

---

[60] Bell (1995).

[61] Examples include the *Women of Trachis*, in which Deianira stabs herself; Euripides's *Suppliants*, in which Evadne jumps into her husband's funeral pyre, and *Oedipus Rex*, in which Jocasta hangs herself. The bloodless act of strangulation appears preferable to the potential bloodshed of rape (Goff [1990: 38]). Loraux (1987: 31–48) suggests that virgins who die are sacrificial victims whose deaths resemble a marriage to Hades (see also Butler [2000: 24]). Goff (1990: 119–20) argues that such sacrifices represent a remedial effect of ritual that is part of a healthy community.

[62] Loraux (1987: 23).

[63] I use the "fatal entanglement of words and deeds" after Butler (2000: 60).

[64] I use the "language of lamentation" after Foley (2001: 28). Treating the politics of lamentation surrounding female tragic characters as outdated, Honig (2013: 196) advises a shift "from a politics of *lamentation* to a *politics* of lamentation."

autonomy assigned to young unmarried women because they yield an incredible outcome despite the odds stacked against them.

Other protagonists in Athenian tragedy use their ability to kill to briefly transgress the restricted space they occupy. For instance, in Euripides's *Medea*, the eponymous protagonist murders her children as a way to punish Jason for taking a new wife in Corinth (1236–1414). Stuck in precarious situations, both the Danaids and Medea must rely on the mercy of others to ensure their safety. Fortunately for the Danaids, they have their father to advocate on their behalf. Unfortunately for Medea, Jason's new marriage strips her of familial protection so she creates her own escape route from her already nullified existence.[65] Instead of terminating her life, Medea opts for a social death that consists of a life of exile. The hero of Sophocles's *Antigone* offers another point of contact for the Danaids. A complex political figure in her own right, Antigone eschews the language of lamentation for a "politics of counter-sovereignty."[66] Her fatal crime begins with her words, in that she defies the limiting paradigm that her uncle Creon has set by openly declaring that she has buried Polynices. Determined to honor her slain brother, Antigone queers the presumed norm of patriarchy in Thebes.[67] Alongside Medea and Antigone, the Danaids are powerful actors who transform their vulnerable bodies into valuable weapons.[68] They carefully negotiate a departure from the confines of the female-centered *oikos* and boldly enter the male-dominated *polis*. Their rewriting of vulnerability into violence indicates that tragic women can inhabit the world of the powerful and the powerless.[69]

---

[65] The nurse fears that Medea will commit suicide by thrusting a sword into her chest (*Med.* 38–43). By assigning to Medea a method of suicide typically associated with men, the nurse implies Medea's potential to bend gender expectations.

[66] I use the "politics of counter-sovereignty" after Honig (2013: 92).

[67] Butler (2000: 82). See also Surtees and Dyer (2020), who propose to queer Classics by integrating feminist, queer, and trans theories into the field.

[68] In one sense, this analogy is imperfect because Medea does not threaten violence against her own person. Her children, however, are a part of her lineage, and their death resembles a suicide in that it ends her family line.

[69] Foley (1982: 6). I use the language of violence and vulnerability after Brill (2009). Other characters engage in this delicate dance, among them Clytemnestra, who seeks revenge for Iphigeneia's death by murdering Agamemnon (Aeschylus's *Agamemnon*). There is a marked difference, however, between Clytemnestra and the Danaids; Clytemnestra overvalues her maternity by avenging Iphigeneia's death while the Danaids undervalue theirs by fleeing marriage (Zeitlin [1996: 150–51]). Medea especially inhabits the world of the powerful when she clasps Jason's hands instead of allowing him to grasp her wrist, an act that positions her as an equal to a man (Mastronarde [2002: 167–68] on *Med.* 20–23).

3.4   **Internal Others in Argos and Athens**

While perturbing the Greek body politic with their intersectional status as Argive Greek *and* Egyptian women, the Danaids also inhabit the role of internal other among the Argive people.[70] Their interstitial status as metics speaks to the multifaceted population of Aeschylus's Athens that exists outside of the mythical confines of the *Suppliants*.[71] That said, scholarship about the play's political significance generally promotes a male-centered outlook rather than a gender-inclusive perspective. For instance, W. G. Forrest compares the Danaids with Thesmistocles, the Athenian *stratēgos* who fled to Argos in 470/69 BCE, and Alan Sommerstein argues that Aeschylus wrote the *Suppliants* to advise Athenians to banish Cimon, an Athenian general who was ostracized in 461 BCE.[72] Rectifying this gendered oversight, Geoffrey Bakewell asserts that the *Suppliants* creates a historical *aition* for the phenomenon of male and female metics in fifth-century Athens. According to Bakewell, this tragedy hints at Athenians' efforts to create their own identity at a time when their city was filled with a heterogeneous population.[73] Therefore, Bakewell equates the successful integration of the Danaids into Argos with the smooth incorporation of metics into Athens. Another persuasive proposal comes from Phiroze Vasunia, who reads the thinly disguised references to democracy as ways to emphasize Ephialtes's developments in the budding Athenian political system.[74] Indeed, Athenian playwrights are attuned to their political environment. In their quest to win tragic competitions, they interact with their lived and

---

[70] See Pelasgus's description of the Danaids as "city-strangers" (ἀστοξένων, *Supp.* 356). Kasimis (2018) and Kennedy (aforementioned forthcoming work discussed in Chp. 1 n. 56) elaborate on the concept of internal other.

[71] Garvie (2006: 141); Mitchell (2006: 220).

[72] Forrest (1960); Sommerstein (1997: 71, 79). Other scholars weigh in on the intersection of politics and tragedy: Podlecki (1966) regards the *Suppliants* as a mirror of Aeschylus's admiration for democracy in Argos; Bernal (1987: 20) treats Danaus as a historical character who symbolizes hostile Egyptian colonization of Greece; Zeitlin (1996: 169) posits that the *Suppliants* concluded with the establishment of a law court; Tzanetou (2012) and Bakewell (2013) generally view Athenian tragedy as a political genre. Garvie (2006: 143) is hesitant to make any grand claims about the political significance in this tragedy because he understands "a playwright [to be] a dramatist, not a political propagandist." Yet Garvie (2006: 162) concedes that the production date of the *Suppliants* (463 BCE) corresponds with a period in which Argos and Athens had a favorable relationship.

[73] Bakewell (2013: ix, 123); Kamen (2013: 43–61) and Kennedy (2014b) on female metics in Athens.

[74] δήμου κρατοῦσα ... τὸ δάμιον, τὸ πτόλιν κρατύνει (*Supp.* 604, 699), discussed in Vasunia (2001: 70). To contextualize these passages: in line 604, the Danaids ask their father what the ruling hand of the Argives (δήμου κρατοῦσα, "ruler of the people") has decided; in line 699, they hope that the Argive rulers (τὸ δάμιον, τὸ πτόλιν κρατύνει, "the people, the ones who rule the city") will guard their honor.

manufactured worlds.[75] Bakewell's and Vasunia's conflation of Argos and Athens obliquely acknowledges the historical amity the two cities shared in 463 BCE. Their conflation also transforms Argos and Athens into a singular Greek *polis* that houses a diverse population.

The Athenian *metoikia* (the establishment of metic status) offers a guide to the obstacles that the Danaids face in Argos. Aeschylus wrote the *Suppliants* in 463 BCE, at the cusp of the *metoikia*'s linguistic transition: the definition of *metoikein* meaning "to migrate," which prevailed in the first half of the fifth century, morphed into "to become a metic" before the century's end.[76] Lynette Mitchell astutely refers to the world of metics as "an ideological space" that exposes the versatile nature of foreignness.[77] In this space, Aeschylus tacks "metic" onto the Danaids' already robust identity, thereby disrupting any attempt to categorize them as foreigners to Argos.[78] Metic-related language first appears when Danaus reports that the Argives have voted to grant metic status to him and his daughters (ἡμᾶς μετοικεῖν [*metoikein*] τῆσδε γῆς ἐλευθέρους, "we are free to be metics in this city," *Supp.* 609). This assignation of metic status transforms the Danaids from frightened suppliants into protected residents, which makes any potential encounter with their terrifying relatives seem

---

[75] Scholars are divided on this issue: Goldhill (1990) treats Athenian tragedy as a genre that both praises and depicts the stress of the *polis*; Griffith (1995) interprets the genre as a negotiator of conflicting class interests between the Greek elite and the masses; Rhodes (2003) cautions against reading tragedy as a distinctive product of Athenian democracy (he champions the equation: "*polis* ≠ democracy"); Wilson's (2009) employment of epigraphy as evidence for democratic expression in the Dionysia encourages Rhodes (2011) to acknowledge that the Dionysia was consciously democratic, but Rhodes attributes this epigraphy solely to the special occasion of the restoration of democracy in the *polis* in 410/9 BCE; Carter (2007) suggests that tragedy asks more political questions relevant to the life of the Greek *polis* than it answers; Sommerstein (2010: 323–24) focuses specifically on the relationship between the *Suppliants* and fifth-century Athens.

[76] Watson (2010: 268); Kennedy (forthcoming). Kamen questions whether the etymology derives from *meta* = "with" or *meta* = "change" (2013: 42 n. 1). As for the orthography, a late sixth-century epigraphic inscription reads *metaoikoi*; this prototype was later replaced by *metoikoi* (Baba [1984: 4]). Bakewell (2013: 122) dates the institution of *metoikia* to the late 470s BCE and asserts that Aeschylus lent legitimacy to this status by linking it to older customs of *xenia* and supplication. Watson (2010: 271) suggests that the delineation between metics and citizens occurred after the passage of Pericles's citizenship laws in 451/50 BCE, which granted Athenian citizenship only to those whose parents held Athenian citizenship. Although Pericles's laws indicated a diverse population in Athens, they do not disprove the presence of metics in the *polis* before 451/50 BCE; rather, they imply that the status of metics was flexible until 451/50 BCE. Therefore, both Bakewell and Watson underscore the flexible status of metics during the first half of the fifth century BCE.

[77] Mitchell (2006: 223). Bakewell (2013: 86) asserts that female metics were dangerous because there was "a possibility of developing an independent subjectivity of their own . . . and the uses to which they might put their moral agency were frightening."

[78] In line with these variable categories of identity, the composition of Aeschylus's audience included citizens, foreigners, enslaved people, and metics (Henderson [1991]). Foley (2001: 3 n. 1) asserts that there were a limited number of women who attended Greek tragic performances.

more manageable.[79] Danaus later prompts his daughters to persevere in a chaste manner and disregard the negative reputation that metics have (πᾶς δ' ἐν μετοίκῳ [*metoikō*] γλῶσσαν εὔτυκον φέρει | κακήν, "each person among the metics has an evil tongue shaped for its purpose," 994–95). Due to the limitations of this protective status, he urges his daughters to avail themselves of a tool in a Greek (and Egyptian) woman's arsenal: the manipulation of sexual desire (996–1005). Their fierce protection of their beauty and charm becomes a weapon with which to offset any potential slander.[80]

More broadly, Aeschylus's metic-related vocabulary draws his fifth-century audience from the distant mythical to their current political world.[81] The assignation of metic status to noncitizen residents who remained in Athens for more than a month had existed since the early fifth century. Rapid economic growth and large-scale immigration mid-century coincided with the formalization of this status.[82] People in this heterogeneous group, which consisted of freeborn and formerly enslaved men and women from various regions, were called "metics" (*metoikoi*).[83] The requirements for metic status consisted of an annual tax (twelve drachmas for men and six for women), a citizen sponsor, attendance at liturgies, and fulfillment of military service. Due to Athenian dependence on metics' labor, the Athenian government permitted these economically indispensable people to temporarily access the benefits of living in Athens while keeping them from more permanent advantages like citizenship.[84] Athenians' discomfort with this reliance potentially encouraged them to strengthen the polarity between metics and themselves.[85] To fortify this distinction, Athenian legislation forbade metics from holding any political position and barred them from owning immoveable property. Metics faced

---

[79] Kennedy (forthcoming) understands the Danaids' welcome into Argos as one step in a process she calls "racializing the metic."

[80] Athenian citizens did not frequently analyze the geographic origin of metics, but Egyptian metics are mentioned in forensic oratory (Hyperides's *Against Athenogenes*) and in an inscription on a sanctuary to Isis in Athens (*Inscriptiones Graecae* II 2, 337.42–45).

[81] Compare Antigone, who uses metic-related vocabulary to define her ambiguous status as a member of the royal family and an impious outsider (Sophocles, *Antigone* 852, 867, 890).

[82] Sosin (2016); Kennedy (forthcoming). For an excellent defense of the use of the term "status" rather than "class" or "order," see Kamen (2013: 1–3, 46).

[83] Bakewell (2013: 3). Refuting Whitehead's (1977: 112–14) oversight regarding gender differences of metics, Kennedy (2014b) highlights the social and economic importance of female metics in Athens.

[84] Bakewell (2013: 18). In his treatise *Constitution of the Athenians* (1.10–13), pseudo-Xenophon briefly sets aside his intense dislike of metics to begrudgingly admit the financial benefits that metics bring to the *polis* in that their *metoikion* ("annual metic tax") counterbalanced the *misthos* ("state payments to citizens").

[85] In the fourth century BCE, a law was passed which prohibited marriage between female metics and Athenian citizens (Kamen [2013: 50]).

the risk of being sold into slavery if they disobeyed any of these rules.[86] Athenians adopted these discriminatory practices, in part to help ensure that they were, and would remain, the powerful in-group.[87] Furthermore, the myth of Athenian autochthony heightened Athenians' claim of special status.[88]

In the world of the *Suppliants*, the Danaids' liminal status as metics greatly affects their standing in Argos. They pose considerable conceptual problems for Pelasgus because they exist at the threshold of citizen and slave as well as native and foreign. He resembles Athenian citizens safeguarding their status when he creates a vast distance between himself and the Danaids. His stout opposition to their malleable identity undermines the overlapping boundaries through which the Danaids glide.[89] Comparable to metics in fifth-century Athens, the Danaids' safety is not guaranteed even after they have proven themselves worthy of Argive Greeks' protection. Despite this challenge, the Danaids effectively rewrite the balance of agency in this Athenian tragedy. They reject binary models that discredit their supple permutations of identity. By troubling the Hellenocentric view of foreigners and imposing a sophisticated system in which notional foreigners control the Greek gaze, Aeschylus has created a layered production that poignantly addresses the complex delineation of identity in the world of the *Suppliants* and that of fifth-century Athens.

[86] Although small in number, privileged groups of metics were able (in order of ascending social status) to own moveable property, pay equal taxes without the *metoikion*, and receive citizenship (Bakewell [2013: 8]; Kamen [2013: 55–61]; Kennedy [forthcoming]). Athenians occasionally granted naturalized citizenship to those who demonstrated *andragathia* ("manly excellence") to the state, which required political connections and high social status. This flexible status boundary required Athenians to work even harder to maintain the illusion that Athenian citizenship corresponded to autochthony (Kamen [2013: 79–86, 111–13]; Watson [2010: 274–75]).

[87] The similarities between metics in the fifth century BCE and undocumented immigrants in the twenty-first century are striking: both leave their hometowns in search for jobs and/or safety, both gain a degree of protection with prominent sponsorship, and both face dire consequences if they do not comply with strict guidelines. Furthermore, the legal systems in both instances are designed to benefit citizens and allot second-class status to metics and undocumented immigrants; legislation such as *graphē aprostatou* (prosecution of metics who do not have a citizen-guardian) and Arizona's SB 1070 (prosecution of undocumented immigrants who do not carry required, government-authorized documents) highlights the unequal treatment of those who lack citizen status. Kasimis (2018) underscores the close relationship between immigration politics and democratic thought in ancient Greece.

[88] Whitehead (1977: 19); Lape (2010: 46); Watson (2010: 274–75). As Edith Hall (1989: 160) explains, a "dynamic manipulation of myth" suited the political atmosphere of Athens, a city that differentiated between Greeks and foreigners after the Persian wars; see also J. Hall (2002).

[89] Gruen (2011). A few examples of fluid identities in ancient Greek literature: Agamemnon as Mycenaean in epic (the *Iliad*) and Lydian in tragedy (Euripides's *Iphigenia at Aulis*); Cadmus as both Theban (Euripides's *Bacchae*) and Tyrian (Euripides's *Phoenician Women*) in tragedy.

3.5   Conclusion: Resisting Monolithic Blackness

The Danaids' performance of a hybrid identity successfully deconstructs Pelasgus's messy category of race (external categorization). Their training for this arduous task begins when Danaus instructs them to keep their distance from their cruel Egyptian relatives and stresses the importance of honoring the Greek gods. In his absence, the Danaids transform from dutiful children into powerful teachers who revel in their hybrid black, Egyptian, and Argive Greek identity. As the playwright writing these characters into existence, Aeschylus invites audiences, both within and outside of the theater, to scrutinize their own understanding of the overlapping relationship between skin color, identity, and race.

In the *Suppliants*, the trope of performance operates on two levels. On a superficial level, the actors playing the Danaids conduct a staged performance in front of an audience of Athenian citizens, metics, and enslaved people. Within the play, the Danaids enact an internal performance for Pelasgus, their audience of one. Aware that Pelasgus's distrust of their claim to Argive Greek identity hinges on their physical appearance, the Danaids externalize their black skin as an innocuous environmental feature. Their savvy manipulation of a metaphorical mask of difference fits into a larger trend of performers who seek creative approaches to challenging situations. Finally, as the Danaids reshape Pelasgus's conception of race to incorporate their hybrid identity, they illuminate the limitations of modern race's color-driven definition. In this way, they bring to the forefront a revelation that clangs against the realities of the twenty-first century: skin color need not be the primary marker of difference.

A closing look at contemporary literature enables readers to situate the Danaids' supple performance alongside twenty-first-century excavations of Blackness. The playwright Suzan-Lori Parks echoes the Danaids' resistance to confining categories in her poetic essay "New Black Math."[90] Writing in answer to the query, "what is a black play?", Parks channels the Danaids' fluid handling of identity.[91] Her diverse personification of her subject upends the idea of monolithic Black experience:

> A black play is tragic.
> A black play is funny as hell.
> A black play has contempt for the other. And love too.
> . . .
> A black play is simple.

---

[90] Parks (2005).

[91] Parks uses "black" (lowercase) to refer to a contemporary group of people while I use "Black" (uppercase) to describe the same group.

> A black play is COMPLICATED.
> A black play is ALL THAT.
> A black play is a piece of work.
> A black play is worth the price of admission.
> A black play is free.[92]

Parks does not offer any easy answers to the guiding question. The Black play occupies contradictory roles in terms of genre, emotion, effort, and expense. Parks's readers cannot assign a straightforward label to this simultaneously shifting and decisive subject. Comparable to the Danaids, whose dynamic performance reshapes Argive Greek identity, Parks reinvents the parameters of a Black production. For Parks, the only fixed element that applies to all Black plays is the demand for continual interrogation. The impetus to question preconceived notions also guides the next chapter, focusing on Herodotus's portrayal of Aithiopia. Exploration of black people in Herodotus's *Histories* prompts readers to reconsider any facile assumptions about the role of blackness in ancient Greek historiography. Furthermore, Herodotus's manipulations of geography and attire challenge myopic tendencies to treat skin color as the sole criterion for race.

---

[92] Parks (2005: 582–83).

CHAPTER 4

Beyond Blackness
Reorienting Greek Geography

In critiquing the gap between black Egyptians and Argive Greeks in Chapter 3, I explored the performance of blackness in an Athenian tragedy. Historiography, the writing of history, is another stage on which subversive performances of blackness occur. On this stage, Herodotus's *Histories*, a nine-tome overview of the Greco-Persian wars, occupies a prominent position. Writing extensively about communities outside of his native Ionia, Herodotus presents Aithiopians as a reverent people who live at the peripheries of the ancient "Greek world," a geographic term I use to emphasize Herodotus's amorphous mapping of Greek-speaking cities (see Figure 4.1).[1] In his *Histories*, Herodotus refers to Aithiopians a dozen times.[2] Three of these instances mention their skin color: he implies that their skin is black (Hdt. 2.104), he calls attention to their black skin (3.101), and he mentions their use of vermilion and white chalk to alter their skin color (7.69). From these examples, it becomes clear that black skin is merely one of several ways that Herodotus describes Aithiopians, thus underscoring the shaky staying power of skin color as it applies to race. Rather, Herodotus points out other ways to categorize Aithiopians that are not bound up in chromatic appearance.

I begin this chapter with an examination of Aithiopia's presence in ancient Greek historiography. Despite my earlier definition of "Aithiopia" as an ethereal land, I employ this term to refer both to a mythical region and a historical country solely to acknowledge the terminology (*Aithiopia*) that ancient Greek historiographers use.[3] After sifting through Herodotus's brief

---

[1] My use of "peripheries" draws inspiration from world-systems analysis (Hall [2014]), a model developed by Immanuel Wallerstein in the 1970s that focuses on systems rather than nation-states. In line with Wallerstein, I focus on the impact of the semi-peripheral and peripheral communities rather than that of a core society. Hestia's geospatial analysis map (https://hestia.open.ac.uk/) provides a helpful visual orientation of the places that Herodotus discusses.

[2] Hdt. 2.29–30, 104, 110, 137–40, 162; 3.17–26, 94, 97; 4.183, 197–98; 7.90; 9.32.

[3] See also my discussion of Aithiopia on p. 168.

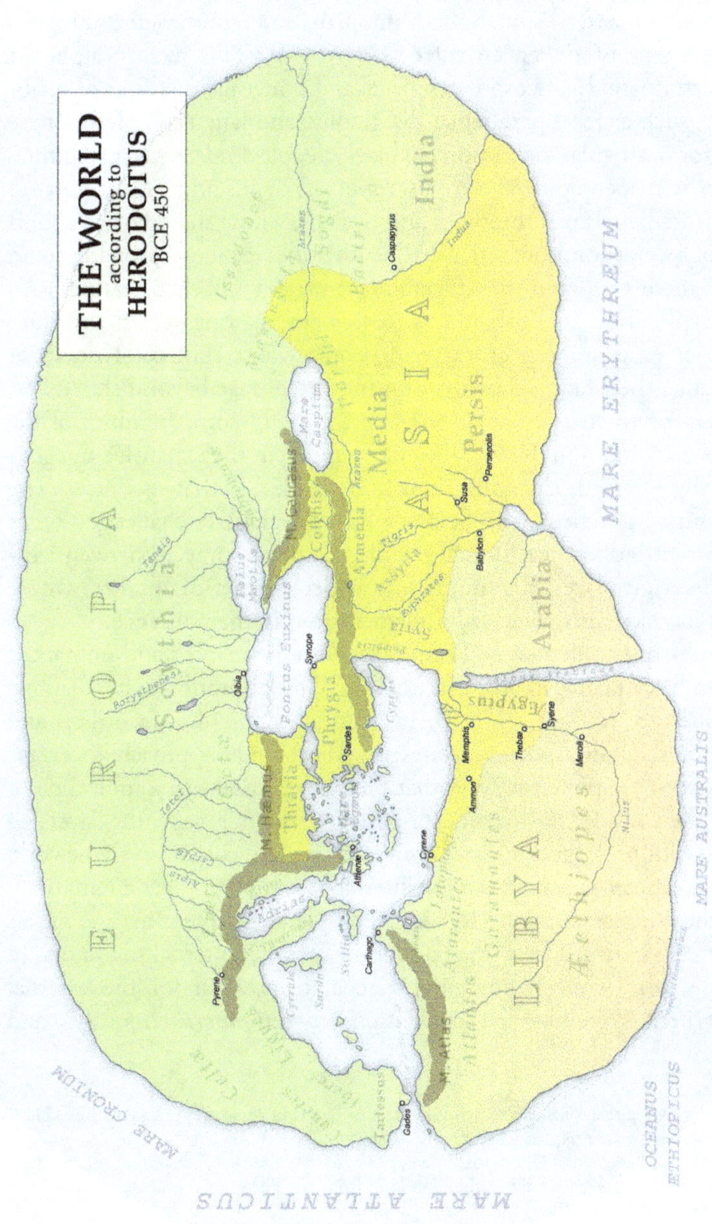

Figure 4.1 Herodotus's map of the world, modified from The Challenger Reports (summary), 1895. © Jonathan O'Rourke/Alamy Stock Photo.

references to Aithiopians, I probe his extended Aithiopian *logos* (3.17–26), a story in which Egyptians from the Elephantine region of the Nile (hereafter referred to as Fish-eaters) spy on the Aithiopians and report their findings to the sixth-century BCE Persian ruler Cambyses II. This reciprocal, albeit mediated, ethnography incorporates visual and nonvisual methods of defining people, such as food preference, geography, and language. Herodotus's resistance of a singular definition of black people leads to cross-cultural encounters with people from various regions. For instance, his report on the similarities between Aithiopians and Indians, whose shared black skin is only one of several commonalities that he identifies, echoes a growing trend of yoking these two countries together in ancient Greek literature.[4] An ensuing exploration of Herodotus's frequent pairing of Egypt and Aithiopia serves as another example of people whose skin color does not overdetermine their race. As part of this inquiry of race beyond skin color, Herodotus's Scythian *logos* (4.76–80) offers a useful comparandum of the ways that visual and nonvisual markers can undercut the expansive category of externally derived categorizations of peoples – that is, race. The Hellenocentric practices of Scyles and Anacharsis challenge other Scythians' rigid adherence to xenophobia. Lastly, a foray into twentieth-century literature places Herodotus in a wider context of thinkers whose characters interact with perceived foreigners even in their absence.

In the subsequent discussion, I scrutinize both the marked and unmarked presences of black people in fifth-century BCE Greek historiography. Daphne Brooks's quest to "read the tension between what the archives record ... and the ruptures and blindspots," inspires my "both/and" approach to extant literary sources; I explore the ways that Herodotus speaks to a multitude of audiences *both* inside *and* outside of his text.[5] In this vein, the layers of narration within Herodotus's *logoi* demand a cohesive framework. Therefore, I differentiate between the internal narrator, who has a temporary role, and the external narrator, Herodotus, who is a permanent fixture. In this way, I am able to address the autonomy of the internal narrators in Herodotus's *logoi* while maintaining a separate position for the external narrator/writer.[6] More broadly, the division between *historiē* ("inquiry") and

---

[4] On the deeply rooted relationship between India and Aithiopia in ancient Greek sources, see Dihle (1964), Schneider (2004, 2015), and Vasunia (2016: 36–39).

[5] Brooks (2006: 10); Greenwood (2009: 102). Here, I refer to the "audiences" instead of the "readers" because Cambyses learns about the Aithiopian king from the Fish-eaters' oral report, not from a written text.

[6] I conflate the writer and external narrator because Herodotus states that he will present the inquiry of Herodotus of Halicarnassus in his proem (1.1).

logos ("story")[7] helps to demarcate the realms of narration in the *Histories*. *Historiē* refers to the domain of the external narrator, and internal narrators are internally autonomous within the *logoi*. In the case of the Aithiopian *logos*, the Fish-eaters and Aithiopians speak authoritatively within the confines of Herodotus's *historiē*. The external narrator perpetually presides in the background of the story, and the internal narrators exist only within their *logos*. They cannot extend their reach to control the *historiē*, which remains contingent on the external narrator.

As the external narrator of the *Histories*, Herodotus confidently leads his readers to various parts of the ancient Greek world. His mode of transmission becomes: "you are there because I was there."[8] Whether or not his mediated report conveys factual information is sometimes impossible to ascertain.[9] He does not always provide explicit clues to determine whose voice emerges from the *historiē* or *logos*. Such vagueness therefore encourages his readers – of any period – to devise their own models with which to analyze representations of black people. Adding to this complexity, Herodotus's black Aithiopians, black Egyptians, and black Indians spill into each other. My use of the verb "spill" invokes Alexis Pauline Gumbs's experimental poetry collection *Spill: Scenes of Black Feminist Fugitivity*. Building on Hortense Spillers,[10] Gumbs seeks to create a sacred space for Black women "who made and broke narrative." Eager to summon Black female writers and characters, Gumbs pours a "libation for the named and the nameless."[11] Her ritual act inspires me as I untangle performances of blackness in Greek historiography, a genre that is part of the disjointed archive of ancient Greek literature. Pushing past analyses that privilege neat distinctions and hegemonic narratives, I also delve into the overlapping categories of external classifications of people (race) and identity as they appear in Herodotus's *Histories*.

4.1 Mapping Aithiopia in the Fifth Century BCE

A summary of Aithiopia's literary lineage contextualizes Herodotus's Aithiopians within fifth-century Greek historiography. Hecataeus's,

---

[7] My translation of *logos* as "story" is specific to the genre of history; I translate *logos* as "speech" in the context of Athenian tragedy and forensic oratory (see Section 3.3). Bakker's narratological lens of *aoidē* ("song") and *epos* ("story") inspires my demarcation. Bakker (2013: 1–12) utilizes *aoidē* and *epos* to distinguish between the Homeric narrator and Homer's Odysseus; *aoidē* represents the stage on which heroes perform and *epos* delineates the speech of characters within the epic.

[8] Clifford (1988: 22); Brandwood (2020).   [9] Fehling (1989).   [10] Spillers (2003).

[11] Gumbs (2016: xii).

Thucydides's, and Xenophon's iterations of Aithiopians evoke Homer's semidivine Aithiopians,[12] but these historians rework the Homeric trope of mythical Aithiopians to put forth their own conceptions of the people from the southern limits of the Greek world.

Hecataeus of Miletus's corpus includes three fragments that mention Aithiopians: the Marmakes Aithiopians, the Aithiopians who live on the small island of Hysaeis, and the Aithiopian Skiapodes. The Marmakes are otherwise unattested, Hysaeis is probably a divine "island of the blessed," and the Skiapodes are a mythical people who live at the peripheries of the Greek world.[13] Henry George Liddell and Robert Scott define the latter as "a fabulous people in the hottest part of Libya, with immense feet which they used as sunshades as they reclined."[14] Hecataeus grafts this mythical iteration of the Skiapodes onto his Aithiopians. Hecataeus's Aithiopian Skiapodes (Σκιάποδες, ἔθνος Αἰθιοπικόν) also calls attention to the Homeric world map (*Od.* 1.23–24) that places Aithiopians in regions where the sun rises and sets – that is, the east and the west. In addition to the Homeric echo, the etymology of "Skiapodes" suggests an affiliation between the sun and skin hue, with the prefix σκιά- implying a shaded (black) skin tone. This coloring coincides with the sun-kissed appearance encapsulated in the etymology of Αἰθιοπικόν (*aithō*, "I blaze" + *ops*, "face"). Conversely, the prefix σκιά- may liken the Aithiopian Skiapodes to people whose upturned feet (πόδες) absorb the sun's rays and prevent their skin color from darkening.[15] The idea that people's skin color reflects the environment in which they live circulates in other fifth-century literature. In the Hippocratic treatise *On Airs, Waters, and Places* (24, 20), environmental determinism results in the physical alteration of people's appearance: people living near hot meadows are black, and a cold environment reddens people's skin.[16] Hecataeus's reworking of this trope complicates

---

[12] Romm (1992: 52–53) provides a compelling reading of the *Iliad* as an extended interruption of an Aithiopian holiday, introduced by Zeus's departure to the Aithiopians (*Il.* 1.423–24) and resolved by Iris's preparations to depart for Aithiopia (*Il.* 23.205–7).

[13] Μάρμακες, ἔθνος Αἰθιοπικόν ... Ὑσαεῖς νῆσος μικρὰ καὶ μεγάλη Αἰθιόπων ... Σκιάποδες, ἔθνος Αἰθιοπικόν, "Marmakes, an Aithiopian people; a small and grand island Hysaeis; Skiapodes, an Aithiopian people" (*Fragmente der griechischen Historiker* 325–327). See also Romm (1992: 55–60) and Skinner (2012: 95–99).

[14] Liddell and Scott (1996: 1610); cf. Skiapodes in Athenian comedy (Aristophanes, *Birds* 1553) and geography (Scylax of Caryanda in Tzetzes, *Chiliades* 7.629). Pliny the Elder cites historian Ctesias's description of the Skiapodes as Indians (*in quadam gente indiae ... monocoli*, "among a certain group of Indians, there are one-legged people," *HN* 7.2.23).

[15] Cf. the distinction between the wealthy man who remains shaded indoors (πλούσιος ἐσκιατροφηκώς) and the poor man who works in the sun (πένης ἡλιωμένος, *Mor.* 556d).

[16] In particular, Scythians have red skin (*Aer.* 20). In addition to the impact that the environment can have on people's skin color, the narrator of the Hippocratic treatise *On Airs, Waters, and Places*

the Aithiopians' relationship with the blazing sun. His Aithiopian Skiapodes need to protect their bodies from excessive exposure to the sun even though their name implies that it has already darkened their skin.

Other historians reimagine the Homeric archetype of Aithiopians as a geographically distant people. When Thucydides (2.48.1–2) cites a report that lists Aithiopia as the source of a deadly plague in Athens, he pushes the origin of this illness to the farthest limits of his world.[17] Xenophon echoes this trope in his portrayal of Aithiopia as the uninhabitable limit of Cyrus's empire (*Cyr.* 8.6.21, 8.8.1).[18] In both instances, Thucydides and Xenophon associate Aithiopia with an undesirable location. Either a hotspot for disease or a barren territory, Aithiopia morphs into a place of danger. Veering away from a faithful rendering of mythical Aithiopia as a vacation destination for the gods (*Il.* 1.423 and *Od.* 1.22–24), Thucydides and Xenophon situate Aithiopia firmly in the mortal domain. If the Athenian plague or Persian encroachment is not curtailed, imminent danger will strike. In effect, Thucydides's and Xenophon's jarring imagery transports Aithiopians from the lofty heavens to the messy world of humans.[19]

In line with his literary counterparts, Herodotus refashions epic renditions of Aithiopians. Setting aside the permutations of Aithiopians that occur in the Aithiopian *logos* (3.17–26), discussed below, the presence of Aithiopians elsewhere in the *Histories* fits into two categories: ethnography

---

explains that people's disposition, health, and physical build are also susceptible to nature. Lo Presti (2012) discusses the gradations of environmental determinism in the treatise.

[17] ἤρξατο δὲ τὸ μὲν πρῶτον, ὡς λέγεται, ἐξ Αἰθιοπίας τῆς ὑπὲρ Αἰγύπτου, ἔπειτα δὲ καὶ ἐς Αἴγυπτον καὶ Λιβύην κατέβη καὶ ἐς τὴν βασιλέως γῆν τὴν πολλήν, "[the plague] first began in Aithiopia, so they say, which is above Egypt. Then, it descended into Egypt and Libya and into most of the king's country" (Thuc. 2.48.1–2). Kim (2010: 38–46) examines other Homeric tropes in Thucydides's *Histories*.

[18] καὶ ἐκ τούτου τὴν ἀρχὴν ὥριζεν αὐτῷ πρὸς ἕω μὲν ἡ Ἐρυθρὰ θάλαττα, πρὸς ἄρκτον δὲ ὁ Εὔξεινος πόντος, πρὸς ἑσπέραν δὲ Κύπρος καὶ Αἴγυπτος, πρὸς μεσημβρίαν δὲ Αἰθιοπία, "and from that time, he [Cyrus] bound the kingdom with the Red Sea in the east, the Black sea in the north, Cyprus and Egypt in the west, and Aithiopia in the south" (*Cyr.* 8.6.21); ὡρίσθη γὰρ πρὸς ἕω μὲν τῇ Ἐρυθρᾷ θαλάττῃ, πρὸς ἄρκτον δὲ τῷ Εὐξείνῳ πόντῳ, πρὸς ἑσπέραν δὲ Κύπρῳ καὶ Αἰγύπτῳ, πρὸς μεσημβρίαν δὲ Αἰθιοπίᾳ, "[the Persian world] was bound by the Red Sea in the east, the Black Sea in the north, Cyprus and Egypt in the west, and Aithiopia in the south" (8.8.1).

[19] In addition to the genre of history, "Aithiopia" appears numerous times in fifth-century BCE medical treatises, epinician poetry, and geography. There are thirty-eight instances of the adjective "Aithiopian" (Αἰθιοπικός) referring to medicinal spices and plants across the following Hippocratic treatises: *Concerning Common Diseases* (once), *Concerning Diseases* 1–3 (once), *Concerning Internal Dispositions* (once), *Concerning Womanly Nature* (nine times), *Concerning the Dispositions of Women* 1–3 (twenty-four times), and *Concerning Superfetation* (twice). In his victory odes, Pindar highlights the heroic ancestry of the Aithiopians with his numerous descriptions of them as the descendants of Memnon, their valiant king (*Olympian Ode* 2.83; *Pyth.* 6.31; *Nemean Ode* 3.62, 6.51–52; *Isthmian Ode* 5.40). In the *Periplus of Hanno*, explorer Hanno of Carthage describes the Aithiopians as a remote group of people living beyond Libya (7, 11).

and political history. In the first grouping, Aithiopia is a country with an abundance of natural resources and beautiful people. The ethereal status of these Aithiopians echoes Homeric descriptions (ἄνδρας μεγίστους καὶ καλλίστους καὶ μακροβιωτάτους, "the biggest, most beautiful, and most long-lived men," Hdt. 3.114; ἀμύμονας Αἰθιοπῆας, "the blameless Aithiopians," *Il.* 1.423). No longer situated at the easternmost and westernmost expanses of the known world (*Od.* 1.23–24), however, Herodotus's Aithiopia is a mappable, albeit difficult-to-reach, location in southern Libya (Hdt. 4.197). Despite his authoritative knowledge about many countries beyond Ionia, Herodotus reaches the southern limit of his travels at Elephantine (2.29) and relies on his numerous contacts to relay information about Aithiopia to his readers.

The second category focuses on Aithiopia's oscillating political strength. Instead of hosting gods at sumptuous feasts like their Homeric counterparts, Herodotus's Aithiopians hinder the tyrannical ambitions of their mortal neighbors. These confrontations include that of the Aithiopian ruler Sabacos who controls Egypt for fifty years, thereby interrupting the longevity of Egyptian rule (Hdt. 2.137–39).[20] Obedient to the prophecy that stipulates he rule for no more than fifty years, Sabacos leaves Egypt of his own accord precisely at the fifty-year mark, and the Egyptian Anysis resumes control. This exchange of rulers pits Aithiopia in an ongoing power struggle with Egypt for control of the Nile region. Despite their tense political clashes, Herodotus lays out comparisons between these two countries. Adding to their close linguistic ties (evident in the Fish-eaters' ability to communicate with the Aithiopian king in the Aithiopian *logos*), the geography and cultural practices of Aithiopia and Egypt spill into each other. Rather than treat Aithiopia and Egypt as interchangeable foils for Attica or Ionia, Herodotus charts a different course in which he outlines the similarities between the two countries without overwriting their differences. For instance, their shared location along the Nile (2.28–30) and their comparable circumcision practices (2.104) do not discount their hostile crusades for power. Herodotus's toggling between the two countries' common elements and fierce antagonism circumvents a singular way to envision Aithiopia. In his *Histories*, Aithiopia is a dynamic place where convergence with and divergence from Egypt coexist.

Extending their political contacts beyond the Nile region, Aithiopians also interact with Persians. Herodotus distinguishes between eastern

---

[20] This passage balances Herodotus's earlier description of Sesostris, an Egyptian ruler who conquered Aithiopia (2.110).

Aithiopians, who pay an annual tribute of 400 talents to Persia, and southern Aithiopians, who give gifts instead of money (Hdt. 3.94, 97). Aithiopians' affiliation with Persians enters the military arena in earnest when they offer their own soldiers and ships to the Persian army (7.69, 90). The provision of financial and human resources likens Aithiopians to historical actors skillfully navigating their local context. Even though they avoid being subsumed into Cambyses's Persian empire, as becomes clear in the Aithiopian *logos*, they eventually adapt to the growing dominance of Xerxes's Persia as a means of survival.[21] Again, Herodotus characterizes Aithiopians as a group of people whose varying responses to their political realities reorients the categories of powerful and powerless.

As part of his extensive world map, Herodotus positions India to the east of Aithiopia. A military alliance pulls them closer together: a subset of eastern Aithiopians fight alongside Indians, whereas their southern counterparts battle alongside Arabians (Hdt. 7.65–70).[22] Herodotus uses attire and equipment to distinguish these troops: eastern Aithiopians wear animal headdresses and wield spears with tips made of gazelle horn, Indians sport cotton clothes and shoot iron-tipped arrows, and southern Aithiopians wear animal skin and carry wooden bows. Herodotus also employs hairstyles to distinguish the Aithiopians eastern Aithiopians have straight hair, and southern Aithiopians have a distinct curl pattern. These vivid descriptions encompass visual elements without focusing on skin color, which broadens readers' perception of Aithiopians and Indians (i.e. their race).[23] Ever the crafty external narrator, Herodotus notes the chromatic similarities between Aithiopians and Indians elsewhere in his *Histories*. In book 3, he asserts that both Aithiopian and Indian men have black skin and ejaculate black sperm (3.101).[24] This curious combination of traits resonates uneasily in a modern context where the hypersexualization of Black people haunts the public sphere. In the realm of Greek antiquity, however, these elements of blackness shared by Herodotus's Aithiopian and Indian men suggest that blackness operates on two registers: external and internal. That is, blackness exists on the outermost surface of their bodies, in their skin color, and within their bodies, in their sperm. Furthermore, this paired description suggests

---

[21] In all my discussions of empires, I use the lowercase "e" to democratize the language of empire. See also Table P.1.

[22] Other notable military overlaps: Indians fight as Persian soldiers (Hdt. 8.113; 9.31); Aithiopians and Egyptians fight together on behalf of Persia (9.32).

[23] The only mention of skin color in this passage refers to external adornment: the gypsum and vermilion that southern Aithiopians smear on their bodies (Hdt. 7.69).

[24] Herodotus adds Egyptians to the list of people who have black skin (2.57, 104); see also Samuels (2015).

that blackness is transferable, in that these men can expel their black sperm and potentially inject it into other people.[25]

Herodotus's uneven convergences of Aithiopians and Indians complicate any attempts to funnel all non-Greek black people into a static group. For example, both Aithiopians and Indians live in a rugged landscape and harvest natural elements such as gold, yet Aithiopians alone collect ebony and ivory (Hdt. 3.97, 106, 114).[26] Aithiopia and India further spill into each other when Herodotus recounts Scylax of Caryanda's scouting expedition to India at the bequest of the Persian ruler Darius. After Scylax's return to Persia, Darius attacks India and annexes it to the Persian empire (4.44). Darius's hegemonic agenda likens him to Cambyses, whose fervent desire to conquer Aithiopia increases after getting confirmation of its fabulous resources (3.17–26). Although Aithiopia and India initially seem to serve as static symbols of Persian rulers' imperial ambitions, Darius's success and Cambyses's failure suggest that the military prowess of Aithiopia trumps that of India. Analogies such as these highlight the relativity of geography. Herodotus's Aithiopians may live in the most remote parts of the ancient Greek world, but this does not restrict their versatility. For his part, Herodotus illuminates a vibrant literary landscape in which Aithiopians juggle various roles. The subsequent inspection of Herodotus's Aithiopian *logos* sheds light on some of their subversive performances.

4.2   Layers of Foreignness in Herodotus's Aithiopian *logos* (Hdt. 3.17–26)

The third book of Herodotus's *Histories* begins with the military expedition of the Persian ruler Cambyses against the Egyptians. After this successful venture, he decides to flex his military might against the Carthaginians, Ammonians, and Aithiopians. As the Aithiopian *logos* unfolds, it becomes clear that the Aithiopians stand in a group of their own. Unlike the Carthaginians and Ammonians, who lack descriptive adjectives, the Aithiopians are "long-lived" people who require careful handling (τοὺς μακροβίους Αἰθίοπας, Hdt. 3.17).[27]

---

[25] I discuss the transferability of color in my discussion of Charicleia's skin color in Section 6.4.

[26] Neither the intense heat of the midday sun nor huge, ferocious ants deter the Indians from harvesting gold dust from the eastern desert (Hdt. 3.94–106). Even though gold is found in Aithiopia (3.97, 114), Herodotus singles out India's large quantities of gold and labor-intensive harvesting practices.

[27] Cambyses opts for a different approach with the Aithiopians in that he sends spies, not the navy or infantry (which he sends to Carthage and Ammon, respectively) to invade Aithiopia. Bosak-Schroeder (2020) investigates the ways that Greek ethnographies of non-Greek environments informed and challenged Greek practices.

Eager to spy on the Aithiopians and determine whether their fabled storehouse of eternal food exists, Cambyses sends the Egyptian Fish-eaters, who live near Elephantine, to Aithiopia in his stead. The Persian ruler chooses the Fish-eaters for this mission because of their fluency in the language of their southern neighbors and that of the Persians. The Fish-eaters attempt to deceive the Aithiopian king by plying him with gifts, but he quickly recognizes the true intent behind their actions and recommends that they curtail their efforts.[28] Even though the Fish-eaters relay this advice to Cambyses, the Persian ruler insists on marching into Aithiopia and eventually aborts his mission.

In the Aithiopian *logos*, Herodotus revamps the Homeric Aithiopians. First, he replaces their generic location in the easternmost and westernmost regions (*Od.* 1.23–24) with the area south of Libya near the Indian Ocean (Hdt. 3.17). The worlds of the *Odyssey* and the *Histories* again collide when the Aithiopian king offers his kingdom to any Persian who can string his bow (Hdt. 3.21), a set-up that evokes Penelope's promise to marry whoever can string Odysseus's bow and use it to pierce twelve axes (*Od.* 21). More than a test of brute strength, the contest reveals Penelope's and the Aithiopian king's desire to forestall widespread violence. Presuming that no one will be able to string the bow, they aim to reduce any potential mayhem to a single activity. The Aithiopian king is more successful in this gamble perhaps because Cambyses embodies only some of Odysseus's traits: he mirrors Odysseus's ethnographic curiosity about places outside of his domain but, rather than surpass the confines of mortality like the "prototypical frontier-man," Cambyses seeks to reach the limits of geography.[29] As another point of divergence, Cambyses does not emulate Odysseus's willingness to heed advice. Instead, Cambyses stubbornly dismisses the Aithiopian king's counsel and charges ahead with his plans to invade Aithiopia. Altogether, these Homeric allusions encourage knowing readers to envision Herodotus as a shrewd recipient of Homeric epics who alludes to Odyssean moments, images, and tropes without directly copying his literary predecessor.[30]

Continuing to chart a new course for Homer's Aithiopians, Herodotus foregrounds their savvy diplomacy. When Cambyses seeks to verify their possession of the Table of the Sun, a magical meadow filled with an endless bounty of food (Hdt. 3.19), he sends the Fish-eaters to serve as his representatives and deliver Persian gifts to the Aithiopian king in a show

---

[28] The Aithiopian king remains unnamed in Herodotus's *Histories*. Morgan (1982: 237–38) and Elmer (2008: 422–25) make a convincing argument that he is Hydaspes, a king in the sixth century BCE and a character in Heliodorus's *Aithiopika*.

[29] Hartog (2001: 3–13).   [30] Irwin (2014: 44).

of goodwill.[31] This act of subterfuge emphasizes the depths of Cambyses's greed, in that he seeks to disarm the Aithiopians with gifts before attempting to overpower them with weapons. Suspicious of Cambyses's ostensible generosity, the Aithiopian king is a genial host to his guests. He shows them the nourishing Table of the Sun and the magical spring from which his people derive their longevity (3.23–24). During this tour, the Aithiopian king shrewdly confirms all of Cambyses's assumptions about Aithiopia while shrouding his own language in a cloak of mystery that Cambyses cannot penetrate. In this way, Herodotus refashions Homer's characterization of Aithiopians as hosts of sumptuous dinner parties (*Il.* 1.423 and *Od.* 1. 22–23). Comparable to his Homeric counterparts, the Aithiopian king opens up his country to outsiders, but he remains keenly aware of the risks that these guests pose.

Channeling the Aithiopian king's decision to sidestep hegemonic projections, the Fish-eaters defy straightforward classification. Herodotus highlights their assignment and purpose as spies (ὀψομένους ... κατοψομένους, 3.17) before introducing them by name as Fish-eaters (Ἰχθυοφάγων ἀνδρῶν, 3.19).[32] In their quest to transmit details (ethnographic or otherwise) from one group to another, spies are masters of deceit. Well versed in surreptitious communication with inhabitants of various regions, spies strive to simultaneously mute their own differences and acutely observe those of others. Although spies may distort the data that they gather, they shorten the distance between communities by transporting information beyond boundaries. Their success depends on their ability to translate their alienation into a new identity that the subjects of their investigation will accept.[33] The Fish-eaters act as spies (κατόπται) once they receive their assignment from Cambyses and embark on an underhanded mission. Surveillance becomes a methodological device that separates the Fish-eaters from the subjects in question even when the two groups encounter each other.

In addition to being masters of subterfuge, the Fish-eaters resemble authoritative translators who speak both the Persian and the Aithiopian language. They navigate interpersonal situations with an impressive level

---

[31] Cambyses awaits the Fish-eaters in Egypt. He is probably stationed in Memphis, having just returned from Sais where he mutilated the corpse of Amasis (Hdt. 3.16).

[32] Each of the three instances of "spies" (κατόπται) in the *Histories* refers to the Fish-eaters (3.17.7, 21.7, 21.10); κατάσκοπος appears twenty-two times and refers to the Fish-eaters four times (3.19.1, 23.5, 23.9, 25.1); and of the fourteen instances of καθοράω, one mention corresponds to the Fish-eaters (3.17.9).

[33] I use the language of translating alienation after Brooks (2006: 3).

of fluency without joining the communities with whom they are in close contact. Similar to the Fish-eaters, who master the strategy of disassociation, Herodotus's readers become ethnographic spies who visit, yet never remain in, countries outside of the Greek world. In the course of their espionage, they snatch glimpses of a place where geography is called into question. In fact, Herodotus's report of this fantastic journey potentially teaches his readers more about Cambyses's crazed desperation than it does about the Aithiopian people.[34] Even still, both groups depend on the Fish-eaters' reports to help them develop their collective ethnographic databases.

By embodying the intersection of spying and translation, the Fish-eaters transform Herodotus's readers into distant knowers. This collision of spying and translation resonates in a contemporary context. The advent of modern ethnography, which developed within the field of anthropology in the 1920s, placed importance on the practice of participant observation.[35] Ethnographers lived in communities they deemed foreign and sought to describe inhabitants in terms familiar to their audience. This mode of fieldwork endowed anthropologists with the power to define remote communities.[36] Scholars in the field have objected to this problematic rendering of non-Western peoples since anthropology's inception. Their ongoing interventions include a rejection of the discipline's myopic portrayal of otherness.[37] As ethnographers of sorts, the Fish-eaters dismantle the category of myopic foreigner because they are (Egyptian) foreigners interacting with (Aithiopian) foreigners who report their findings to (Persian) foreigners. Despite the fact that Herodotus, the ultimate proto-ethnographer, recounts these stories, the Fish-eaters alone have geographic and linguistic proximity to the Aithiopians. Part and parcel of their savvy fieldwork, the Fish-eaters speak on behalf of all Persians, and they eventually influence Cambyses's view of the Aithiopians. Even though Cambyses

---

[34] Cambyses's perilous march to Aithiopia mirrors his descendant Xerxes's quest to subdue Greece (Hdt. 7.4–9.122, esp. 7.108–12 and 8.113–20; see also Bridges [2015]). Persia dominates Xerxes's *logos*, but diverse alliances abound: Persians use Phoenician flax and Egyptian papyrus cables to build bridges (7.34–36), the Persian army and fleet consist of people from numerous regions (7.61–99), and Xerxes throws wine and a golden bowl into the sea (7.54; note the overlap with the gifts that the Fish-eaters bring to the Aithiopian king in 3.20). Taken together, these *logoi* (3.17–26 and 7.4–9.122) present Aithiopia and Greece as inaccessible locations that the Persians hope to reach.

[35] Clifford (1988: 30–32); Redfield (1985). Longo (1987: 19) refers to the Fish-eaters as cultural ambassadors.

[36] For examples of early anthropological fieldwork that refuted these colonial practices, see Hurston (1994); Hurston (2018); Miner (1956).

[37] Among those offering anthropological interventions are Stocking (1982); Baker (1998, 2010); Caspari (2003); Kyllingstad (2014); and King (2019).

authorized them to travel on his behalf, they are not beholden to their trip's sponsor.

During their examination of the Aithiopians, the Fish-eaters do not focus on their skin color as a noteworthy element of their race. The etymology of Aithiopian provides the only insight into their color: *aithō* ("I blaze") + *ops* ("face"). Elsewhere in the *Histories*, Herodotus directly addresses the Aithiopians' black skin, a chromatic observation that reworks the popular iconographic trend by which "white = Greek female" and "black = Greek male." In the Aithiopian *logos*, the absence of color-based vocabulary in relation to the Aithiopians' appearance suggests that their skin color was so well known that it did not require repeating. Furthermore, Herodotus's focus on elements other than skin color in this *logos* destabilizes any reductive reading of color as the sole marker of group categorization. The Aithiopians' diverse markers of alterity spur readers to look beyond color-based clues to learn about these people.[38] When describing the Aithiopians' race (an outward-derived categorization), Herodotus draws attention to their juxtaposed features: they are semidivine yet bound by geography, their king possesses both arrogance and modesty, their king somehow knows in advance that Cambyses is intent on invading his country yet still invites the Fish-eaters to see the Table of the Sun. In this last regard, Herodotus distances the perspicacious Aithiopian king from the category of ignorant foreigner into which he thrusts Cambyses.[39] The Aithiopian king does not conform to any preconceived model of alterity. Rather, he subverts the label "foreigner" all the while remaining within its parameters.

4.2.1   *Reframing Race and Identity*

A wily ethnographer in his own right, the Aithiopian king inquires about Persian habits and shares insight about his own people:

> ἐπείρετο ὅ τι τε σιτέεται ὁ βασιλεὺς καὶ χρόνον ὁκόσον μακρότατον ἀνὴρ
> Πέρσης ζώει. οἱ δὲ σιτέεσθαι μὲν τὸν ἄρτον εἶπον, ἐξηγησάμενοι τῶν πυρῶν

---

[38] Nonetheless, fifth-century Greek iconography of black people exists, such as a musician depicted on a shield painted on a wine jar (*amphora*), attendants to Andromeda on a water jar (*hydria*), a pygmy fighting a crane on a horn-shaped cup (*rhyton*), a crouching warrior on a perfume flask (*alabastron*), and Busiris on a squat mixing vessel (*stamnos*; Snowden [1970: 51, 54, 98, 223, 232]). See also Chapter 2.

[39] Elsewhere in the *Histories*, Herodotus challenges this binary framework by allowing the Persian ruler Darius to espouse a popular Greek view, that every nation sees itself as superior and looks down upon alien practices, to the Greeks themselves (3.38). See also Egyptians' preference of their own customs (2.79), and everyone's predilection for their own practices (3.38).

τὴν φύσιν, ὀγδώκοντα δὲ ἔτεα ζόης πλήρωμα ἀνδρὶ μακρότατον προκεῖσθαι … ἀντειρομένων δὲ τὸν βασιλέα τῶν Ἰχθυοφάγων τῆς ζόης καὶ τῆς διαίτης πέρι, <εἶπε> ἔτεα μὲν ἐς εἴκοσί τε καὶ ἑκατὸν τοὺς πολλοὺς αὐτῶν ἀπικνέεσθαι, ὑπερβάλλειν δέ τινας καὶ ταῦτα, σίτησιν δὲ εἶναι κρέα ἑφθὰ καὶ πόμα γάλα.

> The king asked what a Persian man eats and what is the maximum age a Persian man lives. They [the Fish-eaters] replied that the Persians eat bread, and they described how wheat is grown, and they said that eighty years is set as the maximum length of a Persian's life … When the Fish-eaters asked the king about his people's lives and diet, he replied that many of his people live to be 120 years old, with some even surpassing this age, and that they eat boiled meat and drink milk. (Hdt. 3.22–23)

In this passage, "foreignness" is a pliant label. Four layers of foreignness interact as an Ionian Greek writer (1) describes a Persian ruler (2) who sends Egyptians (3) to speak with the Aithiopian king (4), who informs his audiences about Aithiopian customs.[40] This stack of subordinations makes it difficult to identify which group is the norm against which all others are calibrated, and the gradation of voices reshapes the category of "foreigner" in unpredictable ways. The information about the Aithiopians has passed through three sets of hands, each presumably affecting the end result. This new, layered model does not necessarily eliminate the idea of "native" and "foreigner." This paradigm instead foregrounds the intersubjective understanding of different groups in Herodotus's *logos*. The Aithiopians and Fish-eaters implicitly agree on a shared template for race (external categorization) with their reciprocal line of questioning. The Aithiopian king reduces the Persians' race to longevity and food, and the Fish-eaters apply the same metric to the Aithiopians' race.

The Fish-eaters mute their identity as Egyptians and morph into pseudo-Persians when they explain the ethnographic customs of Persia. They later speak on behalf of the Aithiopians when they recount details about Aithiopia to Cambyses. Despite his vantage point outside of the world of the *logos*, the external narrator uses the deictic pronoun *houtoi* to help Cambyses visualize the Aithiopians (οἱ δὲ Αἰθίοπες οὗτοι, "*these* Aithiopians," Hdt. 3.20).[41] This trope of witnessing reverberates throughout the Fish-eaters' sojourn into Aithiopia. They repeatedly transmit information about what they have observed back to Cambyses: **θεησάμενοι** δὲ καὶ τὸ δεσμωτήριον … τελευταίας **ἐθεήσαντο** τὰς θήκας

---

[40] I discuss this passage in Derbew (2021).
[41] See also Pelasgus's use of a deictic pronoun, discussed in Section 3.3.

αὐτῶν . . . **θεησάμενοι** δὲ τὰ πάντα οἱ κατάσκοποι ("the Fish-eaters *saw* the prison, they *saw* the graves of dead people, they *saw* everything," 3.23–25). Although Cambyses has not seen Aithiopia with his own eyes, the external narrator's autopsy-driven vocabulary offers him a view of the country.[42]

Aware of the limitations of vision, the Aithiopian king does not allow his sight to cloud his judgment. Upon his inspection of the Persian gifts that the Fish-eaters bring to him, most lack any allure: πορφύρεόν τε εἶμα καὶ χρύσεον στρεπτὸν περιαυχένιον καὶ ψέλια καὶ μύρου ἀλάβαστρον καὶ Φοινικηΐου οἴνου κάδον ("a purple cloak, a gold necklace and bracelets, an alabaster of myrrh, and palm wine," Hdt. 3.20). Barring his delight at the wine, the Aithiopian king scoffs at this colorful bounty.[43] He expresses irritation at gifts that conceal color and smell, thus hiding their true nature. In particular, the dyeing of the cloak masks its true color, and fragrant perfume covers up any displeasing odor.[44] In rejecting these gifts, the Aithiopian king spurns Cambyses's plan to lure him into a false friendship.[45] Furthermore, the king's dismissal of these clothes and perfume is compatible with Athenian ethical discourse that disapproves of inherent deception.[46] The Aithiopian king's invocation of Athenian diplomacy may reflect the transferability of Athenian traits. At the same time, this two-way ethnographic mirror potentially indicates the futility of assuming strict distinctions between Athenians and Aithiopians.

The Aithiopian king's reaction to the purple cloak reveals one way in which clothes can disclose a hidden message: the dyed clothes mirror Cambyses's

---

[42] Konstan (1987: 66–67) discusses Herodotus's use of autopsy-driven vocabulary.

[43] This bestowing of wine likens Cambyses to Greeks, who frequently use wine to conduct unfair diplomacy. Love of wine leads to ruin for the Massagetae (Hdt. 1.211) and the Cyclops (*Od.* 9, discussed in Romm [1992: 57–58]). In addition, Cambyses's fondness for wine incites him to violent acts (Hdt. 3.34–36), and the Spartan ruler Cleomenes becomes insane after drinking undiluted wine (6.84). The Aithiopian king's initial rejection of a Greek beverage suggests that he avoids following other rulers' dangerous precedents (Hobden [2013: 94]). But his later admiration of this concentrated beverage signals his non-Greek status, especially since he does not follow the Greek practice of mixing wine with water.

[44] See also Charicleia's use of disguise to mask her beauty in Section 6.4.

[45] Even though the Phoenicians have opted out of Cambyses's expansionist projects, he co-opts them into this expedition by sending a purple cloak as a gift, a color that is linked to Phoenician dyeing practices (Hdt. 3.19). The distinction between "manufactured" and "natural" becomes pronounced as the Persians strive to get through artifice what the Aithiopians receive from the environment, such as meat and the life-nourishing water of the spring. The Aithiopian king's repudiation of Cambyses's gifts potentially symbolizes an attack on what Romm (1992: 57) deems the "most basic underpinnings of Mediterranean technology and material culture . . . [such as] the artifice behind such products as dyed cloth and refined myrrh . . . [and] the use of gold for cosmetic rather than practical purposes."

[46] Cf. Socrates's ethical stance against men's use of perfume (Xenophon, *Symposium*, 2.3–7).

fraudulent intentions. Such surreptitious signaling poses metatheatrical provocations in other literary genres as well. More than mere coverings for people's bodies, clothes can symbolize a semiotic marker of identity.[47] As early as the Homeric epics, fixed sartorial epithets jostle against numerous alterations of attire designed to conceal characters' identity.[48] Characters in Athenian drama also (de)construct components of their identities via their clothes.[49] Herodotus spotlights the signifying power of clothes in his Scythian *logos* (4.76–80). The story of two Hellenophilic Scythian men, Anacharsis and Scyles, elaborates upon the ways that clothes can deliver unintended messages to viewers. In this tragic Scythian *logos*, Scythian people vary in their reliance on clothes as irrefutable evidence of their identity, which leads to unfortunate consequences for some members of their community whose conception of themselves does not correspond to other people's views of them. In other words, some of Herodotus's Scythian characters struggle to find acceptance among fellow Scythians when their (internal) identity and (external) race do not coincide.[50]

From the first words of the Scythian *logos*, the main point of contention is apparent: foreign customs (ξεινικοῖσι δὲ νομαίοισι, Hdt. 4.76).[51]

---

[47] Lee (2015: 1–32, esp. 24). I adopt Wyles's (2011: 4) focus on "clothes" (instead of "costume") to highlight the role of characters existing within the *logos*, rather than figures standing outside of it. My choice of vocabulary is also informed by Roach-Higgins and Eicher's (1992: 1, 2 n. 1) concept of "dress" as "a gender-neutral collective noun … [that is] unambiguous, free of personal or social valuing or bias, [and] usable in descriptions across national and cultural boundaries."

[48] Two examples of sartorial epithets in Homeric epics: "Hector with his gleaming helmet" (*Il.* 6.467–70) and "gold-sandaled Hermes" (*Od.* 5.44–46). Odysseus stands out as the consummate master of disguise who uses clothes to conceal his identity on numerous occasions (Yamagata [2005: 540]). Other notable examples in Homeric epics: Patroclus's assumption of Achilles's armor (*Il.* 16); Athena's numerous disguises (as Mentes in *Od.* 1, Mentor in *Od.* 2–3, Penelope's sister in *Od.* 4, Nausicaa's agemate in *Od.* 6, a young girl in *Od.* 7, a shepherd in *Od.* 13, a woman in *Od.* 16 and 20, and Mentor again in *Od.* 22 and 24).

[49] Examples of the signifying power of clothes include the following: in Euripides's tragedy *Hypsipyle*, the simple, modern clothes of Amphiaraus reflect his simple, modern character (as discussed in Battezzato [1999: 353]); in Euripides's *Bacchae*, Cadmus and Tiresias transform from sluggish old men into rejuvenated worshippers when they wear Dionysus's insignia; in Aristophanes's comedy *Thesmophoriazusae*, Mnesilochus dresses in women's attire in order to infiltrate an all-female religious gathering. See also Muecke (1982).

[50] Agnolon (2020) discusses the tragic elements in this Scythian *logos*. Other Herodotean examples of people adopting other people's sartorial standards: the Persians display their aesthetic preferences for Median and Egyptian clothes (1.135); Macedonian men wear women's clothes to disguise themselves as Persians and kill their lecherous Persian guests (5.17–21); and Athenian women are prohibited from wearing Ionian *chitōns* because some of them had allegedly used brooches from their *chitōns* to stab an Athenian man to death (5.87).

[51] Note the ring composition surrounding this *logos*: **ξεινικοῖσι δὲ νομαίοισι** καὶ οὗτοι αἰνῶς χρᾶσθαι φεύγουσι … οὕτω μὲν περιστέλλουσι τὰ σφέτερα νόμαια Σκύθαι, τοῖσι δὲ παρακτωμένοισι **ξεινικοὺς νόμους** τοιαῦτα ἐπιτίμια διδοῦσι, "and these men refrain exceedingly from using *foreign customs* … therefore the Scythians maintain their own customs, and they assign such penalties to those who acquire *foreign customs*" (Hdt. 4.76, 4.80).

According to most Scythians, all non-Scythian practices are undesirable. The lack of specificity regarding which cities or which rituals most offend them heightens the extent of the Scythians' animosity. Anacharsis is the first Scythian to commit the crime of displaying foreign habits (4.76–78). During his travels, he witnesses the people of Cyzicus worshipping the Phrygian Greek goddess Cybele, and he vows to worship her if he arrives home safely.[52] This promise marks the commencement of Anacharsis's straying from the formula of "Scythia = pure." After celebrating his safe return with music and dance, he fastens images of Cybele to his clothes (ἐκδησάμενος ἀγάλματα, 4.76), which alters the ways in which other Scythians classify him. Namely, Anacharsis's affixing of non-Scythian iconography onto his Scythian body refutes the xenophobia to which other Scythians firmly adhere. For Anacharsis's fellow Scythians, the portability of these images does not lessen their impact. They understand Anacharsis's individual performance of Phrygian Greek religion as an attempt to redefine the parameters of their own Scythian identity. Unfortunately for Anacharsis, his fellow Scythians cannot divorce his (external) race from his (internal) identity. In other words, they lack Anacharsis's robust ability to separate the perceptions of others from the perception of self. In fact, when the Scythian king sees Anacharsis in the act of worshipping Cybele, he immediately kills him to avert the perceived infiltration of a Greek identity into his people's Scythian identity.[53]

The Scythian ruler Scyles is the second transgressor of his people's xenophobic beliefs (Hdt. 4.78–80). Unlike Anacharsis, whose eyes encourage his interest in foreign customs, Scyles falls prey to words. His bilingual household is the first harbinger of his downfall, in that he grows dissatisfied with Scythian practices after his mother teaches him the Greek language.[54] This linguistic capability echoes a theme that Herodotus articulates before and after this *logos*: the perverse affiliation between bilingualism and

---

[52] Cyzicus is a city in northwest Ionia near Propontis; Cybele is a Phrygian mother-goddess whom Greek colonists in Ionia adopted as their own. Herodotus refers to Cybele as "Mother of the God" rather than by her name, an omission that Hartog (1988: 244–45) treats as a prolepsis that looks ahead to the Ionians' destruction of Cybele's temple (Hdt. 5.102) or a linguistic problem in terms of the gap between this name in the Phrygian language and in Ionic Greek.

[53] It is curious to note the flexibility of this perceived Greek identity, in that Anacharsis engages in diverse Greek religious practices when he worships a Hellenized Phrygian goddess in Ionia.

[54] Scyles's mother is from Istria, a coastal city north of Tomis. The city that indirectly helped him foster love of the Greek language leads to his death, in that his captor in Istria hands him over to his brother, Octamasades, who immediately beheads him (Hdt. 4.80). Through his mixed parentage (Greek mother and Scythian father), Anacharsis was also bilingual; his linguistic competency may have played a role in his interest in Greece (Braund [2008: 350]).

death.[55] Unable to engage publicly in foreign practices, Scyles satisfies his interest in a Greek lifestyle within the gated walls of Olbia.[56] Here, he replaces his Scythian clothes with Greek attire and worships Greek gods.[57] His rejection of Scythian clothes and assumption of Greek dress signal his flexible relationship with his Scythian identity. His practice of Greek rituals becomes part of a performance that does not nullify his Scythian identity. As long as he remains enclosed in the city walls and away from the prying eyes of other Scythians, he believes that his sartorially inspired performance will go unchallenged. This geographic presumption speaks to Herodotus's masterful reshaping of physical distance. That is, comparable to the shifting parameters of geography that thwart Cambyses's failed trip to Aithiopia, distance remains a malleable category in the Scythian *logos*. No amount of distance can protect Scyles from fast-traveling Scythian xenophobia. On encountering him, other Scythians perceive his choice of dress as an insidious symbol of his preferences and loyalties: Scythia is no longer his top priority.[58] From their perspective, Scyles's Scythian identity has undergone a semiotic death, and his new dress is symbolic of a new life.[59] To offset the damage that Scyles has wreaked upon the joint Scythian race/identity of his compatriots, his brother murders him.[60]

Scyles's sartorial choices call to mind the Danaids' attire in Aeschylus's *Suppliants* (Chapter 3). Unlike Scyles's secretive assumption of attire, the Danaids openly acknowledge their sartorial difference. They affirm Pelasgus's statement that their clothes look different but insist that this does not affect their Argive Greek identity (εἴρηκας ἀμφὶ κόσμον ἀψευδῆ

---

[55] Other instances of bilingualism leading to violence: Scythians murder bilingual Median children in order to take revenge on the Median ruler who insulted their hunting skills (Hdt. 1.73); the Pelasgians murder bilingual children of Pelasgian fathers and Athenian mothers as a way to curtail the arrogance that Athenian mothers inculcated into their children (6.138); see also Harrison (1998) and Munson (2005: 69). Somehow, the trilingualism of the Fish-eaters increases their efficacy and does not lead to their demise.

[56] Olbia was a commercial center near the river of Borysthenes inhabited by Ionian Greeks (Hdt. 4.2). During their extended wait outside of the city walls waiting for Scyles to finish entertaining himself within the city, the Scythians presumably encounter Borysthenites. Curiously enough, Herodotus's conversation with the Scythian guard Tymnes (one of his sources about Anacharsis's demise) perhaps took place outside these city walls (Braund [2008: 355–56]).

[57] While in Olbia, Scyles also marries a Borysthenite woman. A few comedic examples of sartorial alterations in homage to adopted loyalties include Athenian ambassadors to Media who adopt Median clothes upon their return home (Aristophanes, *Acharnians* 64–99), and Laconophilic Athenians who grow their hair long as a way to express their admiration of Sparta (Aristophanes, *Clouds* 1098–1101).

[58] Munson (2001: 128).   [59] I use the concept of a semiotic death after Wyles (2011: 65–66).

[60] Tymnes's reconstruction of Anacharsis's family tree suggests that Anacharsis also died at the hands of his brother (Hdt. 4.76).

λόγον, "you have spoken not falsely about our clothes," *Supp.* 246).[61] They rely on verbal, rather than visual, markers to convince Pelasgus that his perception of them and their own conception of themselves coincide. Stuck in a world where vision has inordinate power, Scyles mistakenly believes that hiding from Scythians will protect him from their inability to disaggregate his internal identity and external race.[62] Once his fellow Scythians see him practicing Bacchic rites, his days are numbered because his transgressive mimesis troubles their conceptualization of identity and race as a shared category.[63] They assume that an individual's sartorial appearance determines who they are, and they treat any deviation from this Scythian belief as a direct attack on their own Scythian identity.

The preference for rigid distinctions at the expense of plural perspectives haunts twentieth-century scholarship about Herodotus's *Histories*. In particular, in his analysis of the lengthy Scythian ethnography (Hdt. 4.1–82), François Hartog maintains that Herodotus's rhetoric of otherness is an operation of translation.[64] While Hartog's argument about the self-reflexive potential of ethnography is helpful, Herodotus goes beyond conveying the "other" as a variant of the "same."[65] He rejects a reductive approach to "foreignness" with his presentation of shrewd characters. The Aithiopian king turns the trope of ignorant foreigner on its head, and Anacharsis and Scyles attempt to strip Greek religion of its foreign connotations. Using different tactics, they arrive at the same goal: to highlight the relativity of foreignness within the purview of the dominant gaze.[66]

---

[61] Herodotus identifies Pelasgians as an autochthonous people from whom the Athenians descend (1.57; Munson [2005: 7–13, esp. 10–11]).

[62] A symmetrical and inverted relationship between Scythia and Egypt runs throughout the *Histories*. In terms of symmetry, Borsythenes is described as the second most powerful river, the Nile as the first (4.53). In terms of inversion, Egypt claims to be the oldest nation (2.2), and Scythia claims to be the youngest (4.5). For more examples, see *Aer.* 18–20; Hartog (1988: 14–15); Redfield (1985: 106–09); and Vasunia (2001: 92–100, esp. 96–98). Thomas (2000: 42–74, 78–79) adds a Scythia-Aithiopia axis to Herodotus's Scythia-Egypt model.

[63] Bhabha (1984: 126) points out that mimicry can never bridge the cultural division between two groups.

[64] "Une rhétorique de l'altérité est dans son fond opération de traduction: elle vise à faire passer l'autre au même (*tradere*)" (Hartog [1980: 249]). Curiously, the inclusion of a single letter (*r*), transforms the Fish-eaters from spies (*katopt-*) into mirrors (*katoptr-*).

[65] In his landmark text that examines Herodotus's presentation of non-Greeks, Hartog scarcely discusses Aithiopians. He refers to them five times to provide auxiliary information about Scythia, Dionysus, wine, and southern nomads (Hartog [1988]: 44, 76, 166, 176–77, 194]).

[66] See also my discussion of Munson (2001, 2005) in Section 4.3 below. In Dewald's (1990: 221) critique of Hartog's binary structure, she helpfully interprets Herodotus's observation about the shifting power dynamics of cities (Hdt. 1.5) as proof that "[Herodotus's] mirrors are not bolted on their walls."

4.3 Rerouting Alterity

In the Aithiopian *logos*, Herodotus portrays Aithiopians as prominent figures. When he explains that the "Aithiopians are said to be the strongest and most beautiful of all people," Herodotus's choice of the passive voice authorizes the Aithiopians to be the subjects of this declarative statement (οἱ δὲ Αἰθίοπες οὗτοι … λέγονται εἶναι μέγιστοι καὶ κάλλιστοι ἀνθρώπων πάντων, 3.20). Further downplaying his authoritative role, Herodotus allows the Aithiopians to speak on their own behalf: νόμοισι δὲ καὶ ἄλλοισι χρᾶσθαι αὐτούς φασι κεχωρισμένοισι τῶν ἄλλων ἀνθρώπων, "they say that they use other laws that are separate from other people" (3.20). In addition to emphasizing his recurring interest in people's laws (νόμοισι), Herodotus recalibrates the categories of center and periphery with this turn of phrase. He bends the trope of alterity as the Aithiopians use "other laws" and then clarify that said laws are separate from "other people." The adjectives *alloisi* and *allōn* underscore this collision. The Aithiopians are extraordinary in relation to their customs (νόμοισι … ἄλλοισι, "*other* laws") and a core community which is separate from other men (τῶν ἄλλων ἀνθρώπων, "of *other* people"). The malleability of "otherness" undercuts the concept of "foreign" because the Aithiopians embody alterity and regard others as separate from them. Simply put, they coexist at the center and margins of the world into which they have been circumscribed.

Exemplifying what Rosaria Vignolo Munson terms an "unstable paradigm of alterity," the Aithiopian king is somehow privy to Cambyses's expansionist plans even though he lives at the extreme limits of the Persian empire (Hdt. 3.21).[67] At this moment of convergence, xenophobia loses any fixed value.[68] Although Herodotus's ultimate authority as external narrator reveals the inherent textual colonization at play when one person writes both about and on behalf of others, it is important to note that he positions the Aithiopian king (and not himself) as the narrator of his own story.[69] This shift transports the king from his nomadic Aithiopian hamlet to the

[67] Munson (2001: 122–23). Munson's paradigm can also apply to the Persians because of their adoption of foreign (non-Persian) customs despite their contempt for foreigners; for example, Persians follow the Greek practice of loving boys, they wear Median clothes, and they don Egyptian corselets (Hdt. 1.135). Despite the broad applicability of Munson's "unstable paradigm of alterity," Munson herself privileges the voice of the external narrator over that of Herodotus's internal narrators.

[68] Munson (2001) fleetingly refers to Aithiopians seven times: five times in her footnotes (pp. 75 n. 88, 98 n. 165, 108 n. 186, 145 n. 31, 167 n. 91), once in the main text as one of many "hard" societies (p. 77), and once as an example of a "soft primitive" society (p. 79). Munson (2005) refers to Aithiopians seven times: thrice in the footnotes (pp. 20 n. 9, 56 n. 113, 79 n. 50) and four times in the main text (pp. 24, 25, 68, 74).

[69] The phrase "textual colonization" builds on Rutledge (2000), who uses it to describe Tacitus's transformation of ancient Britain into a Roman space via negation and appropriation (i.e. tools of textual colonization) in the *Agricola*. Modern anthropologists endeavor to prevent this from occurring by relegating their roles to that of "participant-observers" in the field and/or including

Egyptian world of the Fish-eaters, the Persian world of Cambyses, and the Greek world of Herodotus.

Herodotus enables the Aithiopians to dictate their own tales through subtle intertextual allusions and ironies. In the passage below, the Aithiopian king presents an ethos of empowerment in the face of Cambyses's intended treachery:

> εἰ γὰρ ἦν δίκαιος, οὔτ' ἂν ἐπεθύμησε χώρης ἄλλης ἢ τῆς ἑωυτοῦ, οὔτ' ἂν ἐς δουλοσύνην ἀνθρώπους ἦγε ὑπ' ὧν μηδὲν ἠδίκηται.

> If he [Cambyses] were just, he would not desire land other than his own, nor would he lead people who have never harmed him into slavery. (Hdt. 3.21)

The Aithiopian king's accusation of deception and injustice suggests a provocative intertextual play that exploits a trope in Persian self-ethnography, specifically Darius I's self-representation as honest and just in the Behistun inscription.[70] Looming approximately sixty meters up a cliff over a spring-fed pool, a trilingual inscription atop a relief on the holy mountain of Behistun depicts Darius's ideology in 522/21 BCE.[71] In the relief, Darius dwarfs everyone as he leads two Persian weapon-bearers and faces a row of nine kings in bondage who stand in chronological order of their defeat (see Figure 4.2).[72] Darius holds a leash in his left hand and extends his right hand upward. Ahuramazda, a prominent Persian god, floats above him, and another defeated king lies trapped beneath his left foot.[73] By describing himself as a humble and righteous ruler who owes his

their subject's voices in their published ethnographies. Postcolonial scholars also challenge textual colonization (Ashcroft, Griffiths, and Tiffin [1989: 78–115, esp. 91–97 and 104–15]).

[70] This rare find is especially exciting in its preservation of a Persian perspective of Persian people, a refreshing alternative to the mostly Greek perspectives of Achaemenid history (Briant [2002]; Lecoq [1974]; Root [1979]; Wiesehöfer [1996]); Kennedy (2013) examines the iconography of Darius in official Achaemenid art. Other extant Persian sources that discuss Aithiopia include a description of a sumptuous feast during which spices were imported from Aithiopia, and a letter from a man in Egypt to his wife in Aithiopia (Kuhrt [2007: 605, 759]).

[71] Behistun corresponds to Bisitun in modern-day Iran. The Behistun relief measures 3 m by 5.5 m. There are minor differences in each part of the trilingual (Elamite, Babylonian Akkadian, and Old Persian) inscription.

[72] The final king (Skunka the Scythian, whom Darius defeated in 519 BCE) was added to the relief in 518 BCE. Although the Aithiopian king is not portrayed in this scene, the depiction of Aithiopians bearing gifts to the Persian ruler in the Apadana relief (discussed in Section 2.2) suggest an established gift-exchange between the two groups (Morkot [1991: 324]).

[73] On the Behistun monument, Darius's compromise between real and idealized renditions of truth is apparent. For instance, his assertion that he defeated nine kings and his restructuring of events privilege positive self-representation over accuracy (Windfuhr [1994: 272]; Kuhrt [2007: 136–40]); see also Darius's delayed acknowledgment of his six co-conspirators until the final paragraph of this inscription and Herodotus's recounting of Darius's trickery in 3.68–88.

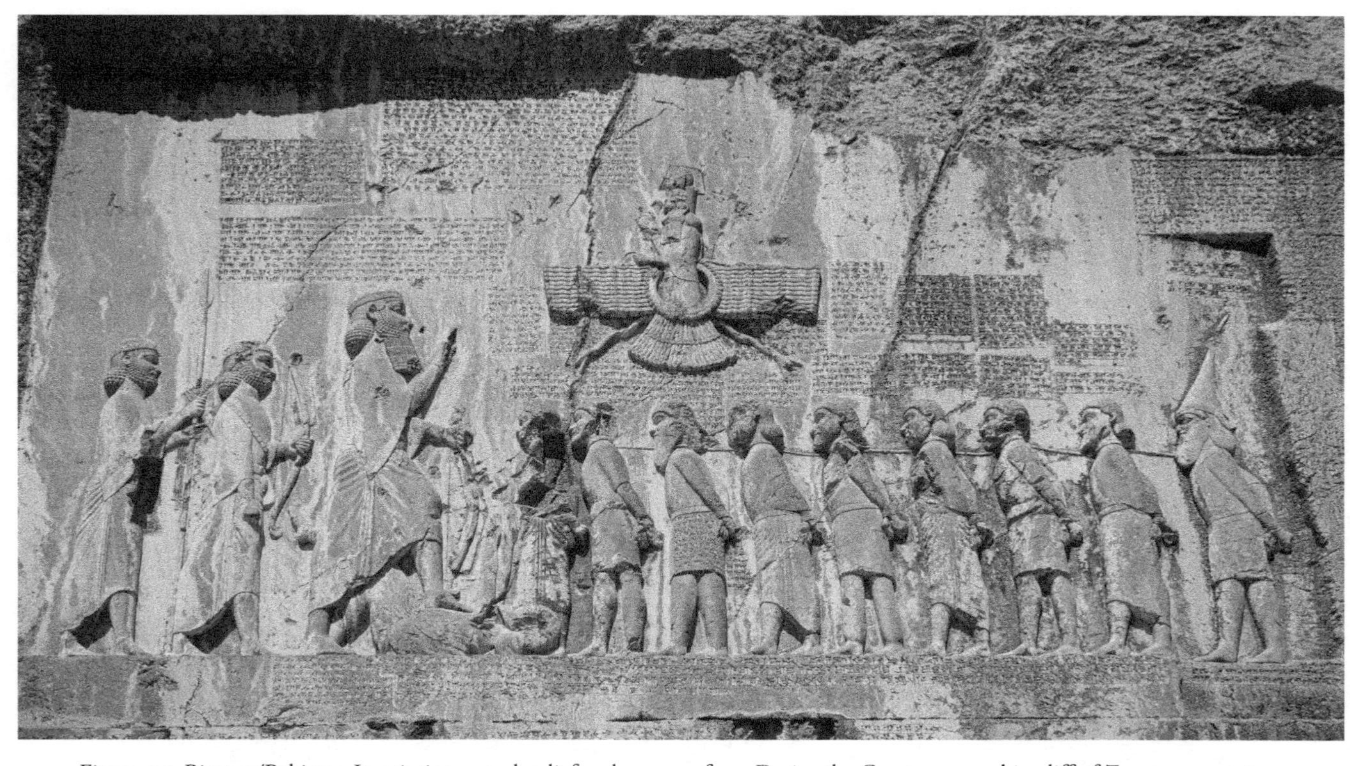

Figure 4.2 Bisotun/Behistun Inscription, a rock relief and message from Darius the Great, engraved in cliff of Zagros mountains, Kermanshah Province, Iran. © Jean-Philippe Tournut/Getty Images.

accomplishments to Ahuramazda in the text inscribed above the relief, Darius strives to manipulate his public image for contemporary and future audiences. He fights against the tenuous nature of empire (and mortality) with a monument that bolsters his image.[74] In chapters 52–57 of this long inscription, he repudiates the "liar kings" who falsely claim descent from the rulers of Persia, Babylon, and Media. Their attempted coups contrast his desire to follow the path of righteousness (chapters 63–64).[75]

By planting Persian ethnographic knowledge in the mouth of the Aithiopian king (εἰ γὰρ ἦν δίκαιος, "if he were just," 3.21), Herodotus briefly nudges his contemporary readers away from the ethereal Aithiopian realm into their historical present in the fifth century BCE. This intertextual allusion spills in the other direction as well, in that the Aithiopian king may be ventriloquizing a Persian voice in order to call his own existence into question. Cambyses may well be on a futile quest to attack a group of people who do not exist. It is also possible that the shared moral values of the Aithiopians and Persians represent a unified threat to the Greek world. In the Aithiopian *logos*, Herodotus has left it to his readers to determine the effect of this allusion. My decision to situate Aithiopia in its own historical context provides a final, subversive analysis of the Aithiopian king's advice to Cambyses. Within this setting, his words amount to a critique of the Persian colonizing project. The king's implicit jab against Cambyses's moral character allows him a chance to write back to the Persian empire.[76] Poking through layers of mediation, the king delivers his "reciprocal critical perception," to employ Renato Rosaldo's language, to deliver a message to Cambyses. "Reciprocal critical perception" describes the phenomenon in which a native person explains her or his community and critically evaluates that of her or his ethnographer.[77] In alignment with

---

[74] Munson (2001: 272–73).

[75] See also Herodotus's list of the three most important traits that Persians value, one of which is honesty (1.136).

[76] My formulation "to write back to the empire" is a rewording of the punning "the empire writes back," coined by Salman Rushdie (1982), which in turn inspired the title to Ashcroft, Griffiths, and Tiffin's *The Empire Writes Back: Theory and Practice in Post-Colonial Literature* (1989). My adoption of this language puts the Aithiopian king in the company of contemporary postcolonial writers who dismantle the binary model of center and periphery. Nonetheless, I remain mindful of Mwangi's (2009) assertion that "writing back to empire" can reproduce one-way development of ideas (from a source text to an empire) and preclude multidirectional movement.

[77] Rosaldo (1989: 64). Munson uses Rosaldo's term to explain the Aithiopian king's distaste for bread (Hdt. 3.22; discussed in Munson [2001: 145 n. 31]). The Aithiopian king's comparison of bread to dung, a fertilizer for wheat crops, potentially reveals his knowledge about cereal cultivation in Persia. In Bosak-Schroeder's (2016: 32–34) examination of what they deem "the ecology of health," they discuss the Aithiopian king's gustatory preferences alongside the collapse of the human diet during the Persians' cannibalistic march.

this term, the Aithiopian king ably defines the habits of his people (Hdt. 3.22–23) and subtly points out the dangers of unchecked ambition.

My emphasis on the Aithiopian king's rerouting of Cambyses's imperial project serves a twofold purpose: it brings the Aithiopians closer to Herodotus's fifth-century readers, *and* it highlights the potential signifying power that those who are deemed foreigners can possess even within restrictive contexts. When the Aithiopian king alludes to Persian customs within a general query about Cambyses's leadership style, he momentarily transforms the Persians into secondary characters who exist in an Aithiopia-centered world.[78] In this way, the Aithiopian king belies his geographical location at the furthest limits of the Persian and Greek worlds. This fits into a larger motif that Herodotus promotes in his Aithiopian *logos*: geography is a trope to exploit, not a location to map.[79] Similarly, the Fish-eaters travel north from Elephantine to Memphis (where Cambyses briefs them) and south from Memphis to Aithiopia, then they double back north to Memphis (where they update Cambyses) and finally return south to Elephantine with ease. But even one-third of this distance becomes an impassibly protracted trek that Cambyses fails to complete on his under-equipped and ill-planned military expedition to Aithiopia.[80] Altogether, these manipulations of vast distances heighten the dramatic tension in the *logos* and dismantle a fixed notion of foreignness.

Herodotus's deft maneuvering of geography spills into his accounts of other sojourns to Aithiopia. In his inquiry on the source of the Nile (Hdt. 2.28–34), he is unable to travel beyond Elephantine. He makes up for physical constraints by acquiring knowledgeable informants who provide him with

---

[78] Overlapping with my claim that the Aithiopian king indirectly reproaches Persian expansion, Török (2014: 125, 130) argues that Aithiopians are "expedient particles of Herodotus' world" who offset Herodotus's inability to create a self-contained Aithiopian *logos*. While Török rightly recognizes the double duty that Herodotus's ethnographies can serve, he overlooks the specific moment of subtle genius in the Aithiopian *logos*. The broad scope of Török's discussion relegates the Aithiopians to a passive role, in which they are only relevant as they apply to the political context in fifth-century Athens, and his overlooking of the agency present in the Aithiopian king's admonition muffles the Aithiopians' voices. Irwin (2014) understands the Aithiopian king's rebuke as representative of a larger trope of political reproach in ancient Greece. Nonetheless, her rendering of the Aithiopian *logos* as a tool with which to analyze the Greek political situation in the fourth century BCE minimizes the significance of the Aithiopian king's subversive intervention. I align my analysis with Moyer (2011: 82), who critiques the tendency to treat non-Greek groups as "passive object[s] of intellectual imperialism, without regard for the cultural self-representations of the supposed object."

[79] See also Mardonius's assertion that Xerxes subdued the Aithiopians (Hdt. 7.9) even though the failure of Cambyses's invasion was well known (7.18); Xerxes's conquered Aithiopians were perhaps a subset of the Aithiopians who lived near the Egyptian border and fought alongside Persia against Greece (7.69).

[80] Powell (1935: 150); Romm (1992: 59); Irwin (2014: 60–63, in which she engages with Powell, who views this conflation of travel as evidence that the Aithiopian *logos* was a later addition to the main story).

details about areas south of the First Cataract.[81] Based on the results of this fact-finding mission, Herodotus vaguely attributes the source of the Nile to the scorching, uninhabited desert southwest of Elephantine, a location that roughly corresponds with the site where Cambyses's men began practicing cannibalism. This intratextual allusion widens the gap between tyranny and geography, in that Cambyses's imperialistic desires cannot bypass an impassible landscape.[82] Unlike Cambyses, Herodotus does not attempt to tame geography to suit his curiosity. Instead, he diverts his attention to the people who live along the Nile, such as the people of Elephantine and Aithiopia.[83]

Concurrent with his geographic imprecision regarding the source of the Nile, Herodotus offers loose categorizations of people living in the vicinity of the First Cataract. He labels Elephantine as the home of the Elephantine Aithiopians (Hdt. 2.29), a group that is distinct from Egyptians and nomadic Aithiopians. He later contradicts the delineation of Elephantine Aithiopians when he explains that the Fish-eaters from Elephantine travel to Aithiopia and learn about Aithiopian habits (3.22–23). Herodotus's slippery handling of Egyptians and Aithiopians recurs when the Egyptian ruler Psammetichus exhorts Egyptian defectors in Aithiopia to return home to their children and wives. In response to Psammetichus's command, one Egyptian man brazenly gestures to his genitals and retorts that the preponderance of his sperm will allow him to establish a new family in his adopted country (2.30).[84] Herodotus's inconsistent rendering of Egyptians and Aithiopians prompts readers to recalibrate any conception of the ancient world that presumes rigid boundaries. In its place, Herodotus reconfigures cartography to measure countries' points of contact rather than physical distance.

4.4 Conclusion: Reframing Absence

In summary, I propose a reorientation of Herodotus's map of the ancient Greek world. At the center, I place Aithiopia, a country whose king stages

---

[81] ἄλλου δὲ οὐδενὸς οὐδὲν ἐδυνάμην πυθέσθαι … τὸ δ' ἀπὸ τούτου ἀκοῇ ἤδη ἱστορέων, "I wasn't able to learn anything from anyone … from this point [at Elephantine], I inquired and listened" (Hdt. 2.29).

[82] In his poetry, Lucan understands tyrants' quest to find the source of the Nile as a manifestation of their imperialistic desire (*Civil War* 10.268–33; discussed in Burstein [1976]). Cf. the ambitions of nineteenth-century British explorers John Hanning Speke and Sir Richard Burton to locate the source of the White Nile, one of the main tributaries of the Nile.

[83] Citing the geographer Agatharchides of Cnidus, Diodorus Siculus (1.41.4–10) attributes the source of the Nile to heavy rainfall from the mountains of Aithiopia. Subsequent geographers correctly identify Lake Tana, in the highlands of northern Ethiopia, as the main reservoir for the Blue Nile.

[84] ἡμερώτεροι γεγόνασι Αἰθίοπες, ἤθεα μαθόντες Αἰγύπτια, "Aithiopians became rather gentle after they learned Egyptian customs" (Hdt. 2.30). According to the geographer Strabo (17.1.2), a woman ruled this squad of defectors.

such a compelling production of Aithiopian knowledge and wealth that Cambyses eagerly seeks to witness its glory for himself. By using an internal narrator who speaks out against imperial threats, Herodotus briefly reduces the degrees of separation between his readers and the characters embedded in his *logos*. The Aithiopian king transforms his people from hollow Homeric projections or mirrors of Greek/Persian imperial ambitions into shrewd internal narrators. Expanding Herodotus's decentered cartography, I include on this map regions where people's appearance overlaps with that of Aithiopians, such as Egypt and India. Another location in this geographic landscape is Scythia, a place where people differ in their assessment of race and identity – namely, Scyles and Anacharsis distinguish between their outward appearance and their self-identification, a broad perspective that they cannot bestow on their Scythian audience. They are trapped in a world where most Scythians rely on sight as singular, unquestioned proof of a merged race and identity. Alongside Herodotus's Aithiopians, these two Scythians reframe the parameters of race, which in turn reshapes the category of foreigner.

Herodotus is part of a community of writers who examine the ongoing instability of "foreigner" in their own contexts. In line with Herodotus's creative descriptions of people and places he has never visited, three twentieth-century writers conceptualize foreigners from a place of absence. Their innovative portrayals of foreigners are not bound up in the foreigners' actual presence.

First, the Greek poet C. P. Cavafy (1863–1933) demonstrates a mutual relationship between an imperial center and those living at the borders in his poem, "Waiting for the Barbarians" (1904):

> What is it that we are waiting for, gathered in the square?
> The barbarians are supposed to arrive today.
>
> Why is there such great idleness inside the Senate house?
> Why are the Senators sitting there, without passing any laws?
> Because the barbarians will arrive today.
> Why should the Senators still be making laws?
> The barbarians, when they come, will legislate.
> . . .
> Why has this uneasiness arisen all at once,
> and this confusion? (How serious the faces have become.)
> Why is it that the streets and squares are emptying so quickly,
> and everyone's returning home in such deep contemplation?
> Because night has fallen and the barbarians haven't come.
> And some people have arrived from the borderlands,
> and said there are no barbarians anymore.

> And now what's to become of us without barbarians.
> Those people were a solution of a sort.[85]

In this poem, the internal narrator pours his anxieties into a reservoir of his own making. These barbarians, "a solution of a sort," answer the narrator's concerns and conversely unsettle his dominance.[86] As the narrator desperately awaits their arrival, the looming threat of the constructed foreigners grows. The barbarians' anticipated presence brings the townspeople together, and their striking absence stirs acute discomfort among them.

Cavafy delivers a simple message in this poem: the barbarians have not arrived. Even so, Cavafy's historical foundation reveals multifaceted ironies. He is a Greek person writing in a poetic idiom both similar to and remote from ancient Greek.[87] That is, he pens his poetry in a city (Alexandria) that has strong historical ties to ancient Greece and a weak association with the modern Greek state. Wendy Belcher's model of discursive possession offers a useful framework with which to approach Cavafy's sophisticated set-up. She envisions historically marginalized people as "producers of discourse" who help to shape representations of their oppressor.[88] Revising Hartog's "rhetoric of otherness" model,[89] she emphasizes the active role that marginalized people play even when they are at the fringes of the dominant discourse. Cavafy's intratextual barbarians fit into Belcher's model of discourse production when he highlights the importance of this peripheral group in relation to the townspeople who have created these projections. The barbarians' disappearance does not occlude their ability to co-constitute the townspeople's identity. In this way, Cavafy's readers enter a circular vortex as they witness the townspeople struggle to exist without the presence of their imagined barbarians.

Cavafy's townspeople are fixated on the idea of barbarians, without whom they cannot edge themselves closer to the political and cultural empire of their circumscribed world. In the act of waiting for people

---

[85] Cavafy (2009: 192–93), translated by Mendelsohn. Krebs (2021) offers a historical example of distant diplomacy in her discussion of Ethiopian embassies traveling to western Europe in the fifteenth and early sixteenth centuries.

[86] Although I am aware of the pejorative use of the modern term "barbarians," I nonetheless employ it in this section solely to signify the authors' nomenclature, not my own. Although Cavafy does not name the town in this poem, the ethnographic model is perhaps a town on the fringes of the Roman empire.

[87] Cavafy's poetic idiom combined the two different dialects of modern Greek: Demotic and Katharevousa.

[88] Belcher (2012: 1). Belcher (2012: 6–18) uses the term "discursive possession" to describe the transcultural model of intertextuality present in Samuel Johnson's *The History of Rasselas: Prince of Abissinia* (1759), a philosophical romance about the peripatetic adventures of an Ethiopian prince.

[89] See Hartog (1988).

geographically and culturally distant from them, the townspeople begin to relegate their control over the foreign presence. This series of uneasy interactions finds an ancient complement in Herodotus's *Histories*. To satisfy his curiosity about Aithiopians, Cambyses is forced to rely on one community of foreigners in order to learn about another. Moreover, Herodotus's intersubjective portrayal of non-Greeks refutes the salience of "the foreigner" as a stable construct. Both he and Cavafy reveal the confounding matrix at play when they write outsiders into literary existence. On a larger scale, Herodotus's Persians, Aithiopians, Egyptians, and Scythians generate a new definition of "foreigner" that does not require a Greek *polis* as its main referent. Despite the fact that they are exteriorized projections of foreigners, these characters subtly attack Hellenocentric perspectives.

Anticipatory encounters between local and foreign people continue to reverberate in J. M. Coetzee's 1980 novel, *Waiting for the Barbarians*. The internal narrator, an aged magistrate at a frontier post, discusses a year of his life during which he and fellow subjects of an unnamed empire anxiously await a barbarian attack on their town. Although the menacing barbarians never materialize, the narrator meets a barbarian woman whom his colleagues eventually kidnap and torture. He hires her to work for him as a cleaner and later becomes "enslaved" to her body.[90] Comparable to Cambyses, who cannot curtail his eagerness to overpower Aithiopia or take responsibility for his rash actions, the narrator attributes his desire for the barbarian woman to her overwhelming nature.[91] His relationship with her leads to his social ostracism and his devolution into a wretched, perpetually hungry creature:

> I cannot wait to be on my rounds, loitering at the barracks gate to sniff the bland watery aroma of oatmeal and wait for the burnt scrapings; cajoling children to throw me down mulberries from the trees; stretching over a garden fence to steal a peach or two ... I eat like a beggar, gobbling down my food with such appetite, wiping my plate so clean that it does the heart good to see it.[92]

During his animal-like quest for food, Coetzee's narrator reveals the tenuousness inherent in the definition of "barbarian." He is no more civilized than his supposedly savage adversaries. Additionally, the soldiers from his town who are tasked with the responsibility of guarding against barbarians transform into brutish vandals who damage the town and

---

[90] Coetzee (1982: 46).   [91] Hayes (2010: 60–71, esp. 67).   [92] Coetzee (1982: 129).

eventually abandon it.[93] In this way, the invisible presence of the dangerous barbarians incites the town to destroy itself. In other words, the unseen barbarians are present within the walls. According to Herodotus, Aithiopians fuel similar sentiments among the Persians. The Fish-eaters' report about bountiful Aithiopia compels Cambyses to lead an ultimately unsuccessful expedition against the Aithiopians. Even though the Aithiopians keep their distance from the Persians, they demolish the monolithic category of foreigners into which Herodotus's readers might be tempted to foist onto them. Their metamorphosis from a remote threat to an uncanny foe reveals the far-reaching power of perception even in the absence of visible evidence.

In a 1985 interview about the ambiguities of *Waiting for the Barbarians*, Coetzee addressed queries about his novel with the response, "everything can be questioned."[94] With this equivocation, he leaves it to his readers to puzzle over whether the town is an allegory for any oppressive state, or no state at all. Considering the resonance of *Waiting for the Barbarians* among various communities fractured by intergroup conflict, Grant Parker suggests that Greco-Roman antiquity "provides a horizon of historical expectation" for the novel.[95] Moving away from a Greco-Roman precedent, Emanuela Tegla interprets the novel as a moral, rather than historical, allegory.[96] Even still, this novel may be an allegory of apartheid South Africa, with the barbarian woman representing Black South African women and men to whom White South Africans meted out various forms of violence. These are all useful lenses with which to understand Coetzee's characters. The fact that no one has complete knowledge of Coetzee's intentions does not disavow any of these conclusions. Similarly, Herodotus's creative characterizations of black people defy simplistic interpretations. His flexible approach to representations of black people invites readers to grapple with plural portrayals of Aithiopians, Egyptians, and Indians.

Naomi Madgett's 1978 poem "In Search of Aunt Jemima (Alias Big Mama)" offers a final comparandum of an eagerly anticipated visitor whose absence speaks volumes. In the closing stanza, Madgett asks:

> Where did Aunt Jemima go? And when
> will she return to reassure us
> that her delicious laughter
> was innocent and wholesome to partake of

---

[93] "[T]he criminals and the civil guards are the same people" (Coetzee [1982: 123]).
[94] Quotation from Dooley (2010: 43).   [95] Parker (2017: 40–41).   [96] Tegla (2011).

and no more subtle
and no more dangerous
than her pancakes?[97]

With these queries, Madgett confronts Americans' one-sided relationship with Aunt Jemima, a minstrel character that Chris Rutt and Charles Underwood repurposed to advertise their pancake mix in 1889. Initially depicted as a grinning Black woman wearing a kerchief (which was replaced with a lace collar and pearl earrings a century later), Aunt Jemima offered middle-class White women what M. M. Manring deems "a slave in a box."[98] That is, Aunt Jemima represented the embodiment of the racist trope that assumes Black women are inherently well placed to serve White families. Channeling the self-serving behavior of Cavafy's and Coetzee's subjects, Madgett's intratextual audience relies on a character who was designed solely to appease them. They reduce Aunt Jemima to her mouth and her pancakes, which allows them to control her body and devour the products of her labor. The audience becomes increasingly desperate for her to return to their kitchens so they can once again consume her "delicious laughter" and nourishing pancakes.[99] Their fragility comes to the fore when they seek to determine whether Aunt Jemima was happy to fill her assigned role or her innocence was a ruse.[100] If the latter is the case, her return may not bode well for them, as her assigned occupation as a kitchen maid would grant her unfettered access into their homes and stomachs.[101] Through her invocation of a manufactured character, Madgett underscores the intense dependency that can exist between a power-hungry audience and someone they label an outsider. In other words, her audience's frenzied longing for a fictional character underscores the monumental role that imaginary characters can have among living people.

Even though the historical context is vastly different for readers in fifth-century BCE Ionia and twentieth-century America, Madgett offers an

---

[97] Madgett (1978: 35).

[98] Manring (1998). See also Harris (1982); Rollins (1985); Turner (1994); Witt (2004); and Johnson (2003: 104–59). Until 2020, the Quaker Oats company defended their use of Aunt Jemima's image to sell ready-made breakfast products. At the time, their website read, "The Aunt Jemima products continue to stand for warmth, nourishment, and trust – qualities you'll find in loving moms from diverse backgrounds who care for and want the very best for their families" (www.auntjemima.com /our-history). After the nationwide protests following George Floyd's murder, the Quaker Oats company replaced the Aunt Jemima brand and logo with the Pearl Milling Company in June 2020.

[99] The intratextual audience's desired acts of consumption resonate eerily in the wake of legalized slavery in twenty-first-century America; I use the language of the wake after Sharpe (2016).

[100] Painter (2010) and DiAngelo (2018) investigate the phenomenon of White fragility.

[101] See also Neely's (2014) subversive rendering of the Aunt Jemima trope.

imaginative way to interpret absence in Herodotus's *Histories*. Her recounting of the departure of an unequivocally constructed character renders absence as an evocative performance.[102] Even after Aunt Jemima exits from the stage of minstrelsy, she still commands her audience's attention. Madgett's reframing of absence encourages modern readers to view Herodotus's Aithiopians as powerful actors who reshape their audiences' perspectives. Even though these Aithiopians are circumscribed within Herodotus's literary world, they manage to tear apart the concept of a singular "foreign" category. In the next chapter, I examine the ways that Lucian builds on Herodotus's disorienting model of foreignness. Turning to satire as his genre of choice, Lucian presents a spectrum of foreignness that includes Scythians, Aithiopians, and Greeks. As a Syrian writing in Greek during a period of Roman rule, Lucian also incorporates his fluid identity into his literary output.

[102] I return to the trope of absence in the conclusion (see Section 7.1).

CHAPTER 5

From Greek Scythians to Black Greeks
A Spectrum of Foreignness in Lucian's Satires

In his second-century CE satires, Lucian presents his readers with a tangled matrix of alterity. As a Syrian writing during the Second Sophistic, a period during which Rome is the dominant power in the Mediterranean, Lucian has an expansive toolbox at his disposal for his literary ventures.[1] His intimate knowledge of the Greek language, the Roman genre of satire, and inhabitants from far-flung parts of the ancient Mediterranean world are on display in his corpus.[2] The various commentators and characters nestled into his approximately eighty satires elude easy categorization. As Lucian writes them, Syrians, Aithiopians, Scythians, and Greeks undermine visual markers as reliable shortcuts to understanding others and themselves. In particular, their uneven reliance on skin color and attire makes for sophisticated performances of race (external categorization) and identity.[3]

---

[1] The intervening years between Herodotus's lifetime (fifth century BCE) and Lucian's (second century CE) yield few extant references to black people in Greek literature. The Hellenistic corpus includes Theophrastus, *Characters* 21.4.2; Theocritus, *Idylls* 3.35, 10.26–28; and Apollonius of Rhodes, *Argonautica* 4.724–29 (discussed Jackie Murray in her forthcoming book *Neikos and the Poetics of Controversy: Apollonius against His Argonautic Predecessors* [Harvard University Press]). I am grateful to her for sharing a draft. The German philologist Erwin Rohde (1876) revived the term "Second Sophistic," first coined by the sophist Philostratus (*Lives of the Sophists* 481) to describe the perceived resurgence of Greek heritage in Greek-speaking cities during the second to fourth centuries CE. Whitmarsh points out the shortcomings of this label, in that it ignores the cultural hybridity that is ever-present in Greek literature written during this period (2011a: 218–19) and anachronistically creates "an impossible idealization of pure, untainted aristocratic Greek tradition" (2013: 3). I echo Whitmarsh's concession that the term is sometimes necessary for clarity and consistency in the discipline of Classics (2001a: 270 n. 4).

[2] Romans touted the genre of satire as their own invention: (*satura quidem tota nostra est*, "however, satire is completely ours," Quintilian, *Institutio Oratoria* 10.1.93) even though traces date back to fifth-century Athens (Hendrickson [1927]; Freudenburg [2005: 1–19]). Freudenburg (2001) and Gowers (2012) offer authoritative introductions to the genre of Roman satire.

[3] In partial agreement with Ní Mheallaigh (2014), Richter (2017), and Rostad (2019), I treat Lucian's non-Syrian characters as literary figures rather than veiled representations of Lucian's own views. Conversely, see Whitmarsh (2001b: 29). Regarding Lucian's career, see Anderson (1976), Branham (1989), Popescu (2009), Ní Mheallaigh (2014), and Bozia (2015).

Rey Chow's concept of the xenophone helps to situate Lucian's diverse literary strategies. As part of his meditation on the ways that Chinua Achebe and Ngũgĩ wa Thiong'o repurpose the English language, Chow defines the xenophone as a linguistic domain in which nonnative writers of English disrupt the presumed monolingualism of the anglophone archive. These writers unleash linguistic multiplicities that speak to a wide range of audiences.[4] Although the criterion of linguistic outsider does not apply to Lucian, who grew up in the multilingual city of Samosata, Lucian does unsettle the category of "foreigner" (*xenos*) via the language (*phōnē*) that he places in the mouth of his characters. His polysemous shaping of language deconstructs the normative parameters of "Greek" within his literary landscape. In other words, he uses language to untether "Greek" from a particular location and refashions the category as a supple literary phenomenon.[5]

In this chapter, I examine Lucian's complicated model of difference.[6] Starting with an overview of his methods of categorizing people in his second-century CE satires, I discuss Lucian's strategies of narratorial self-presentation in the religious treatise *On the Syrian Goddess*. I also draw attention to Lucian's treatment of black Aithiopians in *The Ignorant Book Collector*, a diatribe against a wealthy Syrian man eager to expand his library, and *Hermotimus*, a philosophical dialogue in which a hypothetical Aithiopian presumes that everyone shares his black skin color.[7] Next, as a trilogy of sorts, Lucian's Scythian satires offer vivid examples of characters whose interpersonal exchanges reveal their nuanced understanding of themselves and others – that is, their understanding of identity and race. Lucian sets the stage for these encounters in his *prolalia* ("preamble") titled *The Scythian or the Consul*, in which he creates a mutable landscape that makes space for both a Syrian and a Scythian

---

[4] Chow (2014: 35–60, esp. 59–60). Achebe (1965) insists on English as his preferred linguistic medium; Ngũgĩ (1986) commits to writing in his native Gĩkũyũ and Swahili (discussed in Chapter 1, p. 1).

[5] Woolf (1994) and Gleason (2006) discuss Greek-speaking provinces in the eastern Roman empire; MacMullen (1966) and the contributions in both Adams, Janse, and Swain (2002) and Mullen and James (2012) explore multilingualism in the Roman empire; Andrade (2013) focuses on Greco-Roman Syria.

[6] Derrida's theory of *différance* warrants mention alongside Lucian's model of difference, in that both acknowledge the conceptual oppositions that can occur within language and the importance of context in deciphering a word's meaning. See also Derrida's (1998) dynamic relationship with language, discussed in Chow (2014: 19–33).

[7] Lucian relies on variants of *aithio-* and *mela-* to describe black people. In addition to the examples discussed in this chapter, other instances of black people in Lucian's corpus include the half-black man (μέλας) whom Ptolemy I captures and brings to Egypt (*A Literary Prometheus* 4) and the sight of black men (μέλανες) among animals in the sea (*Dialogue of the Sea-Gods* 15). See also Lucian's iterations of *mela-* to describe animals and ghosts (*The Liar* 24 and 31, respectively).

man in Macedon. A continuation of this story, *Toxaris: A Friendship Dialogue*, explores the reconciliation of dissimilarities between a Scythian and a Greek man who both stubbornly insist upon the superiority of their own countrymen. Concluding these Scythian-Greek pairings, *Anacharsis* recounts a conversation between the Scythian traveler Anacharsis and the Athenian sage Solon while they observe Athenian athletes training in the gymnasium. Throughout this dialogue, Anacharsis treats the Athenians' athletic regimen as an epitome of a Greek identity. Unlike Herodotus's iteration of Anacharsis as a worshipper of the Phrygian Greek goddess Cybele (4.76–78),[8] Lucian's Anacharsis refuses to admire the transformative exercises that turn Athenian men into black, sun-kissed Greeks. Altogether, this trio of texts reveals Lucian's recurring preoccupation with the parameters of foreignness in his literary world. As a nod to satire's continued relationship with identity and skin color, I will close the chapter with a look at Paul Beatty's novel, *The Sellout* (2015), which offers a complementary take on the absurd masquerade of Blackness in the twenty-first century.

5.1 Performance of *paideia* in the Second Century CE

Writing at the height of the Roman empire, Lucian pushes the already flexible categories of topography, belonging, and indicators of recognition to extreme limits.[9] In the second-century CE, Greek identity is no longer embedded in religion, as had been the case for the Danaids (see Chapter 3), nor does physical location occupy an important role in identity formation, as it did for Herodotus's characters (Chapter 4). Instead, the mastery of Greek learning (*paideia*) enables people with divergent religions and homelands to transform into members of the generic category of "Greeks." For his part, Lucian wields his erudite education as a tool with which he openly ridicules sixth-century BCE Greek xenophobia, thereby alerting his readers to the ways in which people's curiosity about others can coincide with the preservation of their own identity.[10] Through his two-way dialogue between past and present worlds, Lucian bridges gaps between two time periods while also building critical distance between

---

[8] Discussed in Chapter 4, p. 114.

[9] In all my discussions of the Roman empire, I use the lowercase "e" to democratize the language of empire. See Table P.1.

[10] I label those who encounter Lucian's satires as his "readers," rather than his "audience," to recognize the written transmission of Lucian's corpus. Nonetheless, he grants a multisensory experience to his readers via his vivid descriptions and performative tropes.

them.[11] In other words, his Janus-like satires pull sixth-century BCE Athens into the second century CE without overlooking the tensions underpinning claims of a Greek identity during the Roman empire.

Lucian invites his readers to enter an imagined sixth-century Greece in which loosely associated city-states have morphed into a collective, dominant entity. Nonetheless, Lucian's readers encounter Roman hegemony poking out through the text, in that Roman occupation of Greek city-states contributes to the creation of the broad category "Greece." For all his railing against Rome, Lucian embraces Rome's unification of Greece in his satires. His vibrant cast of characters participates in the self-fashioned process of "becoming Greek," to paraphrase Maud Gleason, via successful performances of *paideia*. While Lucian's Syrians, Aithiopians, and Scythians engage with the tangled reciprocity of a "Greek" identity in a circumscribed world, Lucian's contemporary readers grapple with this complex trope in real time. Despite any attempts to weave themselves into the tapestry of sixth-century Greece, they remain subjects of the Roman empire.[12]

The diverse performances of Lucian's fictional sixth-century BCE characters resonate in his second-century CE world. Nathanael Andrade elaborates:

> If origins, models, genres, and pasts were not so much imitated as "staged" and "produced" in Lucian's corpus, it was in part because Lucian's texts represented a world in which performance generated origins, models, pasts, and thereby identities and social categories. They framed the world as a "theater" or "stage" (*theatron* or *skēnē*) in which identities, social categories, and pasts were produced through spectacles of performance in which actors (*hypokritai*) created "characters" (*schēmata*) and "faces/masks" (*prosōpa*).[13]

Calling to mind Saidiya Hartman's innovative rendering of performative spaces, Andrade draws attention to the phenomenon of performance that is

---

[11] Branham (1989); Bozia (2015: 76). See also Richter (2017), who treats Lucian's tripartite exploration of Syrianness, Greekness, and Romanness as an interconnected literary trope.

[12] Gleason (1995). The transformative process of "becoming Greek" also complements my discussion of Doležal's "becoming Black," in Chapter 1, p. 7. Whitmarsh (2005b: 23–40) provides a helpful overview of performance culture during the Second Sophistic. Camerotto (1998), Andrade and Rush (2016), and Gallogly (2019) focus on the various performance contexts embedded within Lucian's satires. In terms of genre, Karavas (2005) and Schmitz (2010) trace Lucian's relationship with tragedy; Peterson (2019: 117–42) explores Lucian's allusions to Old Comedy; Konstan (2010) highlights tragic and comedic undertones in Lucian's corpus; and Lada-Richards (2007) examines Lucian's use of pantomime dancing.

[13] Andrade (2013: 271–72).

particularly acute in the context of the Second Sophistic.[14] By crafting characters who engage with multiple identities while reserving the right to critique them, Lucian orchestrates a production that mirrors intricate identity formations in Roman-ruled Greece. On the stage of satire, characters redraw the boundaries of foreignness, which in turn inspires a dynamic reworking of race (external categorization). Different identities morph into masks that they try on and make their own.[15] In fact, Lucian's characters employ the Danaids' stratagem as they repurpose a mask of difference in ways that challenge the already vexed status of "Greek identity" among their internal audience and external readers. As Lucian's Scythians, Aithiopians, and Athenians perform different iterations of Greek identity, his contemporaries witness these productions in real time.

Turning his focus inward, Lucian transforms his own narratorial presence into a mask that he molds at will.[16] Apposite to my earlier distinction between Herodotus's perspective within and outside of the *Histories*, I differentiate between Lucian the narrator who wedges himself into an imagined Greek world and Lucian the writer who lives in a Roman-ruled one. Lucian's masks work as a unit: the quotidian performances orchestrated by Lucian the narrator amplify the *paideia* of Lucian the writer. For example, at the beginning and end of *On the Syrian Goddess*, an account of Lucian the narrator's pilgrimage to Hierapolis, the narrator proudly acknowledges his Syrian identity.[17] Nonetheless, he relies solely on Greek names to discuss Hierapolitan deities. Furthermore, his use of the Ionic dialect, autopsy, and secondhand information likens his satire to a Herodotean ethnography.[18] Exploiting an opportunity to flaunt his education in the treatise's closing chapter, the narrator outlines Syrian rituals regarding hair (*Syr. D.* 60). Echoing the Greek custom, young Syrian men dedicate the first shaving of their beard to the gods. Unique to Syria, Syrian children place a lock of hair that they have grown since

---

[14] Hartman (1997). See also Section 1.2 above.

[15] Anderson (1976: 18–19); Whitmarsh (2001b: 247–95).

[16] Goldhill (2002) examines Lucian's interest in masks.

[17] Lightfoot (2003: 174–84); Swain (1996: 307–08); Elsner (2001). γράφω δὲ Ἀσσύριος ἐών, "I write as a Syrian" (Luc. *Syr. D.* 1); μευ ἐν τῷ ἱρῷ καὶ ὁ πλόκαμος καὶ τὸ οὔνομα, "both my hair and my name are [inscribed] in the [Syrian] temple" (*Syr. D.* 60). Elsner (2001: 126–27) elaborates on the inconsistencies in the opening chapter of *On the Syrian Goddess*. Barring the title of the text (Περὶ τῆς Συρίης θεοῦ) the narrator consistently uses *Assyrios* as an adjective and *Syriē* as a noun (Lightfoot [2003: 287]). Elsner (2001: 124 n. 6) and Lightfoot (2003: 184–208) discuss the controversy surrounding the authorship of *On the Syrian Goddess*.

[18] Another example of the Greek linguistic predominance occurs when the narrator refers to Atagartis as Syrian Hera (τῆς Ἥρης τῆς Ἀσσυρίης, *Syr. D.* 1). Elsner (2001: 126–28), Goldhill (2002: 78–82), and Lightfoot (2003: 184–208) examine other Herodotean allusions in *On the Syrian Goddess*.

birth in a silver or gold jar.[19] They nail the jar, inscribed with their names, to the wall of the temple. Well versed in rituals of his own people and others, the narrator lists a Greek ritual alongside a non-Greek one. In effect, his convergence of these two religions reworks the boundaries of foreignness.

Ever the cunning narrator, Lucian's reticence to name himself is part of his furtive performance of self-presentation.[20] Steering clear of reflexive onomastics, he inches closer to pinning down his name at the end of *On the Syrian Goddess*. In the final chapter, Lucian the narrator describes the act of his own (unspecified) name being inscribed onto the wall of the Syrian temple at Hierapolis as part of a Syrian tonsorial practice: καὶ ἔτι μευ ἐν τῷ ἱρῷ καὶ ὁ πλόκαμος καὶ τὸ οὔνομα ("even now, both my hair and my name are [inscribed] in the [Syrian] temple," *Syr. D.* 60). His explicit affiliation with Syrian rituals ensures a concluding homage to his Syrian identity.[21] This anonymous Syrian mask allows Lucian the writer to resist the self-promotional ideology of his lived world while staking his claim as somebody important within it. At the same time, Lucian's name game dislocates the categorization of "other" in the literary sphere. He privileges Syria as a religious center that is mediated through the linguistic medium of Ionic Greek. This mutual codependency between Syria and Greek Ionia weakens the distinction between "foreigner" and "Greek." As a final twist, despite the realities of Roman imperial might in the second century CE, Lucian devises an interdependent worldview that is devoid of Roman intervention. This selective cosmopolitanism is emblematic of Lucian's revivalist approach to Greek literature. Tinkering with the components of his *paideia*, he constructs a unified Greece that is both a product of Rome and far removed from Rome's historical purview.

In *On the Syrian Goddess*, Lucian's narratorial self-presentation discourages readers from labeling him as solely Syrian or solely Greek. He redirects his readers' perception of difference by introducing them to a character who determines his own parameters of Syrian identity. Lucian the narrator faces fresh scrutiny when he asks his esteemed Macedonian audience to look beyond his Syrian identity and assign him a Scythian one instead

---

[19] The presence of gold in Syrian temples suggests that India and Aithiopia are part of Syria's trading networks (*Syr. D.* 1, 2, 16). See also Hdt. 3.94–106, 114.

[20] Goldhill (2002: 60–107) identifies and analyzes the six instances in which Lucian names himself; Elsner (2001) insists that *On the Syrian Goddess* is an act of cultural translation.

[21] The last word of *On the Syrian Goddess*, *to ounoma* ("the name"), suggests self-identification with Lucian the writer. If Lucian's name were inscribed at the end of the book roll, this closing phrase would serve as a sphragis (discussed in Lightfoot [2003: 534, as an uncited comment by Bowie]). See also Heliodorus's self-identifying sphragis at the end of his *Aithiopika* (10.41.4).

(*Scyth.* 9).[22] In addition to unsettling his narratorial identity, Lucian invites his Macedonian audience to participate in the process of his identity formation. The interplay between internal and external perspectives becomes especially apparent in Lucian's Scythian satires, as Athenians categorize Anacharsis as Scythian based on his attire and language (*Scyth.* 7), even though his later travels and learned erudition mirror those of Solon (Hdt. 1.30). In line with Anacharsis's Scythian attire signaling to Athenians that he is a foreigner, his countryman Toxaris's adoption of Greek attire results in people mistaking him for a Greek (*Scyth.* 3).[23] In both instances, neither man asserts a Greek identity, yet those who see them regard clothes in concert with other prosthetic markers of self-presentation as synonymous with race. Taken together, these instances of seeing through a specific lens coincide with W. J. T. Mitchell's treatment of modern race as a medium through which people understand the perceived alterity of others. Encompassing the visual and verbal spheres, Mitchell draws attention to modern race's "shape-shifting" qualities.[24] In a similar vein, Lucian's satires feature characters who wield race and identity as filters through which they experience and accommodate otherness. They reshape the contours of their own foreignness, which contributes to their permeable understanding of others. Lucian introduces teasing ambiguities that emphasize the reciprocity of foreignness when he puts distant Scythians and Syrians into conversation with Greek people.[25] He promotes a two-way encounter in which one group, then the other, temporarily has the power to label those who differ from them.

5.2 Perceptive Outsiders: Aithiopians and Scythians

Turning now to skin color, another flexible element in the landscape of race and identity, I posit that Lucian renders it as nothing more than a *thauma* (a marvel) with a signifying power that varies among those unaccustomed to appearances that differ from their own. Lucian's pliable approach to skin color especially applies to his iteration of black Aithiopians. In the *Ignorant Book Collector*, Lucian alludes to Aesop's proverb about the futility of washing an Aithiopian clean. He manipulates the indelible nature of skin color presented in this proverb to his own ends, using Aesop's aphorism to mock a book

---

[22] Knowing allusions to the Macedonians' contested status as Greeks in the sixth century BCE lurk in the background of the narrator's address to his Macedonian audience.

[23] Throughout his *Carousal (Symposium) or the Lapiths*, Lucian points out the unreliable link between philosophers' visual appearance and their identity (discussed in Trapp [2017: 53–56]).

[24] Mitchell (2012: 4–19).   [25] Branham (1989: 4–6, 214–15).

collector's resolute resistance to any of his advice: οἶδα ὡς μάτην ταῦτά μοι λελήρηται καὶ κατὰ τὴν παροιμίαν Αἰθίοπα σμήχειν ἐπιχειρῶ ("I know that I have spoken foolishly in vain and, like the proverb, I am trying to wash an Aithiopian [clean]," *Ind.* 28).[26] In a different vein, Lucian has one of the characters in *Hermotimus* use a hypothetical Aithiopian to focalize an argument about the inanity of making value-laden judgments based on skin color. As part of his scathing attack on philosophy, Lycinus announces to his Stoicism-loving friend Hermotimus:

> ἢ τάχ᾽ ἄν τις αὐτῶν καὶ προσέροιτό "εἰπέ μοι" λέγων, "ὦ Λυκῖνε, εἴ τις Αἰθίοψ μηδεπώποτε ἄλλους ἀνθρώπους ἰδών, οἷοι ἡμεῖς ἐσμεν, διὰ τὸ μὴ ἀποδεδημηκέναι τὸ παράπαν, ἔν τινι συλλόγῳ τῶν Αἰθιόπων διισχυρίζοιτο καὶ λέγοι μηδαμόθι τῆς γῆς ἀνθρώπους εἶναι λευκοὺς ἢ ξανθοὺς μηδὲ ἄλλο τι ἢ μέλανας, ἆρα πιστεύοιτ᾽ ἂν ὑπ᾽ αὐτῶν;" ἢ εἴποι τις ἂν πρὸς αὐτὸν τῶν πρεσβυτέρων Αἰθιόπων, "σὺ δὲ δὴ πόθεν ταῦτα, ὦ θρασύτατε, οἶσθα; οὐ γὰρ ἀπεδήμησας[27] παρ᾽ ἡμῶν οὐδαμόσε οὐδὲ εἶδες νὴ Δία τὰ παρὰ τοῖς ἄλλοις ὁποῖά ἐστι." φαίην ἂν ἔγωγε δίκαια ἐρωτῆσαι τὸν πρεσβύτην.

> One of [the philosophers] would quickly say to me, "Speak and tell me, Lycinus, if some Aithiopian, who has never seen any people resembling us because he has not been abroad at all, should confidently state and assert to an Aithiopian assembly that nowhere in the world are there men who are white or yellow or any color other than black, would they believe him? Or would one of the Aithiopian elders say to him, 'You are extremely bold; how do you know these things? For you have not traveled away from our country nor have you seen, by Zeus, the sorts (of skin color) that exist among other people.'" For my part, I would assert that the elder had questioned him fairly. (Lucian, *Hermotimus* 31)

In this hypothetical query, an Aithiopian assumes that his black skin is a worldwide norm because of his lack of travel experience. He relies on skin

---

[26] Aesop, *Fables* 34 (cited in Loomba and Burton [2007: 39]). Kindstrand (1981: 76) compares Aesop with Anacharsis, in that both men are wise, itinerant outsiders in Greece. See also Jeremiah 13:23 (discussed in Selden [2013]): εἰ ἀλλάξεται Αἰθίοψ τὸ δέρμα αὐτοῦ καὶ πάρδαλις τὰ ποικίλματα αὐτῆς, καὶ ὑμεῖς δυνήσεσθε εὖ ποιῆσαι μεμαθηκότες τὰ κακά, "if an Aithiopian [can] change his skin and a leopard his spots, even you shall be able to fare well although you have learned evil things." Sixteenth-century writers of English emblem books transformed this proverb into a racist trope: they render a Black man, described as a "Man of Inde" or "blackamoor," inferior to a White man (translations by Thomas Palmer and Geffrey Whitney, respectively, cited in Loomba and Burton [2007: 98–99, 119–20]). Massing (1995) draws attention to racist overtones present in nineteenth-century soap advertisements that feature Black people washing the pigmentation off their bodies.

[27] The verb *apodēmeō* is integral to both Lucian's and Herodotus's discussion of "frontier-men," to use Hartog's language (Hartog [2001: 3–13]): travelers who have spent time away from home are well placed to challenge others' chauvinistic assumptions and traditions.

color as visual evidence to support his shortsighted conjecture. Of all of the characters Lucian could have used to voice this theory, it is significant that he has chosen to stage this conversation among people whose name implies precisely this kind of chromatic fixation (*aithō*, "I blaze"). Lucian's decision to insert commentary about black skin into the mouths of Aithiopians compels his readers to recognize that a foreigner (*xenos*) speaking the Greek language (*phōnē*) can articulate ideas that coincide with Greek sentiments. Within the domain of the xenophone, there is no fixed preeminence or division. Everyone can easily assume themselves to be the wise majority if they interact only with their own people.[28] Extensive travel can offer a newfound visibility of the world. Until people depart from their homelands, however, ignorance governs their findings. In this vein, Lucian's cross-cultural message undergirds the ever-changing interpretation of skin color even within a single community. One Aithiopian can confidently declare the pervasiveness of black skin, while another can quickly refute this rigid perspective. Divergent intragroup dynamics disallow readers from treating one character's opinion as an indicator of group consensus.

Another group whose foreign status belies their intellect is Lucian's Scythians, who inspect communities outside of their own and draw conclusions based on their findings. The first of Lucian's Scythian satires, *The Scythian or the Consul*, describes Anacharsis's trip to Athens.[29] Upon his arrival, the Scythian traveler converses with his Hellenophilic countryman Toxaris and the Athenian sage Solon.[30] During their chat, Toxaris quips that Solon can make Greeks out of foreigners: εἰ τοίνυν ἐγὼ Σόλωνα οἶδα, οὕτω ποιήσεις καὶ προξενήσεις αὐτοῦ καὶ πολίτην γνήσιον ἀποφανεῖς τῆς Ἑλλάδος ("moreover, if I know you, Solon, you will do this in this way. You will be his patron and you will produce a true citizen of Greece," *Scyth.* 7). The very phraseology of this remark hints at a parodic play: Toxaris introduces the nonsensical idea of being an authentic citizen of Greece in an implied historical period during which someone can be a citizen of a state (i.e. of Athens) but not of Greece. With this comment, Toxaris's poor grasp of Greek politics is laid bare, even though he is supposedly an

---

[28] Heliodorus's characterization of Charicleia, a white Aithiopian, further destabilizes the argument proposed by the myopic Aithiopian in *Hermotimus* (discussed in Chapter 6, below).

[29] While it is difficult to pinpoint in what order Lucian wrote his three Scythian satires, I consider *The Scythian or the Consul* to be first based on the plot structure.

[30] As Bozia (2015: 74) puts it, "estrangement in reverse" occurs when Anacharsis and Toxaris first communicate because they speak in the language of Scythians, which Lucian recounts in Greek. It is curious to note that Anacharsis's name itself could be a Greek invention, deriving from *ana-* ("throughout") and *charis* ("grace") or *chara* ("joy"). See Mestre (2003: 308); Kindstrand (1981: 13 n. 27).

insider. Furthermore, he throws into disarray any attempts at formulating a strict blueprint for Greekness with his proposition that Solon can produce legitimate Greek citizens by sheer will. This model suggests that Anacharsis's Scythian elements – his attire and language – are modest deviations that he can overcome.[31]

Channeling Solon's transformative skills, Lucian the narrator appropriates a Scythian identity in the closing paragraphs of *The Scythian or the Consul*. Eager to secure the company of the most eloquent Macedonians in his midst, he morphs into Anacharsis, a wide-eyed foreigner searching for a generous patron (*Scyth.* 9). Lucian's close association with Anacharsis encourages his Macedonian audience to liken their wisdom to that of Anacharsis's teacher Solon. As an additional boon for Lucian, if the Macedonians adopt Solon's propensity for blurring the lines between seemingly disparate people, Lucian can easily subsume a Scythian identity into his Syrian one. Lucian's reliance on Anacharsis as an exemplum of the foreigner who deserves acceptance in Athens indicates the writer's ongoing negotiation between his vulnerability as a Syrian and his mastery of Greek *paideia*. Hedged in by Roman political might and Greek cultural capital, Lucian the writer must proceed carefully. Therefore, as a narrator, he downplays his intelligence, which lulls his potential patrons into a false sense of superiority, while concurrently reordering any presumed hegemony of intelligence with his account of a meeting between a naïve Scythian and a wise Scythian-turned-Greek.[32] These disparate examples render Lucian's *paideia* a broadly mapped site where patriotic localism and Greek allegiance coexist.[33] The geographical location of learned people ranges from Greece to Scythia to Syria.

Lucian continues to destabilize the boundaries between insider and outsider in *Toxaris: A Friendship Dialogue*. This satire gives an account of a storytelling competition between Toxaris and his Greek friend Mnesippus, each of whom insists that his countrymen best embody friendship. The competition eventually devolves into a pledge of friendship

---

[31] Rostad (2019: 347). Rostad distills Lucian's numerous references to Scythians into three categories: vagrancy, archery, and savagery.

[32] In this way, Lucian maps out two exempla of Scythians, unlearned Anacharsis and smart Toxaris (Braund [2004: 17–20]). Near Toxaris's tomb, a statue of a man with a bow in his left hand and what appears to be a book in his right potentially offers a visual exemplum of Scythian *paideia* (*Scyth.* 2); nonetheless, the "book" may have actually been a quiver (Braund [2004: 21–23]).

[33] Swain (1996: 329, 411–12); Nasrallah (2005); Gleason (1995: xxi). Although *paideia* can lead to social and economic benefits, its fluctuating value frustrates some of Lucian's characters, such as the Syrian book collector who buys copious amounts of books in a misguided attempt to purchase *paideia* (*Ind.*, discussed in Popescu [2009: 227–38]).

on both men's part. This intercultural friendship between a Scythian and a Greek allows Lucian's readers to approach Greek misapprehension of non-Greeks from a layered viewpoint.[34] As readers tackle Scythian and Greek perspectives filtered through the mouth of a Syrian, Lucian's deft storytelling demolishes unchecked assumptions about either group. Intercultural encounters that rejig people's presumed opinions look back to earlier discussions regarding Pelasgus's reformed take on the Danaids' hybrid identity (see Chapter 3) and the Aithiopian king's awareness of Cambyses's dishonest intentions (see Chapter 4).[35] A closer look at Lucian's reconfiguration of the difference between Athenian athletes and their Scythian counterparts reinforces his omnivorous stance.

5.3 Muddy, Sun-Kissed Athenians

Anacharsis recounts a conversation between two friends, the Scythian traveler Anacharsis and his Athenian guide Solon, while they watch Athenian men train in the gymnasium.[36] Although this dialogue takes place in the sixth century BCE, the gymnasium remained an important site for the performance of Greek identity in the Hellenistic and Roman imperial periods. By the time Lucian pens these satires, training in the gymnasium has become so integral to the performance of Greek identity that even non-Greeks adopt the practice.[37] As the spectacle of athletic training unfolds before Anacharsis, he constantly looks to Solon to explain the purpose of the exercises. Every bit the inquisitive spectator, Anacharsis criticizes each element of the athletic ritual, from the unnecessary violence

---

[34] Bozia (2015: 70).

[35] As another point of convergence between Lucian's characters and the Danaids, the insatiably thirsty serpent in his *The Thirst-Snake* calls to mind the latter, who endlessly carry leaky water jars in the underworld (Popescu [2009: 161–68]).

[36] The recounting of Anacharsis's and Solon's conversation appears in other Greek texts, including Plutarch, *Solon* 5 and Diog. Laert. 1.8.101–05. Coinciding with Lucian's portrayal of skeptical Anacharsis, biographers Plutarch and Diogenes Laertius describe Anacharsis's disbelief regarding Solon's implementation of Athenian law. Diogenes Laertius (1.8.104) takes (Lucian's) Anacharsis's dislike of oil-smeared athletes a step further with his suggestion that oil is a madness-inducing drug. Diverging from Lucian's portrayal of Anacharsis, both Plutarch and Diogenes Laertius recount Solon's admiration of Anacharsis's wit upon their first meeting, and Diogenes Laertius posits that Anacharsis died during a hunting trip with his brother. See also Hartog (2001: 107–16).

[37] König (2005: 45–49); König (2017: 156–64); Knox (1985: 24–25). For instance, after Antiochus Epiphanes authorized the construction of a gymnasium in Judaea, Jewish people began to exercise naked in the gymnasium as part of the Hellenizing process (Josephus, *Antiquities of the Jews* 12.237; discussed in Kerkeslager [1997] and Koskenniemi [2019]). Conversely, some of Lucian's contemporaries believed that the development of the body occurred at the expense of the mind (Ath. 413c–f, discussed in Branham [1989: 87]; Galen, *Protrepticus* 11, discussed in Robinson [1955: 192–94]).

to the apathetic spectatorship (*Anach.* 1, 11). Comparable to Lucian's Aithiopians in *Hermotimus*, Anacharsis occupies the domain of the xeno-phone. That is, Anacharsis's non-Greek remarks (i.e. his *xeno-phōnē*) about the performance unfolding in front of him compel Solon to consider his perspective seriously. Even though Anacharsis's curiosity about Greek practices fuels his trip to Athens, he insists that the Athenians' training regimen is inferior to that of the Scythians.[38] Simply put, his desire for *paideia* does not predetermine his reaction to Athenian athletic practices.

Lucian's characterization of Anacharsis calls to mind Herodotus's rendition (4.76–78). Veering away from Herodotus's portrayal of Anacharsis as a worldly traveler who embraces Greek religious rites, Lucian's Anacharsis is a budding explorer who steadfastly refuses to see any merit in the Athenians' curious training regimen. Focusing on the early stages of Anacharsis's journey in *Anacharsis*, Lucian presents a man who is unwilling to compromise his stance on Athenian athletics. This Anacharsis has not yet traveled the world and begun his journey home, after which he clandestinely affixes an image of the Phrygian Greek goddess Cybele onto his clothes. In fact, Anacharsis's intense dislike of Athenian athletic practices coincides with his fellow Scythians' hostility towards Greek customs in Herodotus's *Histories*. A morbid resonance lies behind this shared isolationism, in that Scythian xenophobia leads to Anacharsis's death in the *Histories*. Although the Anacharsis in Lucian's dialogue is oblivious to his violent fate, readers familiar with Herodotus's story will recall that the mere sight of Cybele's image on Anacharsis's clothes warrants his death.

Lucian's take on Herodotus's story offers useful timestamps of the development of Anacharsis's formulation of identity. Having just begun his adventures, Lucian's Anacharsis has not yet inserted Greek practices into his lexicon of identity. He eagerly takes in the sight of the Athenian athletic spectacle, but he refuses to mirror it in his own life. Upon his return to Scythia, however, he freely engages in Greek religious rites with no explicit remorse. To borrow R. Bracht Branham's language, the "Januslike [*sic*] character of the Anacharsis legend" looks backward and forward.[39] The laughing Anacharsis who mocks Greek rituals in *Anacharsis* jostles against the fervent Anacharsis who laps up information about

---

[38] *Anacharsis* and *Toxaris: A Friendship Dialogue* are a "contrived pair" (to quote Anderson [1976: 82]) of complementary dialogues, in that both begin with a critique of the speaker's foreign practices: *Anacharsis* begins with a Scythian person's critique of Greek practices, and *Toxaris* begins with a Greek person's critique of Scythian practices.

[39] Branham (1989: 85).

Greece in *The Scythian or the Consul* and the wizened Anacharsis who participates in Greek practices in Herodotus's *Histories*. Resembling symposiasts who adopt a variety of roles through the janiform cups they use to drink wine (discussed in Section 2.2), each version of Anacharsis offers unique insight into Greek practices from a particular perspective.

During his conversation with Solon, Anacharsis acknowledges that certain sartorial choices emphasize his Scythian identity. Therefore, he opts to leave his Scythian hat at home, lest he look like a foreigner (ξενίζοιμι, *Anach.* 16.27), yet he openly acknowledges his status as an outsider (βάρβαρον, 18.28). At the same time, Anacharsis reminds Solon that the category of foreigner is relative by addressing Solon as a *xenos* in Solon's own city (14.17). The translation of *xenos* poses a challenge because of its dual meaning, "guest-friend" and "foreigner," in ancient Greek. This ambiguity makes it equally plausible to assume Solon's gracious reception of Anacharsis in conjunction with Solon's foreign status in relation to Anacharsis. As for Solon, he is unequivocal about Anacharsis's foreign status (ξένος ... βαρβάρου καὶ ξένου, 17). Despite this assertion, Solon presents a spectrum of foreignness when he explains that Athenian athletes have embraced foreign customs (ξένα, 6).[40] This comment calls into question how many "foreign" customs one can practice while preserving one's identity. In the case of the Athenian athletes, their adoption of foreign (i.e. non-Greek) practices disregards any claims of purity surrounding a Greek identity.

Armed with wily rhetorical moves, Lucian sifts through the permeable category of foreigner to create a composite model. Echoing Herodotus's strategies of decentering Greek *poleis*, Lucian assigns foreigner status to the Greeks themselves.[41] For instance, Anacharsis laughs at the paltry prizes for Athenian athletes (*Anach.* 9). His scoffing mirrors the Persians' astonishment that Greeks compete for a mere olive wreath (Hdt. 8.26.3). This intertextual alliance grants Anacharsis a compatriot in his disbelief at Greek practices. Both he and the Persians find the preeminence of honor to be an ill-fitting reward. Embodying the Persians' dismissal of Greek prizes, Anacharsis compels Solon to reimagine what constitutes the categories of

---

[40] The vocabulary of foreignness appears eight times in *Anacharsis*: in reference to Solon (*xenon*, 14.17), Anacharsis (*xenizoimi*, 16.27; *xenos*, 17.17; *xenou*, 17.24; *barbarou*, 17.24; *barbaron*, 18.28), Athenian athletes' practices (*xena*, 6.2), and generic non-Greek exercises (*xenika*, 39.12). More broadly, these words appear in Lucian's other Scythian satires: five iterations in *Toxaris* (*xen-*: 5.8, 57.16, 63.8; *barbar-*: 4.7, 5.2) and sixteen in *Scythian* (*xen-*: 1.12, 3.3, 4.6, 4.21, 4.23, 5.5, 6.6, 6.7, 7.1, 7.12, 10.11, 10.21; *barbar-*: 3.4, 8.16, 9.9, 10.9).

[41] Anacharsis's scrutiny of Athenian athletic practices calls to mind Solon's critique of happiness following his tour of Sardis (Hdt. 1.29–34).

native and foreign. In any event, Anacharsis's budding friendship with Solon, and his later adoption of Greek religious practices, stands in contrast to the Persians' rigid, Hellenophobic perspective. Still, the dissimilarities between Scythians and Persians do not overshadow the shared impact of their rebukes. Each of their singular castigations strikes a collective blow against Hellenocentrism.

As part of Anacharsis's ongoing critiques of the Athenian athletes, he reprimands them for altering their appearance with mud.[42] The Athenians' application of mud to their bodies gives rise to various intertextual allusions that transport the athletes to a subhuman realm: they resemble muddy pigs and slippery eels that wallow in mud and ferociously attack each other (*Anach.* 1–5). From Anacharsis's point of view, these athletes live in a topsy-turvy world where men are indistinguishable from animals. Anacharsis's description of the Athenian athletes as pigs (1) recalls another unnatural journey from human to animal in which the boundary between men and pigs disappears: when Odysseus's men eat Circe's magical food and turn into sniveling hogs (*Od.* 10.203–399). Although Anacharsis lacks supernatural abilities, he evokes Circe's power when he reshapes Athenian athletes into rowdy animals. Moreover, Anacharsis mirrors Circe's liminal position outside of the world of Greek heroes. Standing literally and figuratively outside of the athletic training grounds, Anacharsis uses his outsider status to his advantage. Under the guise of amicable incredulity, he dissolves Greek myopia regarding their practices.[43]

Despite his lack of protection against the harsh sunlight, Anacharsis does not use mud to protect his skin. Maintaining his stubborn stance, he opts to seek shade to ease his discomfort (*Anach.* 16). His preference for shade brings to mind the Skiapodes, a mythical people whom Hecataeus of Miletus identifies as Aithiopians (*FGrH* 325–27). In fact, the etymology of Aithiopia, *aithō* ("I blaze") and *ops* ("face"), encapsulates precisely the situation that Anacharsis finds himself in during his conversation with Solon: the sun is blazing down on his head.[44] To counter the harsh

---

[42] These muddy bodies may allude to Aesop's proverb about Aithiopians' inability to wash themselves clean (discussed above in n. 26). In addition to discussing the benefits of muddy bodies, Solon promotes the salutary effects of dust (*Anach.* 29), which may indicate an intertextual link with cremation (Musgrave [1990]; see also Philostratus, *On Gymnastics* 56).

[43] Branham (1989: 83, 101–04) and Rostad (2019: 342) both point out overlaps between *Anacharsis* and Platonic dialogue. Chapman (1931), Anderson (1976), Ní Mheallaigh (2005), Schlapbach (2010), and Pass (2016) analyze Lucian's broader appropriations of Plato's dialogues. Peterson (2010) argues that Lucian's use of comic dialogue resolves the contention between Old Comedy and Platonic dialogue.

[44] Anacharsis's stout rejection of mud bears consideration alongside the Aithiopian king's general dislike of Persian gifts in Herodotus's *Histories* (3.17–26, discussed in Section 4.2). It is curious to

sunlight, Anacharsis adopts the strategy of the Skiapodes who shelter in the shadows (σκία) of their huge feet (πόδες). These Aithiopian undertones suggest that Anacharsis's xenophobia is limited to Greek customs, and by extension, to Hellenocentrism itself. Contrary to his lengthy critiques of Athenian practices, Anacharsis is surprisingly reticent to provide substantive information about what Scythian training entails (40). Rerouting Greeks' subjective treatment of non-Greek customs, Anacharsis reserves his judgmental observations solely for the Athenians in whose midst he finds himself.

In a futile attempt to sway his obstinate friend, Solon retorts that the mud-covered athletes can wash off caked-on mud and restore their unsullied appearance once they depart from the gymnasium (*Anach.* 29). To use the language of performance, the mud functions as a temporary mask.[45] It contributes to the athletes' physical prowess, which in turn feeds into their successful performance of Greek identity without demanding any permanent bodily alteration. For Solon, this impermanent symbol of virility marks Athenian athletes as superior to lazy, white men:

> καὶ ἔγωγε ἡδέως ἂν παραστησάμενος πλησίον τῶν τε λευκῶν τινα ἐκείνων καὶ ὑπὸ σκιᾷ δεδιῃτημένων καὶ ὃν ἂν ἕλῃ τῶν ἐν τῷ Λυκείῳ γυμναζομένων, ἀποπλύνας τὴν κόνιν καὶ τὸν πηλόν,[46] ἐροίμην ἄν σε ποτέρῳ ἂν ὅμοιος εὔξαιο γενέσθαι.

> And I would gladly ask you [Anacharsis] whom you would hope to resemble, placing [two men] in front of you – one of those white men who live in the shade and an athlete of your choice from the Lyceum – after I had wiped off the dust and dirt. (Luc. *Anach.* 29)

Solon's query calls to mind the schematic shorthand in Greek iconography that distinguishes between virile Greek men, whose outdoor adventures lead to darkened skin, and elite Greek women, whose indoor

---

note that wine, the only gift that the Aithiopian king enjoyed, is frequently associated with Scythians, especially when unmixed and drunk in excess, as noted in the etymology of *skythizō*, "I drink immoderately (like a Scythian)" (Hdt. 6.84; Hobden [2013: 83–100]; Lissarrague [2001: 111]; Skinner [2012: 68–78]). Another similarity between Aithiopians and Scythians: both eat boiled meat and drink milk (Hdt. 3.23; *Aer.* 18). See also an unidentified fragment from the comic playwright Menander: ὃς ἂν εὖ γεγονὼς ᾖ τῇ φύσει πρὸς τἀγαθά, | κἂν Αἰθίοψ ᾖ, μῆτερ, ἐστὶν εὐγενής. | Σκύθης τις; ὄλεθρος· ὁ δ᾽Ἀνάχαρσις οὐ Σκύθης, "he who is born well has a good nature, even if he is Aithiopian, mother, he is well born. What about a Scythian? He is wretched, but Anacharsis is not Scythian" (fr. 533k lines 11–13, as numbered in Allinson [1921: 48]; discussed in Snowden [1948: 38–39]).

[45] Conversely, most ancient Greek physiognomic texts treat skin color as an unalterable feature (Goldman [2015]).

[46] See also my discussion of mud (*pēlon*) in Section 6.4.

domestic activities result in a pale complexion.[47] According to Solon, the gendered dichotomy of tanned skin and pale skin lends an air of femininity to men without sun-kissed skin. In this vein, Athenian athletes offer a preferable exemplum to white men (*tōn te leukōn*) who lack the muscles and outdoor training needed to be stalwart defenders of their country.[48] Class connotations also undergird Solon's description, in that rich men reserve the right to eschew physical labor and prevent the sun from desiccating their bodies.[49] Anacharsis pokes fun at the power that Solon assigns to mud-caked skin by retorting that darkened skin will not protect men from the lethal weapons and brute violence of their enemies (*Anach.* 31). With this remark, Anacharsis foregrounds the absurdity of a correlation between skin color and strength, thereby nudging Solon to reconsider his privileging of such muddy practices.

5.3.1　Solar Detours

Defending athletes' mud-smattered bodies from another angle, Solon focuses on mud's protective properties. Namely, he highlights mud-covered athletes' ability to withstand extended solar exposure (*Anach.* 16). Solon's explicit mention of the sun alongside a means of solar protection warrants a slight detour to other Lucianic satires that pair the sun with a group of people. In particular, *On Astrology* names the Aithiopians as the first people to study the sky and learn about astrology (3, 5). Due to their supreme wisdom, which Lucian partly attributes to their benign climate and clear skies, Aithiopians credit the moon's brightness to the sun (*Astr.* 3).

Lucian puts a satirical spin on this association between the sun and the moon in *True Stories*. During the narrator's protoglobal journey to places that other geographers can barely map, a powerful whirlwind transports him to the uppermost realms of the sky, where he becomes embroiled in the moon people's battle against the sun people (*Ver. hist.* 1.10–28).[50] Here,

---

[47] As noted in Chapter 2, the visual contrast between black and white in Greek iconography did not map directly onto people living in Greek *poleis*; see also Dee (2003–04). A few literary examples include Socratic dialogue (Xenophon, *Oeconomicus* 7.21–33) and Athenian comedy (Aristophanes, *Ecclesiazusae* 63–64, 699). Both strains of the "tanned/pale" dichotomy appear in Greek epic: Athena restores Odysseus's striking looks by darkening his skin and beautifies Penelope by lightening her skin (*Od.* 16.175–76, 18.195–96).

[48] Conversely, Greek literature offers references to working women with black skin, such as the Hellenistic poet Theocritus's *Idylls* (ἐριθακὶς ἁ μελανόχρως, "the black day-laborer," 3.35).

[49] Sassi (2001) elaborates on the close relationship between external elements, such as the environment, and people's character in the Greco-Roman world.

[50] Dench (2017: 99). Ní Mheallaigh (2014: 216) describes the moon in *True Stories* as a hyperbolic mirror world that enables "a fascinating interplay between the real and the mimetic"; Ní Mheallaigh

the narrator introduces readers to Phaethon, the ruler of a celestial people who live on the surface of the glaring sun. The presence of Phaethon encourages slippage between the sun people and the Aithiopians for a few reasons. To start with, the brightness inherent in the adjective *phaethōn* ("radiant") and the prefix *aithō* ("I blaze") suggest a correlation with the sun. Additionally, the myth surrounding Phaethon intimates a close relationship between Aithiopians and the sun. As Ovid recounts in the *Metamorphoses*, Phaethon, the son of the sun god, rode his father's chariot too close to the land of mortals and scorched their homeland. Eventually, Jupiter shot him down from the sky with his thunderbolt (*Met.* 1.750–2.400). Aithiopians later attributed their black skin color to the blood that rushed to the surface of their skin following Phaethon's chariot ride (*nigrum ... colorem, Met.* 2.236).[51] On a genealogical note, the Aithiopians traced their lineage to Phaethon, whose adoptive father was King Merops, ruler of the Aithiopians. Altogether, these intertextual callbacks to the sun underscore Lucian's uncanny ability to recast solar endurance as an element of astrology, historiography, and mythology. In addition, the allusive pairing of Aithiopians and the sun invites readers of *Anacharsis* to affiliate the sun-kissed Athenian athletes with a new location.

In *True Stories*, Phaethon wields impressive command of the sun. In terms of geography, Phaethon's location on the sun's surface places him in a region of the world that is unfathomably far away from both land and sea.[52] This insurmountable distance likens Phaethon's homeland to the location of the Homeric Aithiopians, who inhabit the most extreme regions of the world (*Od.* 1.23–24). Only the gods are able to visit these distant people, and only a satirical character can reach the heights of the sun. Even when the narrator arrives in the sky, he does not choose to visit the sun. Rather, due to the

(2020) elaborates on the significance of the moon in the ancient Greek imagination; and Anderson (2019: 167–76) broadly examines the role of fantasy in *True Stories*.

[51] Retellings of this myth appear in fragments from Euripides's tragedy *Phaethon*, as reconstructed by Diggle (1970); Plato's philosophical dialogue *Timaeus* (22c); and Apollonius of Rhodes's epic *Argonautica* (4.595–611). Perennially a shrewd reader, Lucian may have been satirizing Ovid's explanation that the gods beg Helios to reconsider his decision to shroud the world in darkness by presenting Phaethon as the recalcitrant bestower of light who eventually acquiesces to the moon king's request. See also the sparkling eyes of Medea, the granddaughter of the sun god (*Argon* 4.724–29, discussed in Murray's aforementioned forthcoming work).

[52] Even though the narrator of *True Stories* explicitly addresses his creative license in his opening remarks, in which he states that everything in his tale is a lie, he remains committed to presenting detailed stories about distant places (*Ver. hist.* 1.4). For instance, despite the vast distance between the sea and the sky, the narrator takes pains to situate the moon carefully on his imaginary map. The precise location of the moon 350 miles above the water satirizes previous ethnographers' quests to reach the furthest limits of their known world (*Ver. hist.* 2.9.2). Cf. Lucian's *Lover of Lies*, in which two characters critique the preponderance of liars around them.

narrator's allegiance to the moon people, the sun people kidnap him and transport him to their kingdom. More than a shorthand for geographical distance, the sun is also a formidable source of power. After bouts of violence sparked by the moon king Endymion's attempts to colonize the star Heosphoros ("Bringer of Dawn"), Phaethon opts to withhold sunlight.[53] Endymion abandons his imperial ambitions and agrees to a peace treaty because his people cannot bear to live in darkness. Such allusive descriptions transform the sun into a powerful entity. With this rendition of the sun in mind, it becomes difficult to trust Solon's insistence that Athenian athletes can endure extreme sunlight. They risk suffering like Endymion when they attempt to protect themselves against solar hegemony.

Skulking beneath the rivalry between Phaethon and Endymion, another allusion sheds light on the sun's signifying power in Lucian's satires – namely, a nod to Herodotus's Aithiopian king and Cambyses, who offer a comparandum for the sun king and moon king, respectively (Hdt. 3.17–26). The Aithiopian king's desire to thwart Persian expansion finds a parallel in Phaethon's disapproval of Endymion's belligerence. Instead of the fabled Table of the Sun with its magical supply of meat that Herodotus's Aithiopians possess, the indomitable Phaethon has at his disposal rays of sunlight that enable the division of days. Despite the obstacles facing the Aithiopian king and Phaethon, both emerge victorious from encounters with underhanded foes. Curiously enough, the narrator of *True Stories* has firsthand access to the sun when he arrives there as a hostage, but he does not remark on the color of the sun people. Phaethon's radiance has enduring importance despite its lack of a chromatic marker. In this way, Herodotean configurations of the Aithiopians' race, via nonchromatic features in the Aithiopian *logos*, find a parallel in the narrator's racing of the sun people. The narrator hints at the Aithiopians' potential blackness by treating sunlight as the defining feature of their race without limiting race to a facile chromatic marker. Lucian applies this pliability to blackness in *Anacharsis* as well, in that the Athenians' sun-kissed skin is not the sole determinant of their race. Furthermore, these intertextual allusions between Aithiopians and the sun again suggest that Solon's Athenian athletes exercising outdoors embrace Aithiopia, along with the rays of sunshine.

---

[53] "Heosphoros" alludes to the eponymous goddess of dawn, Eos, whose lineage suggests a connection between the sun and black skin because by the time that Lucian penned *True Stories*, the color-based epithet of Eos's son Memnon was in circulation: *nigri Memnonis*, "black Memnon" (Vergil, *Aeneid* 1.489; Ovid, *Amores* 1.8.3–4); *Memnon niger*, "black Memnon" (Seneca the Younger, *Agamemnon* 212).

Preoccupied with seizing the star Heosphoros, Endymion bears parodic resemblance to the Cambyses of Herodotus's Aithiopian *logos*. Specifically, Endymion's campaign to expand his celestial empire corresponds to Cambyses's ill-fated quest to invade Aithiopia. Endymion takes Cambyses's zealousness even further with his desire to populate an entire star with his people. As a pair, Endymion and Cambyses symbolize the desperation of those who seek to lay claim to people affiliated with the sun. They follow in the footsteps of Ovid's Phaethon, whose ardent desire to control the sun ends up boding ill for him, rather than Lucian's Phaethon, who puts a stop to others' imperial ambitions.[54] In sum, these mimetic echoes bring together Herodotus's Aithiopians, Lucian's sun people, and Lucian's Athenian athletes without denying readers the pleasure of deduction. In addition to rewarding readers who look beyond the superficial appearance of muddy, sun-enduring Athenian athletes in *Anacharsis* to detect sophisticated rhetorical moves, these allusions fuel Anacharsis's small-scale mockery of Athenian men and large-scale ridicule of Greek people.

5.4 Shadow Costume

Unlike the Athenian athletes whose darkened skin can withstand the noonday sun, Anacharsis needs a break from the intense sunlight (*Anach.* 18). He has left his hat at home so pauses his deliberation with Solon to find a shady spot.[55] Unbothered by the unrelenting sun, Solon remarks that grueling Athenian training practices build up cranial resilience to the sun's harsh rays. This emphasis on resilient heads recalls Herodotus's commentary about Egyptians' and Persians' skull thickness, which itself looks back to fifth-century medical treatises:[56]

αἱ μὲν τῶν Περσέων κεφαλαί εἰσι ἀσθενέες οὕτω ὥστε, εἰ θέλοις ψήφῳ μούνῃ βαλεῖν, διατετρανέεις, αἱ δὲ τῶν Αἰγυπτίων οὕτω δή τι ἰσχυραί, μόγις ἂν λίθῳ παίσας διαρρήξειας. αἴτιον δὲ τούτου τόδε ἔλεγον, καὶ ἐμέ γ᾽ εὐπετέως ἔπειθον, ὅτι Αἰγύπτιοι μὲν αὐτίκα ἀπὸ παιδίων ἀρξάμενοι ξυρῶνται τὰς κεφαλὰς καὶ πρὸς τὸν ἥλιον παχύνεται τὸ ὀστέον. τὠυτὸ δὲ τοῦτο καὶ τοῦ

---

[54] The narrator of *True Stories* provides an ethnography of the moon people that bears comparison with Herodotus's Scythians (*Ver. hist.* 1.23; Hdt. 1.202, 4.75).

[55] Anacharsis's preference for shade likens him to Athenian philosophers who meet in a shady grove (Plato, *Phaedrus* 229a–b; discussed in Goldhill [2001a: 2–3]; see also n. 43 above). In other words, Anacharsis's resistance to one element of Greek identity (athletics) does not preclude his acceptance of another element (philosophy).

[56] The presence of the Macrocephali ("Elongated-heads") in *Aer.* 14 informs Herodotus's observations about the link between their customs and nature (Thomas [2000: 31–32, 127–29]; Kennedy [2016]).

μὴ φαλακροῦσθαι αἴτιόν ἐστι· Αἰγυπτίων γὰρ ἄν τις ἐλαχίστους ἴδοιτο
φαλακρούς πάντων ἀνθρώπων. τούτοισι μὲν δὴ τοῦτό ἐστι αἴτιον ἰσχυρὰς
φορέειν τὰς κεφαλάς, τοῖσι δὲ Πέρσῃσι ὅτι ἀσθενέας φορέουσι τὰς κεφαλὰς
αἴτιον τόδε· σκιητροφέουσι ἐξ ἀρχῆς πίλους τιάρας φορέοντες.

The heads of the Persians are so weak that, if you wished to throw a mere
pebble at their heads, you would bore a hole through them. But somehow, the
heads of Egyptians are so strong that you would break their heads only if you
struck them with a lot of effort. [The Egyptians] explained that the reason for
this, and they easily persuaded me, is because, beginning early in their childhood, they shave their heads, and their bones grow thick under the sun. This is
the same reason why they are not bald: one may observe that Egyptians are the
least bald of all men. For these Egyptians, this is certainly the reason why their
heads are strong. For Persians, on the other hand, this is the reason why they
have weak heads: from the beginning of their lives, they cover their heads with
felt hats and wear royal Persian headdresses. (Hdt. 3.12.1–4)

Similar to Herodotus's Egyptians, who derive their strength from frequent exposure to the sun, Lucian's Athenian athletes gain mental acuity
and physical prowess from the sun's penetrative rays. For both groups,
temporary customs (*nomoi*) permanently alter their nature (*physis*).[57]
Thanks to this solar interference, Herodotus's Egyptians and Lucian's
Athenians do not have weak heads and bodies, respectively.

The shared stamina of hard-headed Athenians and Egyptians decentralizes
Solon's insistence on Athenian Greeks as the stable norm in *Anacharsis*.
Adding to the blurred distinctions between "Greek" and "foreign," both the
Athenians and Egyptians draw on their environment to change their physical
appearance. If Anacharsis were to follow the logic espoused by Solon, prolonged exposure to the sun and avid mud wrestling would transform him into
an Athenian athlete, and therefore a Greek man. Nonetheless, Anacharsis's
decision to come to Athens without his hat prevents Lucian's readers from
directly applying this line of reasoning to him. Deviating from Herodotus's
two options for solar protection, Anacharsis decides against the Egyptians'
strategy for developing a hard head; he also discards the Scythian practice of
wearing a felt hat (πῖλόν, *Anach*. 16), which coincides with the Persian use of
the same (πίλους, Hdt. 3.12) to protect their sensitive scalps.[58] Even so,

---

[57] A marked difference between the two: sunlight penetrates the Egyptians' skin and reaches their
bones (πρὸς τὸν ἥλιον παχύνεται τὸ ὀστέον, Hdt. 3.12), while it stays on the epidermal level for the
Athenian athletes (*Anach*. 25).

[58] Departing from the practice of treating Herodotus's *pilous tiaras* as a hendiadys (de Sélincourt [2003:
174]) or in apposition to each other (Godley [1921: 14–15]), I separate these words into two distinct
nouns ("felt hats and royal Persian headdresses") to heighten the depths of the Persians' weakness, as
suggested by Herodotus. That is, the Persians require two types of external covering, felt hats *and*

Anacharsis's rejection of his hat bears consideration alongside Herodotus's Egyptians because both manipulate the environment to their benefit. Rather than use the broiling sun to strengthen his scalp like Herodotus's Egyptians (and Lucian's Athenian athletes), Anacharsis draws strength from the shade of his external environment by moving to a less sunny outdoor area.

Without any prompting on Solon's part, Anacharsis proffers a reason for his current hatless state. Eager to shed visible signs of his non-Greek identity in Greece, Anacharsis abandoned his felt hat before departing from Scythia (*Anach.* 16). Nevertheless, it is precisely this shadow costume that confirms his identity as non-Greek. I develop the concept of the shadow costume from Kevin Young's "shadow book," a taxonomy of unwritten, removed, and lost books from the Black archive. Young directs his readers' gaze to elaborate on this point: after relaying Colson Whitehead's enjoyment of the music of Afrika Bambaataa, Young leaves a third of a page devoid of text to invite his readers to insert their own riff on what they have just read or heard.[59] My construction of a "shadow costume" similarly illuminates the significance of what has seemingly been erased. The absence of Anacharsis's hat does not negate its importance. In fact, Anacharsis's shadow costume resonates on two levels. Superficially, it implies his lack of sartorial protection against excessive sunlight. More subtly, his shadow costume signals the encroaching dangers of assimilation. In his hatless state, Anacharsis risks altering his head's skin color to that of the sun-kissed Athenian athletes. Without his hat, a means of solar protection and visual marker of his Scythian identity, Anacharsis risks being viewed as a non-Scythian. Therefore, his reference to his hat ensures that his Scythian identity remains hyper-visible even in the absence of a symbolic marker.

After Anacharsis settles into a shady resting spot, he ceases his complaints and returns to his careful study of the athletes in his vicinity. As he

---

headdresses worn by royalty, to achieve adequate protection against the sun. Herodotus's discussion of Persians who externally shade their bodies (σκιητροφέουσι, Hdt. 3.12.4) calls to mind iconography of Persians' shade-producing parasols (τὰ σκιάδεια). Depictions of parasols in Persian and Greek art attributes elite status to the person whom the parasol covers. In Achaemenid Persia, male attendants served as parasol-bearers for men of authority, while Athenians' representations generally depicted enslaved women holding parasols for their female owners (Miller [1992]; Miller [1997: 192–98]).

[59] Young (2012: 11–19). Afrika Bambaataa (born Lance Taylor) is a seminal hip-hop DJ whose career began in the 1970s. Cf. other radical orthographic practices, such as redactions (Sharpe [2016: 8, 113–120]) and crossed-out words (in Basquiat's paintings, discussed in Young [2012: 13]), both of which pique the reader's curiosity about what was deemed worthy of temporary (in Basquiat's case) or complete (in Sharpe's case) removal.

learns from Solon, powerful rays of sunlight fortify the Athenian athletes' skin:

> οὗτοι δὲ ἡμῖν ὑπέρυθροι εἰς τὸ μελάντερον ὑπὸ τοῦ ἡλίου κεχρωσμένοι καὶ ἀρρενωποί, πολὺ τὸ ἔμψυχον καὶ θερμὸν καὶ ἀνδρῶδες ἐπιφαίνοντες, τοσαύτης εὐεξίας ἀπολάμποντες, οὔτε ῥικνοὶ καὶ κατεσκληκότες οὔτε περιπληθεῖς εἰς βάρος, ἀλλὰ εἰς τὸ σύμμετρον περιγεγραμμένοι, τὸ μὲν ἀχρεῖον τῶν σαρκῶν καὶ περιττὸν τοῖς ἱδρῶσιν ἐξαναλωκότες, ὃ δὲ ἰσχὺν καὶ τόνον παρεῖχεν ἀμιγὲς τοῦ φαύλου περιλελειμμένον ἐρρωμένως φυλάττοντες.

> But these men of ours range from somewhat red to rather black because they have been colored and toughened up by the sun. They also appear very manly in respect to their animated and fiery nature, and they beam with such great health. They are neither shriveled and parched nor filled with heavy weight, but they have been drawn with the right proportions. They have eliminated the useless and excess parts of their bodies through sweaty exercise, and they have vigorously guarded the remaining parts of their bodies from ruin, the parts which display pure strength and toil. (Luc. *Anach.* 25)

Looming in the backdrop of this passage, the luminescent sun delivers lasting effects to people's temperament and skin color. Solon suffuses his description of these sun-kissed Athenian athletes with vocabulary that helps readers visualize them. To begin, Solon's use of the deictic pronoun "these" (οὗτοι) paves the way for a vivid narration. Comparable to Pelasgus's initial query about the appearance of the Danaids, to whom he refers to as "this people" (τόδ᾽ ... γένος, *Supp.* 278, discussed in Section 3.3), Solon's vocabulary draws attention to the visual spectacle before him and Anacharsis. Eager to identify the athletes as exemplary Athenian men before elaborating on their physical features, Solon draws them closer to his own identity with his repetition of first-person plural pronouns *houtoi de hēmin* ("these men of ours"). Here, Solon reinforces Anacharsis's outsider status and heightens his own proximate relationship with the Athenian athletes. In addition, Solon's sleight of hand co-opts Lucian's readers into a group of prominent men that includes Solon.[60] Such a conflation transforms all of Lucian's readers into Greeks for the duration of their reading experience.

Next, Solon paints a vivid picture of the Athenian athletes as *hyperythroi eis to melanteron*. H. W. Fowler and F. G. Fowler and A. M. Harmon

---

[60] Although the pronoun *hēmin* can be translated as "our men" (dative of possession), I prefer to translate it as "[these] men of ours" to emphasize the deictic force of the pronoun οὗτοι.

combine their description of the athletes' health and color with their translation of *hyperythroi*, deriving from the standard color adjective *hypo* + *erythros*, as "ruddy."[61] My translation, "somewhat red," acknowledges the limiting element of the prefix *hypo-* and the gradation of skin color among the athletes, dependent upon rigorous exercise and environmental factors. The influence of external determinants on people's physical appearance echoes arguments found in the Hippocratic treatise *On Airs, Waters, and Places*. Attuned to the range of skin colors that exist in his lived world, the narrator of the treatise identifies connections between people's skin color and the environment. Elements of nature, such as the cold weather, hot winds, and hot water, spur chromatic changes on the surface of people's bodies. Unlike the sun that reddens the skin of Athenian athletes in the passage above, frigid weather turns the Scythians' skin red (*Aer.* 20).[62] This correlation between Scythians and red skin likens them to both Athenian athletes, because of their skin color, and Anacharsis, because of his Scythian identity. This fuzzy connection between seemingly opposed identities underscores Lucian's craftiness. In his satires, skin color is a complex signifier that continually recalibrates the categories of insider and outsider.

The polyvalence of skin color extends to the second part of the phrase *hyperythroi eis to melanteron*. Formed from the rare comparative adjective *melanteros*, the substantive adjective *to melanteron* elicits distinct interpretations. Fowler and Fowler conflate *to melanteron* with the phrase that follows, *hypo tou hēliou kechrōsmenoi*, which they translate all together as "sunburnt."[63] Their compact translation hearkens back to the fifth-century BCE relationship between blackness and the environment, such as the discussion of steamy winds and hot streams affecting black people's skin color in *On Airs, Waters, and Places* 24.[64] When the narrator of the treatise points out that volatile seasons produce golden-hued people as opposed to

---

[61] Fowler and Fowler (1905: 203); Harmon (1925: 42–43).

[62] πυρρὸν δὲ τὸ γένος ἐστὶ τὸ Σκυθικὸν διὰ τὸ ψῦχος, "the Scythian people are red because of the cold" (*Aer.* 20).

[63] See also Anacharsis's description of the athletes: κεχρωσμένων πρὸς τὸν ἥλιον ("colored by sunlight," *Anach.* 31), which Fowler and Fowler (1905) translate as "sunburnt," and Harmon (1925) translates as "tanned as you are by the sun."

[64] ὁκόσοι δὲ κοῖλα χωρία καὶ λειμακώδεα καὶ πνιγηρὰ καὶ τῶν θερμῶν πνευμάτων πλέον μέρος μετέχουσιν ἢ τῶν ψυχρῶν, ὕδασί τε χρέονται θερμοῖσιν ... αὐτοὶ μέλανες μᾶλλον ἢ λευκότεροι, "those who inhabit hollow, stifling, meadow-like regions in areas with hot winds rather than cold ones, and those who use hot waters ... they are black rather than an intense pale" (*Aer.* 24.9–13). Other texts may be interceding in *Anacharsis* as well, such as Aristotle's take on the temperate character of Greeks (*Politics* 1327b23–36; discussed in Secord [2016]) and the didactic poet Manilius's account of brown Greek athletes (*perque coloratas subtilis Graecia gentes | gymnasium praefert vultu fortisque palaestras*, "and through [Greece's] brown people, Greece subtly displays its powerful gymnasium and wrestling grounds," *Astronomica* 4.720–21).

black people, the narrator uses comparative adjectives to make his argument: *xanthotera ē melantera* ("more gold rather than more black," *Aer.* 24.26).[65] Operating at the opposite end of the historical spectrum, Fowler and Fowler's language choice is refracted through the prism of twentieth-century science. Racecraft has crept into their translation. That is, they have catapulted Lucian's characters out of their literary context and into a modern world in which prolonged exposure to the sun has become synonymous with a painful affliction for people with low levels of melanin. In this way, Fowler's and Fowler's decision to render Athenian athletes as "sunburnt" foists the category of Whiteness onto ancient Athenian athletes. This anachronistic leap overlooks Lucian's exploration of diverse identities beyond color-based distinctions. It discounts the physical exercises that Athenian athletes undergo as part of their performance of a Greek identity.

As a welcome alternative to Fowler and Fowler's translation, Harmon tacks *to melanteron* onto what follows, *hypo tou hēliou*, which he renders as: "coloured darker by the sun." Here, he captures the comparative aspect of *melanteron* without explicitly identifying a referent against which "darker" is compared. His open-ended language suggests that gradations of color are at play. Conceivably, some of the Athenian athletes already had "dark" skin, and the sun has made it even "darker." Harmon's translation of the prepositional phrase *hypo tou hēliou* in relation to its preceding clause implies a close connection between the sun and the athletes' skin color. The sun offers a visual shortcut to Greek identity that works in tandem with other activities befitting Greek men, such as outdoor exercise.

My translation of *to melanteron* as "rather black" calls for an expansive color wheel that denies absolute colors. This open-ended field of comparison underscores the coexistence of swirling identities in Lucian's Scythian satires. His recurring interest in foreignness from the perspectives of Syrians, Scythians, and Athenian Greeks undermines the fixed preeminence of each group. Departing from Fowler's and Fowler's and Harmon's pairing of the athletes' skin color with the sun, I incorporate the sun into the prepositional clause that follows *to melanteron*: *hypo tou hēliou kechrōsmenoi*, "because they have been colored by the sun." My translation of *kechrōsmenoi* as "colored" replaces the painful skin condition suggested by "sunburnt" with a more benign interaction between the sun and the

---

[65] Lucian's inclusion of a comparative adjective (*melanteron*) in his description of the Athenian athletes suggests that he is parodying scientific ethnographies such as *On Airs, Waters, and Places*.

athletes' skin.[66] My placement of their color ("somewhat red to rather black") before its qualifier ("because they have been colored by the sun") offers readers a vibrant color palette before determining the cause of their hue. Color and its justification merge in this description of athletes who display a range of colors, from red to black, due to their exposure to the sun.[67] With their chromatic range, these athletes resemble those who live farthest from Greece: (red) Scythians in the north and (black) Aithiopians in the south. By applying these two colors to Athenian athletes, Lucian subtly critiques the tendency to conflate skin color and identity, a shorthand that had gained popularity in fifth-century BCE medical treatises.

Nestled into his vivid description of the athletes, Solon heightens the tension between his sun-kissed Athenians and other men. He invests in a rigid framework when he gives lavish praise to Greek men and rebukes non-Greek men. According to Solon, Athenian athletes are healthy and well-proportioned while other men are shrunken down or inflated in size. The placement of the Greeks' physique between extreme want and satiated excess fits into a larger theory of attributing people's character traits to their environment. In *On Airs, Waters, and Places* 5, the narrator labels those who face the rising sun as even-tempered and intelligent.[68] Similarly, the narrator of the pseudo-Aristotelian handbook *Physiognomies* describes extremely black people and white people as excessively cowardly by nature (οἱ ἄγαν μέλανες ... οἱ δὲ λευκοὶ ἄγαν δειλοί, 812a).[69] According to the narrator, the hue of brave people falls in between these two shades. It is unsurprising that the intermediaries between these two extremes are people who are filled with courage, a trait that Greek men were eager to ascribe to themselves.[70] An undercurrent of this

---

[66] The effects of the shining sun reverberate later in this passage with the participle *apolampontes* ("[the athletes] beam"). Cf. Danaus's description of Argive soldiers whose arms are darkened by the sun (*Supp.* 746–47).

[67] Berlin and Kay (1969) hypothesize that all spoken languages with at least three basic color terms distinguish between dark, light, and red; their World Color Survey supports these findings (Kay et al. [2009: 25–41]). Irwin (1974), Sassi (2001), and Eaverly (2013) examine the contrast between dark and light in the ancient Greek context.

[68] Conversely, the pseudo-Aristotelian treatise *Problemata* describes inhabitants of warm regions as cowardly (909–10).

[69] The narrator of this pseudo-Aristotelian treatise categorizes women as white and Aithiopians and Egyptians as black. As an extension of this theory, the narrator insists that a ruddy complexion demarcates one's character: depending on which part of people's bodies is red, this color is associated with insanity, ill temper, bashfulness, or drunkenness ([*Phgn.*] 812a–b). In other Greek and Latin treatises, white skin is often conflated with excessive phlegm and blood, both of which generate foolhardy confidence (Ptolemy, *Tetrabiblios* 2.2; Vitruvius, *On Architecture* 6.1.3–5, 6.1.8–11; Vegetius, *On Military Matters* 1.2).

[70] Aristotle remarks that Greeks occupy a happy medium in terms of their geography and temperament (*Politics* 1327b; discussed in Secord [2016]). See also Grundmann's (2019) discussion of the

long-standing conflation occurs when Solon distances emaciated and corpulent men from Athenian athletes. Either the sun has shone too brightly, leading to their weak and shriveled state, or they have eschewed outdoor activities, culminating in their portliness and lazy nature. Solon continues to foreground vivid displays of excellence when he emphasizes a balance found among Athenian athletes via their correct proportions (*to symmetron*): they have received an ideal amount of sunlight that has darkened their skin and enlivened their bodies. As the sun pierces through their bodies, this penetrative sunlight fortifies their spirit and warms (*thermon*) their soul, which in turn leads to their physical excellence (*Anach.* 25).

By the end of the dialogue, Solon turns away from his disagreement with Anacharsis and seeks information from him about the Scythians' athletic regimen. This final twist reverses their roles: Solon, the sage advisor, becomes a student of Scythian ethnography, and Anacharsis, the curious novice, transforms into a sage.[71] In effect, Anacharsis again disrupts the domain of the xenophone while operating as a foreign (*xenos*) speaker (*phōnē*). This culminating role reversal reinforces Lucian's earlier pairings of seemingly incongruent categories: admiration and ridicule, knowledge and ignorance, Greek and Scythian, the world of reality and the world of performance. These sophisticated subtleties feed into Lucian's broader interest in the permeability of race (external categorization) and identity. His polyvalent approach results in characters who inhabit multiple, sometimes overlapping, identities despite other people's attempts to label them otherwise. To return to the language of shadows, sunlight and mud create shadow identities that illustrate the pull between polarity and proximity in this satire.

5.5 Conclusion: Ludicrous Masquerades of Skin Color

Lucian's biting take on blackness, in which each instance of absurdity further distances his characters from his readers, liberates his performances from thematic or conceptual limitations. Every attempt to reduce black skin to a single place or group of people falls apart. As his characters witness hybrid presentations of black people on a cosmopolitan stage, they integrate more than overt markers of skin color into their understanding of

relationship between alterable skin color and emotional temperament in ancient Greek medical texts.

[71] The trope of a wise Anacharsis also appears in Plato, *Republic* 600a4 and Plutarch, *Moralia* 146e–164d. Mestre (2003: 306) draws a link between Scythian nomadism and cleverness: the lack of a permanent home prevents enemies from sacking Scythia.

others.[72] For Anacharsis, the blackness of Athenian athletes stands along-side their animal-like behavior and simulated violence. For Solon, the athletes' skin color is part of a larger performance of physical prowess that confirms their Greek identity. Taken together, they inspire collective questioning of blackness in relation to Greek identity under the guise of humor.

In the twenty-first century, scholars have pounced on the flexibility afforded by the genre of satire to critique the ludicrous masquerade of skin color in relation to modern race.[73] Paul Beatty's take on the shifting performance of modern race via Blackness writ large provides a final way for readers to reframe Lucian's variable manipulations of blackness. In his novel *The Sellout* (2015), which builds on William E. Cross's 1971 essay, "The Negro-to-Black Conversion Experience,"[74] a Black man named Me ends up in front of the US Supreme Court charged with human enslavement and violation of the Civil Rights Act.[75] After recounting his lonely childhood as a home-schooled boy whose savant father wove the Black Power movement and disturbing psychological experiments into his son's curriculum, Me witnesses his father's death at the hands of a police officer. Unyielding demand from his community compels Me to take on his father's former job as "Negro-whisperer," an occupation that consists of coaxing people on the precipice of suicide to renege on their plans. By granting his protagonist the power to preserve the lives of Black people under the guise of folksy tradition, Beatty spins modern racist ideology on its head. In his role as "Negro-whisperer," Me saves the life of Hominy, an elderly Black man and former minstrel star who unsuccessfully tries to hang himself in an act of pseudo-lynching.[76] In an act of gratitude, Hominy insists on becoming Me's slave. Hominy's new role as a slave turns into a farcical, layered performance in which he engages in

---

[72] Whitmarsh (2011a) elaborates on the trope of hybridity in Greek literature from the Second Sophistic onward.

[73] Such as Dickson-Carr (2001), Haggins (2007), Carpio (2008), Maus and Donahue (2014), and Crawford (2017). It is plausible to regard nineteenth-century minstrelsy as a protosatirical genre.

[74] Cross (1971).

[75] Astrada (2017) discusses the construction of Me's identity and his eventual appropriation of the role into which he has been thrust. Cf. the relationship between characters' names and their personalities in Ngũgĩ wa Thiong'o's satirical novel *Mũrogi wa Kagogo* (translated as *The Wizard of the Crow*, 2006): the greedy politicians Sikiokuu ("major ear" in Swahili), Machokali ("harsh eyes"), and Tajirika ("become rich"; discussed in Mack [2019: 169–94]).

[76] Hominy's suicide attempt is extremely disturbing. When Me discovers him hanging from a wooden beam, Hominy sputters a request: he wants Me to cut off his penis and shove it into his mouth. This scene evokes the inhumane acts that occurred at lynchings (Beatty [2015: 74]; on lynchings, see Wolters [2004]).

dehumanizing acts, such as begging for a whipping and groveling before Me.[77] His performance of abject self-fashioning is so convincing that it eventually results in Me's day in court.[78]

Wandering around Washington, DC before his trial, Me mocks the city's pretensions to emulate ancient Rome:

> Washington, D.C., with its wide streets, confounding roundabouts, marble statues, Doric columns and domes, is supposed to feel like ancient Rome (that is, if the streets of ancient Rome were lined with homeless people, bomb-sniffing dogs, tour buses, and cherry blossoms). Yesterday afternoon, like some sandal-shod Ethiop from the sticks of the darkest of the Los Angeles jungles, I ventured from the hotel and joined the hajj of blue-jeaned yokels that paraded slowly and patriotically past the empire's historical landmarks.[79]

Me interrogates the successful transference of glamour required to transport his readers to ancient Rome. Despite its antiquated layout and architecture, Washington, D.C. cannot escape its decidedly modern elements.[80] Me's pronouncements evoke Lucian's image of Athens in the sixth century BCE – a time when the city had become, in Laura Nasrallah's language, "a haunt of those who claim to be true philosophers and rhetoricians, but are lacking; even a Syrian can show them up."[81] More versatile than other people in the city, Me resists the starry-eyed throng of tourists around him to chart his own course. Echoing the ease with which Lucian the narrator identifies as Scythian in *The Scythian or the Consul*, Me casts himself as a "sandal-shod Ethiop" emerging from the depths of Los Angeles. In line with Lucian's temporal flexibility, Me conflates an ancient referent with his lived reality. Leapfrogging over any association with the transatlantic slave trade, Me embraces a blended timeline in which a sartorially distinct "Ethiop" can descend from "the sticks of the darkest of the Los Angeles jungles."

---

[77] Beatty (2015: 73–80). In and of itself, slavery is a performance of power distribution that masqueraded as an objective norm for hundreds of years. See also my discussion of scenes of resistance in Section 1.2.

[78] In addition to allegedly enslaving Hominy, Me is on trial for reinstituting segregation in his hometown of Dickens (a neighborhood in Los Angeles whose cartographical presence Me takes great pains to restore after its sudden disappearance).

[79] Beatty (2015: 4). See also the narrator's shrewd deliberation about whether or not to use his knowledge of Latin to create Latin mottos for Black people (Beatty [2015: 11–13, 194]).

[80] The fact that Benjamin Banneker, a free African American, was instrumental in surveying Washington, DC, adds to the irony of Me's critique.

[81] Nasrallah (2005: 298).

Combined with his use of antiquated language ("Ethiop"), Me's humble attire and unpretentious hometown provide a sharp contrast with the lofty illusions of Washington, DC. Me's language also signals an unexpected resolution at the intersection of past blackness, through the etymology of "Ethiop" (*aithō*, "I blaze"), and present Blackness, through his lived experience.[82] Flashpoints such as these correspond with Lucian's flexible approach to time, geography, and skin color. In the next chapter, I explore another writer's fascination with these themes. In his fourth-century CE novel *Aithiopika*, Heliodorus chronicles the journey of Charicleia, a white Aithiopian princess who eventually learns about her royal black parentage. An overlap between others' categorization of Charicleia and her own self-identification becomes pertinent to her survival. Furthermore, her extensive travels enable readers to visit Meroe, the historic and religious capital of Nubia (c. 300BCE–300CE) and a locus of power in its own right.

---

[82] Cf. Fran Ross's *Oreo* (1974), a satirical novel in which the main character, a Black Jewish girl from Philadelphia, bears similarities to the mythical figure Theseus (discussed in Cook and Tatum [2010: 292–309]).

CHAPTER 6

Black Disguises in an Aithiopian Novel

Writing approximately two centuries after Lucian, Heliodorus similarly presents black people as compelling, nuanced performers. His ten-book novel *Aithiopika* (c. fourth century CE) underscores the resurgence of interest in sixth-/fifth-century BCE Greek literature during the Second Sophistic.[1] Expanding Herodotus's geographical survey of the land around Meroe (Hdt. 2.29–31), Heliodorus creates a full story around the Meroites.[2] His presentation of the people of Meroe, whom he refers to as Aithiopians, subverts any fixed notion of black people. Furthermore, he troubles a geographical hierarchy that presumes Greece to be at the summit, which in turn shortens the distance between Aithiopia and Greece. This novel, the earliest example written in Greek of a plot in which black skin confers cultural privilege, is not constrained by linguistic, geographic, or temporal boundaries. Its characters grapple with various interpretations of black skin, which some of them believe to be a key determinant of the Aithiopian people. These diverse encounters reveal skin color to be

[1] Scholars vary on the date of Heliodorus's *Aithiopika*. Swain interprets the historical decline of Emesa, Heliodorus's hometown in Syria, after c. 270 CE, as evidence of an early third-century date; as for the similarities between Heliodorus's account of the fictional siege of Syene (9) and the Roman emperor Julian's account of the historical siege of Nisibis in 357 CE (*Orations*, 1, 3), Swain (1996: 423–24) insists that Heliodorus was Julian's source. Conversely, Morgan (2008) and Bowersock (1994) use the siege passages to argue for a fourth-century date. Bowersock (1994: 153–60) further supports his claim by drawing parallels between Heliod. *Aeth.* 10 and the fourth-century CE *Historia Augusta*. Whitmarsh (1999: 33–34 [with n. 2 on p. 33]; 2011b: 5), Hägg (2000: 195), and Ross (2015) also agree with the fourth-century date. Turning to the novel for additional evidence (in Heliod. *Aeth.* 10.27, the Aksumites are the Meroites' distinguished guests), I concur with Morgan (2008: 577 n. 247), who explains that hints of Aksum's later importance "may be intended in the exceptional status of Aksum among Hydaspes's allies." I read the non-tributary status of the Aksumites as a way to allow readers to imagine a privileged relationship with Aksumites that is vastly different from the historical context in the fourth century BCE, during which Aksum destroyed Meroe and potentially annexed Meroe to its empire.

[2] Morgan (2005: 310) and Elmer (2008: 422–25) note similarities between two men: Hydaspes, Heliodorus' Aithiopian king, and Sabacos, the Aithiopian ruler discussed in Hdt. 2.139–40. Morgan (1982: 237–38) also suggests a connection between Hydaspes and Herodotus's Aithiopian king discussed in Hdt. 3.17–26.

a negotiable ethnographic tool that *can,* but does not have to, denote one's identity.[3]

In the *Aithiopika*, Heliodorus takes his readers on a winding journey through Greece, Egypt, and Aithiopia, a trip during which they interrogate the parameters of belonging based on visual and nonvisual clues.[4] His readers follow the peripatetic journey of Charicleia, a sixth-/fifth-century BCE Aithiopian princess abandoned at birth because of the dissonance between her white skin and her parents' black skin.[5] During an arduous trek that eventually leads her back to Aithiopia, Charicleia faces various trials that threaten to derail her completely. Although Charicleia and her companions are fictional characters, her hometown of Meroe is real: it was the thriving capital city of Nubia and a trading partner of Greece and Rome. Intent on expanding his readers' worldview, Heliodorus portrays Charicleia as more than a Greek woman and Meroe as more than a mirror of Greece.[6] He creates a quadripolar vision of the world that eventually includes Greece, Aithiopia, Persia, and Egypt.[7] In this fabricated world, Heliodorus pushes back against a binary model to incorporate a more complex one that toggles between categories such as admirable foreigner and chauvinistic Greek, as well as black Aithiopian and white Aithiopian. Charicleia embodies this quadripolar vision with her various travels, fathers, and performances of identity.

To address my ongoing interrogation of Greece's normative status, I begin with a linguistic proposition: the *Aithiopika* is an Aithiopian novel written in Greek, not a Greek novel about Aithiopia. Next, I discuss the novel's jarring opening scene that situates the reader in the aftermath of a grisly battle (Heliod. *Aeth.* 1.1.1–3.3) as Charicleia uses visual clues to describe the pirates around her. This scene offers an entry point

---

[3] Bradley (2009: 145–60) addresses similar chromatic resonances in Latin literature, in that color signals one's origins and disposition, yet blushing, tanning, and/or intermarrying enable people to alter their color.

[4] While I use the nomenclature "reader" to stress the decoding of signs on the page, I am aware that some of Heliodorus's readers may have listened to an oral presentation of the novel. Stephens (1994), Bowie (1994), and Sanz Morales (2018) discuss the readership of ancient novels written in Greek.

[5] Herodotus's chronology of the *hetaira* Rhodopis (Hdt. 2.134–35), who also appears in the *Aithiopika*, supports the late sixth/early fifth-century BCE date (Morgan [1982: 236 n. 46]; Morgan [2008: 350]; Elmer [2008: 424–25]).

[6] Conversely, some scholars treat Aithiopia or non-Greek places as generic, hollow referents for Greece (Rostovtzeff as quoted in Burstein [1995: 112]; Morgan [2014: 264]; Hartog [1988]). Although there was no general hostility to foreign rule in Meroe, there was no political integration or harmony either (Swain [1996: 411–12]). Heliodorus enhances the Greek perspective of the south in the same way that Antonius Diogenes enhances the Greek view of the north in his novel *Wonders beyond Thule* (Feuillâtre [1966: 145]).

[7] Lonis (1992: 238). Musié (2018) examines the role of Persia in the *Aithiopika*.

into the messy categories of skin color, external categorization (race), and identity that Charicleia negotiates during her travels. An ensuing inspection of Meroe, Charicleia's birthplace, in imperial Greek literature illuminates the ways that Heliodorus masterfully reworks his literary predecessors' rendering of the city. Subsequently, Charicleia's use of soot and mud as a disguise (6.11.3), alongside the inability of Theagenes, her Greek lover, to recognize her (7.7.6–7), highlights the ways that she harnesses blackness as a mobile marker of identity at pivotal moments. Charicleia's temporary adoption of black skin implies an instability of blackness that requires resolution before her family will accept her.[8] This interplay between blackness, disguise, and perception distorts the ways that readers of the *Aithiopika* interpret skin color in the novel. In line with this discussion, I examine the prophecy that merges Charicleia's white skin and Aithiopian identity (2.35.5), further upending the status of black skin as a fixed semiotic marker of identity. I end with a discussion of Pauline Hopkins's novel *Of One Blood*, originally serialized in 1902–03, in which characters use tactics similar to Charicleia's, exploiting their skin color to cross boundaries.

6.1   Hermeneutic Hooliganism

Heliodorus lived and wrote within the rapidly changing topography of the Greek world under Roman rule. Although Heliodorus's sphragis is the sole source of information about the narrator's identity as a Phoenician from Emesa, Syria (Heliod. *Aeth.* 10.41.4),[9] the broad assignation of Roman citizenship issued by the *constitutio Antoniniana* spurred newly minted Roman subjects to negotiate overlapping loyalties to their homeland alongside the rapidly expanding Roman empire.[10] By the time of Heliodorus's birth in the fourth century CE, Roman power had become

---

[8]   Hilton (1998: 91); Perkins (1999: 198).

[9]   Quinn (2017: xviii, 135, 149–51) argues that the term "Phoenician" was a Greek invention and points to Heliodorus as the only self-attested Phoenician in Greco-Roman antiquity. The ecclesiastical historian Socrates claims that Heliodorus was a Christian bishop in Thessaly; Byzantine historians speculate that Heliodorus chose to renounce his post as bishop rather than disown his novel (Morgan [2008: 352]). Swain (1996: 423–24) provocatively identifies Heliodorus as "Heliodorus the Arab" who receives favors from Caracalla (*Lives of the Sophists* 625–27). Without evidence to support such claims, these remain attractive yet unsubstantiated guesses.

[10] The surge of popularity of Christianity also contributes to Heliodorus's diverse landscape. Quiroga (2007) classifies the fourth century CE as the "Third Sophistic," a time during which writers creatively engage with their historical realities, such as the growing presence of Christianity. Andújar (2013) argues that Heliodorus draws inspiration from the second-century Christian text *Acts of Paul and Thecla*.

firmly entrenched in the eastern part of the empire with the new Roman capital of Constantinople. The trope of time travel also permeated the Second Sophistic, as Roman subjects were able to interact with sixth-/fifth-century BCE Athens via their interest in *paideia*. For his part, Heliodorus taps into the flexibility that *paideia* affords its proponents. Merging his reconstruction of a region beyond the southernmost limits of the Roman empire with a timeline that precedes his lived experience by at least nine hundred years, he offers his readers a speculative approach to a world geographically and temporally distant from their own. Nonetheless, the variable identities and extensive travel that he pens into existence coincide with the realities of his lived environment.[11]

Heliodorus's jarring narrative tactics in the *Aithiopika* complement the shifting realities of his lived world. For example, the *Aithiopika* begins *in medias res* with readers accompanying Egyptian pirates who witness Charicleia weeping over her wounded lover Theagenes. At this juncture in her travels, she is in Egypt with Theagenes after fleeing from Delphi. This disorienting framework prevents Heliodorus's readers from learning about Charicleia's lineage – her parents are the king and queen of Aithiopia – until later in the novel (4.8–13). Such maneuvers give the impression that Heliodorus intentionally seeks to baffle his readers, dropping them into a strange world without giving them the tools to make sense of it. Judith Perkins draws an intriguing parallel between the reader's shock upon discovering that Charicleia is not Greek and the reader's surprise at Heliodorus's admission that he is Phoenician at the end of the novel.[12] Indeed, Heliodorus's constant pivots and withholding tactics apply to both his characters and his own identity within the text. He inserts other instances of hermeneutic hooliganism into the contorted narrative structure of his novel, such as his characters' propensity for deception via disguise and their tendency to misread signs of race (external categorization). His ability to insert and resolve numerous occurrences of instability throughout the novel marks the *Aithiopika* as a unique literary project.

Toni Morrison's description of the experience she sought to create for her readers in the foreword to her 1987 novel, *Beloved*, overlaps with Heliodorus's program of narrative alienation. Morrison describes how

---

[11] I limit my discussion of black people as historical subjects in the late Roman empire for two main reasons: the lack of first-hand perspectives means that any conclusions about their role will be speculative, and the need to prove their relevance reflects contemporary anxieties about skin color rather than historical realities, as evidenced in the discussion, p. 163 below, of the quotation from Hägg evincing an adoption of an anachronistic color wheel.

[12] Perkins (1999: 202–03). Anderson (1997) elaborates on Heliodorus's elusive narrative engineering.

she composed her novel in such a way as to cause her readers' mimetic displacement: "I wanted the reader to be kidnapped, thrown ruthlessly into an alien environment as the first step into a shared experience with the book's population – just as the characters were snatched from one place to another, from any place to any other, without preparation or defense."[13] The topsy-turvy world into which Morrison seeks to throw her readers has parallels with Heliodorus's literary setting. Both writers liken their readers to characters who must extricate themselves from challenging, unfamiliar situations. Their shared disavowal of initial narrative guidance compels readers to come to their own conclusions regarding important issues. Nonetheless, Morrison and Heliodorus differ in the ways in which they (mis)lead their readers. Writing within a historical context that is shaped by an unnatural interest in skin color, Morrison challenges the chasm between life and death as it is embodied in one Black character, Beloved, who flits between the two worlds. For his part, Heliodorus reroutes his readers' expectations of what Aithiopians look like with his nuanced exploration of skin color. He forces his readers to engage with a world in which skin color and identity coexist in unpredictable ways. As his characters approach Meroe, polycentrism and physical appearance unearth deep-seated notions of what it means to be Aithiopian.[14] In this vein, Charicleia's radical alteration of blackness is concurrent with the diminishing presence of her adopted homeland, Greece, and the centralized position of Meroe, the land of her birth.

6.2   An Aithiopian Novel Written in Greek

Channeling Heliodorus's decentering of Hellenocentrism, I scrutinize the generally accepted description of the *Aithiopika* as a "Greek" novel and call into question the privileged status of Greece in modern scholarship about the *Aithiopika*.[15] For example, despite J. R. Morgan's incisive insights about the novel, his remark that the *Aithiopika* is an "endorsement, assertion, and extension of Hellenism" overdetermines the impact of Greece on Heliodorus's novel.[16] Morgan's treatment of Aithiopia as a hollow

---

[13] Morrison (2004: xviii). Another point of convergence between Morrison and Heliodorus lies in Morrison's careful treatment of color; for example, the color red (discussed in Bast [2011]).

[14] Cioffi (2013: 2, 173).

[15] The title of the novel has also been the subject of scholarly investigation. Byzantine readers referred to the novel as "Charicleia," and some may have referred to it as "Charicleia and Theagenes" (Morgan [2013: 227]; Whitmarsh [1999: 36 n. 31]).

[16] Morgan (2014: 264). Morgan (2014: 262) also suggests that Meroe is a metaphorical Emesa because of the Aithiopian royal family's descent from the sun god. Stephens (2008: 70) observes that through

intertextual construct denies the country any signifying power of its own. Moreover, twenty-first-century biases have seeped into Tomas Hägg's argument that Charicleia's white skin made her more relatable to Greek readers: "considerations regarding the Greek readership of the novel may have prevented [Heliodorus] from presenting a black heroine; it would have made it less easy for them to identify with her . . . It was easier for him to produce and explain a white Aithiopian than to accommodate a black heroine."[17] Hägg's adoption of an anachronistic color wheel detracts from the malleable rendering of skin color in Heliodorus's novel. Without necessary contextualization, Charicleia becomes a stand-in for contemporary Black female performers who continue to wrestle with the uneven implications of their presence in front of their audience.[18]

In *Dirty Love: The Genealogy of the Ancient Greek Novel* (2018), Tim Whitmarsh helpfully moves away from the myth of a monolithic Greek tradition and focuses instead on the hybrid genealogy of the novel. His formulation of polygenesis is an important starting place from which to conceptualize the diverse portrayal of Aithiopians in the *Aithiopika*. The story of an Aithiopian protagonist whose skin color is white, because her mother looked at a painting of Andromeda (in which the mythical character is depicted with white skin) precisely at the moment of conception, throws doubt on the efficacy of a rigid color palette for Aithiopians.[19] Charicleia's manipulations of temporary markers of blackness and her permanent black birthmark further demand a composite approach to skin color.

With these sophisticated permutations of Aithiopian identity in mind, I propose changing the description of the *Aithiopika* from "a Greek novel" to "an Aithiopian novel written in Greek."[20] This slight shift of focalization treats Hellenocentrism as a subject of inquiry rather than a fixed presumption. This reorientation contests the Hellenocentric lens that threatens to overshadow other prominent communities in the novel. To

---

the *Aithiopika*, Heliodorus "allows both the author and the readers [to] indulge in 'what if,' cushioned by the safety of the text."

[17] Hägg (2000: 216).

[18] I discuss the ways that Black female performers upend limiting categories in Derbew (2019).

[19] Conversely, McGrath (1992) draws attention to the trope of black Andromeda that predates Heliodorus's lifetime, namely in *Her.* 15.36 and *Ars am.* 1.53 (see Chapter 2, n. 45). In dialogue with McGrath, artist Kimathi Donkor (2020: 190–91) reimagines Andromeda as "defiantly black" in his 2011 painting "The Rescue of Andromeda." Irrespective of Andromeda's skin color, her wandering (from east to south) bears similarities with Charicleia's travels.

[20] I align my use of "novel" with Whitmarsh (2011b: 255), who describes it as "a narrative of identity metamorphoses."

be sure, this proposition does not presuppose that Heliodorus is an Aithiopian writer with an indigenous perspective. Rather, the Phoenician narrator from Emesa reworks the concept of linguistic sovereignty in a way that makes space for Aithiopia. His deft writing transforms the southern-most region of the Greek world (under Roman rule) into a heterogeneous land filled with characters who inhabit more than one realm. The prominent position of "Aithiopia" also underscores the importance of this country in the novel, in that the disconnect between Charicleia's appearance and her Aithiopian identity pushes the novel forward and serves as its ideological climax.

The first three words of my proposed nomenclature, "an Aithiopian novel," draw inspiration from Mũkoma wa Ngũgĩ's rethinking of what constitutes the parameters of a genre. In *The Rise of the African Novel: Politics of Language, Identity, and Ownership* (2018), Mũkoma wa Ngũgĩ reconsiders the current African literary archive, which privileges African literature written in English. His corrective genealogy points to the extensive trajectory of literature written in African languages that pre-dates European colonialism.[21] To name a few examples: in 1672, the Ethiopian priest Galawdewos (ገላውዴዎስ) penned the hagiobiography of Welete Petros (ወለተ ጴጥሮስ) in Ge'ez (classical Ethiopic).[22] In 1895, Fesseha Giyorgis Abiyäzgi published *Impressions: An Account of a Voyage from Ethiopia to Italy* in Tigrinya, a language spoken in northern Ethiopia and southern Eritrea; in 1931, Thomas Mofolo published *Chaka, an Historical Romance* in Sesotho, spoken in Lesotho, South Africa, and Zimbabwe; and in 1934, Muhammadu Bello Kagara wrote *Gandaki* in Hausa, spoken in northwestern Nigeria and southern Niger. As part of his commitment to foregrounding Africa's diverse literary output, Mũkoma wa Ngũgĩ issues a call for wider communities to engage with African literature written in African languages.[23] His insistence on a rich linguistic landscape overlaps with his father Ngũgĩ wa Thiong'o's manifesto for literary emancipation from European languages (as I discuss

---

[21] I refer to Mũkoma wa Ngũgĩ by his full name, while I refer to his father, Ngũgĩ wa Thiong'o, as "Ngũgĩ."

[22] Ge'ez is an ancient Semitic language that was once spoken in Ethiopia. Since the seventh century CE, it has been the primary language of the Ethiopian Orthodox Tewahedo (ተዋሕዶ) church.

[23] See the translation and commentary of Galawdewos's hagiobiography ([1672] 2015) by Belcher and Kleiner; Habtu (2000) translates Fesseha Giyorgis's *Impressions*. As part of his advocacy for African literature in African languages, Mũkoma wa Ngũgĩ co-founded the Mabati Cornell Kiswahili Prize for African Literature in 2014, an annual award that recognizes the best literature written in Swahili. In 2021, he worked with colleagues to change the name of Cornell University's English Department to "Department of Literatures in English."

above, in Chapter 1).[24] Although I am eager to prioritize the study of literature written in indigenous languages, the incomplete decipherment of Meroitic script compels me to rely on Greek sources in my investigation of literary Aithiopia.[25] Furthermore, the fact that Heliodorus transmits the entire novel in Greek prevents me from sifting through the different languages associated with the communities in the *Aithiopika*. Nonetheless, Mũkoma wa Ngũgĩ's reframing of African literature influences my proposal of "an Aithiopian novel" because it allows Aithiopia to stand at the center of the story and relegates Greece to the role of distant neighbor.

Mũkoma wa Ngũgĩ's reshuffling of linguistic hegemonies also undergirds "written in Greek," the second half of the label I propose. The phrase encapsulates the projections of Aithiopia within Greek literature without discounting the mediated perspective of Aithiopians. As it stands, my relegation of "Greek" into a participial phrase ("written in Greek") aims to unsettle any assumptions that the language in which a text is written predetermines its content or loyalties. Heliodorus's linguistic choice does not signal the objective superiority of Greece in the novel. In fact, Heliodorus disrupts the seeming preeminence of the Greek language by drawing attention to linguistic challenges. For instance, in the opening scene of the novel, Charicleia has difficulty communicating with two groups of pirates she comes across because they do not know Greek, and she does not speak their language.[26] Other Aithiopians, however, including her father Hydaspes and the wise gymnosophist Sisimithres, speak both the language of the Greeks and that of the Aithiopians.[27] Another case in point: the Meroitic crowd is ignorant of the Greek language (10.9.6), yet Heliodorus grants them momentary and inexplicable comprehension of the conversation being held among the royal family in Greek (10.38.3).[28]

---

[24] Ngũgĩ wa Thiong'o (1987).

[25] Rowan (2006) and Rilly and de Voogt (2012) offer useful introductions to Meroitic phonology and the Meroitic writing system, respectively.

[26] Perkins (1999: 204–06); Slater (2005: 107–08); Whitmarsh (2005a). On linguistic problems in the *Aithiopika*'s multilingual world, see Morgan (1982: 258–59); Winkler (1982: 104–06); Saïd (1992); and Groves (2012).

[27] Hydaspes's fluency in Greek may reflect his royal education (Hägg [2000: 204]). The linguistic capabilities of non-Greek characters appear in fifth-century BCE Athenian tragedy (Greek-speaking Persians in Aeschylus's *Persians*) and imperial Greek literature (Philostratus's description of an enslaved Indian who speaks Greek in an Indian dialect and an Indian king who is fluent in Greek, *V A* 2.27. Philostratus's explicit interrogation of the Indian king's linguistic abilities, however, questions the regularity of this phenomenon). Cioffi (2013: 202 n. 689) suggests that Hydaspes's multilingual fluency draws attention to the multiple countries present in the novel.

[28] Heliodorus challenges any shallow observation of linguistic fluency with characters who express their inability to understand other languages (Thyamis cannot speak Greek, *Aeth.* 1.19.3) and those

Straddling numerous linguistic axes, Heliodorus firmly moves away from a Hellenocentric perspective and nudges Aithiopia closer to the novel's origin, center, and *telos*. The Greek language is the vehicle that carries this novel to its readers, but the plot and characters of the *Aithiopika* are less invested in the Greek *polis*.

At the start of this Aithiopian novel written in Greek, Charicleia encounters a band of Egyptian men near the Nile Delta. Lacking any background information, readers rely on the narrator and Charicleia to understand the race (external categorization) of these men:

> καὶ μέλανας ἰδοῦσα τὴν χροιὰν καὶ τὴν ὄψιν αὐχμηρούς, "εἰ μὲν εἴδωλα τῶν κειμένων ἐστέ," φησίν "οὐκ ἐν δίκῃ παρενοχλεῖτε ἡμῖν … εἰ δέ τινες τῶν ζώντων ἐστέ, λῃστρικὸς μὲν ὑμῖν ὡς ἔοικεν ὁ βίος, εἰς καιρὸν δὲ ἥκετε."

> And she looked up and saw the appearance of men with black skin who were covered in dust. She said, "If you are ghosts of men who lie dead, you trouble us unfairly … But if you are living men, you lead the life of pirates, it seems. You have come at the right time." (Heliod. *Aeth.* 1.3.1)

Different clues point readers in different directions. The narrator highlights the skin color of the men standing before Charicleia (μέλανας … τὴν χροιὰν, "men with black skin"). Based on the narrator's etiology for their appearance (αὐχμηρούς, "dust"), these Egyptian men derive their appearance from their environment, thereby resembling the Athenian athletes whom Solon and Anacharsis observed (Chapter 5). In addition, the narrator's pairing of blackness and dust suggests that skin color is not a reliable criterion with which to categorize people (i.e. to determine their race). At this point in Charicleia's journey, she does not dwell directly on skin color's vast signifying possibilities. Rather, she refers to the men's occupation, which obliquely hints at their skin color, thereby drawing a loose connection between ghosts, pirates, and blackness.[29]

During this exchange, the Egyptian men proffer no information about their race (external categorization). Therefore, the readers encounter them solely through the eyes of Charicleia, focalized by the narrator (ἰδοῦσα … ὄψιν, "she saw the appearance of men"). As a result of this guidance, readers construct the race of these men based on what is immediately visible. This fragmentary, vision-based approach to the categorization of

---

who learn foreign languages (Cnemon and Theagenes learn the Egyptian language during their time in Egypt, 1.19, 8.17.3).

[29] In his discussion of Lollianus's novel *Phoinikika*, fr. B, as labeled in Heinrichs (1972), Winkler (1980: 157–65) concludes that ghosts regularly frighten humans by using the colors black or white as suitable disguises.

others resonates in the postcolonial context. In his *Black Skin, White Masks* (1952), Frantz Fanon offers complementary insight into the interplay between sight and subjectivity during interpersonal meetings. Fanon wryly notes:

> The white gaze, the only valid one, is already dissecting me. I am *fixed*. Once their microtomes are sharpened, the Whites objectively cut sections of my reality. I have been betrayed. I sense, I see in this white gaze that it's the arrival not of a new man, but of a new type of man, a new species. A Negro, in fact! ... When they like me, they tell me my color has nothing to do with it. When they hate me, they add that it's not because of my color. Either way, I am a prisoner of the vicious cycle.[30]

Tools in hand, the White community cuts Fanon up and pieces him together as a newly palatable person. Their piercing gaze creates a new species that only they have the power to define. What is clear to the "valid" White community is arbitrary to the object of their gaze, the "prisoner of the vicious cycle." The vivid scientific terms ("dissecting ... microtomes are sharpened ... objectively cut sections") contribute to the presumptuous and lofty position of the viewers. Fanon sarcastically frames their gaze as one devoid of opinions and solely based on unassailable facts. The perspective of the viewers trumps that of the viewed. In this way, the viewers have "betray[ed]" the object of their gaze, Fanon, by stripping him of the ability to label himself.

Charicleia flirts with the very role of ultimate arbiter against which Fanon rails when she attempts to label the men as pirates. The unbowed protagonist's brief encounter with these men has given her enough information to classify them. Nonetheless, Charicleia differs from the all-powerful White people in Fanon's lexicon because she is in a precarious situation. The narrator reminds readers that the men's strength in numbers and weapons threatens Charicleia's safety. Additionally, her use of the impersonal phrase "as it seems" (ὡς ἔοικεν) and the repeated conjunction "if" (εἰ) hints at her uncertainty among these men. More broadly, Charicleia's attempt to parse the men's race (external categorization) partly based on their appearance fits into her larger project of sorting out the components of race during her sojourn. As she continues her journey, she

---

[30] Fanon (2008: 95–96), translation Philcox. Fanon (1952: 93–94): "Déjà les regards blancs, les seuls vrais, me dissèquent. Je suis *fixé*. Ayant accommodé leur microtome, ils réalisent objectivement des coupes de ma réalité. Je suis trahi. Je sens, je vois dans ces regards blancs que ce n'est pas un nouvel homme qui entre, mais un nouveau type d'homme, un nouveau genre. Un nègre, quoi! ... Quand on m'aime, on me dit que c'est malgré ma couleur. Quand on me déteste, on ajoute que ce n'est pas à cause de ma couleur ... Ici ou là, je suis prisonnier du cercle infernal."

begins to envision a compound framework for classifying people, which bodes well for her own successful performance of her Aithiopian identity.

6.3   Situating Aithiopia and Nubia in Roman Greece

Although Charicleia's sixth-/fifth-century BCE world does not correspond directly to his lived reality, Heliodorus's fictional rendering of her birthplace, Meroe, speaks to the wider phenomenon of geographic and temporal slipperiness in Greek-speaking provinces of the Roman empire.[31] Writing in the fourth century CE, Heliodorus lives in a cosmopolitan world where travel to and ensuing literature about distant regions of the Greek world is increasing in popularity. He lends flexibility to these boundaries with his inclusion of Meroe, the historical and religious capital city of Nubia from c. 300 BCE to 300 CE, in a novel set in Aithiopia in the sixth/fifth century BCE.[32] Heliodorus's collapse between historical Nubia and literary Aithiopia transforms Meroe into both the Fish-eaters' semi-mythical destination in Herodotus's Aithiopian *logos* and an important trading partner with Rome. Another flagrant anachronism that heightens Heliodorus's interconnected timeline is the presence of Aksumites in the novel (*Aeth.* 10.27). The kingdom of Aksum (c. 150 BCE–700 CE), whose eponymous capital was in the Ethiopian highlands, held sway over the Red Sea and Upper Nile Valley.[33] In the fourth century CE, the Aksumite king Ezana repeatedly attacked Meroe and his kingdom potentially eclipsed Meroe as the trading powerhouse of the region. The fictional harmony between Meroe and Aksum in the *Aithiopika*, as evidenced by their military alliance and exchange of gifts, is antithetical to the violent relationship they later developed. Overall, Heliodorus's refashioned chronology alerts his readers to his creative license regarding the mythical and historical legacy of Aithiopia.

As I explained in Section 3 of Chapter 1, "Ethiopia" and "Aithiopia" are distinct regions. In the fourth century CE, Aksumite rulers adopted the label "Ethiopia" in part to forge a link between themselves and the semidivine

---

[31] Feuillâtre (1966: 145), Morgan (1982: 248), and Saïd (1994: 218) examine realistic elements within the novel.

[32] As early as the sixth century BCE and well beyond the fourth century CE, a town existed at the site of Meroe. Nubians moved their capital city there, upstream from Napata (near the Fourth Cataract), in c. 592 BCE, but Napata remained the religious capital of Nubia until the fourth century BCE (Edwards [2004: 143]; Shinnie [1967: 32–33]).

[33] Various environmental and social factors contributed to Aksum's demise in the seventh century CE, among them overcropping, erratic precipitation, and migrations from the eastern desert and the Arabian peninsula (Fattovich, Bard, Petrassi, and Pisano [2000: 24–25]; Munro-Hay [1991: 258–59]).

Aithiopians from the Homeric and biblical traditions.[34] In this chapter, I foreground the term "Aithiopia" to acknowledge the geopoetics of Heliodorus's language. That is, Heliodorus narrates a story that takes place in the sixth/fifth century BCE, a time in which "Aithiopia" was a quasi-mythical country. Despite my best efforts to signal a literary shift from the imaginary world of Aithiopia to the physical world of Nubia, my differentiation clashes with ancient writers, such as Diodorus Siculus and Philostratus, discussed below, who use the term "Aithiopia" to encapsulate both an imaginary oasis and the land of mortal men. Their preference for "Meroe" adds to this temporal confusion because they deploy the label to denote the capital of both a mythical and a historical region. For the sake of a smooth reading experience that avoids mid-sentence toggling, I do not graft "Nubia" onto their slippery terminology of "Aithiopia," even when they refer to the physically grounded country.

From approximately the third century BCE to the third century CE, Nubia's geographical limits spanned from the First to the Sixth Cataract of the Nile (see Figure 6.1 below). During this period, Meroe, located between the Fifth and Sixth Cataracts, was its capital. Situated at the crossroads between the savannah and the Nile, Meroe drew on both its agricultural and pastoral potential. Its location on a navigable stretch of the Nile and its proximity to the Red Sea ensured that it was well positioned for trade. Additionally, natural resources such as iron ore and timber helped the region thrive. Meroe's decline in the third century CE was intimately linked with the rise of Aksum. Trilingual inscriptions (Greek, Sabaean, and Ge'ez) found in Aksum indicate that the Aksumite kingdom was in contact with its neighbors.[35] In terms of Nubia's northern neighbors, attested relations between Nubia and Greek Egypt were sporadic until the advent of the Hellenistic period.[36] Ptolemy II's Nubian campaigns in c. 270 BCE, during which he sought elephants from Nubia in order to strengthen his army, spurred contact.[37] Concurrent with Ptolemy's expeditions for elephants, long-distance trade was important because the Ptolemies desired ivory, gold, and incense from Nubia, while

---

[34] Selden (2013: 327–28, 333–43); Vasunia (2016: 39); Uhlig (2003: 163–65).

[35] *FHN* III 1094–1103. Burstein (1998: 97–100) and Bowersock (2013) examine Greek inscriptions found in Aksum.

[36] An example of a pre-Hellenistic interaction is the Greek epigraph (593 BCE), scratched onto the left leg of a statue of Ramses II, describing the campaign of Greek soldiers sent by Psamtek II to fight in Nubia (*FHN* I 286–89).

[37] Diod. Sic. 1.37.5, discussed in Burstein (1995: 179). The Seleucids' stronghold in India prevented the Ptolemies from gaining access to Indian elephants (Burstein [1995: 108–09]).

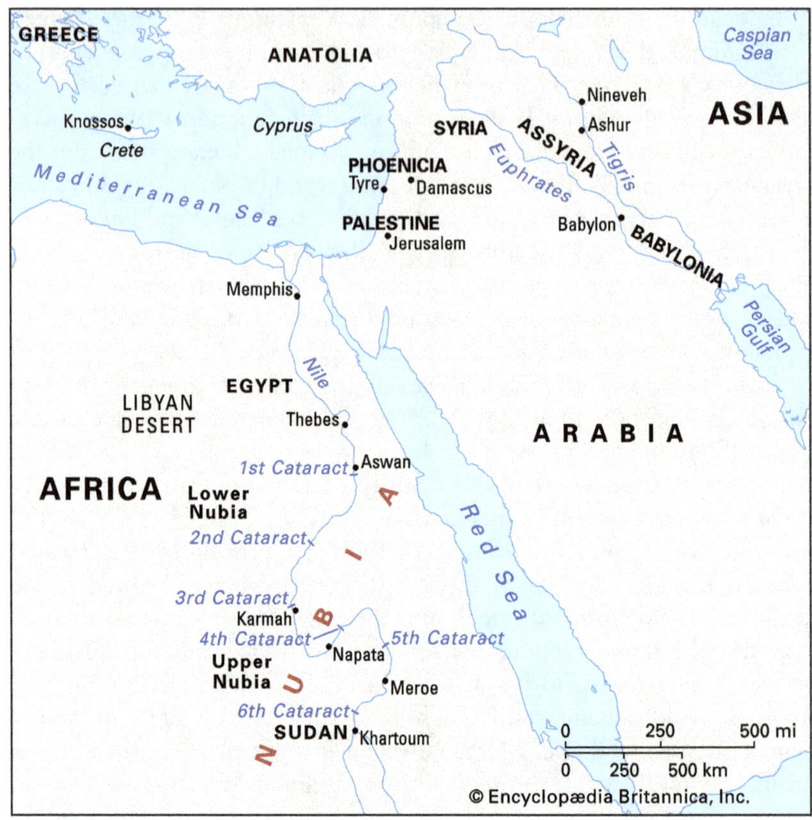

Figure 6.1 A map of Egypt and Nubia. Reprinted with permission from Encyclopædia Britannica. © 2015 Encyclopædia Britannica, Inc.

faience, ceramics, and wooden furniture were among the goods that the Nubians imported.[38]

When Rome gained control of Egypt in 30 BCE, Nubia's relationship with its northern neighbors saw a second peak. Material finds, such as the discovery of a bronze head of Augustus in Meroe, highlight interaction between the two regions. Relying on ancient sources to unravel the mystery surrounding this Roman object's location, Thorsten Opper proposes that the Meroites transported the bust from Roman Egypt to Meroe, where they buried it beneath a victory shrine. This proposed location granted

---

[38] Edwards (2004: 167); Burstein (1989: 1). Burstein (2008b) maintains that Nubian adoption of these Greek elements did not signal a shift towards Hellenization.

Meroites the power to trample on Rome, both physically and symbolically.[39] Even with the uncertainty surrounding the transportation of this head to Meroe, Augustus's economic interest in this part of the world is undeniable. The geographer Strabo recounts that Augustus and the Meroitic queen Amanirenas's ambassadors agreed to the Treaty of Samos in 20 BCE, in which Augustus promised to remit Meroe's tribute payments and recognize Dodecaschoenus, the contested territory between Roman Egypt and Nubia, as a neutral buffer zone.[40]

Due to limited comprehension of the Meroitic script, other languages offer useful source material with which to outline the resurgence of interactions between Greece and Nubia. Written in Greek, Latin, and Egyptian hieroglyphs, the inscription of Cornelius Gallus, the first Roman prefect of Egypt, describes Roman military triumphs in Nubia.[41] Curious discrepancies in Gallus's trilingual inscription underscore the importance of critical readership. Namely, the reader's choice of language greatly affects her or his interpretation of the power dynamics between Rome and Nubia. The Greek text suggests an amicable relationship between Gallus and the Meroitic ruler (προξενίαν παρὰ τοῦ βασιλέως λαβών, "[Gallus] seized public friendship from the [Aithiopian] king"), while the Latin version implies Gallus's dominance over the Meroitic ruler (*eodem rege in tutelam recepto*, "when the same [Aithiopian] king was placed under [Gallus's] protection").[42] Left unexamined, such linguistic discrepancies can recast partial histories as indisputable facts. A modern counterpart illustrates the high stakes associated with uneven translations. In Article XVII of the 1889 Treaty of Wuchale between Menelik II of Ethiopia and Pietro Antonelli of Italy, the Amharic version stated that Ethiopia *could* seek Italy's advice before participating in foreign affairs, while the Italian version stated that Ethiopia *must* solicit Italy's input in advance of any international dealings. The Italian version's restrictive verb contributed to Emperor Menelik II's denunciation of the treaty and led to the Battle of Adwa between Ethiopia and Italy seven years later.

---

[39] Opper (2014: 26–29); Burstein (1995: 165–76; 1998: 57); Török (1989–90: 181–85). The head of Augustus is currently part of the British Museum's collections (discussed in Section 2.4). The statue of Lady Sennuwy offers an illuminating comparandum: in 1600 BCE, Nubians took the statue of Lady Sennuwy, carved during the reign of Senwosret I (1971–1926 BCE), from Egypt to Nubia and buried it in the royal tomb of a Nubian ruler.

[40] Strabo 17.1.54, discussed in Burstein (2001: 138–41); Sidebotham (2011: 3); Roller (2018: 973).

[41] *Orientis Graeci Inscriptiones Selectae* 654. Greek and Latin texts recount the fight against Nubians led by Cornelius Gallus's successor, Petronius: historian Cassius Dio (*Roman History* 54.5.4–6) and encyclopedist Pliny the Elder (*HN* 6.181–82).

[42] Török (2009: 432–35); Burstein (1995: 165–66); Edwards (2004: 145).

Beyond military accounts, a wide range of Greek-speaking writers express sustained interest in Nubia during the Roman imperial period. Comparable to Heliodorus, their status as Roman subjects does not curtail their interest in regions outside of the Roman empire. The ensuing explorations of these historians, geographers, and biographers situate Heliodorus's account of the royal family of Meroe within a larger trajectory of sustained literary interest in Nubia.[43] In Diodorus Siculus's account of Aithiopians, the narrator describes them as black people, thereby evoking Xenophanes of Colophon's vivid portrayal of Aithiopians who fashion black gods in their own image.[44] Diodorus's Aithiopians bear a superficial resemblance to Heliodorus's black Aithiopians, but Charicleia's insistence on her Aithiopian identity despite her white skin requires a more nuanced model than Diodorus Siculus allows. Conversely, Dionysius of Alexandria opens up the category of "Aithiopians" (αἴθω, "I blaze"+ ὄψ, "face") to include a broader group of people, such as Indians (κυανέουσι, "they are dark," Dionys. Per. 1112), Blemmyes (αἰθαλέων, "they are blazing," 220), and Erembi (μελαίνεται, "they are becoming black," 966).[45] Dionysius's merging of distinct groups into one category complements Heliodorus's description of an Aithiopian royal family whose dissimilar skin color does not negate their kinship.

As Heliodorus pushes for a polycentric map of the ancient Greek world, he echoes his predecessors who reworked their own literary inheritances. For instance, Diodorus reshapes Cambyses's expansionist ambitions in Herodotus' *Histories* into a sedate piety when he explains that Cambyses founded a city and named it in honor of his mother Meroe.[46] Opting for Greek linguistic games instead of Persian ones, Heliodorus presents Greek etymologies of non-Greek entities with little regard for geographic boundaries in the *Aithiopika*: Homer's origin in Egypt does not correspond to his Greek-derived name (ὁ μηρός, "the thigh," Heliod. *Aeth.* 3.14); the "Nile"

---

[43] Other historical examples include the work of an unnamed Greco-Egyptian merchant, *Periplus of the Red Sea* 2; Ptolemy, *Geography* (cited in *FHN* III 926–32); and Pausanias, *Description of Greece* 1.33.3–5, 5.7.4. Fictional accounts include the *Alexander Romance* and Dio Chrysostom, *Discourses* 11.50. The Hellenistic writer Bion of Soloi also wrote a historical text entitled *Aithiopika*, of which only fragments survive (Hägg [2000: 199]).

[44] Diod. Sic. 3.8.2; Xenophanes of Colophon, fr. 16. Diodorus also quotes Homer's description of pious Aithiopia (Diod. Sic. 3.2; *Il.* 1.423–24). Keen to highlight a less glamorous subset of Aithiopians as well, Diodorus labels some as screaming, dirty beasts (3.8.2–6).

[45] The first extant appearance of the Erembi occurs in Menelaus's account of his travels (*Od.* 4.84).

[46] Hdt. 3.17–26; Diod. Sic. 1.33.1–4. Diodorus Siculus 3.11.2 lists Agatharchides of Cnidus as an important source for information about Meroe, especially the second book of Agatharchides's *On Affairs in Asia*. Agatharchides's *On the Erythraean Sea* also presents a detailed account of aspects of Meroitic customs (Burstein [1989: 15–16, 36]).

is a conflation of two words, "new soil" (νέαν ἰλύν, 9.22.5); and the Aksumite "cameleopard" derives its name from two animals (κάμηλος "camel" + πάρδαλις "leopard," 10.27.1).[47] These loosely enforced delineations between countries form the basis of Heliodorus's extensive world map, which includes Greece, Egypt, and Aithiopia. Another layered allusion lurks beneath Heliodorus's description of Aithiopian soldiers (9.1). Namely, his portrayal of courageous Aithiopians evokes Strabo's account of the Aithiopians' valiant campaign against the Romans (17.1.53–54), which in turn points to Herodotus's description of Aithiopian troops fighting on behalf of Persia (7.69–70). Both Herodotus's and Strabo's Aithiopians inform Heliodorus's rendition, in that their stalwart warriors resurface as independent actors who fight against Persians during the siege of Syene (Heliod. *Aeth.* 9.1).

Subtle allusions to India form another part of Heliodorus's expansive world map. Namely, Philostratus's presentation of Indian gymnosophists in his *Life of Apollonius of Tyana* provides an important model for Heliodorus's rendition of wise men in the *Aithiopika.*[48] Nonetheless, Heliodorus reorders Philostratus's hierarchy of wisdom (*V A* 6.6) that reveres Indians as the wisest gymnosophists, followed by Aithiopians, and finally Egyptians.[49] Pushing aside the Indian exemplar, Heliodorus privileges the counsel of Sisimithres, the Aithiopian gymnosophist who uses his intelligence and prudence to save Charicleia's life on numerous occasions. Heliodorus marries venerable wisdom with blackness in his characterization of the learned, black Sisimithres (2.30.1). Sisimithres's intellect enters the visual realm as he ably explains Charicleia's skin color with what Michael Reeve terms the Andromeda effect – the theory that a mother can affect her child's physical appearance depending on what she views at the moment of conception (10.14.7).[50] Heliodorus's characterization of Sisimithres further nuances a rigid assessment of skin color when

---

[47] Cioffi (2013: 193). See also Plutarch's proposed Greek etymologies of non-Greek words: "Isis" from the Greek verb *oida* ("I know"), and "Serapis" from *sairein* ("to sweep"; Plutarch, *Isis and Osiris* 2 [351f] and 29 [362c]).

[48] Morgan (2009); conversely, Robiano (1992). Philostratus recounts Apollonius's trip to visit gymnosophists in India, Egypt, and Aithiopia (*Life of Apollonius of Tyana*, 2.1–3.50, 6.1–27). Echoing Hdt. 3.101 and Strabo 15.1.13, Philostratus describes Indians, Egyptians, and Aithiopians as black people (*V A* 2.22.4, 6.2).

[49] Morgan (1982: 237; 2008: 404 n. 6). Charicleia and Theagenes's journey mirrors the sacred hierarchy of the priests, as Heliodorus deems it: dim Charicles in Greece, shrewd Calasiris in Egypt, and supremely enlightened Sisimithres in Aithiopia (Whitmarsh [1999: 24]).

[50] Reeve (1989). Earlier instances of the theory of maternal impression are found in Genesis 30:25–43; later endorsements of this theory appear among doctors and philosophers in sixteenth-century France (Ndiaye [2016: 159–60 n. 6]).

Sisimithres tells the Aithiopian royal couple, Hydaspes and Persinna, that a smart man does not judge people by their appearance (10.10.4). Sisimithres recognizes that appearances can be misleading, a logical inference for a man who believes that Charicleia is Aithiopian, even though her skin color suggests otherwise. Along with Sisimithres's wisdom, the etymology of his name indicates another innovation on Heliodorus's part. By giving a Hellenized Persian name to an Aithiopian man, Heliodorus increases the distance between Sisimithres and his Indian gymnosophistic counterparts.[51] Even when Heliodorus includes India in his etymologies, as is the case for Hydaspes, whose name corresponds to an Indian river or enslaved Indian person, this linguistic connection promotes the cosmopolitan nature of the novel without imposing an Indocentric worldview.[52]

Heliodorus alludes to his Roman-era counterparts in a time of diverse interactions, a time when an Emesan subject of the Roman empire could produce an Aithiopian novel written in Greek.[53] The blurred boundaries of the fourth century CE provide a fitting backdrop for Heliodorus to manipulate his literary inheritance. His sophisticated presentation of skin color and identity demands that his readers rethink any assumptions about the relationship between Greece and Aithiopia, white and black, native and foreigner. In what follows, I discuss the ways that Heliodorus articulates the slipperiness of color through Charicleia's shrewd manipulation of her skin tone, which perturbs assumptions about clear-cut, consistent distinctions between her appearance and her identity.

6.4   Literal and Metaphorical Blackness

In an effort to protect themselves during their trip to Bessa (a town in Upper Egypt), Charicleia and her third foster father, Calasiris[54], disfigure their bodies:

> ἡ Χαρίκλεια δὲ καὶ ὁ Καλάσιρις πρῶτα μὲν εἰς τὸ πτωχικὸν πλάσμα μετημφιέννυντο ῥάκεσιν ἑαυτοὺς προπαρεσκευασμένοις ἐξευτελίσαντες, ἔπειτα ἡ μὲν Χαρίκλεια τό τε πρόσωπον ἐνύβριζεν ἀσβόλου τε ἐντρίψει

---

[51] Hägg (2000: 207).   [52] Whitmarsh (2011b: 124); Schneider (2004: 133).

[53] Morgan (2005: 313–16) suggests that Heliodorus surpasses the Christian discourse of white skin and purity, and conversely black skin and the devil, by activating two semiotic systems in relation to Aithiopia: land of piety and land of sin.

[54] Charicleia's first foster father is Sisimithres; her second is Charicles. At this point in the novel, Charicleia and Calasiris are heading to Bessa to find Theagenes and Thyamis (Theagenes's captor and Calasiris's son). See also the scene in which Theagenes suggests that he and Charicleia disguise themselves as beggars (Heliod. *Aeth.* 2.19.1).

καὶ πηλοῦ καταχρίσει μολύνασα καὶ κρηδέμνου ῥυπῶντος τὸ κράσπεδον ἀπὸ μετώπου κατὰ θατέρου τοῖν ὀφθαλμοῖν εἰς ἄτακτον προκάλυμμα ἐπισοβοῦσα, πήραν τε ὑπὸ μάλης, οὑτωσὶ μὲν ἰδεῖν ψωμῶν τινῶν καὶ ἀκόλων δῆθεν ταμιεῖον χρειωδέστερον δὲ τῆς ἱερᾶς ἐκ Δελφῶν ἐσθῆτος καὶ τῶν στεμμάτων τῶν τε συνεκτεθέντων μητρῴων κειμηλίων καὶ γνωρισμάτων εἰς ὑποδοχήν, ἐξῆπτο.

First Charicleia and Calasiris changed into a beggarly guise, disparaging themselves with rags that they had prepared. Then Charicleia sullied her face, smearing it with soot and mud, and she placed the hem of a filthy headdress on one side of her forehead like a shabby veil over her eyes. She carried a wallet under her arm, ostensibly to provide a receptacle for some morsels and bits of food, but in reality, it was an essential storehouse for her sacred robes from Delphi, the garlands that were laid beside her when she was abandoned, and the treasures and tokens from her mother. (Heliod. *Aeth.* 6.11.3)

Once Charicleia has masked her beauty with soot and mud, she resembles the pirates from the Nile Delta (1.3.1).[55] Unlike the conflation of blackness and Aithiopian identity that appears in other parts of the novel, Charicleia's dirt-covered skin has no geographic referent in this episode. Her new appearance implies a filthy lifestyle, but she can dispose of this temporary disguise when her viewers no longer threaten her safety.[56] In fact, she abandons this pretense after it masks her identity in a way she does not desire (Heliod. *Aeth.* 7.7.6).[57] Moreover, the word *plasma* in this passage indicates an interplay between the plasticity of identity and the plastic arts, as discussed in Chapter 2. Both Charicleia and fifth-century BCE artists shape a new, disorienting visual experience for their audiences. Disguises, via soot or a janiform cup, offer a gateway to a world in which characters can distort the politics of viewing.

The next passage reveals the rich interplay between eyes and words that reunites the two lovers when Charicleia attempts to convince Theagenes of

---

[55] Charicleia's manipulation of her appearance calls to mind Aesop's proverb about washing an Aithiopian clean (see Section 5.2) and the description of muddy Athenian athletes in *Anacharsis* (sections 5.3–4). Calasiris's disguise of an exaggerated gait and hunched back bears comparison with Odysseus's disguise as a wrinkly, bleary-eyed, ill-clad figure (Heliod. *Aeth.* 6.11.4; *Od.* 13.430–38).

[56] Newell (2020) offers an excellent analysis of the interpretive category of dirt, albeit in the vastly different setting of colonial and postcolonial Lagos, Nigeria.

[57] Beyond visual disguises, Charicleia's acumen extends to her economic prowess: she makes calculating promises in order to delay her would-be consumers (suitors) from redeeming their purchase (marriage), then she reneges on their agreed-upon exchange (Whitmarsh [2011b: 218–19]).

her identity as his beloved. Her disguise of soot and mud is so effective that he initially cannot determine who stands before him:

ὁ δὲ οἷον εἰκὸς ὄψιν τε ῥυπῶσαν καὶ πρὸς τὸ αἰσχρότερον ἐπιτετηδευμένην ἰδὼν καὶ ἐσθῆτα τετρυχωμένην καὶ κατερρωγυῖαν, ὥσπερ τινὰ τῶν ἀγειρουσῶν καὶ ἀληθῶς ἀλῆτιν διωθεῖτο καὶ παρηγκωνίζετο ... ἡ δὲ "ὦ Πύθιε" ἔφη πρὸς αὐτὸν ἠρέμα "οὐδὲ τοῦ λαμπαδίου μέμνησαι;" καὶ τότε ὁ Θεαγένης ὥσπερ βέλει τῷ ῥήματι βληθεὶς καὶ τῶν συγκειμένων αὐτοῖς συμβόλων τὸ λαμπάδιον γνωρίσας, ἐνατενίσας τε καὶ ταῖς βολαῖς τῶν ὀφθαλμῶν τῆς Χαρικλείας ὥσπερ ὑπ' ἀκτῖνος ἐκ νεφῶν διαττούσης καταυγασθείς, περιέβαλλέ τε καὶ ἐνηγκαλίζετο.

When Theagenes saw such an image, the sight [of Charicleia] made filthy in a rather ugly way with worn out, ripped clothes, he pushed her away and shoved her with his elbow as if she were truly some derelict beggar ... "Pythian," she whispered to him, "don't you remember the torch?" At once, Theagenes was struck by her words as if they were arrows, and he recognized the torch as one of the signs that they had agreed upon. He stared at Charicleia and was stunned by her piercing glance, as if her eyes were beams of light darting forth from the clouds. Then he threw his arms around her and embraced her. (Heliod. *Aeth.* 7.7.6–7)

Here, Heliodorus presents an intricate interplay between the visual and verbal spheres. Theagenes observes the sight of Charicleia (ἰδὼν ... ὄψιν) before he hears her words. Despite the unreliability of vision, Theagenes allows his eyes to be his leading guide.[58] Heliodorus ensures that his readers are aware of Theagenes's visual shortcomings by referring to Charicleia as a spectacle (ὄψιν). The gap between the reader's knowledge and that of Theagenes grows as the reader is privy to the identity of the person behind the disguise while Theagenes remains ignorant. In other words, he is subject to a type of narrative alienation that Heliodorus's readers are able to circumvent. Theagenes is unaware of Charicleia's presence beneath her rags because he treats her skin color and clothes as visual manifestations of her race (i.e. external categorization). In this way, she successfully performs the role of pitiful beggar before an audience of one.[59] Charicleia has altered her appearance in order to confuse myopic strangers, but Theagenes was never her intended target. The task of identifying her is especially difficult for Theagenes because he is in the process of uncoupling the link between

---

[58] Eyes are an important part of part of erotic discourse in the *Aithiopika* (Goldhill [2001b: 170–72]). See also Theagenes's mistaken identification of Thisbe's dead body as Charicleia (Heliod. *Aeth.* 2.1.2), and Penelope's reaction to Odysseus (*Od.* 23).

[59] Perkins (1999: 201). See also Philostratus's description of an Aithiopian man discarding his clothes alongside his identity (*VA* 6.11.13).

his vision and his knowledge. Initially he cannot know a person until he sees said person, but in this scene, he develops a perspicacity that enables him to look beyond visual cues.

Heliodorus ostensibly sympathizes with Theagenes in the face of this challenge when he describes Charicleia's rags as "truly" (ἀληθῶς) beggar-like. The adverb "truly" hints at the success of Charicleia's spectacular performance. Combined with her phenomenal acting skills, she has momentarily convinced the narrator that she is a wandering vagrant. By nestling the description of Charicleia's false disguise as real within a figure of speech (ὥσπερ, "as if"), however, Heliodorus returns to the realm of narrative alienation. That is, Heliodorus emphasizes to his readers that Charicleia is performing the role of beggar. If Theagenes had access to Heliodorus's linguistic signposts, he too would recognize Charicleia in front of him. As it stands, Theagenes can see only Charicleia's external race, marking her as a pauper, while Heliodorus invites his readers to recall earlier iterations of her identity. Together, Heliodorus and his readers become co-viewers of the spectacle in which Theagenes slowly acclimatizes to Charicleia's performance.[60]

In these two passages, Heliodorus elevates Charicleia to the role of wily protagonist. Like her intellectual forebear Odysseus (*Od.* 23), she fools her lover into misidentifying her based on her ripped, dirty clothes.[61] Charicleia further exploits the weak correlation between vision and recognition for her own ends when she utters her and Theagenes's password "torch" (τὸ λαμπάδιον). The password itself reveals subtle sophistication. It hearkens back to their first meeting, during which Charicleia carried a torch (Heliod. *Aeth.* 3.4.6) and forward to their marriage torch (10.39.2).[62] Once Theagenes recognizes that vision is not a reliable shortcut to recognition, he recalibrates his perspective and takes a second look at her. Charicleia's use of a linguistic symbol (σύμβολον) rather than a visual one draws attention to the confounding linguistic-visual nexus in this Aithiopian novel written in Greek.[63] Her words become physical entities

---

[60] Bartsch (1989: 109–43). Morgan (1998: 77) and Montiglio (2012: 106–58) elaborate on (mis) recognition scenes in the *Aithiopika*.

[61] Whitmarsh (1999: 20–23); Elmer (2008: 414–18). Charicleia and Odysseus also both have identifiable marks that they have had since birth: a black blotch on Charicleia's arm and a scar on Odysseus's leg (*Od.* 19.386–475). Whitmarsh (2002: 119) and Montiglio (2012: 114–16) discuss other Homeric allusions in the *Aithiopika*; Paulsen (1992) discusses the novel's tragic and comic allusions.

[62] Winkler (1982: 156–57). The torch also functions as a metaphor for Heliodorus's novel, and brightness indicates a broader thematic polarity of light and darkness that permeates the novel from the title (Ἡλιοδώρου [*helio-*, "sun"] Αἰθιοπικά [*aithio-*, "blaze"]) onward (Bowie [1998: 18]).

[63] Mueller (2016: 75–108) traces the presence of visual signs (σύμβολα) in Athenian tragedy.

that strike Theagenes like arrows (ὥσπερ βέλει, 7.7.6). This exchange transforms Charicleia from an ugly beggar to a beautiful maiden and Theagenes from a violent man to a kind lover. They can resume their journey to Meroe only after these metamorphoses are complete.

Despite Charicleia's mastery of words in the passage above, her linguistic fluency does not remain constant in this Aithiopian novel written in Greek. In fact, interactions between the Aithiopian and Greek languages contribute to a shifting model of cultural superiority. Charicleia grapples with her linguistic limitations when she confronts the Aithiopic script on her ribbon. After she moved from Meroe to Delphi at the age of seven, she lost her fluency in the Aithiopian language, which prevents her from deciphering her mother's message. Akin to Cambyses, who cannot communicate with the Aithiopians on his own (Hdt. 3.17–26), Charicleia requires assistance in order to learn about the circumstances of her birth. Her linguistic dependency is at odds with her brave acts of leadership, such as her use of disguise.[64] As the mastermind behind these linguistic plays, Heliodorus coaxes his readers to identify with Charicleia in their shared reliance on a mediator who can help them access unknown languages.

Heliodorus's collision of various modes of communication indicates that both autopsy and *akoē* help characters understand the perturbed link between color and identity. For Theagenes, sight and sound merge when his and Charicleia's shared password works in tandem with her glowing eyes to restore his sight. The simile that introduces Theagenes's moment of clarity evokes the world of light, in that Charicleia's identity becomes as clear as a sunbeam peeking through the clouds (ὥσπερ ὑπ᾽ ἀκτῖνος ἐκ νεφῶν διαττούσης, "as if [her eyes] were beams of light darting forth from the clouds"). This illuminating vocabulary reveals that deceit and truth can coexist in visual markers. In other words, this contradictory occurrence compels readers to question which markers of authenticity are trustworthy. Heliodorus's manipulation of black skin implies that no marker is fixed. Unstable color and sounds engender unreliable recognition. Nonetheless, Charicleia learns to activate different identities at different times, and multiple identities at once. In this way, she can be a docile woman *and* the leader of her entourage, as well as a Greek *and* an Aithiopian.[65]

---

[64] Groves (2012: 29–35). Linguistic capability is the one arena in which Charicleia's lover Theagenes supersedes her, in that his bilingualism stands in contrast to her monolingualism. Perkins (1999: 204–07) interprets Charicleia's loss of the Aithiopian language and adoption of that of Greece as a reflection of Greece's linguistic hegemony in Heliodorus's fourth-century CE world.

[65] Lye (2016: 258) notes the development of "'hybrid' ethnic loyalties" as Heliodorus complicates the dichotomy between Greece and regions east of its borders.

Charicleia and Theagenes's heightened exchange reveals a seeming incongruence between her appearance and her self-proclaimed identity. Charicleia successfully redefines Theagenes's parameters of recognition, thereby calling to the reader's mind her tragic counterparts, the Danaids, who successfully maneuver this lopsided nexus. The similarities between the Danaids and Charicleia extend to the threat of attack that hangs over both, especially when they are separated from their father figures. Additionally, both carry tokens that support their assertions of identity: suppliant boughs for the Danaids, and the ribbon for Charicleia. These tokens provide clarity for their audience of one, Pelasgus and Hydaspes, respectively, and safety for themselves. Pelasgus's observation of the Danaids' suppliant boughs alongside their unGreek attire does not advance his ability to comprehend their Argive Greek identity. Instead, their appearance remains an impenetrable disguise which requires renegotiation before they can seek refuge in his city. Comparable to Pelasgus, Hydaspes stubbornly refuses to accept Charicleia's assertion that she is Aithiopian.[66] Despite the glaring example of a white Aithiopian princess, Andromeda, in the painting hanging in his bedroom, he does not budge. It is only after he sees Charicleia's birthmark, the ultimate reassuring token, that he accepts her Aithiopian identity.

The revelation of Charicleia's black birthmark leads to a final chromatic twist within this Aithiopian novel written in Greek. After Sisimithres tells Charicleia to bare her arm, she obediently pulls up her left sleeve: ἐγύμνωσεν αὐτίκα ἡ Χαρίκλεια τὴν λαιάν, καὶ ἦν τις ὥσπερ ἔβενος περίδρομος ἐλέφαντα τὸν βραχίονα μιαίνων ("at once Charicleia bore her left arm, and there was a mark staining her arm, as if ebony were running around ivory," 10.15.2).[67] This vivid imagery alludes to the Homeric simile comparing the bloody wound on Menelaus's thigh with a Maeonian or Carian woman staining a piece of ivory with red dye (*Il.* 4.141–47).[68] The artifice of this Homeric

---

[66] Unlike Pelasgus, however, Hydaspes decenters Hellenocentrism with a world map centered on Aithiopia that situates Delphi at its extreme limits (Heliod. *Aeth.* 10.16.6; discussed in Whitmarsh [1999: 23]). See also Whitmarsh's (1998) inverted Hellenocentric model that pits Greece against Aithiopia.

[67] The novel begins with Charicleia resting her cheek on her right arm (Heliod. *Aeth.* 1.2.2). In the final scene, she reveals her left arm (10.15.2), thereby allowing readers to metaphorically traverse across her body. Cf. an Indian woman whose skin is black from her breasts upward and white from her breasts downward (*VA* 3.3).

[68] Morgan (2008: 569 n. 241; 2013: 231–32). The crimson staining the ivory (ἐλέφαντα ... φοίνικι μιήνῃ, "she stains the ivory with red dye," *Il.* 4.142) mirrors the opening scene of the *Aithiopika* in which red blood runs down Theagenes's white cheeks (Heliod. *Aeth.* 1.2.3). To describe Theagenes's cheeks, Heliodorus uses the participle *phoinittomenē* ("turned red"), which alludes to his self-proclaimed identity as *phoinix* ("Phoenician"). In this way, Heliodorus generates a ring composition with an intratextual reference, and he links his novel to a foundational text of Greek literature with an

imagery is apparent, in that the narrator likens Menelaus's wound to a chromatically altered object – dyed ivory. In line with the Homeric simile, Heliodorus grafts onto Charicleia's body the image of ebony amidst ivory. The contrasting colors on Charicleia's arm imply another grounded comparison: the dark ink on light papyrus in which the novel is written. In effect, Charicleia embodies both meanings of *graphē*: as she strips her arm, she embodies a written novel and a black-and-white painting.[69] Her skin color is itself an artifice based on the painting of Andromeda, the archetype for Aithiopian royalty, that Persinna views at the precise moment of conception. The ease of this transference further illuminates the dynamism of skin color. The effortless transmission of skin color via sight weakens its role as a reliable marker of race (external categorization).

Heliodorus's readers experience a final moment of narrative alienation when he prompts them to accept Charicleia's birthmark as authentic even though he has already primed them to question the reliability of blackness (Heliod. *Aeth.* 6.11.3).[70] The repetition of blackness may reflect Heliodorus's attempts to convince doubtful readers of the validity of Charicleia's birthmark: *melani . . . espilōto . . . ebenos . . . miainōn* ("black . . . it had been stained . . . ebony . . . dyeing," 10.15.2). Regardless of Heliodorus's intentions, the disjuncture between the portability of Charicleia's disguise earlier in her journey and the permanence of her birthmark at its close highlights the vast signifying power of blackness. Its concealing and revelatory qualities serve Charicleia well in dire situations: blackness via soot temporarily masks her beauty in the company of lecherous men, and blackness via her birthmark affords her permanent safety among her Aithiopian family.[71]

6.4.1   White on Black

Beyond the colors visible on Charicleia's body, the congruence of black and white connotes religious symbolism in the Pythian oracle's prophecy:

τὴν χάριν ἐν πρώτοις αὐτὰρ κλέος ὕστατ᾽ ἔχουσαν
φράζεσθ᾽, ὦ Δελφοί, τὸν θεᾶς γενέτην.

intertextual allusion. Bowie (1998) discusses varied uses of *phoinix* (φοῖνιξ) in the *Aithiopika*: to signify a deep red color, date palm, phoenix bird, or Phoenician person.

[69]   Morgan (2013: 232). On Charicleia as a walking ecphrasis, see Whitmarsh (2002: 111) and Elmer (2008: 43).

[70]   See also the incongruity between outward appearance and underlying nature in Greek epic: in the *Odyssey*, people repeatedly misrecognize Odysseus; and comparable to Theagenes, who disregards Charicleia's disguise once he hears her speak (Heliod. *Aeth.* 7.7.7), Antenor marvels at Odysseus's powerful voice despite Odysseus's humble appearance (*Il.* 216–24).

[71]   I also analyze Charicleia's birthmark in Derbew (2021).

οἵ νηὸν προλίποντες ἐμὸν καὶ κῦμα τεμόντες
ἵξοντ᾽ ἠελίου πρὸς χθόνα κυανέην,
τῇ περ ἀριστοβίων μέγ᾽ ἀέθλιον ἐξάψονται
λευκὸν ἐπὶ κροτάφων στέμμα μελαινομένων.

Observe the one who begins with grace and ends in glory,
Delphi, and the one born from a goddess!
After they leave my temple and cleave through the waves,
They will settle in the black land of the sun,
Where they will receive a great prize for the most virtuous people:
A white crown on temples (of the forehead) that are becoming black.

(Heliod. Aeth. 2.35.5)

The etymology of the lovers' names is woven into this prophecy: "*charin . . . kleos*" and "*theas . . . genetēn*." This divine pronouncement welcomes the travelers who proceed from Apollo's temple in Delphi to the land of the Sun God in Meroe. Charicleia's successful journey from Delphi, presumably the religious center of the mythical Greek world, to Meroe, ostensibly at its extremity, redefines the categories of center and periphery.[72] Delphi is not a fundamental referent against which to measure Meroe; both Delphi and Meroe occupy a prominent role in Charicleia's reconciliation of her Aithiopian identity.

The dynamism of blackness is evident in the grounded imagery of the black land of the sun, perhaps referring to the color of the earth's soil, and the metaphorical rendering of Charicleia's and Theagenes's black heads.[73] The translation of the present participle *melainomenōn* as "becoming black" emphasizes the progressive nature of their transformation. By the time of this prophecy's reiteration, the ongoing metamorphosis of the valence of blackness has been resolved (Heliod. *Aeth.* 10.41.2).[74] That being said, no immutable physical alteration of their skin color occurs.

---

[72] Even though the presence of a "prize" (ἀέθλιον) in this prophecy alludes to Meroe's athletic reputation, the religious aspect is more relevant, especially because Charicleia and Theagenes receive a crown of victory (στέμμα) without engaging in any competition. Nonetheless, undertones of agonistic elements come to the fore when Theagenes competes in the Pythian games in Delphi (Heliod. *Aeth.* 4.2–4) and fights an Aithiopian wrestler in Meroe (10.31.5–8; discussed in Morgan [1998: 72–77]).

[73] The whiteness in this prophecy operates on two registers: the white wreath indicates Charicleia's skin color and symbolizes the ritual purity of the wearer. *Leukos* can also appear as an epithet of beautiful women and goddesses (*leukōlenos*) in Greek epic and iconography (Irwin [1974: 112–13, 180]; Sassi [2001]; Eaverly [2013]). Grand-Clément (2020) examines the correlation between certain colors (white, black, and purple) and emotion in Greek religious practices.

[74] Thanks to David Elmer and Tim Whitmarsh for pointing out that the present participle *melainomenōn* indicates an incremental process ("becoming black"), which mirrors Charicleia's slow progress from Delphi to Meroe.

Instead, the temples of the crown-wearers that are becoming black (*melainomenōn*) signify the symbolic status of blackness in the novel.[75] That is, blackness represents the roles of Sun Priestess and Priest that Charicleia and Theagenes will assume after they have left Delphi, cleaved through the waves, and reached the black (*kuaneēn*) land of the sun (*hēliou*). The theme of departure and arrival in this prophecy echoes the sojourns of Odysseus, the prototypical traveler. Unlike Odysseus's trip, which starts and ends in Greece, Charicleia begins and concludes her adventure in Aithiopia.[76] In this way, Heliodorus has crafted a non-Greek rewrite of Homer's epic that reorients the reader to place Aithiopia at the center of the protagonist's *nostos*.[77]

The tangible point of contact between black and white in this prophecy foreshadows the tranquil reconciliation between Greece and Aithiopia that becomes evident by the novel's closing episode.[78] The two chariots drawn by white oxen lead the characters to a new beginning: Charicleia and Persinna in one, Theagenes and Hydaspes in the other, and Sisimithres and Charicleia's second foster father, Charicles, closing the procession (Heliod. *Aeth.* 10.41.3). By ending the novel at the place where Charicleia's blackness begins, Heliodorus ushers in a resolution of a complex chromatic framework, embodied in the variety of skin color in each chariot.

6.5   Conclusion: Afterlives of Passing

This Aithiopian novel written in Greek traces a number of journeys: a disorienting trek from the mouth of the Nile to Meroe (Heliod. *Aeth.* 1, 10), a personal transformation from a presumably Greek identity to an indisputably Aithiopian one, and an emotional leap from a foster father to a birth family.[79] David Elmer reads the Nile itself as a metaphor for the diversity woven in the novel: "Each time Kharikleia acquires a new father-figure – each time she moves closer to her paternal origin – the shift is occasioned by Nilotic *historia*, an association that exploits the

---

[75] Selden (1998: 182) reads this participle as a marker that "clearly designates Heliodorus's account as a progressive ethnico-somatic crossing."

[76] Although the novel begins near the mouth of the Nile Delta, Charicleia's travails begin with her birth in Aithiopia.

[77] Whitmarsh (2011b: 112–17).

[78] Morgan (2005: 317). This reconciliation suggests an end to the epic feud between Memnon, Charicleia's Aithiopian ancestor, and Achilles, Theagenes's Greek ancestor (Harris [2001: 383]).

[79] Charicleia's foster fathers each represent a country through which she passes: Greece via Charicles, Egypt via Calasiris, and Aithiopia via Sisimithres (Elmer [2008: 428]; Whitmarsh [1998: 107–09]).

obvious parallel between the search for the sources of the Nile and the search for Kharikleia's true father."[80]

Even Charicleia's final destination has a tripartite structure: three rivers – the Nile, Astaborrhas, and Asasobas – converge at Meroe.[81] On a chromatic level, readers find themselves ending where they began, in that they first encounter Charicleia among black Egyptian pirates (Heliod. *Aeth.* 1.1.1– 1.3.3), and they leave her among black Aithiopians (10.41.3). Despite this ring composition, the role of blackness morphs throughout the novel. After Charicleia disguises herself with soot and mud, she comes to terms with a dynamic identity that encompasses blackness, whiteness, Greece, and Aithiopia. Her black birthmark grants this identity broad legibility, for besides being a literal mark of blackness on Charicleia's body, it symbolically connects her to the Sun cult, a cult of which she eventually becomes priestess.

Ricocheting off the walls of Greco-Roman antiquity, the trope of skin color manipulations as a sophisticated plot device resonates in later centuries. The alteration of skin color to gain acceptance into another community – that is, passing – has had rich afterlives.[82] According to Perkins, Charicleia's assumption of a Greek identity is *the* prototypical act of passing.[83] This is not to say that Greek identity and white skin were synonymous, nor does it mean that Charicleia relies on her white skin to pass as Greek. Rather, her skin color openly contradicts Aithiopians' widespread belief that whiteness and Aithiopian identity are antithetical. Her peripatetic childhood allows this falsehood to go unquestioned. Once she moves to Delphi, Charicleia's linguistic and religious training overrides her Aithiopian identity and she unknowingly passes as a Greek woman. As another manifestation of the passing trope, Charicleia's disguise of soot and mud grants her access to a world of beggars in which she seeks refuge (Heliod. *Aeth.* 6.11.3). Her act of passing as a beggar is so successful that it even convinces unintended audiences. Altogether, Charicleia's acts of passing are part of a long literary tradition. In nineteenth- and twentieth-century African American literature, Black women and men resist the laws of hypodescent that assign them

---

[80] Elmer (2008: 434).

[81] Elmer (2008: 438). The tripartite structure also applies to the various genres integrated into the novel (epic, tragedy, and history; Elmer [2008: 413]). Groves (2012: 58) also points out the limitations of using a binary model to investigate the world of the novel.

[82] Scholars have examined later receptions of the *Aithiopika* in early Christian narratives (Andújar [2013]), Renaissance literature (Spiller [2011: 79–111]), theatrical productions in early modern France and England (Ndiaye [2016]), and late nineteenth-/early twentieth-century African American literature (Selden [1998: 200–09]).

[83] Perkins (1999).

membership in the Black community. They pass as White hoping to secure acceptance into the White community and advancement in their personal lives.[84] Regardless of their convincing performances, the constant threat of exposure looms over them.

An examination of Pauline Hopkins's *Of One Blood* (1902–03) puts Charicleia in dialogue with other characters who traverse boundaries via their revamping of (external) race and (internal) identity.[85] In Hopkins's novel, a young Black doctor named Reuel Briggs resuscitates and eventually marries Dianthe Lusk, a beautiful Black woman with mysterious lapses of consciousness and memory. Both pass as White, a move that affords them social and financial mobility. In an attempt to earn money for his new family, Reuel joins an archaeological expedition heading to Meroe. While in Meroe, Reuel mistakenly believes that Dianthe has died when, in reality, his best friend Aubrey Livingston has connived to take her as his wife. During Reuel's period of mourning, he stumbles across an ancient kingdom and discovers he is its long-lost king. Nonetheless, he learns that Dianthe is still alive and rushes home to her. She dies soon after because Aubrey has forced her to drink poison. After ensuring that Aubrey pays for his crimes, Reuel returns to Meroe where the queen of the kingdom eagerly receives him. Towards the end of the novel, readers learn that Reuel, Dianthe, and Aubrey are siblings whose mother was an enslaved Black woman and whose father was their owner. Reuel and Dianthe knowingly pass as White, while Aubrey, who was switched at birth with his mistress' dead child, believes himself to be White.

Numerous elements from Heliodorus's novel resurface in *Of One Blood*. In terms of plot, both follow a pair of lovers who attempt to overcome various obstacles and enjoy marital happiness. Desperate to abandon their hardships, both couples hide their identity when it suits them. An insidious link pulls Charicleia and Dianthe closer together, in that both women wear veils that grant them a brief departure from their vulnerable identities: Charicleia adorns herself with a dirty, tattered veil that hides her magnetic beauty from would-be captors (Heliod. *Aeth.* 6.11.3), while Dianthe protects her Black womanhood with the veil of Whiteness.[86] Conversely, the two novels intersect in their moments of delightful escapism. Hopkins and

---

[84] Fictional accounts penned by James Weldon Johnson (1999) and Philip Roth (2000) explore the passing trope among Black men; Nella Larsen (2007) and Jessie Redmon Fauset (1999) trace this trope among Black women.

[85] Knight (2012) and Nurhussein (2019: 51–71) discuss Hopkins's rich literary career; Wald (2000) expounds on the legacy of boundary crossing.

[86] Hopkins (2004: 40). On Hopkins's redeployment of veiling, see Brooks (2006: 289–325).

Heliodorus do not allow any temporal or geographical limitations to curtail their praise of Meroe. Despite the distance between themselves and the subjects of their tales, both writers ensure that their protagonists, Reuel and Charicleia, eventually claim their rightful seat in the royal palace at Meroe.

Hopkins's and Heliodorus's ethereal bent also applies to their female characters. At the beginning of the *Aithiopika*, the Egyptian pirates initially assume that Charicleia is a goddess. Her extravagant clothes and golden hair liken her to Artemis, while her pose cradling Theagenes resembles Isis caring for Osiris (Heliod. *Aeth.* 1.2.2–6). In a similar vein, Dianthe overwhelms her intratextual audience upon her first appearance. As she begins to sing African American spirituals, her sonorous voice delights the rapturous crowd who witness her performance.[87] Instead of the visual nod to the divine world that guides the pirates' interpretation of Charicleia, auditory clues signal to Dianthe's audience and Hopkins's readers that she is not of the mortal world:

> There fell a voice upon the listening ear, in celestial showers of silver that passed all conceptions, all comparisons, all dreams; a voice beyond belief – a great soprano of unimaginable beauty, soaring heavenward in mighty intervals.[88]

Hopkins emphasizes the holy power of Dianthe's voice with lavish descriptions: the "celestial showers of silver," "a voice beyond belief … soaring heavenward." During Dianthe's temporary residence in the realm of the divine, her voice nearly surpasses the limits of utterable language. In this ephemeral moment, the sound of Dianthe singing transports Reuel outside of his body.[89] As he revels in this supernatural experience, Reuel concludes that he must have fallen asleep and entered a dream world.

The heavenly aura of Dianthe's voice does not protect her from real-life challenges. Readers witness her enjoy a short respite when she passes as White, but adverse consequences, namely deep unhappiness and premature death, await her. Unlike Charicleia, who learns to mask her beauty in order to remain safe, Dianthe can extinguish only her Black identity; her attractiveness remains on full display. This divergence of characterization is unsurprising, as Hopkins contends with historically entrenched tropes of hypersexualizing and objectifying Black women that do not apply to Heliodorus. For those with intersectional identities as Black people *and*

---

[87] Selden (1998: 204–09) and Harris (2001) trace additional connections between *Of One Blood* and the *Aithiopika*.

[88] Hopkins (2004: 14).   [89] Hopkins (2004: 15).

women living in anti-Black, misogynistic societies, safety becomes harder to acquire.

Despite writing a work of fiction, Hopkins does not offer Dianthe a way out of this intersectional conundrum. Instead, she is forced to reckon with the real-life consequences of passing in nineteenth-century America. As an offset of sorts to this sobering reality, Hopkins injects fantastical elements into her novel with her rendition of an ancient, semi-magical kingdom south of Egypt.[90] The homeland of Meroe is an enticing alternative to the brutally harsh power dynamics that Dianthe faces in America. Nonetheless, unlike Charicleia, Dianthe never has the chance to reclaim ties with her majestic, ancestral home. For her, Meroe remains an elusive utopia.

---

[90] Gillman (1996) elaborates on Hopkins's revisionist history.

CHAPTER 7

Conclusion
(Re)placing Blackness in Greek Antiquity

In turning away from reductive classifications of black people in ancient Greek literature and art, I have sought to lay bare uncritical analyses of black skin color that have long informed scholarship in Classics. To counter the invisible ontologies of modern race that have governed scholars' rapid conflations of black people and inferior foreigners, in each chapter I have offered a metatheatrical stage on which characters enact performances of blackness. The jovial atmosphere of the symposium is one such stage on which vibrant performances of blackness occur. The theatricality of blackness also appears in Athenian tragedy, when, in Aeschylus's *Suppliants*, the Danaids' performance of verbal acuity enables them to reconcile the seeming incongruity between their Argive Greek identity and their black skin. On the stage of history, Herodotus focuses on the Aithiopian king's uncanny intelligence and bountiful resources as meaningful indicators of his race, not his skin color. Writing in Roman-ruled Greece, Lucian assigns black skin to Athenians in his satires, thereby refuting the idea that blackness and the performance of Greek identity are antithetical. Opting for pigmental polarities in his Aithiopian novel written in Greek, Heliodorus crafts characters who struggle to reconcile Charicleia's white skin and Aithiopian lineage.[1] Charicleia further complicates a one-to-one correlation between skin color and race when she assumes the role of a beggar, covered with black soot and mud.

In writing this book, I have attempted to offer a fresh starting point for a renewed analysis of blackness that complicates static notions of "Greek antiquity." My theorization of "race" invites both Classicists and critical race theorists to confront the messy category of skin color in its own context without precluding transhistorical dialogue. As it stands, manifold tensions between the present and the past have striking implications for the

---

[1] I use the language of pigmental polarities after Whitmarsh (2018: 169).

discipline of Classics.[2] Nonetheless, careless attempts to negotiate the temporal divide have done a disservice to the field. In the words of Frank Snowden, Jr., some scholars "have regarded the black man of antiquity as a kind of Ralph Ellisonian 'invisible man': they have refused to see him."[3] Intent on addressing this erasure, I have drawn from a wide range of thinkers who share a vested interest in the permutations of black skin. My literary intervention has promoted a deep history of blackness in which precision and plurality override unsubstantiated assumptions.

7.1   Performances of Liberation: A Poetic Invitation

Mindful of the gap between fictional black characters and their historical counterparts, I turn to poetry as a final lens with which to view performances of blackness. Poets Langston Hughes and Gwendolyn Brooks prompt me to recover what "has been disappeared" from Greek antiquity without overlooking specific historicities of the Black experience in their twentieth-century world.[4] My intentional use of the passive voice, "has been disappeared," acknowledges the near impossibility of pinpointing those responsible for the archival dearth of representations of black people in Greek antiquity while sidestepping the impulse to dwell on the indeterminate reasons for this absence. That is, the passive voice reroutes attention to the subjects of disappearance – black people as they appear in ancient Greek literature and art – rather than the potential perpetrators of their disappearance. "Has been disappeared" also draws attention to the expansive nature of time. In other words, those who focus solely on "disappeared" in the simple aspect reduce this act of disappearance to a specific moment in time. Countering the oversimplified shorthand, I use the perfect tense ("*has been* disappeared") to highlight the ongoing process of disappearance.

---

[2] The cultural politics surrounding the marble whiteness of ancient Greek sculptures reveals the ways in which color can complicate notions of "Greek" antiquity. Brinkmann, Dreyfus, and Koch-Brinkmann (2017) and Skovmøller (2020) offer refreshing alternatives to the monochromatic norm popularized by art historian and archaeologist Johann Winckelmann in the eighteenth century; Stager (2018) rightly encourages museum curators to push "the pendulum of pigment" further to acknowledge the intersectional elements of ancient Greco-Roman iconography; and Bindman (2002: 51–58) helpfully emphasizes the role of the perceiver's aesthetics in her or his evaluation of artistic subjects.

[3] Snowden (1988: 63–64). Nonetheless, Snowden's choice of noun ("man") completely overlooks women. Rankine (2006: 121–92) elaborates on the dialogue between Classics and the protagonist from Ellison's *Invisible Man* (1952).

[4] I use the language of "having been disappeared" after Painter (2018), who uses the phrase to describe her experience of attending art school as a sixty-four-year-old Black woman.

In Hughes's "The Black Clown" (1931) and Brooks's "To All My Sisters Who Kept Their Naturals" (1980), the poets provide a blueprint for unearthing silences. Through their sophisticated wordplay, they dispute mean-spirited descriptions of a Black identity. Furthermore, Hughes's and Brooks's disruptions of asymmetrical power relations offer a valuable lesson for unlearning normative ways of knowing based upon physical appearance. Under the careful tutelage of writers like Hughes and Brooks, readers are primed to look beyond predetermined parameters to access performances of liberation.

Langston Hughes's poem "The Black Clown" is composed of two parts, "The Mood" and "The Poem." His audience witnesses the initial subjugation of the narrator, a Black man, and the eventual proclamation of his manhood.[5] The poem's structure, arranged in two parallel columns, presents a pair of narrators side by side: the director of the dramatic monologue, who sets the stage for his narrator (in "The Mood"), and the chronicler of a Black man's experience, who slowly disrupts his audience's preconceived notions (in "The Poem"). "The Poem" begins with a direct address: "You laugh. Because I'm poor and Black and funny."[6] With this opening quip, the narrator isolates his audience's reaction to his presence. He identifies the presumed reasons for their mirth, which coincide with the multisensory role they have assigned him. That is, his audience believes that the sight of his poverty and Blackness, along with the sound of his jokes, define the contours of his performance. Rather than immediately reject their limited and limiting outlook, the narrator distances himself from their prejudice with the distinction between the second person "you" and the first person "I." The narrator's placement of "you" before "I" ostensibly privileges the costume of subjugation over the reality of shared humanity, but behind these words there lurks an acknowledgment of his audience's myopia. The narrator sees his audience gazing at him, and he detects the hidden preconceptions that drive their laughter. His audience, on the other hand, has reduced the narrator to a spectacle whose sole purpose is their entertainment. The audience cannot repurpose the language of humor into that of liberation.

---

[5] Rampersad (1995: 150–51). The trope of the sad clown looks back to Pierrot, a character in Molière's *Don Juan* (c. 1665) who became a stock character in the Italian theatrical form *commedia dell'arte*. Hughes wrote two poems from the perspective of Pierrot: "Heart" and "A Black Pierrot" (Deshmukh [2004]). Gates and Appiah (1993) compile a wide range of reviews of Hughes's extensive corpus.

[6] James Baldwin said, "It was my great luck to be born poor and black in America because it meant that I couldn't lie about what America really was" (as told to Caryl Phillips in the documentary *No Complaints*, BBC Radio 4, November 1984, quoted in Pitts [2019: 301]).

The rumblings of Fields and Fields's racecraft grow louder as subjective observations ("I'm poor and Black and funny") morph into infallible statements.[7] Despite the intratextual audience's attempts to undermine the narrator's agency under the banner of humor, he slowly discards his role as mere spectacle. He concludes his lesson of unlearning with an encomium to Black men in the last lines of "The Poem": "I was once a black clown / But now – / I'm a man!"[8] Refusing to participate in his audience's attempts to obliterate his manhood, the narrator proclaims his self-worth without subscribing to their convergence of difference and inferiority.

Comparable to Hughes's performance of liberation, Gwendolyn Brooks's "To Those of My Sisters Who Kept Their Naturals" aims to free Black women from any doubts of their intrinsic worth.[9] In an ode to Black women and their unprocessed hair, the Black female narrator turns away from the society within which disrespect for Black women runs rampant:

> To Those of My Sisters Who Kept Their Naturals
> *Never to look*
> *a hot comb in its teeth.*
>
> Sisters!
> I love you.
> Because you love you.
> Because you are erect.
> Because you are also bent.
> In season, stern, kind.
> Crisp, soft – in season.
> And you withhold.
> And you extend.
> And you Step out.
> And you go back.
> And you extend again.[10]

---

[7] See Fields and Fields (2014); see also my discussion of racecraft in Section 1.3.1.

[8] Cf. James Baldwin's keen self-awareness: "You give me a terrifying advantage. You never had to look at me. I had to look at you. I know more about you than you know about me" (Peck [2017: 103]. As an advance warning for those who look into this reference, Peck includes a disturbing photograph of Laura Nelson, a Black woman from Oklahoma, after a lynch mob killed her; Wolters [2004: 413–22], discusses the violence of White supremacy in relation to this image).

[9] Hughes and Brooks had a mutual admiration of each other's work. Hughes was one of the dedicatees of Brooks's *In the Mecca* (1968), and Hughes dedicated his book of short stories, *Something in Common* (1963), to her. Lansana and Popoff (2017) and Jackson (2017) discuss Brooks's influential role in the Black Arts Movement.

[10] Brooks (1980: 12, vv. 1–12). As discussed in earlier chapters, the trope of curly hair also appears in ancient Greek literature and art.

Resisting societal pressure to hail the hot comb, the narrator develops an inclusive project of hair politics.[11] The punctuation undergirds the shared sisterhood in this undertaking. First, the narrator's opening exclamation ("Sisters!") demands that her intended listeners heed her call. The succinct sentence that follows ("I love you") encapsulates the narrator's message of adoration. The period at the end of each ensuing clause allows each of the sisters' loving qualities to stand on its own, while the repeated conjunctions ("because ... and") situate each clause as part of a collective unit. In addition to the camaraderie undergirding Brooks's opening lines, the poem's visual presentation lends itself to comparison with a single strand of curly hair. Readers who turn their head to the side when reading the entire poem will notice that it resembles an undulating curl pattern. From this angle, each staccato phrase contributes to the long curlicue of hair.

The narrator uses hair as a vehicle through which to praise the resilience of Black women. Her oscillating observations enumerate the positive qualities of Black women via their hair: straight or curly, harsh or gentle, rigid or pliable, all are worthy of her love. Her embrace of passive and active vocabulary ("you are also bent," "you Step out") further demonstrates the versatility of her subjects.[12] Despite the unnamed forces that have bent them, they insist on forging ahead. Moreover, the narrator's repetition of verbs of movement ("you Step out ... you go back") counteracts the immobility that has driven some women to "look a hot comb in its teeth." The narrator's message of solidarity encourages her sisters to embark on a restorative journey towards their own liberation.

Hughes's and Brooks's poetic reorientations of Black identity offer creative ways to approach silences in the generative, multisourced ancient Greek archive. In concert with Ngũgĩ's appeal for literature written in African languages, with which I began this book, Hughes and Brooks demand that the realm of performance make space for productions that prioritize the voices of Black people. Buoyed by Ngũgĩ's, Hughes's, and Brooks's inclusive ethos, I have carved out some space for versatile, nuanced, and multidimensional performances of blackness in ancient Greek literature and art. It is my hope that in the future, scholars of

---

[11] Rooks (1996), Banks (2000), and Byrd and Tharps (2014) offer an ethnography of Black women's hair; see also Mercer (1994: 97–130) and Knudsen and Rahbek (2016: 235–63). For an introduction to Black women's studies, see Hull, Bell-Scott, and Smith (2015); James, Foster, and Guy-Sheftall (2009); and Brewer (2011).

[12] Brooks's vivid evocation of "bent" women finds echoes in the title of Moraga and Anzaldúa's collection, *This Bridge Called My Back: Writings by Radical Women of Color* (2015).

antiquity will examine their convictions and context to ensure that they are not perpetuating silences or prejudices. To be sure, the task ahead is a challenging one. Opening up reductive presumptions, teasing apart overlapping representations – not to mention addressing voices that have been disappeared from the archive – requires committed confrontation. Nonetheless, it is only with vigorous and persistent revision of static presumptions across disciplines that we can equitably untangle the past.

This list consists of objects that have been archived and catalogued in the online Beazley Archive. I used the following entries to conduct an advanced search: "decoration description: heads" and "decorated area: FIG." I have omitted horned drinking cups (*rhyta*) that depict the full body of a black person being devoured by a crocodile due to my focus on iconographic representations of faces. Under "Type," I have provided the descriptions from the Beazley Archive. Generally, these descriptions focus on the age (youth) of the black face and the gender (female) of the brown face on the opposite side.

Type	Approximate Date (BCE)	Finding Site[1]	Provenance	Current Collection	URL/Source
Red-figure stout perfume bottle (*aryballos*) (6)					
black youth + woman	500–450	NL	Athenian	London, British Museum: 1005	www.beazley.ox.ac.uk/record/1734CC82-9F8A-4381-AB97-F0A4B365DE66
black youth + woman	475–425	NL	Athenian	London, British Museum: 47.8–6.35	www.beazley.ox.ac.uk/record/D87B79FB-8410-440B-9397-AFC2811884F6
black youth + woman	400–300	Greece	Athenian	Paris, Louvre: CA987	www.beazley.ox.ac.uk/record/00C8734E-5F19-4EC6-ABB2-C93C18716633
black youth + woman	400–300	Attica, Anavyssos	Athenian	Athens, National Archaeological Museum, M. Vlasto	www.beazley.ox.ac.uk/record/B9D3F04D-BB00-46B4-B643-1FFB7FDD35B3
black youth + black youth	400–300	NL	Athenian	Boston, Museum of Fine Arts: 98.888	www.beazley.ox.ac.uk/record/58E35727-A8AF-4119-A98E-47E16216C3A5
black man + satyr [both faces made from the same mold]	400–300	NL	Athenian	New York, Metropolitan Museum of Art: 06.1021.204	www.beazley.ox.ac.uk/xdb/ASP/browse.asp?tableName=qryData&newwindow=true&id={E34D7775-7EFE-414A-B7A9-E3B1B4BA598B}

[1] NL = not listed

Red-figure wine jug (*oinochoē*) (3)

black youth + woman	500–450	NL	Athenian	Basel, market (Münzen und Medaillen A. G.)	www.beazley.ox.ac.uk/record/6A6 3572B-6F02-4A4B-8453-644777AD6DA9
black youth + woman	500–450	NL	Athenian	Brussels, Musées royaux: R434	www.beazley.ox.ac.uk/record/E30 D4B1F-5A5E-4E82-AA67-2C8987FECA88
black youth + woman	400–300	NL	Athenian	Paris, Louvre: H62	www.beazley.ox.ac.uk/record/059 9C7B8-B784-4C00-A62E-EB13DF25BBFD

Black-figure cup (*kantharos*) (1)

black woman + woman [Figure 2.1a–c][2]	400–300	NL	Athenian	Boston, Museum of Fine Arts: 98.926	www.beazley.ox.ac.uk/record/62E FF28A-A0AC-4D97-A5B7-2DDF01AC9FE4

Red-figure cup (*kantharos*) (13)

black youth + woman	525–475	NL	Athenian	London, market (Christie's)	www.beazley.ox.ac.uk/record/F89 FC3B5-F3C0-4914-BDA1-B34689648573
black man + satyr	500–450	NL	Athenian	Cleveland, Museum of Art: 1979.69	www.beazley.ox.ac.uk/record/1459 254D-1C27-4A67-B572-6E45BD56E846

[2] Listed as "high-handled drinking cup (kantharos) in the form of two heads" in the online catalogue of the Boston Museum of Fine Arts (https://collections.mfa.org /objects/153959).

(cont.)

Type	Approximate Date (BCE)	Finding Site	Provenance	Current Collection	URL/Source
black youth + Hercules	500–450	NL	Athenian	San Antonio, Museum of Art: 91.24	www.beazley.ox.ac.uk/record/F5F15D40-15DF-48D7-A783-7DD001EF1077
black woman + woman	500–450	NL	Athenian	London, market (Christie's)	www.beazley.ox.ac.uk/record/26A91A7F-75E6-4386-B482-70D1D08C6908
black woman + woman	500–450	Macedonia (Aiani Kodzanis)	Athenian	Macedonia, Aiani Archaeological Museum: 9024130	www.beazley.ox.ac.uk/record/D81C1BE1-DE3B-4923-80C6-42D605A646F3
black satyr + woman	500–450	Italy, Corchiano	Athenian	San Simeon, Hearst Historical State Monument: 9904	www.beazley.ox.ac.uk/record/5EF10448-2E0C-4C3F-9475-006B8D54E2A3
black youth + Hercules	475–425	NL	Athenian	Vatican City, Museo Gregoriano Etrusco Vaticano: 16539	www.beazley.ox.ac.uk/record/87247BAE-413B-4459-A705-7CFFEBB720C8
black woman + woman [Figure 2.3a–c][3]	475–425	NL	Athenian	Cambridge, Fitzwilliam Museum: GR. 2.1999	www.beazley.ox.ac.uk/record/9F2F80CC-56F9-4BC9-BA4D-1B790B922CCE
black youth + woman [Figure 2.4a–c][4]	400–300	NL	Athenian	Princeton, Art Museum: 33.45	www.beazley.ox.ac.uk/record/05B7295A-F38D-4ADC-AB9D-EBBC6A9A3C72

[3] Listed as "Attic red-figure janiform kantharos, Class G of the head vases; the London Class" in the online catalogue of the Fitzwilliam Museum (https://collection.beta.fitz.ms/id/object/125494).

[4] Listed as "Janiform kantharos with addorsed heads of a male African and female Greek, ca. 480–470 B.C." in the online catalogue of the Princeton University Art Museum (https://artmuseum.princeton.edu/collections/objects/20038).

black youth + woman [Figure 2.5a–c][5]	400–300	Chalkidike, Akanthos	Athenian	Polygyros, Archaeological Museum: I.D.Y.8	www.beazley.ox.ac.uk/record/4D1FA240-C5CE-4EAF-B60C-A69D7B95A462
black youth + woman	400–300	Bologna	Athenian	Bologna, Museo Civico Archeologico: 466	www.beazley.ox.ac.uk/record/74A0D986-931B-4C4F-874D-EC900112F5EA
black woman + woman	400–300	Etruria, Tarquinia	Athenian	Rome, Museo Nazionale Etrusco: 50571	www.beazley.ox.ac.uk/record/3CA2AA51-4FA3-447E-99B7-408D5501EC68
black woman + woman	400–300	Boeotia, Thespiai	Athenian	Athens, National Archaeological Museum: N1232	www.beazley.ox.ac.uk/record/2BEE753A-8B48-4198-BF1F-A7D8A9CBB2F7
Red-figure cup (unspecified shape) (3)					
black youth + woman	525–475	NL	Athenian	Beverly Hills, Summa Galleries: 11676	www.beazley.ox.ac.uk/record/94BA74AA-BC05-476C-A4C6-9D484474D5BC
black youth + woman	500–450	NL	Athenian	Munich, Staatliche Antikensammlungen: 9535	www.beazley.ox.ac.uk/record/F531B7B4-9020-45DE-966A-1A432142FA85
black youth + woman	500–450	NL	Athenian	Athens, Kanellopoulos Museum: 83	www.beazley.ox.ac.uk/record/CCA3C5CD-E15B-422C-B104-8B9C88A002B8

[5] Listed as "*kantharos* with the heads of a young woman and a negro from Akanthos" in the catalogue of the Polygyros Museum.

This list consists of objects that have been archived, photographed, and catalogued on the Beazley database. I used the following entries to conduct an advanced search: "decorated area: FIG" and "decoration description: black." Under "Type," I have provided the descriptions from the Beazley Archive. Generally, these descriptions disregard the gender of the black face.

Type	Approximate Date (BCE)	Finding Site[1]	Provenance	Current Collection	URL/Source
Red-figure stout perfume bottle (*aryballos*) (8)					
head of black youth	550–500	NL	Athenian	Hannover, Kestner Museum: 1893.7	www.beazley.ox.ac.uk/record/1F0 8CB8D-5859-450E-A98A -38BD44D25D6E
head of black youth	525–475	NL	Athenian	Baltimore, Walters Art Gallery: 48.2017	www.beazley.ox.ac.uk/record/DB FC92A3-62E4-4E80-818D- 760EEAB60866
head of black youth	525–475	NL	Athenian	Athens, National Archaeological Museum: 2385	www.beazley.ox.ac.uk/record/5B6 94130-26 CD-45DC-B92A- BBCA34629B72
head of black youth	500–450	NL	Athenian	Basel, market (Münzen und Medaillen A. G.)	www.beazley.ox.ac.uk/record/68B 41F2 F-BD43-44A0-88E8- A28FB3CDFC18
head of black youth	475–425	Attica	Athenian	Berlin, Staatliche Antikensammlung: F4049	www.beazley.ox.ac.uk/record/A88 8B360-9663-4BA6-9FF8- B0FFE519BFB2
head of black youth	400–300	NL	Athenian	Athens, National Archaeological Museum: N1228	www.beazley.ox.ac.uk/record/D D8C4385-AF5 C-48E1-960 F-E24ADE5B664D

[1] NL = not listed

(*cont.*)

Type	Approximate Date (BCE)	Finding Site	Provenance	Current Collection	URL/Source
head of black youth	400–300	Etruria, Vulci	Athenian	London, British Museum: 1836.2–24.359	www.beazley.ox.ac.uk/record/FABAE7F4-A1FF-4D76-89AE-B0E4CF3CBAE9
head of black youth	400–300	NL	Athenian	Athens, National Archaeological Museum: 2050	www.beazley.ox.ac.uk/record/9A59CCE7-9046-4E2 C-A2AF-17B7BB175901
Red-figure wine jug (*oinochoē*) (6)					
head of black youth	525–475	NL	Athenian	Malibu, J. Paul Getty Museum: 83.A3.229	www.beazley.ox.ac.uk/record/B2BF6F14-86A2-46D4-AFB9-803554B63D8C
head of black youth	525–475	NL	Athenian	Malibu, J. Paul Getty Museum: 78.AE.304	www.beazley.ox.ac.uk/record/A22EF183-5377-48EE-8FE3-DC36E3C01A06
head of black youth	525–475	NL	Athenian	Basel, market (Münzen und Medaillen A. G.)	www.beazley.ox.ac.uk/record/9AE54071-0294-4B9B-A7A5-5B522F92CA4F
head of black youth	500–450	NL	Athenian	San Simeon, Hearst Historical State Monument: 5618	www.beazley.ox.ac.uk/record/E181507B-F6F4-4F96-8B68-B3B5FA1D601C
head of black youth	475–425	Boeotia, Tanagra	Athenian	London, British Museum: 91.4–22.2	www.beazley.ox.ac.uk/record/93EA5871-D995-4CAA-B214-AC913A06FCFB
head of black youth	400–300	Etruria	Athenian	London, British Museum: 1915.15–29.1	www.beazley.ox.ac.uk/record/2AB7FC82-7BC6-4905-BDCB-B5FDB617D608

Red-figure cup (*kantharos*) (3)					
head of black woman	525–475	NL	Athenian	St. Louis, Washington University Museum: WU3284	www.beazley.ox.ac.uk/xdb/ASP/browse.asp?tableName=qryData&newwindow=true&id={21B20B88-4E97-45ED-9A1A-ED6477FF8CBB}
head of black youth	450–400	NL	Athenian	Frankfurt, Museum für Vor- und Frühgeschichte: B422	www.beazley.ox.ac.uk/record/EE3C66CA-8A92-4F37-A3F8-B369BBE40D6E
head of black woman	400–300	Etruria, Cerveteri	Athenian	Vienna, Kunsthistorisches Museum: 3714	www.beazley.ox.ac.uk/record/661BED67-83 CD-46F8-92F0-6DF85E67C91F
Red-figure single-handled, wide-mouthed cup (*skyphos*) (2)					
head of black woman wearing a Persian cap	425–375	NL	Athenian	Oxford, Ashmolean Museum: 554	www.beazley.ox.ac.uk/record/242EE53A-9154-4A56-B25A-CE20FDD889F4
head of black youth[2]	400–300	NL	Athenian	Boston, Museum of Fine Arts: 00.332	www.beazley.ox.ac.uk/record/A851D769-03FB-44AD-B377-AD9D312F8EB5

[2] It is curious that even black faces with wrinkles, such as the one on this cup, are classified as youthful.

Recommended Translations of Primary Greek Texts

Aeschylus, *Suppliants*

Collard, Christopher (trans.). 2008. *Aeschylus:* Persians *and Other Plays*. Oxford: Oxford University Press.

Heliodorus, *Aithiopika*

Morgan, John R. (trans.). 2008. "Heliodorus: An Ethiopian Story." In *Collected Ancient Greek Novels*, edited by Bryan P. Reardon, 349–588, new ed. Berkeley: University of California Press.

Herodotus, *Histories*

Sélincourt, Aubrey de (trans.). 2003. *Herodotus*: The Histories. Rev. ed. New York: Penguin.

Lucian, *Anacharsis*

Harmon, Austin M. (ed. and trans.). 1925. *Lucian*, vols. 4–6. Cambridge, MA: Harvard University Press.

Bibliography

Abel, Lionel. 1963. *Metatheatre: A New View of Dramatic Form*. New York: Hill and Wang.

2003. *Tragedy and Metatheatre: Essays on Dramatic Form*. New York: Holmes and Meier.

Achebe, Chinua. 1965. "English and the African Writer." *Transition* 18: 27–30.

Adams, James Noel, Mark Janse, and Simon Swain (eds.). 2002. *Bilingualism in Ancient Society: Language Contact and the Written Text*. Oxford: Oxford University Press.

Adler, Eric. 2016. *Classics, the Culture Wars, and Beyond*. Ann Arbor: University of Michigan Press.

Agnolon, Alexandre. 2020. "Cosmopolitanism and Contingency in Herodotus: Myth and Tragedy in the Book IV of the *Histories*." In *Ethnicity and Identity in Herodotus*, edited by Thomas Figueira and Carmen Soares, 159–77. London: Routledge.

Ako-Adounvo, Gifty. 1999. "Studies in the Iconography of Blacks in Roman Art." PhD diss., McMaster University.

Albin, Andrew, Mary C. Erler, Thomas O'Donnell, Nicholas L. Paul, and Nina Rowe (eds.). 2019. *Whose Middle Ages? Teachable Moments for an Ill-Used Past*. New York: Fordham University Press.

Allinson, Francis (ed.). 1921. *Menander: The Principal Fragments*. New York: G. P. Putnam's Sons.

Anderson, Graham. 1976. *Lucian: Theme and Variation in the Second Sophistic*. Leiden: Brill.

2019. *Fantasy in Greek and Roman Literature*. London: Routledge.

Anderson, Michael J. 1997. "The ΣΩΦΡΟΣΥΝΗ of Persinna and the Romantic Strategy of Heliodorus' *Aethiopica*." *Classical Philology* 92 (4): 303–22.

Andrade, Nathanael J. 2013. *Syrian Identity in the Greco-Roman World*. Cambridge: Cambridge University Press.

Andrade, Nathanael J., and Emily Rush. 2016. "Introduction: Lucian, a Protean *Pepaideumenos*." *Illinois Classical Studies* 41 (1): 151–84.

Andújar, Rosa M. 2013. "Charicleia the Martyr: Heliodorus and Early Christian Narrative." In *The Ancient Novel and Early Christian and Jewish Narrative: Fictional Intersections*, edited by Marília P. Futre Pinheiro, Judith Perkins, and Richard Pervo, 139–52. Groningen: Barkhuis.

Appiah, Kwame Anthony. 1992. *In My Father's House: Africa in the Philosophy of Culture*. Oxford: Oxford University Press.

2018. *The Lies That Bind: Rethinking Identity*. New York: Liveright.

Asante, Molefi Kete. 2007. *An Afrocentric Manifesto: Toward an African Renaissance*. Cambridge: Polity.

Ashby, Solange. 2020. *Calling Out to Isis: The Enduring Nubian Presence at Philae*. Piscataway: Gorgias Press.

Ashcroft, Bill, Gareth Griffiths, and Helen Tiffin (eds.). 1989. *The Empire Writes Back: Theory and Practice in Post-Colonial Literatures*. London: Routledge.

Asso, Paolo. 2011. "The Idea of Africa in Lucan." In *African Athena: New Agendas*, edited by Daniel Orrells, Gurminder K. Bhambra, and Tessa Roynon, 225–38. Oxford: Oxford University Press.

Astrada, Scott. 2017. "Home and Dwelling: Re-Examining Race and Identity through Octavia Butler's *Kindred* and Paul Beatty's *The Sellout*." *Journal of French and Francophone Philosophy* 25 (1): 105–20.

Austin, John L. 2016. "How to Do Things with Words: Lecture II." In *The Performance Studies Reader*, edited by Henry Bial and Sara Brady, 205–10. 3rd ed. London: Routledge. [Originally published in *How to Do Things with Words*, edited by James O. Urmson and Marina Sbisá, 1962.]

Baba, Keiji. 1984. "On Kerameikos Inv. I 388 (*SEG* xxii, 79): A Note on the Formation of the Athenian Metic-Status." *Annual of the British School at Athens* 79: 1–5.

Bäbler, Balbina. 1998. *Fleissige Thrakerinnen und wehrhafte Skythen: Nichtgriechen im klassischen Athen und ihre archäologische Hinterlassenschaft*. Berlin: De Gruyter.

Bachvarova, Mary R. 2009. "Suppliant Danaids and Argive Nymphs in Aeschylus." *Classical Journal* 104 (4): 289–310.

Baker, Lee D. 1998. *From Savage to Negro: Anthropology and the Construction of Race, 1896–1954*. Berkeley: University of California Press.

2010. *Anthropology and the Racial Politics of Culture*. Durham, NC: Duke University Press.

Bakewell, Geoffrey W. 2013. *Aeschylus's* Suppliant Women*: The Tragedy of Immigration*. Madison: University of Wisconsin Press.

Bakker, Egbert J. 2013. *The Meaning of Meat and the Structure of the* Odyssey. Cambridge: Cambridge University Press.

Balachandran, Sanchita. 2019. "Bringing Back the (Ancient) Bodies: The Potters' Sensory Experiences and the Firing of Red, Black and Purple Greek Vases." *Arts* 8 (2): 1–24.

Baldwin, Brooke. 1981. "The Cakewalk: A Study in Stereotype and Reality." *Journal of Social History* 15 (2): 205–18.

Banks, Ingrid. 2000. *Hair Matters: Beauty, Power, and Black Women's Consciousness*. New York: New York University Press.

Bard, Kathryn A. 1996. "Ancient Egyptians and the Issue of Race." In *Black Athena Revisited*, edited by Mary R. Lefkowitz and Guy MacLean Rogers, 103–11. Chapel Hill: University of North Carolina Press.

Barnard, John Levi. 2018. *Empire of Ruin: Black Classicism and American Imperial Culture*. Oxford: Oxford University Press.

Bartsch, Shadi. 1989. *Decoding the Ancient Novel: The Reader and the Role of Description in Heliodorus and Achilles Tatius*. Princeton: Princeton University Press.

Bast, Florian. 2011. "Reading Red: The Troping of Trauma in Toni Morrison's *Beloved*." *Callaloo* 34 (4): 1069–86.

Battezzato, Luigi. 1999. "Dorian Dress in Greek Tragedy." *Illinois Classical Studies* 24–25: 343–62.

Beardsley, Grace Hadley. 1929. *The Negro in Greek and Roman Civilization: A Study of the Ethiopian Type*. Baltimore: Johns Hopkins University Press.

Beatty, Paul. 2015. *The Sellout*. New York: Picador.

Beazley, John D. 1927. "Icarus." *Journal of Hellenic Studies* 47 (2): 222–33.

———. 1929. "Charinos." *Journal of Hellenic Studies* 49 (1): 38–78.

Bedigan, Kirsten M. 2008. "Boeotian Kabeiric Ware: The Significance of the Ceramic Offerings at the Theban Kabeirion in Boeotia." PhD diss., University of Glasgow.

———. 2013. "Parodying the Divine: Exploring the Iconography of the Cult of the Kabeiroi in the Ancient Greek World." In *Daimonic Imagination: Uncanny Intelligence*, edited by Angela Voss and William Rowlandson, 43–63. Newcastle upon Tyne: Cambridge Scholars.

Bednarowski, K. Paul. 2010. "The Danaids' Threat: Obscurity, Suspense and the Shedding of Tradition in Aeschylus' *Suppliants*." *Classical Journal* 105 (3): 193–212.

Belcher, Wendy Laura. 2012. *Abyssinia's Samuel Johnson: Ethiopian Thought in the Making of an English Author*. Oxford: Oxford University Press.

Bell, Derrick A., Jr. 1995. "*Brown v. Board of Education* and the Interest Convergence Dilemma." In *Critical Race Theory: The Key Writings That Formed the Movement*, edited by Kimberlé Crenshaw, Neil Gotanda, Gary Peller, and Kendall Thomas, 20–28. New York: New Press.

Bell, Sinclair. [in press]. "Images and Interpretations of Africans in Roman Art and Social Practice." In *The Oxford Handbook of Roman Imagery and Iconography*, edited by Lea K. Cline and Nathan T. Elkins. Oxford: Oxford University Press.

Bello, Muhammadu. 1934. *Gandoki*. Zaria: Translation Bureau.

Benston, Kimberly W. 2000. *Performing Blackness: Enactments of African-American Modernism*. London: Routledge.

Bérard, Claude. 2000. "The Image of the Other and the Foreign Hero." In *Not the Classical Ideal: Athens and the Construction of the Other in Greek Art*, edited by Beth Cohen, 390–412. Leiden: Brill.

Berlin, Brent, and Paul Kay. 1969. *Basic Color Terms: Their Universality and Evolution*. Berkeley: University of California Press.

Berlinerblau, Jacques. 1999. *Heresy in the University: The Black Athena Controversy and the Responsibilities of American Intellectuals*. New Brunswick: Rutgers University Press.

Bernal, Martin. 1987. *Black Athena: The Afroasiatic Roots of Classical Civilization*, Vol. 1: *The Fabrication of Ancient Greece, 1785–1985*. New Brunswick: Rutgers University Press.

   1989. "*Black Athena* and the APA." *Arethusa* 22: 17–38.

   1991. *Black Athena: The Afroasiatic Roots of Classical Civilization*, Vol. 2: *The Archaeological and Documentary Evidence*. New Brunswick: Rutgers University Press.

   2006. *Black Athena: The Afroasiatic Roots of Classical Civilization*, Vol. 3: *The Linguistic Evidence*. New Brunswick: Rutgers University Press.

Besterman, Tristram. 2011. "Cultural Equity in the Sustainable Museum." In *Routledge Companion to Museum Ethics: Redefining Ethics for the Twenty-First Century Museum*, edited by Janet Marstine, 239–55. London: Routledge.

Bethencourt, Francisco, and Adrian J. Pearce (eds.). 2012. *Racism and Ethnic Relations in the Portuguese-Speaking World*. Oxford: Oxford University Press.

Bhabha, Homi K. 1984. "Of Mimicry and Man: The Ambivalence of Colonial Discourse." *October* 28: 125–33.

Bielenberg, Aliosha Pittaka. 2018. "A Bronze Bust and its Legacy at the RISD Museum." Personal blog, December 13. https://alioshabielenberg.com/a-bronze-bust-and-its-legacy-at-the-risd-museum/.

Bindman, David. 2002. *Ape to Apollo: Aesthetics and the Idea of Race in the 18th Century*. Ithaca: Cornell University Press.

Bindman, David, and Henry Louis Gates, Jr. (eds.). 2010. *The Image of the Black in Western Art*, Vol. 1: *From the Pharaohs to the Fall of the Roman Empire*. New ed. Cambridge, MA: Harvard University Press.

The Black Public Sphere Collective (ed.). 1995. *The Black Public Sphere: A Public Culture Book*. Chicago: University of Chicago Press.

Blakely, Sandra. 2006. *Myth, Ritual, and Metallurgy in Ancient Greece and Recent Africa*. Cambridge: Cambridge University Press.

Blyden, Edward Wilmot. 1869. *The Negro in Ancient History*. Washington, DC: M'Gill and Witherow.

Bond, Sarah. 2017. "Whitewashing Ancient Statues: Whiteness, Racism and Color in the Ancient World." *Forbes*, April 27. www.forbes.com/sites/drsarahbond/2017/04/27/whitewashing-ancient-statues-whiteness-racism-and-color-in-the-ancient-world/?sh=1165832c75ad.

Bosak-Schroeder, Clara. 2016. "The Ecology of Health in Herodotus, Dicaearchus, and Agatharchides." In *The Routledge Handbook of Identity and the Environment in the Classical and Medieval Worlds*, edited by Rebecca Futo Kennedy and Molly Jones-Lewis, 29–44. London: Routledge.

   2020. *Other Natures: Environmental Encounters with Ancient Greek Ethnography*. Oakland: University of California Press.

Bowersock, Glen Warren. 1994. *Fiction as History: Nero to Julian*. Berkeley: University of California Press.

   2013. *The Throne of Adulis: Red Sea Wars on the Eve of Islam*. Oxford: Oxford University Press.

Bowie, Ewen. 1994. "The Readership of Greek Novels in the Ancient World." In *The Search for the Ancient Novel*, edited by James Tatum, 435–59. Baltimore: Johns Hopkins University Press.

1998. "Phoenician Games in Heliodorus' *Aithiopika*." In *Studies in Heliodorus*, edited by Richard L. Hunter, 1–18. Cambridge: Cambridge Philological Society.

Boxill, Bernard (ed.). 2001. *Race and Racism*. Oxford: Oxford University Press.

Bozia, Eleni. 2015. *Lucian and His Roman Voices: Cultural Exchanges and Conflicts in the Late Roman Empire*. London: Routledge.

Bradley, Mark. 2009. *Colour and Meaning in Ancient Rome*. Cambridge: Cambridge University Press.

Brandwood, Steven. 2020. "Herodotus' *Hermēneus* and the Translation of Culture in the *Histories*." In *Ethnicity and Identity in Herodotus*, edited by Thomas Figueira and Carmen Soares, 15–42. London: Routledge.

Branham, Robert Bracht. 1989. *Unruly Eloquence: Lucian and the Comedy of Traditions*. Cambridge, MA: Harvard University Press.

Braund, David. 2004. "Scythians in the Cerameicus: Lucian's *Toxaris*." In *Pontus and the Outside World: Studies in Black Sea History, Historiography, and Archaeology*, edited by Christopher J. Tuplin, 17–24. Leiden: Brill.

2008. "Royal Scythians and the Slave-Trade in Herodotus' Scythia." *Antichthon* 42: 1–19.

Braxton, Joanne M. (ed.). 1993. *The Collected Poetry of Paul Laurence Dunbar*. Charlottesville: University of Virginia Press.

Brewer, Rose M. 2011. "Black Women's Studies: From Theory to Transformative Practice." *Socialism and Democracy* 25 (1): 146–56.

Brewer, William M. 1929. Review of *The Negro in Greek and Roman Civilization: A Study of the Ethiopian Type*, by Grace Hadley Beardsley. *Journal of Negro History* 1 (4): 531–34.

Briant, Pierre. 2002. *From Cyrus to Alexander: A History of the Persian Empire*, translated by Peter T. Daniels. Winona Lake: Eisenbrauns.

Bridges, Emma. 2015. *Imagining Xerxes: Ancient Perspectives on a Persian King*. London: Bloomsbury.

Brill, Sara. 2009. "Violence and Vulnerability in Aeschylus's *Suppliants*." In *Logos and Muthos: Philosophical Essays in Greek Literature*, edited by William Robert Wians, 161–80. Albany: State University of New York Press.

Brinkmann, Vinzenz, Renée Dreyfus, and Ulrike Koch-Brinkmann (eds.). 2017. *Gods in Color: Polychromy in the Ancient World*. San Francisco: Fine Arts Museums of San Francisco.

Brody, Jennifer DeVere. 1998. *Impossible Purities: Blackness, Femininity, and Victorian Culture*. Durham, NC: Duke University Press.

2008. *Punctuation: Art, Politics, and Play*. Durham, NC: Duke University Press.

Brooks, Daphne A. 2006. *Bodies in Dissent: Spectacular Performances of Race and Freedom, 1850–1910*. Durham, NC: Duke University Press.

Brooks, Gwendolyn. 1968. *In the Mecca*. New York: Harper and Row.

1980. *Primer for Blacks*. Chicago: Black Position Press.

Brown, Jayna. 2008. *Babylon Girls: Black Women Performers and the Shaping of the Modern*. Durham, NC: Duke University Press.

Brownson, Laura, dir. 2018. *The Rachel Divide*. Documentary film. Los Gatos: Netflix.

Burstein, Stanley M. 1976. "Alexander, Callisthenes and the Source of the Nile." *Greek, Roman and Byzantine Studies* 17 (2): 135–46.

1981. "Axum and the Fall of Meroe." *Journal of the American Research Center in Egypt* 18: 47–50.

(ed. and trans.). 1989. *Agatharchides of Cnidus:* On the Erythraean Sea. London: Hakluyt Society.

1995. *Graeco-Africana: Studies in the History of Greek Relations with Egypt and Nubia*. New Rochelle: Aristide D. Caratzas.

1998. *Ancient African Civilizations: Kush and Axum*. Princeton: M. Wiener.

2001. "The Kingdom of Meroe." In *Africa and Africans in Antiquity*, edited by Edwin M. Yamauchi, 132–58. East Lansing: Michigan State University Press.

2002. "A Contested History: Egypt, Greece and Afrocentrism." In *Current Issues and the Study of Ancient History*, edited by Carol Thomas, 9–30. Claremont: Regina Books.

2008a. "Elephants for Ptolemy II: Ptolemaic Policy in Nubia in the Third Century BC." In *Ptolemy II Philadelphus and His World*, edited by Paul McKechnie and Philippe Guillaume, 135–48. Leiden: Brill.

2008b. "When Greek Was an African Language: The Role of Greek Culture in Ancient and Medieval Nubia." *Journal of World History* 19 (1): 41–61.

Burton, Joan. 1998. "Women's Commensality in the Ancient Greek World." *Greece and Rome* 45 (2): 143–65.

Butler, Judith. 2000. *Antigone's Claim: Kinship between Life and Death*. New York: Columbia University Press.

Butler, Shelley Ruth. 2011. *Contested Representations: Revisiting "Into the Heart of Africa."* Toronto: University of Toronto Press.

Buzon, Michele R. 2011. "Nubian Identity in the Bronze Age." *Bioarchaeology of the Near East* 5: 19–40.

Byrd, Ayana, and Lori Tharps. 2014. *Hair Story: Untangling the Roots of Black Hair in America*. 2nd rev. ed. New York: St. Martin's Griffin.

Byron, Gay L. 2002. *Symbolic Blackness and Ethnic Difference in Early Christian Literature*. London: Routledge.

Cahana-Blum, Jonathan, and Karmen MacKendrick (eds.). 2019. *We and They: Decolonizing Greco-Roman and Biblical Antiquities*. Aarhus: Aarhus University Press.

Cameron, Alan. 1998. "Black and White: A Note on Ancient Nicknames." *American Journal of Philology* 119 (1): 113–17.

Camerotto, Alberto. 1998. *Le metamorfosi della parola: Studi sulla parodia in Luciano di Samosata*. Pisa: Istituti editoriali e poligrafici internazionali.

Campbell, David A. (ed. and trans.). 1988. *Greek Lyric*, Vol. 2: *Anacreon, Anacreontea, Choral Lyric from Olympus to Alcman*. Cambridge, MA: Harvard University Press.

Caron, Christina. 2018. "A Black Yale Student Was Napping, and a White Student Called the Police." *New York Times*, May 9. www.nytimes.com/2018/05/09/nyregion/yale-black-student-nap.html.

Carpio, Glenda. 2008. *Laughing Fit to Kill: Black Humor in the Fictions of Slavery*. Oxford: Oxford University Press.

Carter, David M. 2007. *The Politics of Greek Tragedy*. Liverpool: Liverpool University Press.

Carter, Marva Griffin. 2008. *Swing Along: The Musical Life of Will Marion Cook*. Oxford: Oxford University Press.

Caspari, Rachel. 2003. "From Types to Populations: A Century of Race, Physical Anthropology, and the American Anthropological Association." *American Anthropologist* 105 (1): 65–76.

Casson, Lionel. 1993. "Ptolemy II and the Hunting of African Elephants." *Transactions of the American Philological Association* 123: 247–60.

Cavafy, Constantine. 2009. "Waiting for the Barbarians." In *Collected Poems*, translated by Daniel Adam Mendelsohn, 192–94. New York: Knopf. [Originally published in 1904]

Caygill, Marjorie. 1992. *The Story of the British Museum*. 2nd ed. London: British Museum Press.

Challis, Debbie. 2013. *The Archaeology of Race: The Eugenic Ideas of Francis Galton and Flinders Petrie*. London: Bloomsbury.

Chapman, John Jay. 1931. *Lucian, Plato and Greek Morals*. Boston: Houghton Mifflin.

Chapman, Michael. 1986. *The Paperbook of South African English Poetry*. Craighall: Ad. Donker.

Chapouthier, Fernand. 1930. Review of *The Negro in Greek and Roman Civilization: A Study of the Ethiopian Type*, by Grace Hadley Beardsley. *Revue des études grecques* 43 (203): 453.

Chow, Rey. 2014. *Not Like a Native Speaker: On Languaging as a Postcolonial Experience*. New York: Columbia University Press.

Cioffi, Robert Louis. 2013. "Imaginary Lands: Ethnicity, Exoticism, and Narrative in the Ancient Novel." PhD diss., Harvard University.

Clarke, John Henrik. 1988. "African Warrior Queens." In *Black Women in Antiquity*, edited by Ivan Van Sertima, 123–34. New Brunswick: Transaction.

Clifford, James. 1988. *The Predicament of Culture: Twentieth-Century Ethnography, Literature, and Art*. Cambridge, MA: Harvard University Press.

Cobb, Matthew A. 2018. *Rome and the Indian Ocean Trade from Augustus to the Early Third Century CE*. Leiden: Brill.

Coetzee, J. M. 1982. *Waiting for the Barbarians*. New York: Penguin. [Originally published in 1980]

Cohen, Ada. 2011. "The Self as Other: Performing Humor in Ancient Greek Art." In *Cultural Identity in the Ancient Mediterranean*, edited by Erich S. Gruen, 465–90. Los Angeles: Getty Research Institute.

Cohen, Beth. 2006. *The Colors of Clay: Special Techniques in Athenian Vases*. Los Angeles: J. Paul Getty Museum.

2012. "The Non-Greek in Greek Art." In *A Companion to Greek Art*, edited by Tyler Jo Smith and Dimitris Plantzos, 456–79. Chichester: Wiley-Blackwell.

Cohen, David. 1989. "Seclusion, Separation, and the Status of Women in Classical Athens." *Greece and Rome* 36 (1): 3–15.

Cohen, William B. 1980. *The French Encounter with Africans: White Response to Blacks, 1530–1880*. Bloomington: Indiana University Press.

Colbert, Soyica Diggs. 2015. "African American Performance." In *Oxford Handbooks Online*. https://doi.org/10.1093/oxfordhb/9780199935338.013.119.

Collard, Christopher, and Martin Cropp (eds. and trans.). 2008. *Euripides. Fragments:* Aegeus–Meleager. Cambridge, MA: Harvard University Press.

(eds. and trans.). 2009. *Euripides. Fragments:* Oedipus–Chrysippus, *Other Fragments*. Cambridge, MA: Harvard University Press.

Conybeare, Catherine. 2015. "Augustini Hipponensis Africitas." *Journal of Medieval Latin* 25: 111–30.

Cook, William W., and James Tatum. 2010. *African American Writers and Classical Tradition*. Chicago: University of Chicago Press.

Coombes, Annie E. 1994. *Reinventing Africa: Museums, Material Culture and Popular Imagination*. New Haven: Yale University Press.

Corner, Sean. 2010. "Transcendent Drinking: The Symposium at Sea Reconsidered." *Classical Quarterly* 60 (2): 352–80.

2012. "Did 'Respectable' Women Attend Symposia?" *Greece and Rome* 59 (1): 34–45.

Crawford, Margo Natalie. 2017. *Black Post-Blackness: The Black Arts Movement and Twenty-First-Century Aesthetics*. Urbana: University of Illinois Press.

Crenshaw, Kimberlé Williams. 1989. "Demarginalizing the Intersection of Race and Sex: A Black Feminist Critique of Antidiscrimination Doctrine, Feminist Theory and Antiracist Politics." *University of Chicago Legal Forum* 1989 (1): 139–67.

1993. "Mapping the Margins: Intersectionality, Identity Politics, and Violence against Women of Color." *Stanford Law Review* 43 (6): 1241–99.

Cross, William E. 1971. "The Negro-to-Black Conversion Experience." *Black World* 20 (9): 13–27.

Cuno, James. 2008. *Who Owns Antiquity? Museums and the Battle Over Our Ancient Heritage*. Princeton: Princeton University Press.

Davé, Shilpa S. 2013. *Indian Accents: Brown Voice and Racial Performance in American Television and Film*. Urbana: University of Illinois Press.

Dee, James H. 2003–04. "Black Odysseus, White Caesar: When Did 'White People' Become 'White'?" *Classical Journal* 99 (2): 157–67.

DeFrantz, Thomas F., and Anita Gonzalez. 2014. "Introduction: From Negro Expression to Black Performance." In *Black Performance Theory*, edited by Thomas F. DeFrantz and Anita Gonzalez, 1–15. Durham, NC: Duke University Press.

Delany, Martin Robison. 1879. *Principia of Ethnology: The Origin of Races and Color*. Philadelphia: Harper & Brother.

Dench, Emma. 2005. *Romulus' Asylum: Roman Identities from the Age of Alexander to the Age of Hadrian*. Oxford: Oxford University Press.

2017. "Ethnicity, Culture, and Identity." In *The Oxford Handbook to the Second Sophistic*, edited by Daniel S. Richter and William A. Johnson, 99–114. Oxford: Oxford University Press.

Dent, Gina (ed.). 1998. *Black Popular Culture: A Project by Michele Wallace*. New York: The New Press.

Derbew, Sarah. 2018. "An Investigation of Black Figures in Classical Greek Art." *Iris Blog: Behind the Scenes at the Getty*, April 25. http://blogs.getty.edu/iris/an-investigation-of-black-figures-in-classical-greek-art/.

2019. "(Re)membering Sara Baartman, Venus, and Aphrodite." *Classical Receptions Journal* 11 (3): 336–54.

2021. "Definitions and Representations of Race in Ancient Greek Literature." In *A Cultural History of Race in Antiquity (500 BCE–800 CE)*, edited by Denise McCoskey, 21–31. London: Bloomsbury.

[in press]. "Race in Aeschylus' *Persians* and *Suppliant Women*." In *Companion to Aeschylus*, edited by Jacques Bromberg and Peter Burian. Chichester: Wiley-Blackwell.

Derrida, Jacques. 1998. *Monolingualism of the Other, or, The Prosthesis of Origin*, translated by Patrick Mensah. Stanford: Stanford University Press.

Deshmukh, Madhuri. 2004. "Langston Hughes as Black Pierrot: A Transatlantic Game of Masks." *Langston Hughes Review* 18: 4–13.

Dewald, Carolyn. 1990. Review of *The Mirror of Herodotus: The Representation of the Other in the Writing of History*, by François Hartog. *Classical Philology* 85 (3): 217–24.

Diamantopoulos, A. 1957. "The Danaid Tetralogy of Aeschylus." *Journal of Hellenic Studies* 77 (2): 220–29.

DiAngelo, Robin. 2018. *White Fragility: Why It's so Hard for White People to Talk About Racism*. Boston: Beacon Press.

Dickson-Carr, Darryl. 2001. *African American Satire: The Sacredly Profane Novel*. Columbia: University of Missouri Press.

Diggle, James (ed.). 1970. *Euripides:* Phaethon. Cambridge: Cambridge University Press.

Dihle, Albrecht. 1964. "The Conception of India in Hellenistic and Roman Literature." *Proceedings of the Cambridge Philological Society* 10: 15–23.

Diop, Cheikh Anta. 1955. *Nations nègres et culture*. Paris: Présence africaine.

Dittenberger, Wilhelm (ed.). 1905. *Orientis Graeci Inscriptiones Selectae: Supplementum Sylloges Inscriptionum Graecarum*, Vol. 2. Leipzig: S. Hirzel.

Dixon, Angela R., and Edward E. Telles. 2017. "Skin Color and Colorism: Global Research, Concepts, and Measurement." *Annual Review of Sociology* 43: 405–24.

Dobrov, Gregory. 2001. *Figures of Play: Greek Drama and Metafictional Poetics*. Oxford: Oxford University Press.

Doležal, Rachel. 2017. *In Full Color: Finding My Place in a Black and White World*. Dallas: BenBella Books.

Donkor, Kimathi. 2020. "Africana Andromeda: Contemporary Painting and the Classical Black Figure." In *Classicisms in the Black Atlantic*, edited by Ian S. Moyer, Adam Lecznar, and Heidi Morse, 163–94. Oxford: Oxford University Press.

Dooley, Gillian. 2010. *J. M. Coetzee and the Power of Narrative*. Amherst: Cambria Press.

Dosoo, Korshi. 2020. "Circe's Ram: Animals in Ancient Greek Magic." In *Animals in Ancient Greek Religion*, edited by Julia Kindt, 260–88. London: Routledge.

Doxey, Denise M., Rita E. Freed, and Lawrence Michael Berman. 2018. *Arts of Ancient Nubia: MFA Highlights*. Boston: MFA Publications, Museum of Fine Arts.

Drake, St. Clair. 1987–90. *Black Folk Here and There: An Essay in History and Anthropology*. 2 vols. Los Angeles: University of California, Los Angeles, Center for Afro-American Studies.

Dubin, Steven C. 2006. "Incivilities in Civil(-ized) Places: 'Culture Wars' in Comparative Perspective." In *A Companion to Museum Studies*, edited by Sharon MacDdonald, 477–93. Oxford: Blackwell.

DuBois, Page. 2008. *Slaves and Other Objects*. Chicago: University of Chicago Press.

Du Bois, William Edward Burghardt. 2007. *The Souls of Black Folk*. New ed. Oxford: Oxford University Press. [Originally published in 1903]

Dugas, Charles. 1930. Review of *The Negro in Greek and Roman Civilization: A Study of the Ethiopian Type*, by Grace Hadley Beardsley. *Revue des études anciennes* 32 (1) : 50–51.

Dunbar, Paul Laurence. 1895. "We Wear the Mask." In *Majors and Minors*. Toledo: Hadley and Hadley.

Duncan, Anne. 2006. *Performance and Identity in the Classical World*. Cambridge: Cambridge University Press.

Dustagheer, Sarah, and Harry Newman. 2018. "Metatheatre and Early Modern Drama." *Shakespeare Bulletin* 36 (1): 3–18.

Easterling, Pat, and Edith Hall (eds.). 2002. *Greek and Roman Actors: Aspects of an Ancient Profession*. Cambridge: Cambridge University Press.

Eaverly, Mary Ann. 2013. *Tan Men/Pale Women: Color and Gender in Archaic Greece and Egypt, A Comparative Approach*. Ann Arbor: University of Michigan Press.

Ebbinghaus, Susanne. 2008. "Of Rams, Women, and Orientals: A Brief of Attic Plastic Vases." In *Papers on Special Techniques in Athenian Vases: Proceedings of a Symposium Held in Connection with the Exhibition* The Colors of Clay: Special Techniques in Athenian Vases, *at the Getty Villa, June 15–17, 2006*, edited by Kenneth D. S. Lapatin, 145–60. Los Angeles: J. Paul Getty Museum.

(ed.). 2018. *Animal-Shaped Vessels from the Ancient World: Feasting with Gods, Heroes, and Kings*. Cambridge, MA: Harvard Art Museums.

Edmonds, John Maxwell. 1931. *Elegy and Iambus with the* Anacreontea. *Part 1: Elegiac Poets from Callinus to Critias*, Vol. 1. London: William Heinemann.

Edwards, David N. 2004. *The Nubian Past: An Archaeology of the Sudan*. London: Routledge.

Eide, Tormod, Tomas Hägg, R. H. Pierce, and László Török (eds.). 1994. Fontes Historiae Nubiorum: *Textual Sources for the History of the Middle Nile Region between the Eighth Century BC and the Sixth Century AD*, Vol. 1: *From the Eighth to the Mid-Fifth Century BC*. Bergen: University of Bergen Press.

Elam, Harry J., Jr., and David Krasner (eds.). 2001. *African American Performance and Theater History: A Critical Reader*. Oxford: Oxford University Press.

Elisei, Anna. 1928. "Le Danaidi nelle *Supplici* di Eschilo." *Studi italiani* 6: 197–219.

Ellison, Ralph. 1995. *Invisible Man*. New York: Random House. [Originally published in 1952]

    1995. "Change the Joke and Slip the Yoke." In *The Collected Essays of Ralph Ellison*, edited by John F. Callahan, 100–12. New York: The Modern Library. [Originally published in the *The Partisan Review*, 1958]

Elmer, David F. 2008. "Heliodoros's 'Sources': Intertextuality, Paternity, and the Nile River in the *Aithiopika*." *Transactions of the American Philological Association* 138 (2): 411–50.

Elsner, Jaś. 2001. "Describing Self in the Language of Other: Pseudo (?) Lucian at the Temple of Hierapolis." In *Being Greek under Rome: Cultural Identity, the Second Sophistic and the Development of Empire*, edited by Simon Goldhill, 123–53. Cambridge: Cambridge University Press.

Emberling, Geoff, and Bruce Beyers Williams. 2020. "Nubia, A Brief Introduction." In *The Oxford Handbook of Ancient Nubia*, edited by Geoff Emberling and Bruce Beyers Williams, 1–4. Oxford: Oxford University Press.

Fanon, Frantz. 1952. *Peau Noire, Masques Blancs*. Éditions du Seuil: Paris.

    2008. *Black Skin, White Masks*, translated by Richard Philcox. New York: Grove Press.

Faraji, Salim. 2016. "Kush and Rome on the Egyptian Southern Frontier: Where Barbarians Worshipped as Romans and Romans Worshipped as Barbarians." In *Romans, Barbarians, and the Transformation of the Roman World: Cultural Interaction and the Creation of Identity in Late Antiquity*, edited by Ralph W. Mathisen and Danuta Shanzer, 223–31. London: Routledge.

Fattovich, Rodolfo, Kathryn Bard, Lorenzo Petrassi, and Vincenzo Pisano. 2000. *The Aksum Archaeological Area: A Preliminary Assessment*. Naples: Istituto Universitario Orientale.

Fauset, Jessie Redmon. 1999. *Plum Bun: A Novel without a Moral*. Boston: Beacon Press. [Originally published in 1929]

Fehling, Detlev. 1989. *Herodotus and His "Sources": Citation, Invention and Narrative Art*, translated by J. G. Howie. Leeds: Francis Cairns.

Feuillâtre, Émile. 1966. *Études sur les "Éthiopiques" d'Héliodore : contribution à la connaissance du roman grec*. Paris: Presses universitaires de France.

Fields, Karen E., and Barbara J. Fields. 2014. *Racecraft: The Soul of Inequality in American Life*. London: Verso.

Figueira, Thomas, and Carmen Soares (eds.). 2020. *Ethnicity and Identity in Herodotus*. London: Routledge.

Firmin, Anténor. 1885. *De l'égalité des races humaines: anthropologie positive*. Paris: F. Pichon.

Flaherty, Colleen. 2020. "More White Lies." *Inside Higher Ed*, September 10. www .insidehighered.com/news/2020/09/10/more-allegations-racial-fraud-academe.

Fleetwood, Nicole R. 2011. *Troubling Vision: Performance, Visuality, and Blackness*. Chicago: University of Chicago Press.

Foley, Helene P. 1982. "The 'Female Intruder' Reconsidered: Women in Aristophanes' *Lysistrata* and *Ecclesiazusae*." *Classical Philology* 77 (1): 1–21.

2001. *Female Acts in Greek Tragedy*. Princeton: Princeton University Press.

Forrest, William G. 1960. "Themistocles and Argos." *Classical Quarterly* 10 (2): 221–41.

Fowler, Henry Watson, and Francis George Fowler, trans. 1905. *The Works of Lucian of Samosata*, Vol. 3. Oxford: Oxford University Press.

Fraser, Alexander David. 1929. Review of *The Negro in Greek and Roman Civilization: A Study of the Ethiopian Type*, by Grace Hadley Beardsley. *Art Bulletin* 11 (4): 426–27.

Freudenburg, Kirk. 2001. *Satires of Rome: Threatening Poses from Lucilius to Juvenal*. Cambridge: Cambridge University Press.

2005. "Introduction: Roman Satire." In *The Cambridge Companion to Roman Satire*, edited by Kirk Freudenburg, 1–30. Cambridge: Cambridge University Press.

von Fritz, Kurt. 1936. "Die Danaidentrilogie des Aeschylus." *Philologus* 91 (1): 121– 36, 249–69.

Frontisi-Ducroux, Françoise. 1989. "In the Mirror of the Mask." In *A City of Images: Iconography and Society in Ancient Greece*, by Claude Bérard et al., translated by Deborah Lyons, 151–65. Princeton: Princeton University Press.

Funke, Melissa. 2018. "Colourblind: The Use of Greek Colour Terminology in Cultural Linguistics in the Late Nineteenth and Early Twentieth Centuries." In *Brill's Companion to Classics and Early Anthropology*, edited by Emily Varto, 255–76. Leiden: Brill.

Futterman, Matthew, and Talya Minsberg. 2020. "After a Killing, 'Running While Black' Stirs Even More Anxiety." *New York Times*, May 8. www .nytimes.com/2020/05/08/sports/Ahmaud-Arbery-running.html.

Gaines, Alisha. 2017. *Black for a Day: White Fantasies of Race and Empathy*. Chapel Hill: University of North Carolina Press.

Gaines, Malik. 2017. *Black Performance on the Outskirts of the Left: A History of the Impossible*. New York: New York University Press.

Gaither, Paula, Elisa McAtee, Kenneth Lapatin, and David Saunders. 2020. "Rethinking Descriptions of Black Africans in Greek, Etruscan, and Roman Art." *Iris Blog: Behind the Scenes at the Getty*, December 15. https://blogs .getty.edu/iris/rethinking-descriptions-of-black-africans-in-greek-etruscan-and- roman-art/.

Galawdewos. 2015. *The Life and Struggles of Our Mother Walatta Petros: A Seventeenth-Century African Biography of an Ethiopian Women*, edited and translated by Wendy Laura Belcher and Michael Kleiner. Princeton: Princeton University Press. [Originally published in 1672]

Gallogly, Lynn D. 2019. "Figures of Speech: Texts, Bodies, and Performance in Lucian." PhD diss., University of California, Berkeley.

Garnett, Anna, and Derek Welsby. 2016. "Exhibitions and Galleries: Refreshing Sudan, Egypt and Nubia at the British Museum." *British Museum Newsletter: Egypt and Sudan* 3: 16–17. www.britishmuseum.org/sites/default/files/2020-06/British-Museum_Egypt_Sudan_Newsletter3_2016.pdf.

Garvey, Marcus. 1925. "Who and What Is a Negro?" In *Philosophy and Opinions of Marcus Garvey*, Vol. 2, edited by Amy Jacques Garvey, 18–21. New York: Universal Publishing.

Garvie, Alexander F. 2006. *Aeschylus' Supplices: Play and Trilogy*. 2nd ed. Bristol: Phoenix.

Gates, Henry Louis, Jr., and Kwame Anthony Appiah (eds.). 1993. *Langston Hughes: Critical Perspectives Past and Present*. New York: Amistad.

Genet, Jean. 1994. *The Blacks: A Clown Show*, translated by Bernard Frechtman. New York: Grove Atlantic.

Gerber, Douglas E. (ed. and trans.). 1999a. *Greek Elegiac Poetry: From the Seventh to the Fifth Centuries BC*. Cambridge, MA: Harvard University Press.

(ed. and trans.). 1999b. *Greek Iambic Poetry: From the Seventh to the Fifth Centuries BC*. Cambridge, MA: Harvard University Press.

Gere, Cathy. 2009. *Knossos and the Prophets of Modernism*. Chicago: University of Chicago Press.

Getty Museum. (n.d.). "Making Greek Vases." YouTube video, 4:20. www.youtube.com/watch?v=WhPW5or07L8.

Gikandi, Simon. 2000. *Ngũgĩ wa Thiong'o*. Cambridge: Cambridge University Press.

Gillman, Susan. 1996. "Pauline Hopkins and the Occult: African-American Revisions of Nineteenth-Century Sciences." *American Literary History* 8 (1): 57–82.

Gilman, Sander L. 1985. *Difference and Pathology: Stereotypes of Sexuality, Race and Madness*. Ithaca: Cornell University Press.

Gilroy, Paul. 1995. "'. . . To Be Real': The Dissident Forms of Black Expressive Culture." In *Let's Get It On: The Politics of Black Performance*, edited by Catherine Ugwu, 12–33. London: Institute of Contemporary Arts.

Giridharadas, Anand. 2018. *Winners Take All: The Elite Charade of Changing the World*. New York: Knopf.

Glasgow, Joshua, Sally Anne Haslanger, Chike Jeffers, and Quayshawn Spencer. 2019. *What Is Race? Four Philosophical Views*. Oxford: Oxford University Press.

Gleason, Maud. 1995. *Making Men: Sophists and Self-Presentation in Ancient Rome*. Princeton: Princeton University Press.

2006. "Greek Cities under Roman Rule." In *A Companion to the Roman Empire*, edited by David S. Potter, 228–49. Oxford: Blackwell.

Godley, Alfred Denis (ed. and trans.). 1921. *Herodotus: The Persian Wars*, Vol. 2: *Books 3–4*. Cambridge, MA: Harvard University Press.

Goff, Barbara E. 1990. *The Noose of Words: Readings of Desire, Violence and Language in Euripides'* Hippolytos. Cambridge: Cambridge University Press.

2013. *"Your Secret Language": Classics in the British Colonies of West Africa.* London: Bloomsbury.

Goff, Barbara E., and Michael Simpson. 2007. *Crossroads in the Black Aegean: Oedipus, Antigone, and Dramas of the African Diaspora.* Oxford: Oxford University Press.

Goldhill, Simon. 1990. "The Great Dionysia and Civic Ideology." In *Nothing to Do with Dionysos? Athenian Drama in Its Social Context,* edited by John J. Winkler and Froma I. Zeitlin, 97–129. Princeton: Princeton University Press.

2001a. "Introduction. Setting an Agenda: 'Everything Is Greece to the Wise'." In *Being Greek under Rome: Cultural Identity, the Second Sophistic and the Development of Empire,* edited by Simon Goldhill, 1–26. Cambridge: Cambridge University Press.

2001b. "The Erotic Eye: Visual Stimulation and Cultural Conflict." In *Being Greek under Rome: Cultural Identity, the Second Sophistic and the Development of Empire,* edited by Simon Goldhill, 154–94. Cambridge: Cambridge University Press.

2002. *Who Needs Greek? Contests in the Cultural History of Hellenism.* Cambridge: Cambridge University Press.

2015. "Is There a History of Prostitution?" In *Sex in Antiquity: Exploring Gender and Sexuality in the Ancient World,* edited by Mark Masterson, Nancy Sorkin Rabinowitz, and James Robson, 179–97. London: Routledge.

Goldman, Max L. 2015. "Associating the *Aulêtris*: Flute Girls and Prostitutes in the Classical Greek Symposium." *Helios* 42 (1): 29–60.

Gordon, Avery F. 2008. *Ghostly Matters: Haunting and the Sociological Imagination.* Minneapolis: University of Minnesota Press.

Gowers, Emily (ed.). 2012. *Horace* Satires*: Book 1.* Cambridge: Cambridge University Press.

Grand-Clément, Adeline. 2020. "'What Color Is the Sacred?' Couleurs et émotions dans les rituels grecs, de l'époque archaïque à l'époque hellénistique." In *Psychologie de la couleur dans le monde gréco-romain : huit exposés suivis de discussions et d'un épilogue,* edited by Katerina Ierodiakonou and Pierre Ducrey, 227–59. Geneva: Fondation Hardt pour l'étude de l'Antiquité classique.

Greenwood, Emily. 2009. "Re-Rooting the Classical Tradition: New Directions in Black Classicism." *Classical Receptions Journal* 1 (1): 87–103.

2010. *Afro-Greeks: Dialogues between Anglophone Caribbean Literature and Classics in the Twentieth Century.* Oxford: Oxford University Press.

2013. "Conjoined Heads and the Split Subject: Response to Jeremy Tanner." Presentation at the Yale University Art Gallery symposium "The Image of the Black in Western Art," May 3.

Griffith, Mark. 1995. "Brilliant Dynasts: Power and Politics in the *Oresteia*." *Classical Antiquity* 14 (1): 62–129.

Groves, Robert W. 2012. "Cross-Language Communication in Heliodorus' *Aethiopica*." PhD diss., University of California, Los Angeles.

Gruen, Erich S. 2011. *Rethinking the Other in Antiquity*. Princeton: Princeton University Press.

Grundmann, Steffi. 2019. *Haut und Haar: Politische und soziale Bedeutungen des Körpers im klassischen Griechenland*. Wiesbaden: Harrassowitz.

Gumbs, Alexis Pauline. 2016. *Spill: Scenes of Black Feminist Fugitivity*. Durham, NC: Duke University Press.

Habib, Imtiaz. 2007. *Black Lives in the English Archives, 1500–1677: Imprints of the Invisible*. London: Routledge.

Habtu, Hailu. 2000. "The Voyage of Däbtära Fesseha Giyorgis to Italy at the End of the 19th Century." *Annales d'Éthiopie* 16: 361–68.

Hägele, Hannelore. 2013. *Colour in Sculpture: A Survey from Ancient Mesopotamia to the Present*. Newcastle upon Tyne: Cambridge Scholars.

Hägg, Tomas. 2000. "The Black Land of the Sun: Meroe in Heliodoros' Romantic Fiction." *Graeco-Arabica* 7–8: 195–220.

Haggins, Bambi. 2007. *Laughing Mad: The Black Comic Persona in Post-Soul America*. New Brunswick: Rutgers University Press.

Hairston, Eric Ashley. 2013. *The Ebony Column: Classics, Civilization, and the African American Reclamation of the West*. Knoxville: University of Tennessee Press.

Haley, Shelley P. 1993. "Black Feminist Thought and Classics: Re-Membering, Re-Claiming, Re-Empowering." In *Feminist Theory and the Classics*, edited by Nancy Sorkin Rabinowitz and Amy Richlin, 23–43. London: Routledge.

2005. Review of *The Invention of Racism in Classical Antiquity*, by Benjamin Isaac. *American Journal of Philology* 126 (3): 451–54.

2009. "Be Not Afraid of the Dark: Critical Race Theory and Classical Studies." In *Prejudice and Christian Beginnings: Investigating Race, Gender, and Ethnicity in Early Christian Studies*, edited by Laura Salah Nasrallah and Elisabeth Schüssler Fiorenza, 27–49. Minneapolis: Fortress Press.

Hall, Edith. 1989. *Inventing the Barbarian: Greek Self-Definition through Tragedy*. Oxford: Oxford University Press.

2002. "When Is a Myth Not a Myth? Bernal's 'Ancient Model.'" In *Greeks and Barbarians*, edited by Thomas Harrison, 133–52. Edinburgh: Edinburgh University Press.

Hall, Jonathan M. 1997. *Ethnic Identity in Greek Antiquity*. Cambridge: Cambridge University Press.

2002. *Hellenicity: Between Ethnicity and Culture*. Chicago: University of Chicago Press.

Hall, Kim F. 1995. *Things of Darkness: Economies of Race and Gender in Early Modern England*. Ithaca: Cornell University Press.

Hall, Thomas D. 2014. "Ethnicity and World-Systems Analysis." In *A Companion to Ethnicity in the Ancient Mediterranean*, edited by Jeremy McInerney, 50–65. Chichester: John Wiley and Sons.

Halliwell, Stephen. 1993. "The Function and Aesthetics of the Greek Tragic Mask." In *Intertextualität in der griechisch-römischen Komödie*, edited by Niall W. Slater and Bernhard Zimmermann, 195–211. Stuttgart: J. B. Metzler.

Halpin, Marjorie. 1983. "Anthropology as Artifact." In *Consciousness and Inquiry: Ethnology and Canadian Realities*, edited by Frank E. Manning, 262–75. Ottawa: National Museums of Canada.

Halsell, Grace. 1969. *Soul Sister*. New York: World Publishing Company.

Hardwick, Lorna. 2003. *Reception Studies*. Oxford: Oxford University Press.

Harloe, Katherine. 2013. *Winckelmann and the Invention of Antiquity: History and Aesthetics in the Age of Altertumswissenschaft*. Oxford: Oxford University Press.

Harmon, Austin M. (ed. and trans.). 1925. *Lucian*, Vol. 4. Cambridge, MA: Harvard University Press.

Harpalani, Vinay. 2015. "To Be White, Black, or Brown? South Asian Americans and the Race-Color Distinction." *Washington University Global Studies Law Review* 14 (4): 609–36.

Harris, Marla. 2001. "Not Black and/or White: Reading Racial Difference in Heliodorus's *Ethiopica* and Pauline Hopkins's *Of One Blood*." *African American Review* 35 (3): 375–90.

Harris, Trudier. 1982. *From Mammies to Militants: Domestics in Black American Literature*. Philadelphia: Temple University Press.

Harrison, Thomas. 1998. "Herodotus' Conception of Foreign Languages." *Histos* 2: 1–45.

Hartman, Saidiya. 1997. *Scenes of Subjection: Terror, Slavery, and Self-Making in Nineteenth-Century America*. Oxford: Oxford University Press.

2008. "Venus in Two Acts." *Small Axe: A Caribbean Journal of Criticism* 12 (2): 1–14.

2019. *Wayward Lives, Beautiful Experiments: Intimate Histories of Riotous Black Girls, Troublesome Women, and Queer Radicals*. New York: Norton.

Hartog, François. 1980. *Le Miroir d'Hérodote : essai sur la représentation de l'autre*. Paris: Gallimard.

1988. *The Mirror of Herodotus: The Representation of the Other in the Writing of History*, translated by Janet Lloyd. Berkeley: University of California Press.

2001. *Memories of Odysseus: Frontier Tales from Ancient Greece*, translated by Janet Lloyd. Chicago: University of Chicago Press.

Haslanger, Sally Anne. 2012. *Resisting Reality: Social Construction and Social Critique*. Oxford: Oxford University Press.

Hatke, George. 2013. *Aksum and Nubia: Warfare, Commerce, and Political Fictions in Ancient Northeast Africa*. New York: New York University Press.

Hayes, Patrick. 2010. *J. M. Coetzee and the Novel: Writing and Politics after Beckett*. Oxford: Oxford University Press.

Heinrichs, Albert. 1972. *Die Phoinikika des Lollianos: Fragmente eines neuen griechischen Romans*. Bonn: R. Habelt.

Hemelrijk, Jaap M. 1984. *Caeretan Hydriae*. Mainz am Rhein: Philipp von Zabern.

Henderson, Jeffrey. 1991. "Women and the Athenian Dramatic Festivals." *Transactions of the American Philological Association* 121: 133–47.

Henderson, Taja-Nia Y., and Jamila Jefferson-Jones. 2020. "#LivingWhileBlack: Blackness as Nuisance." *American University Law Review* 69 (3): 863–914.

Hendrickson, George L. 1927. "Satura tota nostra est." *Classical Philology* 22 (1): 46–60.

Heng, Geraldine. 2018. *The Invention of Race in the European Middle Ages.* Cambridge: Cambridge University Press.

Hering Torres, Max S., María Elena Martínez, and David Nirenberg (eds.). 2012. *Race and Blood in the Iberian World.* Zürich: LIT Verlag.

Hicks, Dan. 2020. *The Brutish Museums: The Benin Bronzes, Colonial Violence and Cultural Restitution.* London: Pluto Press.

Hilton, John. 1998. "An Ethiopian Paradox: Heliodorus, *Aithiopika* 4.8." In *Studies in Heliodorus*, edited by Richard Hunter, 79–92. Cambridge: Cambridge Philological Society.

Hobbs, Allyson. 2014. *A Chosen Exile: A History of Racial Passing in American Life.* Cambridge, MA: Harvard University Press.

——— 2015. "Rachel Dolezal's Unintended Gift to America." *New York Times*, June 17. www.nytimes.com/2015/06/17/opinion/rachel-dolezals-unintended-gift-to-america.html.

Hobden, Fiona. 2009. "The Politics of the *Sumposion*." In *The Oxford Handbook of Hellenic Studies*, edited by George Boys-Stones, Barbara Graziosi, and Phiroze Vasunia, 271–80. Oxford: Oxford University Press.

——— 2013. *The Symposion in Ancient Greek Society and Thought.* Cambridge: Cambridge University Press.

Hodder, Ian. 2011. "Wheels of Time: Some Aspects of Entanglement Theory and the Secondary Products Revolution." *Journal of World Prehistory* 24 (2–3): 175–87.

——— 2012. *Entangled: An Archaeology of the Relationships between Humans and Things.* Chichester: Wiley-Blackwell.

——— 2016. *Studies in Human-Thing Entanglement.* Stanford: Ian Hodder.

Honig, Bonnie. 2013. *Antigone, Interrupted.* Cambridge: Cambridge University Press.

Hooper-Greenhill, Eilean. 2006. "Studying Visitors." In *A Companion to Museum Studies*, edited by Sharon Macdonald, 362–76. Oxford: Blackwell.

Hopkins, Pauline. 2004. *Of One Blood: Or, The Hidden Self.* New York: Washington Square Press. [Originally serialized in the December 1902 and January 1903 issues of the *Colored American Magazine*]

Houston, Drusilla Dunjee. 1926. *Wonderful Ethiopians of the Ancient Cushite Empire.* Oklahoma City: Universal Publishing.

Howe, Stephen. 1998. *Afrocentrism: Mythical Pasts and Imagined Homes.* London: Verso.

Hughes, Langston. 1963. *Something in Common.* New York: Hill and Wang.

——— 1995. "The Black Clown." In *The Collected Poems of Langston Hughes*, edited by Arnold Rampersad, 150–52. New York: Knopf. [Originally published in 1931]

Hull, Akasha (Gloria T.), Patricia Bell-Scott, and Barbara Smith (eds.). 2015. *All the Women Are White, All the Black Are Men, But Some of Us Are Brave: Black Women's Studies*. 2nd ed. New York: Feminist Press.

Humphrey, Jeff. 2015. "KXLY Exclusive: Rachel Dolezal Responds to Race Allegations." YouTube video, 0:42, posted by 4 News Now, June 11. www.youtube.com/watch?v=_7Gb9kK8HGk.

Hurston, Zora Neale. 1994. *Mules and Men*. New York: Harper Perennial. [Originally published in 1935]

    1998. "Characteristics of Negro Expression." In *The Jazz Cadence of American Culture*, edited by Robert G. O'Meally, 298–310. New York: Columbia University Press. [Originally published in *Negro: An Anthology*, edited by Nancy Cunard, 1934]

    2018. *Barracoon: The Story of the Last "Black Cargo."* Edited by Deborah G. Plant. New York: Amistad. [Based on Hurston's fieldwork in 1927]

Irwin, Eleanor. 1974. *Colour Terms in Greek Poetry*. Toronto: Hakkert.

Irwin, Elizabeth. 2014. "Ethnography and Empire: Homer and the Hippocratics in Herodotus' Ethiopian *Logos* 3.17–26." *Histos* 8: 25–75.

Isaac, Benjamin. 2004. *The Invention of Racism in Classical Antiquity*. Princeton: Princeton University Press.

    2009. "Racism: A Rationalization of Prejudice in Greece and Rome." In *The Origins of Racism in the West*, edited by Miriam Eliav-Feldon, Benjamin Isaac, and Joseph Ziegler, 32–56. Cambridge: Cambridge University Press.

    2017. *Empire and Ideology in the Graeco-Roman World: Selected Papers*. Cambridge: Cambridge University Press.

Jackson, Angela. 2017. *A Surprised Queenhood in the New Black Sun: The Life and Legacy of Gwendolyn Brooks*. Boston: Beacon Press.

Jacobson, Matthew Frye. 1998. *Whiteness of a Different Color: European Immigrants and the Alchemy of Race*. Cambridge, MA: Harvard University Press.

James, Stanlie M., Frances Smith Foster, and Beverly Guy-Sheftall (eds.). 2009. *Still Brave: The Evolution of Black Women's Studies*. New York: Feminist Press.

Jasanoff, Jay H., and Alan Nussbaum. 1996. "Word Games: The Linguistic Evidence in *Black Athena*." In *Black Athena Revisited*, edited by Mary R. Lefkowitz and Guy MacLean Rogers, 177–205. Chapel Hill: University of North Carolina Press.

Jenkins, Tiffany. 2016. *Keeping Their Marbles: How the Treasures of the Past Ended up in Museums … and Why They Should Stay There*. Oxford: Oxford University Press.

Jess, Tyehimba. 2016. *Olio*. Seattle: Wave Books.

Johansen, H. Friis, and Edward W. Whittle (eds.). 1980. *Aeschylus: The Suppliants*, Vol. 2. Copenhagen: Gyldendal Publishing House.

Johnson, E. Patrick. 2003. *Appropriating Blackness: Performance and the Politics of Authenticity*. Durham, NC: Duke University Press.

    2006. "Black Performance Studies: Genealogies, Politics, Futures." In *The Sage Handbook of Performance Studies*, edited by D. Soyini Madison and Judith Hamera, 446–63. Thousand Oaks: Sage.

Johnson, James Weldon. 1999. *The Autobiography of an Ex-Coloured Man.* New York: Hill and Wang. [Originally published in 1912]

Johnston, Andrew C. 2017. *The Sons of Remus: Identity in Roman Gaul and Spain.* Cambridge, MA: Harvard University Press.

Jones, Christopher P. 1996. "ἔθνος and γένος in Herodotus." *Classical Quarterly* 46 (2): 315–20.

Jones, Gregory. 2014. "Voice of the People: Popular Symposia and the Non-elite Origins of the Attic *Skolia.*" *Transactions of the American Philological Association* 144 (2): 229–62.

Joseph-Gabriel, Annette K. 2020. *Reimagining Liberation: How Black Women Transformed Citizenship in the French Empire.* Urbana: University of Illinois Press.

Kaiser, Alan. 2015. *Archaeology, Sexism, and Scandal: The Long-Suppressed Story of One Woman's Discoveries and the Man Who Stole Credit for Them.* Lanham: Rowman and Littlefield.

Kamen, Deborah. 2013. *Status in Classical Athens.* Princeton: Princeton University Press.

Kamugisha, Aaron. 2003. "Finally in Africa? Egypt, from Diop to Celenko." *Race and Class* 45 (1): 31–60.

Karavas, Orestis. 2005. *Lucien et la tragédie.* Berlin: De Gruyter.

Karp, Ivan, and Corinne A. Kratz. 2000. "Reflections on the Fate of Tippoo's Tiger: Defining Cultures through Public Display." In *Cultural Encounters: Representing "Otherness,"* edited by Elizabeth Hallam and Brian V. Street, 194–223. London: Routledge.

——— 2006. "Introduction: Museum Frictions: Public Cultures/Global Transformations." In *Museum Frictions: Public Cultures/Global Transformations,* edited by Ivan Karp, Corinne A. Kratz, Lynn Szwaja, and Tomás Ybarra-Frausto, 1–31. Durham, NC: Duke University Press.

Karp, Ivan, and Fred Wilson. 1996. "Constructing the Spectacle of Culture in Museums." In *Thinking about Exhibitions,* edited by Reesa Greenberg, Bruce W. Ferguson, and Sandy Nairne, 251–67. London: Routledge.

Kasimis, Demetra. 2018. *The Perpetual Immigrant and the Limits of Athenian Democracy.* Cambridge: Cambridge University Press.

Kay, Paul, Brent Berlin, Luisa Maffi, William R. Merrifield, and Richard Cook. 2009. *The World Color Survey.* Stanford: Center for the Study of Language and Information.

Keita, Maghan. 2000. *Race and the Writing of History: Riddling the Sphinx.* Oxford: Oxford University Press.

Kennedy, Rebecca Futo. 2013. "A Tale of Two Kings: Competing Aspects of Power in Aeschylus' *Persians.*" *Ramus* 42 (1/2): 64–88.

——— 2014a. "Geography in Greek Tragedy." In *The Encyclopedia of Greek Tragedy,* Vol. 2, edited by Hanna M. Roisman, 570–74. Chichester: Wiley-Blackwell.

——— 2014b. *Immigrant Women in Athens: Gender, Ethnicity, and Citizenship in the Classical City.* London: Routledge.

2015. "Elite Citizen Women and the Origins of the *hetaira* in Classical Athens." *Helios* 42 (1): 61–79.

2016. "Airs, Waters, Metals, Earth: People and Environment in Archaic and Classical Greek Thought." In *The Routledge Handbook of Identity and the Environment in the Classical and Medieval Worlds*, edited by Rebecca Futo Kennedy and Molly Jones-Lewis, 9–28. London: Routledge.

Kennedy, Rebecca Futo, C. Sydnor Roy, and Max L. Goldman (trans.). 2013. *Race and Ethnicity in the Classical World: An Anthology of Primary Sources in Translation*. Indianapolis: Hackett.

Kerkeslager, Allen. 1997. "Maintaining Jewish Identity in the Greek Gymnasium: A 'Jewish Load' in *CPJ* 3.519 (= *P. Schub.* 37 = *P. Berol.* 13406)." *Journal for the Study of Judaism in the Persian, Hellenistic, and Roman Period* 28 (1): 12–33.

Keuls, Eva. 1974. *The Water Carriers in Hades: A Study of Catharsis through Toil in Classical Antiquity*. Amsterdam: A. M. Hakkert.

1986. "*Danaides* and *Danaos*." In *Lexicon Iconographicum Mythologiae Classicae*, Vol. 3.1: *Atherion–Eros*, 337–43. Zürich: Artemis.

Kidd, Colin. 2006. *The Forging of Races: Race and Scripture in the Protestant Atlantic World, 1600–2000*. Cambridge: Cambridge University Press.

Kim, Lawrence. 2010. *Homer between History and Fiction in Imperial Greek Literature*. Cambridge: Cambridge University Press.

Kindstrand, Jan Fredrik. 1981. *Anacharsis, the Legend and the Apophthegmata*. Uppsala: Almqvist and Wiksell International.

King, Charles. 2019. *The Reinvention of Humanity: A Story of Race, Sex, Gender and the Discovery of Culture*. London: Bodley Head.

Knight, Alisha R. 2012. *Pauline Hopkins and the American Dream: An African American Writer's (Re)visionary Gospel of Success*. Knoxville: University of Tennessee Press.

Knox, Bernard. 1985. "Books and Readers in the Greek World." In *The Cambridge History of Classical Literature*, Vol. 1: *Greek Literature*, edited by P. E. Easterling and Bernard M. W. Knox, 1–41. Cambridge: Cambridge University Press.

1993. *The Oldest Dead White European Males and Other Reflections on the Classics*. New York: Norton.

Knudsen, Eva Rask, and Ulla Rahbek. 2016. *In Search of the Afropolitan: Encounters, Conversations, and Contemporary Diasporic African Literature*. Lanham: Rowman and Littlefield.

König, Jason. 2005. *Athletics and Literature in the Roman Empire*. Cambridge: Cambridge University Press.

2017. "Athletes and Trainers." In *The Oxford Handbook to the Second Sophistic*, edited by Daniel S. Richter and William A. Johnson, 155–68. Oxford: Oxford University Press.

Konstan, David. 1987. "Persians, Greeks and Empire." *Arethusa* 20 (1–2): 59–73.

2010. "Anacharsis the Roman, or Reality vs. Play." In *Lucian of Samosata, Greek Writer and Roman Citizen*, edited by Francesca Mestre and Pilar Gómez, 183–90. Barcelona: University of Barcelona.

Koskenniemi, Erkki. 2019. *Greek Writers and Philosophers in Philo and Josephus: A Study of Their Secular Education and Educational Ideals.* Leiden: Brill.

Krebs, Verena. 2021. *Medieval Ethiopian Kingship, Craft, and Diplomacy with Latin Europe.* Cham: Palgrave Macmillan.

Kreps, Christina. 2015. "Appropriate Museology and the 'New Museum Ethics': Honoring Diversity." *Nordisk Museologi* 2: 4–16.

Kuhrt, Amélie. 2007. *The Persian Empire: A Corpus of Sources from the Achaemenid Period*, Vol. 2. London: Routledge.

Kyllingstad, Jon Røyne. 2014. *Measuring the Master Race: Physical Anthropology in Norway, 1890–1945.* Cambridge: Open Book.

Lada-Richards, Ismene. 2007. *Silent Eloquence: Lucian and Pantomime Dancing.* London: Duckworth.

LaFraniere, Sharon, and Andrew W. Lehren. 2015. "The Disproportionate Risks of Driving While Black." *New York Times*, October 24. www.nytimes.com /2015/10/25/us/racial-disparity-traffic-stops-driving-black.html.

Lambert, Michael. 2005. "Proto-Racism." Review of *The Invention of Racism in Classical Antiquity*, by Benjamin Isaac. *Classical Review* 55 (2): 658–62.

Lape, Susan. 2010. *Race and Citizen Identity in the Classical Athenian Democracy.* Cambridge: Cambridge University Press.

Larsen, Nella. 2007. *Passing.* New York: Norton. [Originally published in 1929]

Lansana, Quraysh Ali, and Georgia A. Popoff (eds.). 2017. *The Whiskey of Our Discontent: Gwendolyn Brooks as Conscience and Change Agent.* Chicago: Haymarket Books.

Lecoq, Pierre. 1974. "Le problème de l'écriture vieux-perse." *Acta Iranica* 3: 25–107.

Lee, Mireille M. 2015. *Body, Dress, and Identity in Ancient Greece.* Cambridge: Cambridge University Press.

Lefkowitz, Mary R. 1992. "Not Out of Africa: The Origins of Greece and the Illusions of Afrocentrists." *New Republic*, February 10: 29–36.

1997. *Not Out of Africa: How Afrocentrism Became an Excuse to Teach Myth as History.* Rev. ed. New York: Harper Collins.

2008. *History Lesson: A Race Odyssey.* New Haven: Yale University Press.

Lefkowitz, Mary R., and Guy MacLean Rogers (eds.). 1996. *Black Athena Revisited.* Chapel Hill: University of North Carolina Press.

Levine, Molly Myerowitz. 1989. "The Challenge of *Black Athena* to Classics Today." *Arethusa* 22: 7–16.

Lewis, Sian. 2002. *The Athenian Woman: An Iconographic Handbook.* London: Routledge.

Lhamon, William T., Jr. 1998. *Raising Cain: Blackface Performance from Jim Crow to Hip Hop.* Cambridge, MA: Harvard University Press.

Liddell, Henry George, and Robert Scott. 1996. *A Greek-English Lexicon.* 9th ed. Oxford: Oxford University Press.

Lightfoot, Jane L. (ed. and trans.). 2003. *Lucian:* On the Syrian Goddess. Oxford: Oxford University Press.

Lissarrague, François. 1994. "*Epiktetos egraphsen*: The Writing on the Cup." In *Art and Text in Ancient Greek Culture*, edited by Simon Goldhill and Robin Osborne, 12–27. Cambridge: Cambridge University Press.

———. 1995. "Identity and Otherness: The Case of Attic Head Vases and Plastic Vases." *Source: Notes in the History of Art* 15 (1): 4–9.

———. 1999. "Publicity and Performance: *Kalos* Inscriptions in Attic Vase-Painting," translated by Robin Osborne. In *Performance Culture and Athenian Democracy*, edited by Simon Goldhill and Robin Osborne, 359–73. Cambridge: Cambridge University Press.

———. 2001. "The Athenian Image of the Foreigner," translated by Antonia Nevill. In *Greeks and Barbarians*, edited by Thomas Harrison, 101–24. Edinburgh: Edinburgh University Press.

Lloyd-Jones, Hugh (ed. and trans.). 1996. *Sophocles: Fragments*. Cambridge, MA: Harvard University Press.

Longo, Oddone. 1987. "I mangiatori di pesci: Regime alimentare e quadro culturale." *Materiali e discussioni per l'analisi dei testi classici* 18: 9–55.

Lonis, Raoul. 1992. "Les Éthiopiens sous le regard d'Héliodore." In *Le monde du roman grec: actes du colloque international tenu à l'École Normale Supérieure (Paris 17–19 décembre 1987)*, edited by Marie-Françoise Baslez, Philippe Hoffmann, and Monique Trédé, 233–41. Paris: Presses de l'École Normale Supérieure.

Loomba, Ania, and Jonathan Burton (eds.). 2007. *Race in Early Modern England: A Documentary Companion*. New York: Palgrave Macmillan.

Lo Presti, Roberto. 2012. "Shaping the Difference: The Medical Inquiry into the Nature of Places and the Early Birth of Anthropology in the Hippocratic Treatise *Airs Waters Places*." In *Medicine and Space: Body, Surroundings and Borders in Antiquity and the Middle Ages*, edited by Patricia A. Baker, Han Nijdam, and Karine van 't Land, 169–96. Leiden: Brill.

Loraux, Nicole. 1987. *Tragic Ways of Killing a Woman*, translated by Anthony Forster. Cambridge, MA: Harvard University Press.

Lott, Eric. 1993. *Love and Theft: Blackface Minstrelsy and the American Working Class*. Oxford: Oxford University Press.

Löwenherz, J. 1861. *Die Aethiopen der altclassischen Kunst*. Göttingen: Commission bei Adalbert Rente.

Lye, Suzanne. 2016. "Gender and Ethnicity in Heliodorus' *Aithiopika*." *Classical World* 109 (2): 235–62.

Mack, Peter. 2019. *Reading Old Books: Writing with Traditions*. Princeton: Princeton University Press.

MacKinnon, John Kenneth. 1978. "The Reason for the Danaids' Flight." *Classical Quarterly* 28 (1): 74–82.

MacMullen, Ramsay. 1966. "Provincial Languages in the Roman Empire." *American Journal of Philology* 87 (1): 1–17.

Madgett, Naomi Long. 1978. *Exits and Entrances*. Detroit: Lotus Press.

Malamud, Margaret. 2016. *African Americans and the Classics: Antiquity, Abolition and Activism*. London: Tauris.

Malkin, Irad. 2011. *A Small Greek World: Networks in the Ancient Mediterranean*. Oxford: Oxford University Press.

Manring, Maurice M. 1998. *Slave in a Box: The Strange Career of Aunt Jemima*. Charlottesville: University Press of Virginia.

Marstine, Janet (ed.). 2011. *Routledge Companion to Museum Ethics: Redefining Ethics for the Twenty-First Century Museum*. London: Routledge.

Marstine, Janet, Alexander A. Bauer, and Chelsea Haines. 2011. "New Directions in Museum Ethics." *Museum Management and Curatorship* 26 (2): 91–95.

(eds.). 2013. *New Directions in Museum Ethics*. London: Routledge.

Martin, S. Rebecca. 2014. "Ethnicity and Representation." In *A Companion to Ethnicity in the Ancient Mediterranean*, edited by Jeremy McInerney, 356–75. Chichester: John Wiley and Sons.

Massing, Jean Michel. 1995. "From Greek Proverb to Soap Advert: Washing the Ethiopian." *Journal of the Warburg and Courtauld Institutes* 58: 180–201.

Mastronarde, Donald (ed.). 2002. *Euripides:* Medea. Cambridge: Cambridge University Press.

Mattingly, David J. 2011. *Imperialism, Power, and Identity: Experiencing the Roman Empire*. Princeton: Princeton University Press.

Maus, Derek C., and James J. Donahue (eds.). 2014. *Post-Soul Satire: Black Identity after Civil Rights*. Jackson: University Press of Mississippi.

McCart, Gregory S. 2007. "Masks in Greek and Roman Theatre." In *The Cambridge Companion to Greek and Roman Theatre*, edited by Marianne McDonald and Michael Walton, 247–67. Cambridge: Cambridge University Press.

McClure, Laura. 1999. *Spoken Like a Woman: Speech and Gender in Athenian Drama*. Princeton: Princeton University Press.

McConnell, Justine. 2013. *Black Odysseys: The Homeric* Odyssey *in the African Diaspora since 1939*. Oxford: Oxford University Press.

McCoskey, Denise. 2003. "By Any Other Name? Ethnicity and the Study of Ancient Identity." *Classical Bulletin* 79 (1): 93–109.

2004. "On *Black Athena*, Hippocratic Medicine, and Roman Imperial Edicts: Egyptians and the Problem of Race in Classical Antiquity." In *Race and Ethnicity: Across Time, Space and Discipline*, edited by Rodney D. Coates, 297–330. Leiden: Brill.

2006. "Naming the Fault in Question: Theorizing Racism among the Greeks and Romans." Review of *The Invention of Race in Classical Antiquity*, by Benjamin Isaac. *International Journal of the Classical Tradition* 13 (2): 243–67.

2012. *Race: Antiquity and Its Legacy*. London: I. B. Tauris.

McGrath, Elizabeth. 1992. "The Black Andromeda." *Journal of the Warburg and Courtauld Institutes* 55: 1–18.

McInerney, Jeremy (ed.). 2014. *A Companion to Ethnicity in the Ancient Mediterranean*. Chichester: John Wiley and Sons.

Meer, Sarah. 2005. *Uncle Tom Mania: Slavery, Minstrelsy and Transatlantic Culture in the 1850s*. Athens: University of Georgia Press.

Mercer, Kobena. 1994. *Welcome to the Jungle: New Positions in Black Cultural Studies*. London: Routledge.

Mestre, Francesca. 2003. "Anacharsis, the Wise Man from Abroad." *Lexis* 21: 303–17.

Metzler, Dieter, and Herbert Hoffmann. 1977. "Zur Theorie und Methode der Erforschung von Rassismus in der Antike." *Kritische Berichte* 5 (1): 5–20.

Miller, Christopher L. 1985. *Blank Darkness: Africanist Discourse in French*. Chicago: University of Chicago Press.

　　1998. *Nationalists and Nomads: Essays on Francophone African Literature and Culture*. Chicago: University of Chicago Press.

Miller, Margaret C. 1992. "The Parasol: An Oriental Status-Symbol in Late Archaic and Classical Athens." *Journal of Hellenic Studies* 112: 91–105.

　　1997. *Athens and Persia in the Fifth Century BC: A Study in Cultural Receptivity*. Cambridge: Cambridge University Press.

　　2000. "The Myth of Bousiris: Ethnicity and Art." In *Not the Classical Ideal: Athens and the Construction of the Other in Greek Art*, edited by Beth Cohen, 413–42. Leiden: Brill.

Mills, Charles W. 1998. *Blackness Visible: Essays on Philosophy and Race*. Ithaca: Cornell University Press.

Miner, Horace. 1956. "Body Ritual among the Nacirema." *American Anthropologist* 58 (3): 503–07.

Mitchell, Alexandre G. 2009. *Greek Vase-Painting and the Origins of Visual Humor*. Cambridge: Cambridge University Press.

Mitchell, Lynette G. 2006. "Greeks, Barbarians and Aeschylus' *Suppliants*." *Greece and Rome* 53 (2): 205–23.

Mitchell, William John Thomas. 2012. *Seeing through Race*. Cambridge, MA: Harvard University Press.

Mofolo, Thomas. 1967. *Chaka, an Historical Romance*, translated by F. H. Dutton. 2nd ed. Oxford: Oxford University Press for the International African Institute. [Originally published in 1931]

Montagu, Ashley. 1997. *Man's Most Dangerous Myth: The Fallacy of Race*. 6th ed. Walnut Creek: AltaMira Press.

Montiglio, Silvia. 2012. *Love and Providence: Recognition in the Ancient Novel*. Oxford: Oxford University Press. [Originally published in 1942].

Moraga, Cherríe, and Gloria Anzaldúa (eds.). 2015. *This Bridge Called My Back: Writings by Radical Women of Color*. 4th ed. Albany: State University of New York Press.

Morgan, John R. 1982. "History, Romance, and Realism in the *Aithiopika* of Heliodorus." *Classical Antiquity* 1 (2): 221–65.

　　1998. "Narrative Doublets in Heliodorus' *Aithiopika*." In *Studies in Heliodorus*, edited by Richard Hunter, 60–78. Cambridge: Cambridge Philological Society.

　　2005. "Le blanc et le noir: perspectives païennes et chrétiennes sur l'Éthiopie d'Héliodore." In *Lieux, décors et paysages de l'ancien roman des origines à Byzance*, edited by Bernard Pouderon, 309–18. Lyon: Maison de l'Orient et de la Méditerranée.

2008. "Heliodorus: An Ethiopian Story." In *Collected Ancient Greek Novels*, edited by Bryan P. Reardon, 349–588. New ed. Berkeley: University of California Press.

2009. "The Emesan Connection: Philostratus and Heliodorus." In *Theios Sophistes: Essays on Flavius Philostratus' Vita Apollonii*, edited by Kristoffel Demoen and Danny Praet, 263–81. Leiden: Brill.

2013. "The Erotics of Reading Fiction: Text and Body in Heliodorus." In *Théorie et pratique de la fiction à l'époque impériale*, edited by Christophe Bréchet, Anne Videau, and Ruth Webb, 225–37. Paris: Éditions Picard.

2014. "Heliodorus the Hellene." In *Defining Greek Narrative*, edited by Douglas Cairns and Ruth Scodel, 260–76. Edinburgh: Edinburgh University Press.

Morkot, Robert. 1991. "Nubia and Achaemenid Persia: Sources and Problems." In *Asia Minor and Egypt: Old Cultures in a New Empire*, edited by Heleen Sancisi-Weerdenburg and Amélie Kuhrt, 321–67. Leiden: Nederlands Instituut voor het Nabije Oosten.

Morris, Sarah P. 1996. "The Legacy of *Black Athena*." In *Black Athena Revisited*, edited by Mary R. Lefkowitz and Guy MacLean Rogers, 167–74. Chapel Hill: University of North Carolina Press.

Morrison, Toni. 1993. *Playing in the Dark: Whiteness and the Literary Imagination*. New York: Vintage International.

2004. *Beloved*. New York: Vintage International. [Originally published in 1987]

Moses, Wilson Jeremiah. 1998. *Afrotopia: The Roots of African American Popular History*. Cambridge: Cambridge University Press.

Moten, Fred. 2003. *In the Break: The Aesthetics of the Black Radical Tradition*. Minneapolis: University of Minnesota Press.

Moyer, Ian S. 2011. *Egypt and the Limits of Hellenism*. Cambridge: Cambridge University Press.

Moyer, Ian S., Adam Lecznar, and Heidi Morse (eds.). 2020. *Classicisms in the Black Atlantic*. Oxford: Oxford University Press.

Mudimbe, Valentin Y. 1994. *The Idea of Africa*. Bloomington: Indiana University Press.

Muecke, Frances. 1982. "'I Know You – By Your Rags': Costume and Disguise in Fifth-Century Drama." *Antichthon* 16: 17–34.

Mueller, Melissa. 2016. *Objects as Actors: Props and the Poetics of Performance in Greek Tragedy*. Chicago: University of Chicago Press.

Mũkoma wa Ngũgĩ. 2018. *The Rise of the African Novel: Politics of Language, Identity, and Ownership*. Ann Arbor: University of Michigan Press.

Mullen, Alex. 2013. *Southern Gaul and the Mediterranean: Multilingualism and Multiple Identities in the Iron Age and Roman Periods*. Cambridge: Cambridge University Press.

Mullen, Alex, and Patrick James (eds.). 2012. *Multilingualism in the Graeco-Roman Worlds*. Cambridge: Cambridge University Press.

Mullen, Harryette. 1994. "Optic White: Blackness and the Production of Whiteness." *Diacritics* 24 (2–3): 71–89.

Munro-Hay, Stuart. 1991. *Aksum: An African Civilisation of Late Antiquity*. Edinburgh: Edinburgh University Press.

Munson, Rosaria Vignolo. 2001. *Telling Wonders: Ethnographic and Political Discourse in the Work of Herodotus*. Ann Arbor: University of Michigan Press.

2005. *Black Doves Speak: Herodotus and the Languages of Barbarians*. Washington, DC: Center for Hellenic Studies.

Murray, Jackie. 2021. "Race and Sexuality: Racecraft in the *Odyssey*." In *A Cultural History of Race in Antiquity*, edited by Denise McCoskey, 137–56. London: Bloomsbury.

[forthcoming]. *Neikos and the Poetics of Controversy: Apollonius against His Argonautic Predecessors*. Cambridge, MA: Harvard University Press.

Murray, Robert Duff. 1958. *The Motif of Io in Aeschylus' Suppliants*. Princeton: Princeton University Press.

Musgrave, Jonathan. 1990. "Dust and Damn'd Oblivion: A Study of Cremation in Ancient Greece." *Annual of the British School at Athens* 85: 271–99.

Musié, Mai (Meharit). 2018. "Representation of Persians in Ancient Greek Novels." PhD diss., Swansea University.

Mveng, Engelbert. 1972. *Les sources grecques de l'histoire négro-africaine depuis Homère jusqu'à Strabon*. Paris: Présence Africaine.

Mwangi, Evan Maina. 2009. *Africa Writes Back to Self: Metafiction, Gender, Sexuality*. Albany: State University of New York Press.

Mylonas, George E. 1929. Review of *The Negro in Greek and Roman Civilization: A Study of the Ethiopian Type*, by Grace Hadley Beardsley. *Classical Philology* 24 (4): 423.

Myres, John Linton. 1930. Review of *The Negro in Greek and Roman Civilization: A Study of the Ethiopian Type*, by Grace Hadley Beardsley. *Antiquity* 4 (16): 513.

Nash, Jennifer C. 2019. *Black Feminism Reimagined: After Intersectionality*. Durham, NC: Duke University Press.

Nasrallah, Laura. 2005. "Mapping the World: Justin, Tatian, Lucian, and the Second Sophistic." *Harvard Theological Review* 98 (3): 283–314.

Ndiaye, Noémie. 2016. "'Everyone Breeds in His Own Image': Staging the *Aethiopica* across the Channel." *Renaissance Drama* 44 (2): 157–85.

Neils, Jenifer. 2000. "Others within the Other: An Intimate Look at Hetairai and Maenads." In *Not the Classical Ideal: Athens and the Construction of the Other in Greek Art*, edited by Beth Cohen, 203–26. Leiden: Brill.

Newell, Stephanie. 2020. *Histories of Dirt: Media and Urban Life in Colonial and Postcolonial Lagos*. Durham, NC: Duke University Press.

Newman, Alana N. 2017. "Queering the Minoans: Gender Performativity and the Aegean Color Convention in Fresco Painting at Knossos." *Journal of Mediterranean Archaeology* 30 (2): 213–36.

Ngũgĩ wa Thiong'o. 1964. *Weep Not, Child*. London: Heinemann.

1973. *Homecoming: Essays on African and Caribbean Literature, Culture and Politics*. New York: Lawrence Hill. [Includes the 1968 memo, "On the Abolition of the English Department" in the appendix, 145–50]

1987. *Decolonising the Mind: The Politics of Language in African Literature*. London: James Currey. [Originally published in 1986]

2006. *Wizard of the Crow*. A translation from Gĩkũyũ by the author. New York: Pantheon Books.

2018. *Wrestling with the Devil: A Prison Memoir*. New York: The New Press.

Ngũgĩ wa Thiong'o, and Ngũgĩ wa Mĩriĩ. 1997. *I Will Marry When I Want*. Portsmouth: Heinemann. [Originally published as *Ngaahika Ndeenda*, 1982]

Ngũgĩ wa Thiong'o, and Micere Githae Mugo. 1976. *The Trial of Dedan Kimathi*. London: East African Educational Publishers.

Ní Mheallaigh, Karen. 2005. "'Plato Alone Was Not There …': Platonic Presences in Lucian." *Hermathena* 179: 89–103.

2014. *Reading Fiction with Lucian: Fakes, Freaks and Hyperreality*. Cambridge: Cambridge University Press.

2020. *The Moon in the Greek and Roman Imagination: Selenography in Myth, Literature, Science and Philosophy*. Cambridge: Cambridge University Press.

Noble, Joseph Veach. 1988. *The Techniques of Painted Attic Pottery*. Rev. ed. London: Thames and Hudson.

Nurhussein, Nadia. 2019. *Black Land: Imperial Ethiopianism and African America*. Princeton: Princeton University Press.

Nyong'o, Tavia. 2009. *The Amalgamation Waltz: Race, Performance, and the Ruses of Memory*. Minneapolis: University of Minnesota Press.

2019. *Afro-fabulations: The Queer Drama of Black Life*. New York: New York University Press.

Oakley, John H. 2000. "Some 'Other' Members of the Athenian Household: Maids and Their Mistresses in Fifth-Century Athenian Art." In *Not the Classical Ideal: Athens and the Construction of the Other in Greek Art*, edited by Beth Cohen, 227–47. Leiden: Brill.

O'Connor, David B. 1993. *Ancient Nubia: Egypt's Rival in Africa*. Philadelphia: University Museum of Archaeology and Anthropology, University of Pennsylvania.

Ogbechie, Sylvester Okwunodu. 2011. *Making History: African Collectors and the Canon of African Art (The Femi Akinsanya African Art Collection)*. Milan: 5 Continents.

Olya, Najee. 2021. "Herakles in Africa: Confronting the Other in Libya and Egypt." *Ancient World Magazine*, February 28. www.ancientworldmagazine.com/art icles/herakles-africa/.

Omi, Michael, and Howard Winant. 1994. *Racial Formation in the United States: From the 1960s to the 1990s*. 2nd ed. London: Routledge.

Opper, Thorsten. 2014. *The Meroë Head of Augustus*. London: British Museum Press.

Orrells, Daniel, Gurminder K. Bhambra, and Tessa Roynon (eds.). 2011. *African Athena: New Agendas*. Oxford: Oxford University Press.

Osborne, Robin. 2014. "Intoxication and Sociality: The Symposium in the Ancient Greek World." *Past and Present* 222 (Suppl. 9): 34–60.

Padilla Peralta, Dan-el. 2020. "Santo Domingo and the Politics of Classical Reception in the Caribbean." In *The Oxford Handbook of Comparative Political Theory*, edited by Leigh K. Jenco, Murad Idris, and Megan C. Thomas, 169–90. Oxford: Oxford University Press.

Painter, Nell Irvin. 2010. *The History of White People*. New York: Norton.

2018. *Old in Art School: A Memoir of Starting Over*. Berkeley: Counterpoint Press.

Parker, Grant. 2008. *The Making of Roman India: Greek Culture in the Roman World*. Cambridge: Cambridge University Press.

2017a. "The Azanian Muse: Classicism in Unexpected Places." In *South Africa, Greece, Rome: Classical Confrontations*, edited by Grant Parker, 3–52. Cambridge: Cambridge University Press.

(ed.). 2017b. *South Africa, Greece, Rome: Classical Confrontations*. Cambridge: Cambridge University Press.

Parks, Suzan-Lori. 2005. "New Black Math." *Theatre Journal* 57 (4): 576–83.

Parmenter, Christopher Stedman. 2021. "'A Happy Coincidence': Race, the Cold War, and Frank M. Snowden, Jr's *Blacks in Antiquity*." *Classical Receptions Journal* 13 (4): 485–506.

Pass, David Blair. 2016. "Buying Books and Choosing Lives: From Agora to Acropolis in Lucian's Transformation of Plato's Emporium of Polities." *American Journal of Philology* 137 (4): 625–54.

Paulsen, Thomas. 1992. *Inszenierung des Schicksals: Tragödie und Komödie im Roman des Heliodor*. Trier: Wissenschaftlicher Verlag.

Peck, Raoul (ed.). 2017. *I Am Not Your Negro (A Major Motion Picture): From Texts by James Baldwin*. New York: Vintage International.

Pedley, John Griffiths. 2012. *Greek Art and Archaeology*. 5th ed. Upper Saddle River: Prentice Hall.

Perkins, Judith. 1999. "An Ancient 'Passing' Novel: Heliodorus' *Aithiopika*." *Arethusa* 32 (2): 197–214.

Peterson, Anna. 2010. "Laughter in the Exchange: Lucian's Invention of the Comic Dialogue." PhD diss., Ohio State University.

2019. *Laughter on the Fringes: The Reception of Old Comedy in the Imperial Greek World*. Oxford: Oxford University Press.

Phelan, Peggy, and Jill Lane (eds.). 1998. *The Ends of Performance*. New York: New York University Press.

Pitts, Johny. 2019. *Afropean: Notes from Black Europe*. London: Allen Lane.

Podlecki, Anthony J. 1966. *The Political Background of Aeschylean Tragedy*. Ann Arbor: University of Michigan Press.

Popescu, Valentina. 2009. "Lucian's *Paradoxa*: Fiction, Aesthetics, and Identity." PhD diss., University of Cincinnati.

The Postclassicisms Collective. 2020. *Postclassicisms*. Chicago: University of Chicago Press.

Powell, John Enoch. 1935. "Notes on Herodotus II." *Classical Quarterly* 29 (3–4): 150–63.

Prashad, Vijay. 2001. *The Karma of Brown Folk*. Minneapolis: University of Minnesota Press.

Provenzo, Eugene F., Jr. (ed.). 2002. *Du Bois on Education*. Lanham: AltaMira Press.

Quinn, Josephine. 2017. *In Search of the Phoenicians*. Princeton: Princeton University Press.

Quiroga, Alberto. 2007. "From *Sophistopolis* to *Episcopolis*: The Case for a Third Sophistic." *Journal for Late Antique Religion and Culture* 1: 31–42.

Rabinowitz, Nancy Sorkin. 2014. "Are Aeschylus' *Suppliants* Women of Color?" Presentation at the 145th American Philological Association Annual Meeting, Chicago, January 3.

The Racial Imaginary Institute. 2017. "The Whiteness Issue." *The Racial Imaginary Institute*, September. https://theracialimaginary.org/issue/the-whiteness-issue/.

Ramgopal, Sailakshmi. 2019. "Mobility." In *A Cultural History of Western Empires in Antiquity*, edited by Carlos F. Noreña, 131–52. London: Bloomsbury.

Rampersad, Arnold (ed.). 1995. *The Collected Poems of Langston Hughes*. New York: Knopf.

Rankine, Patrice D. 2006. *Ulysses in Black: Ralph Ellison, Classicism, and African American Literature*. Madison: University of Wisconsin Press.

Raue, Dietrich. 2019. "Introduction: A Rather Young Discipline." In *Handbook of Ancient Nubia*, edited by Dietrich Raue, 3–13. Berlin: De Gruyter.

Redfield, James. 1985. "Herodotus the Tourist." *Classical Philology* 80 (2): 97–118.

Reed, Christopher Robert. 2000. *"All the World Is Here!" The Black Presence at White City*. Bloomington: Indiana University Press.

Reeve, Michael. 1989. "Conceptions." *Proceedings of the Cambridge Philological Society* 35 (215): 81–112.

Reid, Donald Malcolm. 2015. *Contesting Antiquity in Egypt: Archaeologies, Museums, and the Struggle for Identities from World War I to Nasser*. Cairo: American University in Cairo Press.

Reimer, Thomas O. 2013. "The Presentation of Gold in the Reliefs of the Eastern Staircase of the Apadana in Persepolis." *Iranian Journal of Archaeological Studies* 3 (1): 57–63.

Revell, Louise. 2016. *Ways of Being Roman: Discourses of Identity in the Roman West*. Oxford: Oxbow Books.

Rhodes, Peter John. 2003. "Nothing to Do with Democracy: Athenian Drama and the Polis." *Journal of Hellenic Studies* 123: 104–19.

2011. "The Dionysia and Democracy Again." *Classical Quarterly* 61 (1): 71–74.

Richlin, Amy. 2019. "Blackface and Drag in the *Palliata*." In *Complex Inferiorities: The Poetics of the Weaker Voice in Latin Literature*, edited by Sebastian Matzner and Stephen Harrison, 49–72. Oxford: Oxford University Press.

Richter, Daniel S. 2017. "Lucian of Samosata." In *The Oxford Handbook to the Second Sophistic*, edited by Daniel S. Richter and William A. Johnson, 327–44. Oxford: Oxford University Press.

Richter, Gisela, and Marjorie J. Milne. 1935. *Shapes and Names of Athenian Vases.* New York: Metropolitan Museum of Art.

Rilly, Claude, and Alex de Voogt. 2012. *The Meroitic Language and Writing System.* Cambridge: Cambridge University Press.

Ringer, Mark. 1998. *Electra and the Empty Urn: Metatheater and Role Playing in Sophocles.* Chapel Hill: University of North Carolina Press.

Rizo, Elisa, and Madeleine Mary Henry (eds.). 2016. *Receptions of the Classics in the African Diaspora of the Hispanophone and Lusophone Worlds: Atlantis Otherwise.* Lanham: Lexington Books.

Roach-Higgins, Mary Ellen, and Joanne B. Eicher. 1992. "Dress and Identity." *Clothing and Textiles Research Journal* 10 (4): 1–8.

Robiano, Patrick. 1992. "Les gymnosophistes éthiopiens chez Philostrate et chez Héliodore." *Revue des études anciennes* 94 (3–4): 413–28.

Robinson, Rachel Sargent. 1955. *Sources for the History of Greek Athletics in English Translation.* Cincinnati: Rachel Sargent Robinson.

Rogers, Joel A. 1946. *World's Great Men of Color: 3000 B.C. to 1946 A.D.* New York: J. A. Rogers.

———. 1967. *Sex and Race: Negro-Caucasian Mixing in All Ages and All Lands.* 9th ed. St. Petersburg: Helga M. Rogers.

Rohde, Erwin. 1876. *Der griechische Roman und seine Vorläufer.* Leipzig: Breitkopf und Härtel.

Roller, Duane W. 2018. *A Historical and Topographical Guide to the Geography of Strabo.* Cambridge: Cambridge University Press.

Rollins, Judith. 1985. *Between Women: Domestics and Their Employers.* Philadelphia: Temple University Press.

Romm, James. 1992. *The Edges of the Earth in Ancient Thought: Geography, Exploration, and Fiction.* Princeton: Princeton University Press.

Ronnick, Michele Valerie. 2016. "Classical Education and the Advancement of African American Women in the Nineteenth and Twentieth Centuries." In *Women Classical Scholars: Unsealing the Fountain from the Renaissance to Jacqueline de Romilly,* edited by Rosie Wyles and Edith Hall, 176–93. Oxford: Oxford University Press.

Rooks, Noliwe M. 1996. *Hair Raising: Beauty, Culture, and African American Women.* New Brunswick: Rutgers University Press.

Root, Margaret C. 1979. *The King and Kingship in Achaemenid Art: Essays on the Creation of an Iconography of Empire.* Leiden: Brill.

Rosaldo, Renato. 1989. *Culture and Truth: The Remaking of Social Analysis.* Boston: Beacon Press.

Rösler, Wolfgang. 2007. "The End of the *Hiketides* and Aischylos' Danaid Trilogy." In *Oxford Readings in Aeschylus,* edited by Michael Lloyd, 174–98. Oxford: Oxford University Press.

Ross, Alan J. 2015. "Syene as Face of Battle: Heliodorus and Late Antique Historiography." *Ancient Narrative* 12: 1–26.

Ross, Fran. 1974. *Oreo.* New York: Greyfalcon House.

Rostad, Aslak. 2019. "Vagrancy, Archery, and Savagery: Lucian's Use of Scythians as a Rhetorical Tool." *Hermes* 147 (3): 333–51.

Roth, Philip. 2000. *The Human Stain*. Boston: Houghton Mifflin.

Rotroff, Susan I. 2014. "A Scorpion and a Smile: Two Vases in the Kemper Museum of Art in St. Louis." In *Athenian Potters and Painters*, Vol. 3, edited by John H. Oakley, 165–74. Oxford: Oxbow Books.

Rowan, Kirsty. 2006. "Meroitic: A Phonological Investigation." PhD diss., University of London.

Rushdie, Salman. 1982. "The Empire Writes Back with a Vengeance." *The Times* (London), July 3: 8.

Rutledge, Steven H. 2000. "Tacitus in Tartan: Textual Colonization and Expansionist Discourse in the *Agricola*." *Helios* 27 (1): 75–95.

Rydell, Robert W. 1987. *All the World's a Fair: Visions of Empire at American International Expositions, 1876–1916*. Chicago: University of Chicago Press.

Said, Edward W. 1978. *Orientalism: Western Conceptions of the Orient*. New York: Pantheon.

Saïd, Suzanne. 1992. "Les langues du roman grec." In *Le monde du roman grec. Actes du colloque international tenu à l'École Normale Supérieure (Paris 17–19 décembre 1987)*, edited by Marie-Françoise Baslez, Philippe Hoffmann, and Monique Trédé, 169–86. Paris: Presses de l'École Normale Supérieure.

1994. "The City in the Greek Novel." In *The Search for the Ancient Novel*, edited by James Tatum, 216–36. Baltimore: Johns Hopkins University Press.

Samuels, Tristan. 2015. "Herodotus and the Black Body: A Critical Race Theory Analysis." *Journal of Black Studies* 46 (7): 723–41.

Sandin, Pär. 2005. *Aeschylus' Supplices: Introduction and Commentary on vv. 1–523*. Corr. ed. Lund: Symmachus.

Sandweiss, Martha A. 2009. *Passing Strange: A Gilded Age Tale of Love and Deception across the Color Line*. New York: Penguin.

Sanz Morales, Manuel. 2018. "Copyists' Versions and the Readership of the Greek Novel." In *Cultural Crossroads in the Ancient Novel*, edited by Marília P. Futre Pinheiro, David Konstan, and Bruce Duncan MacQueen, 183–94. Berlin: De Gruyter.

Sassi, Maria Michela. 2001. *The Science of Man in Ancient Greece*, translated by Paul Tucker. Chicago: University of Chicago Press.

Scarborough, William Sanders. 2005. *The Autobiography of William Sanders Scarborough: An American Journey from Slavery to Scholarship*. Edited by Michele V. Ronnick. Detroit: Wayne State University Press.

2006. *The Works of William Sanders Scarborough: Black Classicist and Race Leader*. Edited by Michele V. Ronnick. New York: Oxford University Press.

2018. *William Sanders Scarborough's First Lessons in Greek: A Facsimile of the 1881 Edition*. Edited by Donald E. Sprague. Mundelein: Bolchazy-Carducci.

Schlapbach, Karin. 2010. "The *Logoi* of Philosophers in Lucian of Samosata." *Classical Antiquity* 29 (2): 250–77.

Schmidt, Erich Friedrich. 1953. *Persepolis*, Vol. 1: *Structures, Reliefs, Inscriptions*. Chicago: University of Chicago Press.

Schmitz, Thomas. 2010. "A Sophist's Drama: Lucian and Classical Tragedy." In *Beyond the Fifth Century: Interactions with Greek Tragedy from the Fourth Century BCE to the Middle Ages*, edited by Ingo Gildenhard and Martin Revermann, 289–312. Berlin: De Gruyter.

Schneider, Pierre. 2004. *L'Éthiopie et l'Inde: interférences et confusions aux extrémités du monde antique*. Rome: École Française de Rome.

2015. "The So-Called Confusion between India and Ethiopia: The Eastern and Southern Edges of the Inhabited World from the Greco-Roman Perspective." In *Brill's Companion to Ancient Geography: The Inhabited World in Greek and Roman Tradition*, edited by Serena Bianchetti, Michele Cataudella, and Hans-Joachim Gehrke, 184–202. Leiden: Brill.

Seaford, Richard (ed.). 2016. *Universe and Inner Self in Early Indian and Early Greek Thought*. Edinburgh: Edinburgh University Press.

Secord, Jared. 2016. "Overcoming Environmental Determinism: Introduced Species, Hybrid Plants and Animals, and Transformed Lands in the Hellenistic and Roman Worlds." In *The Routledge Handbook of Identity and the Environment in the Classical and Medieval Worlds*, edited by Rebecca Futo Kennedy and Molly Jones-Lewis, 210–29. London: Routledge.

Selden, Daniel L. 1998. "*Aithiopika* and Ethiopianism." In *Studies in Heliodorus*, edited by Richard Hunter, 182–217. Cambridge: Cambridge Philological Society.

2013. "How the Ethiopian Changed His Skin." *Classical Antiquity* 32 (2): 322–77.

Seligman, Charles Gabriel. 1930. *Races of Africa*. London: T. Butterworth.

de Sélincourt, Aubrey (trans.). 2003. *Herodotus:* The Histories. Rev. ed. New York: Penguin.

Sellassie, Sergew Hable. 1972. *Ancient and Medieval Ethiopian History to 1270*. Addis Ababa: United Printers.

Serrell, Beverly. 2015. *Exhibit Labels: An Interpretive Approach*. 2nd ed. Lanham: Rowman and Littlefield.

Shapiro, Alan. 1987. "*Kalos*-Inscriptions with Patronymic." *Zeitschrift für Papyrologie und Epigraphik* 68: 107–18.

Sharpe, Christina Elizabeth. 2016. *In the Wake: On Blackness and Being*. Durham, NC: Duke University Press.

Sharpley-Whiting, Tracy Denean. 2002. *Negritude Women*. Minneapolis: University of Minnesota Press.

Shinnie, Peter Lewis. 1967. *Meroe: A Civilization of the Sudan*. London: Thames and Hudson.

Shipp, Jesse. 1903. *In Dahomey, a Negro Musical Comedy*. London: Keith, Prowse and Co.

Shipton, Matthew. 2018. *The Politics of Youth in Greek Tragedy: Gangs of Athens*. London: Bloomsbury.

Sicherl, Martin. 1986. "Die Tragik der Danaiden." *Museum Helveticum* 43 (2): 81–110.

Sicherman, Carol. 1990. *Ngugi wa Thiong'o: The Making of a Rebel. A Sourcebook in Kenyan Literature and Resistance*. London: Hans Zell.

Sidebotham, Steven E. 2011. *Berenike and the Ancient Maritime Spice Route*. Berkeley: University of California Press.

Skinner, Joseph E. 2012. *The Invention of Greek Ethnography: From Homer to Herodotus*. Oxford: Oxford University Press.

Skovmøller, Amalie. 2020. *Facing the Colours of Roman Portraiture: Exploring the Materiality of Ancient Polychrome Forms*. Berlin: De Gruyter.

Slater, Niall W. 2005. "And There's Another Country: Translation as Metaphor in Heliodorus." In *Metaphor and the Ancient Novel*, edited by Stephen Harrison, Michael Paschalis, and Stavros Frangoulidis, 106–22. Groningen: Barkhuis.

Smith, Henry Roy William. 1930. Review of *The Negro in Greek and Roman Civilization: A Study of the Ethiopian Type*, by Grace Hadley Beardsley. *American Journal of Archaeology* 34 (4): 511.

Smith, Stuart Tyson. 2003. *Wretched Kush: Ethnic Identities and Boundaries in Egypt's Nubian Empire*. London: Routledge.

Snell, Bruno, Richard Kannicht, and Stefan L. Radt (eds.). 1971–2004. *Tragicorum Graecorum Fragmenta*. 6 vols. Göttingen: Vandenhoeck and Ruprecht.

Snowden, Frank M., Jr. 1947. "The Negro in Classical Italy." *American Journal of Philology* 68 (3): 266–92.

1948. "The Negro in Ancient Greece." *American Anthropologist* 50 (1): 31–44.

1970. *Blacks in Antiquity: Ethiopians in the Greco-Roman Experience*. Cambridge, MA: Harvard University Press.

1981. "Aithiopes." In *Lexicon Iconographicum Mythologiae Classicae*, Vol. 1.1: *Aara–Aphlad*, 413–19. Zürich: Artemis.

1983. *Before Color Prejudice: The Ancient View of Blacks*. Cambridge, MA: Harvard University Press.

1988. "Μέλας-λευκός and *Niger-candidus* Contrasts in Classical Literature." *Ancient History Bulletin* 2: 60–64.

1997. "Greeks and Ethiopians." In *Greeks and Barbarians: Essays on the Interactions between Greeks and Non-Greeks in Antiquity and the Consequences for Eurocentrism*, edited by John E. Coleman and Clark A. Walz, 103–26. Bethesda: CDL Press.

2001. "Attitudes towards Blacks in the Greek and Roman World: Misinterpretations of the Evidence." In *Africa and Africans in Antiquity*, edited by Edwin M. Yamauchi, 246–75. East Lansing: Michigan State University Press.

2010. "Iconographical Evidence on the Black Populations in Greco-Roman Antiquity." In *The Image of the Black in Western Art*, Vol. 1: *From the Pharaohs to the Fall of the Roman Empire*, edited by David Bindman and Henry Louis Gates, Jr., 141–250. New ed. Cambridge, MA: Harvard University Press.

Sommerstein, Alan H. 1997. "The Theatre Audience, the *Demos*, and the *Suppliants* of Aeschylus." In *Greek Tragedy and the Historian*, edited by Christopher Pelling, 63–79. Oxford: Oxford University Press.

(ed. and trans.). 2008. *Aeschylus:* Persians, Seven against Thebes, Suppliants, Prometheus Bound. Cambridge, MA: Harvard University Press.

2010. *Aeschylean Tragedy*. 2nd ed. London: Duckworth.

(ed.). 2019. *Aeschylus:* Suppliants. Cambridge: Cambridge University Press.

Sorsby, Bert D., and S. D. Horne. 1980. "The Readability of Museum Labels." *Museums Journal* 80 (3): 157–59.

Sosin, Joshua D. 2016. "A Metic Was a Metic." *Historia: Zeitschrift für Alte Geschichte* 65: 2–13.

Spatz, Lois. 1982. *Aeschylus*. Boston: Twayne.

Spiller, Elizabeth. 2011. *Reading and the History of Race in the Renaissance.* Cambridge: Cambridge University Press.

Spillers, Hortense J. 2003. "Black, White and in Color, or Learning How to Paint: Toward an Intramural Protocol of Reading." In *Black, White, and in Color: Essays on American Literature and Culture*, edited by Hortense Spillers, 203–29. Chicago: University of Chicago Press.

Spivak, Gayatri Chakravorty. 1994. "Can the Subaltern Speak?" In *Colonial Discourse and Post-Colonial Theory: A Reader*, edited by Patrick Williams and Laura Chrisman, 66–111. New York: Columbia University Press.

Sprigle, Ray. 1949. *In the Land of Jim Crow*. New York: Simon and Schuster.

Spring, Christopher, Nigel Barley, and Julie Hudson. 2001. "The Sainsbury African Galleries at the British Museum." *African Arts* 34 (3): 18–37, 93.

Stager, Jennifer. 2018. "The Unbearable Whiteness of Whiteness." *Art Practical* (blog), January 16. www.artpractical.com/column/feature-the-unbearable-whiteness-of-whiteness/.

Steiner, Ann. 2002. "Private and Public: Links between *Symposion* and *Syssition* in Fifth-Century Athens." *Classical Antiquity* 21 (2): 347–90.

Stephens, Susan. 1994. "Who Reads Ancient Novels?" In *The Search for the Ancient Novel*, edited by James Tatum, 405–18. Baltimore: Johns Hopkins University Press.

2003. *Seeing Double: Intercultural Poetics in Ptolemaic Alexandria*. Berkeley: University of California Press.

2008. "Cultural Identity." In *The Cambridge Companion to the Greek and Roman Novel*, edited by Tim Whitmarsh, 56–71. Cambridge: Cambridge University Press.

Stepto, Robert B. 1991. *From Behind the Veil: A Study of Afro-American Narrative*. 2nd ed. Urbana: University of Illinois Press.

Stocking, George W., Jr. 1982. *Race, Culture, and Evolution: Essays in the History of Anthropology*. Chicago: University of Chicago Press.

Stoneman, Richard. 2019. *The Greek Experience of India: From Alexander to the Indo-Greeks*. Princeton: Princeton University Press.

Surtees, Allison, and Jennifer Dyer. 2020. "Introduction: Queering Classics." In *Exploring Gender Diversity in the Ancient World*, edited by Allison Surtees and Jennifer Dyer, 1–25. Edinburgh: Edinburgh University Press.

Swain, Simon. 1996. *Hellenism and Empire: Language, Classicism, and Power in the Greek World, AD 50–250*. Oxford: Clarendon Press.

Tanner, Jeremy. 2010. "Introduction to the New Edition. Race and Representation in Ancient Art: *Black Athena* and After." In *The Image of the Black in Western Art*, Vol. 1: *From the Pharaohs to the Fall of the Roman Empire*, edited by David Bindman and Henry Louis, Jr., 1–39. New ed. Cambridge, MA: Harvard University Press.

Taplin, Oliver. 1977. *The Stagecraft of Aeschylus: The Dramatic Use of Exits and Entrances in Greek Tragedy*. Oxford: Clarendon Press.

Taylor, Paul, Linda Alcoff, and Luvell Anderson (eds.). 2018. *The Routledge Companion to the Philosophy of Race*. London: Routledge.

Tegla, Emanuela. 2011. "*Waiting for the Barbarians*: The Journey from Duty to Moral Choice." *English: Journal of the English Association* 60 (228): 68–91.

Thomas, Bridget M. 1998. "Negotiable Identities: The Interpretation of Color, Gender, and Ethnicity in Aeschylus' *Suppliants*." PhD diss., Ohio State University.

Thomas, Rosalind. 2000. *Herodotus in Context: Ethnography, Science and the Art of Persuasion*. Cambridge: Cambridge University Press.

Thompson, Ayanna. 2021. *Blackface*. London: Bloomsbury.

Thompson, Lloyd. 1989. *Romans and Blacks*. Norman: University of Oklahoma Press.

1993. "Roman Perceptions of Blacks." *Scholia: Studies in Classical Antiquity* 2: 17–30.

Toll, Robert C. 1974. *Blacking Up: The Minstrel Show in Nineteenth-Century America*. New York: Oxford University Press.

Topper, Kathryn. 2012. *The Imagery of the Athenian Symposium*. Cambridge: Cambridge University Press.

Török, László. 1989–90. "Augustus and Meroe." *Orientalia Suecana* 38–39: 171–90.

1997. *The Kingdom of Kush: Handbook of the Napatan-Meroitic Civilization*. Leiden: Brill.

2009. *Between Two Worlds: The Frontier Region between Ancient Nubia and Egypt 3700 BC–500 AD*. Leiden: Brill.

2014. *Herodotus in Nubia*. Leiden: Brill.

Trafton, Scott. 2004. *Egypt Land: Race and Nineteenth-Century American Egyptomania*. Durham, NC: Duke University Press.

Trapp, Michael. 2017. "Philosophical Authority in the Imperial Period." In *Authority and Expertise in Ancient Scientific Culture*, edited by Jason König and Greg Woolf, 27–57. Cambridge: Cambridge University Press.

True, Marion. 2006. "Athenian Potters and the Production of Plastic Vases." In *The Colors of Clay: Special Techniques in Athenian Vases*, by Beth Cohen, 240–49. Los Angeles: J. Paul Getty Museum.

Tuck, Eve, and K. Wayne Yang. 2012. "Decolonization Is Not a Metaphor." *Decolonization: Indigeneity, Education and Society* 1 (1): 1–40.

Turner, Patricia A. 1994. *Ceramic Uncles and Celluloid Mammies: Black Images and Their Influence on Culture*. New York: Anchor.

Tuvel, Rebecca. 2017. "In Defense of Transracialism." *Hypatia* 32 (2): 263–78.

Tzanetou, Angeliki. 2012. *City of Suppliants: Tragedy and the Athenian Empire*. Austin: University of Texas Press.

Tziovas, Dimitris (ed.). 2014. *Re-Imagining the Past: Antiquity and Modern Greek Culture*. Oxford: Oxford University Press.

Uhlig, Siegbert (ed.). 2003. *Encyclopaedia Aethiopica*, Vol. 1: *A–C*. Wiesbaden: Harrassowitz.

Umachandran, Mathura. 2019. "More than a Common Tongue: Dividing Race and Classics across the Atlantic." *Eidolon*, June 11. https://eidolon.pub/more-than-a-common-tongue-cfd7edeb6368.

UNESCO (ed.). 1969a. "Statement on Race, Paris, July 1950." In *Four Statements on the Race Question*, 30–35. Paris: UNESCO.

    1969b. "Statement on the Nature of Race and Race Differences, Paris, June 1951." In *Four Statements on the Race Question*, 36–43. Paris: UNESCO.

    1978. "Declaration on Race and Racial Prejudice." November 27. https://unesdoc.unesco.org/ark:/48223/pf0000114032.page=60.

Valdez, Raul, and Robert G. Tuck, Jr. 1980. "On the Identification of the Animals Accompanying the 'Ethiopian' Delegation in the Bas-Reliefs of the Apadana at Persepolis." *Iran: Journal of the British Institute of Persian Studies* 18: 156–57.

Vasunia, Phiroze. 2001. *The Gift of the Nile: Hellenizing Egypt from Aeschylus to Alexander*. Berkeley: University of California Press.

    2013. *The Classics and Colonial India*. Oxford: Oxford University Press.

    2016. "Ethiopia and India: Fusion and Confusion in British Orientalism." *Les Cahiers d'Afrique de l'Est* 51: 21–43.

Verhoogen, Violette. 1932. Review of *The Negro in Greek and Roman Civilization: A Study of the Ethiopian Type*, by Grace Hadley Beardsley. *Revue belge de philologie et d'histoire* 11 (1–2): 218–20.

Vidal-Naquet, Pierre. 1988. "Aeschylus, the Past and the Present." In *Myth and Tragedy in Ancient Greece*, by Jean-Pierre Vernant and Pierre Vidal-Naquet, translated by Janet Lloyd, 249–72. New York: Zone Books.

Vokotopoulou, Ioulia. 1996. *Guide to the Archaeological Museum of Thessalonike*, translated by David Hardy. Athens: Kapon Editions.

Volz, Andreas. 2012. "Janiforme Darstellungen im interkulturellen Vergleich." *Tribus (Jahrbuch des Linden-Museums)* 61: 114–55.

Walcott, Derek. 1990. *Omeros*. New York: Farrar, Straus and Giroux.

Wald, Gayle. 2000. *Crossing the Line: Racial Passing in Twentieth-Century U.S. Literature and Culture*. Durham, NC: Duke University Press.

Walters, Tracey Lorraine. 2007. *African American Literature and the Classicist Tradition: Black Women Writers from Wheatley to Morrison*. New York: Palgrave Macmillan.

Warner, Tobias. 2019. *The Tongue-Tied Imagination: Decolonizing Literary Modernity in Senegal*. New York: Fordham University Press.

Watson, James. 2010. "The Origin of Metic Status at Athens." *Cambridge Classical Journal* 56: 259–278.

Welsby, Derek. 1996. *The Kingdom of Kush: The Napatan and Meroitic Empires*. London: British Museum Press.

West, Martin L. (ed. and trans.). 2003. *Greek Epic Fragments*. Cambridge, MA: Harvard University Press.

Wetmore, Kevin J., Jr. 2002. *The Athenian Sun in an African Sky: Modern African Adaptations of Classical Greek Tragedy*. Jefferson: McFarland.

Wheatley, Phillis. 1773. *Poems on Various Subjects, Religious and Moral*. London: A. Bell.

Whitaker, Cord J. 2019. *Black Metaphors: How Modern Racism Emerged from Medieval Race-Thinking*. Philadelphia: University of Pennsylvania Press.

Whitehead, David. 1977. *The Ideology of the Athenian Metic*. Cambridge: Cambridge Philological Society.

Whitmarsh, Tim. 1998. "The Birth of a Prodigy: Heliodorus and the Genealogy of Hellenism." In *Studies in Heliodorus*, edited by Richard Hunter, 93–124. Cambridge: Cambridge Philological Society.

1999. "The Writes of Passage: Cultural Initiation in Heliodorus' *Aethiopica*." In *Constructing Identities in Late Antiquity*, edited by Richard Miles, 16–40. London: Routledge.

2001a. "'Greece Is the World': Exile and Identity in the Second Sophistic." In *Being Greek Under Rome*, edited by Simon Goldhill, 269–305. Cambridge: Cambridge University Press.

2001b. *Greek Literature and the Roman Empire: The Politics of Imitation*. Oxford: Oxford University Press.

2002. "Written on the Body: Ekphrasis, Perception and Deception in Heliodorus' *Aethiopica*." *Ramus* 31 (1–2): 111–25.

2005a. "Heliodorus Smiles." In *Metaphor and the Ancient Novel*, edited by Stephen Harrison, Michael Paschalis, and Stavros Frangoulidis, 87–105. Groningen: Barkhuis.

2005b. *The Second Sophistic*. Oxford: Oxford University Press.

(ed.). 2010. *Local Knowledge and Microidentities in the Imperial Greek World*. Cambridge: Cambridge University Press.

2011a. "Hellenism, Nationalism, Hybridity: The Invention of the Novel." In *African Athena: New Agendas*, edited by Daniel Orrells, Gurminder K. Bhambra, and Tessa Roynon, 210–24. Oxford: Oxford University Press.

2011b. *Narrative and Identity in the Ancient Greek Novel: Returning Romance*. Cambridge: Cambridge University Press.

2013. *Beyond the Second Sophistic: Adventures in Greek Postclassicism*. Berkeley: University of California Press.

2018. *Dirty Love: The Genealogy of the Ancient Greek Novel*. Oxford: Oxford University Press.

Wiesehöfer, Josef. 1996. *Ancient Persia: From 550 BC to 650 AD*, translated by Azizeh Azodi. London: Tauris.

Wiles, David. 2007. *Mask and Performance in Greek Tragedy: From Ancient Festival to Modern Experimentation*. Cambridge: Cambridge University Press.

Wilson, David M. 2002. *The British Museum: A History*. London: British Museum Press.

Wilson, Peter. 2009. "Tragic Honours and Democracy: Neglected Evidence for the Politics of the Athenian Dionysia." *Classical Quarterly* 59 (1): 8–29.

Windfuhr, Gernot L. 1994. "Saith Darius: Dialectic, Numbers, Time and Space at Behistun (DB, Old Persian Version)." In *Continuity and Change: Proceedings of the Last Achaemenid History Workshop, April 6–8, 1990, Ann Arbor, Michigan*, edited by Heleen Sancisi-Weerdenburg, Amélie Kuhrt, and Margaret C. Root, 265–81. Leiden: Nederlands Instituut voor het Nabije Oosten.

Winkler, John J. 1980. "Lollianos and the Desperadoes." *Journal of Hellenic Studies* 100: 155–81.

——— 1982. "The Mendacity of Kalasiris and the Narrative Strategy of Heliodoros' *Aithiopika*." In *Later Greek Literature*, edited by John J. Winkler and Gordon Willis Williams, 93–158. Cambridge: Cambridge University Press.

Winnington-Ingram, Reginald P. 1961. "The Danaid Trilogy of Aeschylus." *Journal of Hellenic Studies* 81: 141–52.

Wintle, Claire. 2013. "Decolonising the Museum: The Case of the Imperial and Commonwealth Institutes." *Museum and Society* 11 (2): 185–201.

Witt, Doris. 2004. *Black Hunger: Soul Food and America*. Minneapolis: University of Minnesota Press.

Wohl, Victoria. 2010. "Suppliant Women and the Democratic State: White Men Saving Brown Women from Brown Men." In *When Worlds Elide: Classics, Politics, Culture*, edited by Karen Bassi and J. Peter Euben, 409–35. Lanham: Lexington Books.

Wolters, Wendy. 2004. "Without Sanctuary: Bearing Witness, Bearing Whiteness." *JAC: A Journal of Composition Theory* 24 (2): 399–425.

Woolf, Greg. 1994. "Becoming Roman, Staying Greek: Culture, Identity and the Civilizing Process in the Roman East." *Proceedings of the Cambridge Philological Society* 40: 116–143.

Wrenhaven, Kelly L. 2011. "Greek Representations of the Slave Body: A Conflict of Ideas?" In *Reading Ancient Slavery*, edited by Richard Alston, Edith Hall, and Laura Proffitt, 97–120. London: Bristol Classical Press.

——— 2012. *Reconstructing the Slave: The Image of the Slave in Ancient Greece*. London: Bristol Classical Press.

Wyles, Rosie. 2011. *Costume in Greek Tragedy*. London: Bristol Classical Press.

Yamagata, Naoko. 2005. "Clothing and Identity in Homer: The Case of Penelope's Web." *Mnemosyne* 58 (4): 539–46.

Young, Harvey. 2010. *Embodying Black Experience: Stillness, Critical Memory, and the Black Body*. Ann Arbor: University of Michigan Press.

Young, Kevin. 2012. *The Grey Album: On the Blackness of Blackness*. Minneapolis: Graywolf Press.

Zeitlin, Froma I. 1996. *Playing the Other: Gender and Society in Classical Greek Literature*. Chicago: University of Chicago Press.

Zhang, Sarah. 2017. "A Kerfuffle about Diversity in the Roman Empire." *The Atlantic*, August 2. www.theatlantic.com/science/archive/2017/08/dna-romans/535701/.

Zuckerberg, Donna. 2016. "How to Be a Good Classicist under a Bad Emperor." *Eidolon*, November 21. https://eidolon.pub/how-to-be-a-good-classicist-under-a-bad-emperor-6b848df6e54a.

For EU product safety concerns, contact us at Calle de José Abascal, 56–1°,
28003 Madrid, Spain or eugpsr@cambridge.org.

www.ingramcontent.com/pod-product-compliance
Lightning Source LLC
Chambersburg PA
CBHW051441050726
47593CB00005B/1871